The Problem with Feeding Cities

The Problem with Feeding Cities

The Social Transformation of Infrastructure, Abundance, and Inequality in America

ANDREW DEENER

The University of Chicago Press
Chicago and London

The University of Chicago Press, Chicago 60637

The University of Chicago Press, Ltd., London

© 2020 by The University of Chicago

All rights reserved. No part of this book may be used or reproduced in any
manner whatsoever without written permission, except in the case of brief
quotations in critical articles and reviews. For more information, contact the
University of Chicago Press, 1427 E. 60th St., Chicago, IL 60637.

Published 2020

Printed in the United States of America

29 28 27 26 25 24 23 22 21 20   1 2 3 4 5

ISBN-13: 978-0-226-70291-9 (cloth)

ISBN-13: 978-0-226-70307-7 (paper)

ISBN-13: 978-0-226-70310-7 (e-book)

DOI: https://doi.org/10.7208/chicago/9780226703107.001.0001

Library of Congress Cataloging-in-Publication Data

Names: Deener, Andrew, author.

Title: The problem with feeding cities : the social transformation of
    infrastructure, abundance, and inequality in America / Andrew Deener.

Description: Chicago : University of Chicago Press, 2020. |
    Includes bibliographical references and index.

Identifiers: LCCN 2020008790 | ISBN 9780226702919 (cloth) |
    ISBN 9780226703077 (paperback) | ISBN 9780226703107 (ebook)

Subjects: LCSH: Food supply—United States. | Food security—United States. |
    Food consumption—United States.

Classification: LCC HD9005 .D37 2020 | DDC 338.1/973091732—dc23

LC record available at https://lccn.loc.gov/2020008790

For Alana, Azalea, and Echo

CONTENTS

PREFACE

My family visits the same supermarket every week and purchases many of the same products on each visit. We keep a list on our phones to remind us of the things we want to replace. We also think about the week ahead as we search through the aisles and make our choices. What special ingredients are necessary for dinners during the weekdays, what do our kids want as snacks, and what will they bring to school for lunch?

As we make our selections, we look at the prices of comparable products. For some of the packaged goods, we look at the ingredients too. We evaluate the color and texture of the fresh foods in front of us. We rarely find something so unfamiliar that we have not seen it before. More often, we find a twist on an already established product that we try out—a new cereal or a different apple variety. We pile the stuff into our shopping cart. It is an exercise of mundane knowledge: recognizing whether the lettuce looks wilted; understanding how the aisles are organized so we can find the exact products and brands; unloading the objects from the shopping cart onto the conveyor belt at the checkout station; paying with a debit card that automatically transfers money from our bank account to the store's account; and bagging up the groceries to take home.

When we explore the sea of products found throughout the aisles, we do not think about how or why all those items are there with such reliability. For most of us, the supermarket is just there, filled with all the stuff we are looking for. This book is, in part, about how that remarkable system of abundance and convenience came into being—the social organization of a high-volume and high-variety market infrastructure.

Yet the rise of this kind of vital infrastructure has also created unexpected consequences. When I started conducting research in Philadelphia in 2010, I met Cynthia Watson, a woman in her early sixties, who has lived in various

West Philadelphia neighborhoods for most of her life. The neighborhood where Cynthia currently resides has dozens of vacant lots and poor housing conditions. As a young black girl growing up in this segregated city, Cynthia walked to a range of nearby shops: a green grocer owned by one of her neighbors and an independently owned grocery store and pharmacy. All of that commerce is gone. The only food shopping option in walking distance from her home is a corner store.

The small shop on Cynthia's block is packed from floor to ceiling with chips, soda, candy, cereal, bread, diapers, cleaning supplies, and other household items. The couple that owns the store tried carrying different fruits and vegetables to fulfill requests of some residents. They purchased cases of bananas, apples, and oranges, and sometimes avocados and potatoes, at a wholesale market. However, difficulties mounted up. Without proper refrigeration or quick turnover, they could not sell most of the product before it rotted. While some residents, like Cynthia, purchased the fresh produce on occasion, the price point was higher than at supermarkets, variety and choice were much more limited, and the quality was poorer.

However, the problems facing this neighborhood and its residents are more complicated than inadequate food shopping options. Cynthia helps to support and feed her grandchildren, preparing most of their dinners. With limited economic resources, she and her family rely on her church's food cupboard for canned vegetables, boxes of rice, and loaves of bread sent over from Philabundance, the city's food bank. For other foods, Cynthia takes a train, bus, or sometimes a taxi several miles to the Reading Terminal Market, the famed vending market and one of Pennsylvania's largest redeemers of Supplemental Nutritional Assistance Program (SNAP) benefits, formerly called food stamps. There, Amish bakers and local sandwich-makers sell their specialties alongside fish mongers, Italian butchers, and discounted produce stalls.

My experience and Cynthia's experience represent different sides of the food distribution equation—one side defined by abundance and convenience, the other by economic insecurity, limited transportation options, and lack of accessibility. Yet the more I learned about healthy food access and local responses to it, the more I questioned whether my starting point in neighborhoods was the right choice for understanding the problem. Even though abandoned properties and a lack of grocery stores are visible indicators of racial and economic disparities throughout Philadelphia, healthy food access is a broader national and global problem related to building the vital infrastructure.

Rather than continuing on this track of how people live, shop, and eat in the city, I started seeking out different parts of the food system to better understand their interconnections. I investigated how markets and cities were developed, how distribution relationships between production, storage, transport, and consumption were constructed, how organizational actors coordinated and evaluated food supplies, and how these factors contributed to problems like limited access to "healthy" food, disruptions of market abundance and convenience, and the entanglements between the prominent market dynamics and the nonprofit organizations managing food insecurity.

Figuring out how an infrastructural system fits into or excludes the local environment was one part of my investigation. But I also wanted to trace the infrastructure backward in time to better understand how different food varieties and qualities were made into high-volume supply chains. The history of industrial food processing built on staple commodities was well documented, but it was less clear how perishable foods—those that public health officials and nutritional experts deemed the healthiest, like fruits and vegetables—became incorporated into the infrastructure of mass consumption. My hunch was that if the policy concerns about food access were really about access to healthy food, then it was necessary to trace the historical links between the healthiest foods and the mass-merchandising system.

The social organization of the food distribution infrastructure is not the typical lens for studying urban change and inequality. Infrastructure's mundane features make it easy to overlook and difficult to pinpoint the interdependencies that matter. Tracking down the social life of infrastructure is even more complicated when dealing with a system that supplies food, not just for Philadelphia, a city with over 1.5 million people, but for an entire nation of more than 300 million.

This book, then, explains how the high-volume and high-variety food system was assembled and how it intersected with a specific urban region, in this case, Philadelphia. Philadelphia—like all cities and regions in the United States—has become inextricably interwoven with a distribution system connecting many regions and countries at the same time. I will explain why the food market system locked into certain places, market dynamics, and distribution scales in ways that have played a major role in food access and public health debates.

I dug deep into the historical record about the reorganization of urban and economic development and food distribution connections from the turn of the twentieth century to the present. I visited multiple archives where I read scientific, policy, and planning reports; political meeting minutes; articles in newspapers, magazines, and journals; political memoranda; and technical and economic feasibility studies. I also built upon 190 interviews with stakeholders from political, business, technology, and nonprofit sectors and toured dozens of facilities: farms, retail and wholesale markets, distribution centers, port facilities, cold storage warehouses, food auctions, food banks, farmers' markets, logistics firms, shipping companies, and more.

What I found changed my analytic sensibilities about how to study the development of cities and regions and their economies. Place matters, of course, in terms of addressing questions about meaning-making, social ties, and economic transactions. However, there would be no urban place-making opportunities without the durable webs of distribution. By unpacking how the food system converged in place, we can then see how the pursuit of market profitability and efficiency became intertwined with a vital infrastructure. This book is the result: an inquiry into the social transformation of infrastructure, abundance, and inequality in America.

ONE

The Transformation of the Food System

Supermarkets represent the modern world of abundance and convenience. The average supermarket is more than 40,000 square feet and carries almost 40,000 different products. The same cans of soup, boxes of cereal, packages of pasta, and frozen pizzas are found in stores across the country. Even highly perishable foods are set up for this shopping format. Butchers have already carved up chicken breasts and pork chops and ground up beef and turkey to expedite our shopping trips. Fresh fruits and vegetables, once constrained by seasonal production cycles, now appear as year-round market displays. Fuji, Granny Smith, Gala, Pink Lady, and Delicious apples are piled high near oblong Roma tomatoes, golf ball–like cherry tomatoes, bite-size grape tomatoes, and cluster tomatoes still "on the vine." Refrigerated cases are always stocked with plastic pouches of baby carrots, baby spinach, and baby kale.

Shoppers of the early 1900s would be astounded by the sheer volume and variety of food supplies found almost everywhere. The United States has more than 38,000 stocked supermarkets. The supermarket produce aisle alone, with its piled-up varieties of fresh fruits and vegetables, would have seemed like science fiction a century ago. Shoppers in those days frequented small neighborhood stores, less than 1,000 square feet in size. Grocery stores were initially family owned, but then later grew into large chain operations. Thousands of outlets fanned out over urban neighborhoods and onto suburban Main Streets.

The corner grocery store was set up according to a completely different logic of consumption than the contemporary supermarket. Almost every neighborhood had one, but they mostly sold dry bulk goods like flour, sugar, coffee, and tea. Canned foods, boxes of cereal, and national brands were still in their early stages of development. Neighborhood shops were not self-service, with customers picking and choosing products off shelves. Grocery clerks packaged up products for customers to take home. Without refrigeration, grocers carried only the most durable fruits and vegetables.[1] Fresh produce was mostly seasonal, stocked in downtown wholesale markets where pushcart peddlers purchased products and then sold them off to neighborhood residents. Out-of-season and tropical fruits and vegetables were an exotic luxury. Residents of large cities and their surrounding suburbs traveled on public transportation to downtown market halls and department stores to buy oranges and pineapples.

It is not just that the 1900-era corner grocery store and the 2000-era supermarket present contrasts in their building sizes, product volumes, and varieties. How food retailers plug into supply chains and into their environmental surroundings has also dramatically changed. The means of distribution have transformed from feeding central cities to feeding regions to feeding nearly the entire population of the United States. The organizational and technical methods of producing, storing, shipping, and marketing foods became interwoven with urban and suburban development, population settlement, and transportation connections.

At the turn of the twentieth century, the infrastructural problems of feeding central cities—by which I mean cities that act as hubs for their regions, like Philadelphia or Chicago or New York—were about increasing product quantities, varieties, and nutrients for large population settlements separated from sites of agricultural production. Health experts concerned about vitamin and nutrient deficiencies advised the public to eat more food and more varieties of it. Produce wholesalers, operating out of dense urban downtowns, started to incorporate fresh fruits and vegetables from beyond local regions. However, shipping methods and rudimentary product preservation techniques constrained the connections between different regions of agricultural production and the urban consumers dependent on them. The urban masses came to rely on the plentiful supplies of packaged, processed, and fortified foods like flour and cereal.[2]

During the twentieth century, the United States food economy and its distribution infrastructure reconfigured around mass merchandising for a suburbanizing nation. Managing the high-volume profit-making system grew in priority over managing the nation's nutritional health. The social organization of the high-volume and high-variety food system has now become so fully ingrained into American consumer culture that it is difficult for people to conceptualize food shopping outside of this mundane infrastructure of abundance and convenience. Even policy experts concerned about communities without healthy food access, what are often referred to as "food deserts," search for solutions in market spaces that are upwards of 60,000 square feet. How far a person lives from massive amounts of products is considered a property of structural advantage or disadvantage.

Water, electricity, and food systems all transformed over the course of the nineteenth and twentieth centuries.[3] A combination of urban development, population growth, and political priorities extended public investment into water and electricity infrastructures while gradually eroding investment in public food markets by the mid-1800s.[4] Yet that does not mean federal and state governments refrained from playing any subsequent role in regulating food access and classifying which foods and combinations were deemed healthiest. In the United States, a wide range of public-private alliances have reached into food industries, classified health and safety protocols, and facilitated consumer trends and social programs.

Building a food distribution infrastructure to supply large population settlements of cities and suburbs presents a unique problem: unlike water or electricity, food is not one "thing." Its material and conceptual diversity involves complicated system-building at every turn.[5] Even the definition of "food" depends on its geographic regions and conditions of production, storage, and consumption, culturally distinct tastes, and combinations of ingredients solidified as food products. Food is influenced as much by politics, science, and economics as it is by culture and tradition. Moreover, determining the "healthiest" combinations and qualities remains elusive.[6]

The heterogeneity of food has informed the composition of the distribution system that surrounds it and the political-economic motivations of those investing in it. The phrase "it's like apples and oranges" is particularly apropos. Even the apple and orange industries have established different organizational and technical methods for growing, storing, and shipping their products. The material compositions of the objects themselves led to different collective approaches for managing their volumes, varieties, and qualities. Supply chains have integrated specialized knowledge about biochemical, physical, and aesthetic properties into routine handling and exchange dynamics so that marketplaces across the country can reassemble familiar-looking aisle arrangements.

The relative autonomy of the material resources continues to shape distribution conventions and consumer expectations. Today almost everyone in the United States, nearly 100 percent of the population, lives in a home networked with electricity and water.[7] The food distribution system may someday be similarly networked into the home through online shopping and grocery delivery services. Yet supermarkets and big box stores remain the primary food shopping hubs. They are the most visible spaces of consumption—the material manifestation for fulfilling the bridge between abundance, convenience, and inequality.

It has become conventional wisdom in the social sciences that changing interdependencies between economic and urban development play an important role in the uneven distribution of resources. Yet when addressing questions about the causes of uneven distribution, researchers focus on the changing systems of production or the contexts of consumption, but rarely on the methods of coordination and connection between them. We tend to blame uneven distribution on the malicious intent of powerful corporations; political-economic ideologies and state regulatory structures; the role of globalization, information technology, and automation in converting cities and towns from manufacturing centers to sites of postindustrial consumerism; or the impact of white flight, middle-class out-migration to the suburbs, and residential redlining on the creation and durability of neighborhood-level race and class inequalities.

While the unequal distribution of resources we see in Philadelphia today emerges from the relationships and entanglements between all the above factors, there is more to the story. This book turns its focus to the formation and transformation of the entanglements themselves and the unintended consequences that grew out of them.[8] The logic of inquiry is to untangle the transformation from feeding cities to feeding regions to feeding an entire nation. We can then see how and why organizations, technical innovations, and land-use developments crystallized in particular social and historical contexts, rearranged the relationships between competing interests and methods for handling product qualities, and locked in the underlying logic of managing market risk—instead of population health risk—into a vital infrastructure.[9]

The rest of this chapter builds the conceptual and methodological framework for studying food distribution in terms of the transformation of infrastructure, abundance, and inequality. The first step is to conceptualize food distribution as infrastructural regimes, the underlying sociotechnical machinery stabilizing distinct periods of economic and urban development. The second step is to conceptualize how organizational actors and decision-makers realigned market profitability and material product qualities in relation to the changing infrastructural dynamics. The food distribution system that was taken for granted in the early 1900s now seems antiquated by today's standard marketplaces and diverse consumer preferences. Likewise, organizational and technical innovations that the public would have viewed as extraordinary or even impossible—like the supermarket produce aisle—have been implemented as part of the routine food shopping experience for those who frequent one of the nearly 40,000 supermarkets across the country.

Food Distribution as Infrastructural Regimes

A central feature of all infrastructure, according to Geoffrey Bowker and Susan Leigh Star, is that it permeates so fully into daily life that it falls into the invisible background.[10] Creating such entrenched infrastructural systems is partly about state planning of the connections between populations and places within an established territory: railroads, highways, money systems, and electric, water, and communication networks.[11] However, people also develop organizational routines, practical skills, technical expertise, methods of classification, and conventions of exchange relationships that adapt to, correspond with, and reinforce the durable physical connections.[12] Under certain historical conditions, the social and technical components lock in the mutually reinforcing interdependencies. In food distribution, these are the infrastructural regimes of feeding cities, feeding regions, and feeding an entire nation.[13]

The rise of modern consumer abundance and convenience has its origins in the social organization, technical control, and political and economic manipulation of the environment. Political, scientific, and economic actors converted nature into instrumental natural resources. They expanded their capabilities and capacities for engineering natural resources into reproducing systems between production and consumption. Martin Heidegger referred to the underlying logic as the "standing reserve." He regarded the technical forms of organization and coordination as foundations of modern society.[14]

The infrastructural ties between agricultural production, manufacturing industries, storage, preservation, communication, and transportation have simplified and sustained human life. In particular, industrial methods and machinery around mass production, storage, and distribution enabled people to overcome a delicate relationship once observed by Thomas Malthus between population growth, agricultural surpluses, and nutritional sustenance. Economists and geographers often see industrialization and its mechanized system of producing excess as overcoming the "Malthusian trap."[15]

The modern political economy of the "standing reserve" created the conditions for new forms of spatial and economic interdependency, but it also gave rise to conflicts over land uses, unequal valuations of natural resources, competing assessments of nutritional characteristics, and disparities in health outcomes. The sociotechnical system enabled organizational actors to profitably realign agricultural sites of food production with urban contexts of demand by controlling product qualities, coordinating distribution temporalities through storage and transportation, and shaping consumer expectations of the high volumes and varieties of products available in the marketplaces.

Strengthening the spatial interdependencies between products and places locked in the environmental distinctiveness of rural and urban settings, but it also created power struggles between them. Land-use distinctions and locational assets became contested economic resources. It was a dual process: people created symbolic and meaningful relationships with their local territories and environmental aesthetics; and they converted places with distinct environmental conditions and natural resources into economic nodes in the physical distribution networks.[16] Infrastructure came to encompass both the hard organizational and technical interdependencies between places and the soft human interactions for coordinating and framing how those connections supported a place's local knowledge and profit-making potential.[17]

The infrastructural regime of feeding cities was built upon a process of mutual adaptation. During the nineteenth century, rural and urban trading partners aligned distinct land uses into routine means of distribution. William Cronon details how farmers of the Great West employed organizational and technical skills to transform untapped fertile land into sites of new agricultural efficiencies, increased storage capacities, and methods of product standardization. Cronon also found that market entrepreneurs in large cities like Chicago managed the growing consumer dependencies in the creation of wholesale markets that heightened the urban demand for agricultural commodities.[18]

Although the relationships between rural and urban environments were reinforced through shared distribution connections, philosophers and social scientists conceptualized urban and rural areas as bounded geographic territories with distinct logics of cultural and economic place-making.[19] In the early 1900s, Georg Simmel referred to the distinct "mental life" of people living in cities, pushed into more calculative associations with strangers and new exchange partners. He wrote, "The city sets up a deep contrast with small town and rural life with reference to the sensory foundations of psychic life." Simmel analyzed urban economic exchange dynamics as having an impersonal rhythm; separating producers from consumers; privileging money and expediency over interpersonal trust; and facilitating routine social interdependencies through the division of labor.[20]

Simmel argued that the quantitative features of population growth and economic exchange in cities were translated into qualitative social forms. Sociologists in the United States expanded on these points, giving rise to the distinct subfields of rural and urban sociology, rather than engaging with and prioritizing their interconnections. Louis Wirth maintained that quantitative features of cities like population density, heterogeneity, and size produced new urban-based features of social life, such as increased anonymity and greater individual autonomy in choosing social networks. He labeled these emerging social patterns as "urbanism as a way of life."[21]

Place-making "urbanism" grew into one of the central objects of social science inquiry, primarily concerned with the study of bounded spatial organization, a kind of "methodological cityism."[22] Paradoxically, in urban studies, a conflict remains over how and where to study urban conditions, in large part because of the unsettled ambiguity of the meaning of the word "urban." One common debate is between those studying the internal compositions of bounded places and those focusing on how places are embedded in social and technical networks and power relationships that are geographically spread across urban and suburban landscapes.[23]

Urban social scientists periodically renew this opposition: "place matters" versus "power matters."[24] As John Logan and Harvey Molotch explain, they both matter, because power and place are interdependent.[25] Nonetheless, the spatial and economic interdependencies and the priorities and scales of power and place have changed over time. The focus on centralized urbanism was not just an intellectual paradigm. Cities—and especially the largest municipalities—accumulated economic resources and advantages in the late nineteenth and early twentieth centuries. Population concentrations, transportation connections, and rural-urban economic ties reinforced provisioning systems for central cities. Lewis Mumford wrote in the 1930s, "Every phase of life in the countryside contributes to the existence of cities . . . converted into instruments of urban living" with "greater possibilities of interchange." The rural-urban interdependencies created the conditions through which organizations in central cities built up their wealth, power, and control over market dynamics and profit-making opportunities.[26]

The food distribution infrastructure at the turn of the twentieth century was dependent on rail transportation. It was based on the political economy of place-based growth machines intersecting in urban centers like New York, Philadelphia, and Chicago, each of which had over a million inhabitants by the end of the 1800s.[27] However, in the next century, the railroad industry experienced crises that led to its gradual demise. The Interstate Commerce Commission heavily regulated railroads. Ford started mass-producing automobiles. Suburban development was on the rise. The Supreme Court broke up Standard Oil into dozens of competing companies that lowered the price of oil. A new auto, oil, and rubber coalition was formed to promote auto transportation. And the federal government subsidized the construction of streets and highways that the public, including the trucking industry, could use for free.[28]

The infrastructural regime of feeding cities was different than the subsequent infrastructural regime of feeding regions of tens of millions of people. During the 1920s, a process of infrastructural decentralization started to materialize. It combined highway construction, the rise of corporate car manufacturers like General Motors, new technologies of energy distribution, shifting modes of information broadcasting and telephone communication, and changes in population settlement.[29] By 1950, the new infrastructural regime reached a critical mass in terms of visibility across cities and regions. For the first time in the history of the United States, more than half of the nation's population lived in either an urban or suburban locale. Robert Fishman writes that the decentralization of development, transportation connections, and population settlements broke apart the "logic that had sustained the big city" and "distribut[ed] its prized functions over whole regions."[30]

Infrastructural centralization produced an ideology of "urbanism as a way of life." Infrastructural decentralization through subsidized highways, trucking and automotive industries, and new organizational and technical methods of coordination gave rise to what Kenneth Jackson terms the "drive-in culture": parking lots, fast-food chains, supermarkets, and shopping centers. Lizbeth Cohen labels the transition in spaces of consumption "from the town center to the shopping center." Douglas Rae calls it the "end of urbanism."[31]

The shifting infrastructural interdependencies gradually reshaped the relationships between humans, the environment, and expectations of convenient consumption. The railroads, their storage and wholesale depots, and pervading neighborhood grocers were the symbolic and material manifestations of their time—the market and distribution model of centralized urbanism.[32] The means of distribution reconfigured around changing urban and economic development patterns. The ties between suburbanization and mass consumption became ever-clearer. In 1946, only eight planned shopping centers had been built in the United States. Between 1950 and the end of the 1970s, 22,000 shopping centers were assembled on highways across the country. Trucking replaced rail distribution. The relationship between suburban development, population settlement, and auto transportation shifted the underlying expectations of food shopping.[33]

The changing infrastructural regime altered people's attachments to places and consumer sensibilities, as well as further obscured the very meaning of "urban." The process of urbanization—the shift from rural to urban habitats—was not bounded by territory, although I am focusing on the United States, where over 80 percent of the population now resides in a so-called urban area. Henri Lefebvre, writing in the 1970s, described the "urban society" dismantling the spatial and cultural boundaries of centralized urbanism. The undulating roads, housing developments, and shopping sites of the suburbs may have looked physically and aesthetically different than the gridded urban centers with their tenements and high-rise apartment buildings. Yet Lefebvre saw them as part of a continuous process of capitalist urban expansion. It was an "implosion" of the previous paradigm, of "the dominance of the city over the country." In Lefebvre's view, the ideology of urbanism as a way of life was no longer bounded by city centers. The infrastructure that supplied and sustained large cities was pushing out toward every corner of the nation. "In this sense," according to Lefebvre, "a vacation home, a highway, a supermarket in the countryside are all part of the urban fabric."[34]

Even as social scientists ideologically tilted their interests toward the study of bounded territories, the changing infrastructural regime revealed something different about spatial and economic interdependencies. The fabric of coordination and connection that was once fundamental to urban centralization was being distributed nearly everywhere in the United States. The spreading out of water, energy, and communication infrastructures was an indication of this urban expansion—an extension of "networked infrastructures."[35] But what about food?

Without centralized political intervention, the spread of supermarkets, and then the rise of Wal-Mart afterward, signaled a similar spatial realignment in the distribution system from the center to the suburbs to consumers across the nation. Sam Walton started a five-and-dime general store chain in a small Arkansas city, but his company slowly evolved into an information and logistics operation fit with satellites and advanced computing capacity. The supermarket infrastructure rearranged the food system for the suburbs, but Wal-Mart became the primary player in the exurban growth machine that brought the mass-produced supply system to new places. In turn, Wal-Mart also became the nation's—and indeed, the world's—largest food retailer. The company built successful distribution centers and shopping centers in less-populated towns that urban and suburban retailers thought could never turn a profit.[36]

Despite the visibility of influential corporations profiting from the expansion of mass consumption, the relationships between power and products were not imposed on populations and places from the top down. A process of mutual adaptation between many different organizations and interests accumulated into a subtle form of cultural and economic power—an inter-locking machinery of reification. The infrastructural logic of coordination and connection formatted the mundane worlds of abundance, convenience, and consumption. It also reinforced how political and economic actors defined food-related problems in terms of market risk, which then shaped how people sought solutions to emerging problems.[37] The infrastructural regimes encompassed how businesses made money from food distribution, how and where people shopped for food, how consumers evaluated product qualities, and how they experienced food access and its disruptions in their busy and complicated lives.

William Cronon writes that agricultural production, rail mobility, and the city centers of the nineteenth century "required that a new human order be superimposed on nature until the two became completely entangled." The "hybrid system" was "second nature to those who lived within it."[38] The more flexible and decentered mobility of the "drive-in culture" set up a different link between convenience and consumerism as second nature.[39] Sharon Zukin writes that the retailing landscape created the "everyday nor-malcy of shopping" that "makes us accept as natural the idea that humans exist to sell and buy." The permeating system "teaches us how to live in a market society."[40]

In neoclassical economic theory, price is related to supply and demand. However, middle-range processes, competing valuations and scales, and or-ganizational and technical machinery configure and align the supplies and demands into "naturalized" market projects.[41] One of the core aspects of mod-ern capitalism is that organizational and technical interdependencies—in factories, in bureaucracies, and across supply chains—manage, measure, and manipulate the temporalities of labor, transit, and product preservation into market standards and consumer expectations. Infrastructural regimes entan-gle what Michel Callon refers to as the calculative "devices," "tools," and "equipment" across wide-ranging situations that lead people to reify "what it is to be 'economic' "—and that includes how to supply and consume food through a framework of economic exchange and mass merchandising.[42]

The food system, unlike the distribution of water and electricity, absorbed an underlying logic of managing profitability through product diversity and high-volume efficiency. Political, technical, and economic actors consistently identified and isolated new spaces and situations of economic value as the core problem to be managed. The value structure of this vital system was not about health optimization. The logic of linking profits, products, and ef-ficiencies permeated across food distribution sectors and into everyday sites of consumption.

However, the market-based pursuit of food distribution efficiency did not inevitably lead to the upgrading evolution of society or to maximized profitability.[43] It led to collective benefits, but it also created unexpected outcomes, organizational mistakes, environmental problems, and health inequalities. In other words, what was deemed most efficient for some actors at particular historical junctures was not necessarily beneficial for others. Changes in the mundane aspects of infrastructure gradually disrupted the relationships between manufacturing, transporting, storage, and retailing industries. These moments of infrastructural uncertainty led to new power struggles over how to define the future of the food system.

The history of food distribution has been filled with many moments of instability since the rise of industrial capitalism. Urban consumers demanded cheaper food supplies and better access to resources; manufacturers, wholesalers, and retailers battled over the control of supply chains; financial investors gained more leverage over the profit/loss dimensions of production and distribution; information technology engineers found new ways to measure supply chain efficiencies and identified previously hidden sites of economic value; and agrarian producers had to strive to make a living off of declining wages and diminished control of local land uses. Over time the very meaning and scale of what is being contested, where it is being contested, and how the rewards are being distributed have dramatically changed.[44]

As the distribution of rewards and resources changed, so did the problem-solving frameworks. Infrastructural regimes have their own internal conflicts and inequalities. The contemporary United States is a particular type of time and place in advanced capitalism where flexible distribution infrastructure, global supply chains, and heightened consumer demand make abundance a part of routine life in more and more places. However, not everyone everywhere, even in the United States, gets access to the same degree of convenience and the same quality of food.

The infrastructure of abundance and convenience has unique problems: spaces where market coverage is noticeably absent; blurred lines between healthy and unhealthy foods in the same marketplaces; scientific confusions about what even counts as healthy food; pesticides, fertilizers, and artificial additives that manipulate product volumes and qualities with unknown implications for public health and the environment; associations between quality, brand, variety, and status; obesity and diabetes epidemics with competing explanations about their causes; and segments of the population simply unable to afford basic nutritional requirements despite widespread abundance.

The organizational and technical relationships have configured the profit-making motives of market-makers, the handling and evaluation of commodity qualities, and the sensibilities of the consuming population. In doing so, they have also created new disruptions, uneven distribution, and problem-solving frameworks for managing market risk that have disregarded concerns for health outcomes and environmental threats. The next step is to explain how the infrastructural regimes have changed and why they have produced unintended consequences.

Complex Systems: From Uncertainty to Unintended Consequences

The United States food distribution infrastructure integrated heterogeneous supply chains and products into one-stop shopping. Building the food system around such a complex web of social and technical ingredients could have happened differently. The transformation of infrastructural regimes is much easier to see in retrospect than in moments of innovation. It was not immediately clear from the points of view of strategic actors embedded in the system which combinations of prototypes would stick together into a reinforcing feedback dynamic between economic and urban development. It was partly that actors had to get the pieces of an infrastructural system to fit together into coherent "sociotechnical ensembles" at certain historical junctures.[45] However, the particular ways the components became adjoined also crystallized and constrained the social, spatial, political, and economic conventions. The relationships between the organizational and material components held the "inertial force."[46]

A key paradox is that infrastructural regimes transformed even though so many discrete social and technical factors conspired toward stabilizing the lock in between them. The contemporary merchandising and distribution system in the United States did not arise all at once. The food distribution system did not instantly shift from small neighborhood grocery stores with a few dry goods to larger stores because someone came up with the idea to create "super" markets. The transportation system did not rapidly change from rail-centered distribution to highway-and-truck-centered distribution because highways were constructed or refrigerated trucks were invented. These changes occurred by adjusting many organizational and technical components, interests, and conflicts into mutually reinforcing relationships with shared understandings and valuations.

The challenge with studying the transformation of a large technical system is to conceptualize and empirically disentangle the historical processes in order to locate and analyze the emerging interactions, contestations, and negotiations between them where new social and technical interdependencies became aligned. It is a challenge of studying the relationship between complex systems and organizational emergence.[47] Complex systems are based on nonlinear and mutually adaptive relationships between interdependent components. As Robert Jervis writes, changes in "some elements or their relations produce changes in other parts of the system." However, it is difficult in situated contexts for organizational decision-makers to forecast how outcomes will accumulate and materialize, because decisions and investments "ripple" through the system of relationships in unpredictable ways.[48]

Heterogeneous organizations, interests, and products were interwoven into a nonlinear complex system. As a result, strategic actors investing in the food system did not impose changes from the top down, not even those occupying the most powerful political and economic positions. In this regard, the transformation of the food system was not a direct outcome of what Michael Mann calls "infrastructural power," through which the state maintains an autonomous problem-solving platform in relation to resource coordination and distribution.[49] Neither was the food system transformation about "biopower," Michel Foucault's term for understanding how "biological features" of population optimization "became the object of political strategy."[50]

State-level policies played a role in shaping the food system, not through strategic efforts to promote health optimization but by facilitating the conditions for decentering market-based problem-solving frameworks. Market technologies permeated through the system into discrete and taken-for-granted interdependencies. In this regard, the state made financial resources available to specific industries through tax incentives, motivated new organizational and supply chain partnerships, and sponsored and facilitated technical and transportation innovations and urban and suburban developments. Likewise, state-level backing of laissez-faire economics and industry deregulations were a key part of the private industrial development equation, explained by Monica Prasad as the faster the growth of credit, the slower the growth of the welfare state.[51]

Nonetheless, the transformation of the food system was not the result of political-economic coercion. Strategic actors pursued profit-making agendas, but they did so, as Marion Fourcade puts it, with neither "ex-ante pressure" nor "ex-post sanction."[52] New spatial and economic interdependencies occurred through contingent interactions between relatively autonomous and geographically distributed streams of knowledge and practice. Scientific, technical, political, and economic actions became entangled in specific contexts around emerging problems related to coordination, connection, profitability, and efficiency. Trial-and-error negotiations between actors with different forms of knowledge gave rise to new problem-solving frameworks for managing market risk.

Collective intelligence was the way of problem-solving. Writing about the "impossible engineering" of the Canal du Midi in seventeenth-century France, Chandra Mukerji shows how "anonymous power" and "distributed reasoning" operated as an early form of collective intelligence. Technical and land-use problems brought together interactions between state authorities, expert engineers, and locals who knew the intricacies of the terrain. The new relationships created an "intellectual scaffolding" that transcended the specific knowledge of each interest group. Together, they solved problems that would have otherwise remained impenetrable at that historical juncture.[53]

Since the rise of urban industrial capitalism, problem-solving through market innovation and technical adaptation accumulated into the system's collective framework, overshadowing other possible problem-solving frames like promoting health optimization. A wide range of interests—scientists, engineers, politicians, farmers, manufacturers, wholesalers, retailers, shippers, and consumers—contributed to building the system of cheap food. They became interwoven around private industry problems related to profit margins, transaction costs, corporate bottom line, mechanization, automation, product preservation, standardization, and urbanization. Different interests competed over how to define situated problems and how to reap rewards from managing them. They found economic solutions in calculative technologies that were gradually applied to more and more situations. As these market techniques permeated across sectors and supply chains, they repositioned how organizations and coalitions then leveraged rewards and constrained future actions.

In order for the food system to transform, decision-makers invested in some innovations over others. Different actors put forth different prototypes around market coordination and physical distribution connections in order to reach more consumers and gain the profit edge: transporting methods, agricultural and manufacturing mechanization, retail store and distribution center sizes and geographic locations, product code mechanisms, computer processers, refrigeration techniques, supply chain partnerships, combinations of products in market aisles, product qualities and brands, and methods of collecting consumer information to better forecast supply and demand.

All of these examples had competing prototypes, but not all of the prototypes were converted into interdependent relationships. Strategic actors looked to edge out their competitors, but they neither easily spread new techniques through the complex system nor directly coerced consumers to shop for food in particular ways. Andrew Pickering argues that studies of sociotechnical change must differentiate between the design of organizational and technical prototypes and their implementations into new interdependencies. For a system to change, actors have to turn novel methods, tools, and techniques into interactive and compatible ties. They have to convert specific technical knowledge into routine exchange sequences, organizational cultures, predictable supply chains, and profit-making conventions.[54]

Implementation entails the ambiguous interaction negotiation of system realignment through situated uncertainty and trial and error. Pickering refers to it as "tuning up" the sociotechnical relationships, as in tuning the radio or tuning up a car. To get to the point of mutually reinforcing agreement between exchange partners, organizational actors first experiment with different prototypes, make mistakes about their applications, follow the economic rewards, and figure out how to get the organizational and technical components to interlock across interests. It is a process of adjustment geared toward finding the right interaction and exchange frequencies out of the range of available alternatives. And there are always emerging and contested alternatives.[55]

The trial-and-error process of realigning the food system has meant that, even when actors were faced with the same economic constraints, organizational mimicry and strategic planning were uncertain processes over elongated periods of years and even decades. The process of isomorphism was not only about transposing schemas across industries and contexts— creating the same look and feel of food shopping everywhere.[56] Implementing calculative devices and organizational methods did not easily translate across sectors and supply chains even when they shared goals of stabilizing high-volume supplies for supermarkets and big box stores.

The isomorphic process appears patterned in retrospect. Yet implementing organizational and technical compatibility in apple supply chains did not create an exact blueprint for orange supply chains, let alone supply chains for more fragile foods like strawberries. In terms of the supermarket system, it was a much different series of organizational and technical steps to convert cereal and canned soup products into routine market formats than it was to fit fresh fruits and vegetables into similar high-volume and high-variety arrangements.

Actors doing the work of supplying food for large central cities faced new challenges and opportunities when the development landscape, transportation methods, storage facilities, and population settlement patterns pushed out beyond the urban center. Collective actors across industries adjusted their distribution and profitability goals to address the growing numbers of consumers in the suburbs and beyond. Diane Vaughan calls it the problem of "environmental uncertainty," in which organizational decision-makers faced difficulties "accurately predicting circumstances that might affect their future activities."[57] Such contingent decision-making contexts—with multiple viable options embedded in the situations—posed challenges for pursuing profitability.[58]

The suburban supermarket system was not set up to harm people by limiting food access or by fostering bad nutrition through unceasing expansions of processed products. Unequal health outcomes were unexpected consequences of mutual adaptations of decision-makers navigating the secular trends in land use, transportation, and population settlement. For example, economic rewards accrued through new organizational and distribution methods, which then constrained older approaches that were initially set up to supply urban centers. Changing profitability methods locked into the distribution infrastructure and created repercussions for consumers living in older urban territories. The transformation of the distribution system gave rise to the food and retail deserts of the 1970s that continued for decades.

Once the distribution methods locked in profit-and-loss conventions across supply chains, "system effects" took down corporations, even the most powerful ones.[59] The Great Atlantic & Pacific Tea Company (A&P), for example, grew to prominence in the first half of the 1900s. The corporation capitalized on market deregulations and new distribution efficiencies in the face of urban concentrations. However, executives of the nation's largest chain operation did not anticipate the pervading suburban supermarket system. In a subsequent era, Woolworth and Kmart mastered different discount store models, mostly by selling huge quantities of inexpensive mass-produced goods to suburban consumers. These once-dominant retailers did not foresee Wal-Mart's logistical and global supply chain methods extending the volume and variety of products to new territories. This iterative and adaptive infrastructural process transcended industries. A number of department stores saw the trend of expanding from city centers to suburban malls but missed the shift toward online shopping. As a result, A&P, Woolworth, and Kmart spiraled into obsolescence and hollowed-out "dead malls" now weigh down towns and cities across the United States.

Decision-makers experienced difficulties in moments of innovation. They had a hard time forecasting which emerging prototypes would turn into the routine market relationships, distribution connections, and mundane consumer expectations. Even the most successful business experts could not predict that Sam Walton and Jeff Bezos would become such powerful change agents. Wal-Mart and Amazon.com were celebrated only when their organizational approaches to pursuing profitability and efficiency matched the accumulating collective momentum of the new infrastructural regime.[60]

Prevailing market formats—neighborhood chain grocers, supermarkets, big box stores, and online shopping—rose to prominence through accumulating changes in the web of coordination and connection. Political and economic actors worked out practical and technical steps into complex recipes that became more easily implemented into new situations.[61] By converting emerging social and technical steps into routine sociotechnical recipes across supply chains, industries were able to replicate the coordination and movement of hundreds of thousands of different products to tens of thousands of marketplaces all over the country and increasingly into the home.

The infrastructural regimes have changed. Methods for managing market risk permeated into the vital infrastructure in ways that the public has now taken for granted. The transformation of the food system created unintended consequences. The infrastructure of abundance and convenience has shaped mundane consumer expectations about what kinds of foods are readily available, what different products look and taste like, how people shop for them, and how public health problems and inequalities related to food production, distribution, and consumption are framed and solved.

The Road Ahead and Its Intersections

The rest of this book untangles the transformation of the American food system by focusing on specific organizational, technical, and spatial relationships in the history of food distribution. The logic of inquiry is to examine the reconfiguring processes in a specific locale—Philadelphia—to see how they intersect, align, combine, and transcend previously established infrastructural regimes. This approach locates the emergence of new organizational and technical methods, the uncertainties and conflicts that arose, how certain interdependencies gained momentum over others, and the consequences and problem-solving efforts that resulted.

The Philadelphia region serves as the site to investigate these issues, but this book is not about Philadelphia in the traditional social science and historical sense of place-making studies of urbanism. Philadelphia has been the subject of some of the most important studies of industrial and urban history, economic change, neighborhood development, and race and class relations and inequalities. This book engages with that research, but there are also sections that focus less on Philadelphia as a municipality or region and more on the locations and processes where organizational and technical innovations and market and supply chain implementations occurred. Philadelphia acts as a key impact site—a point of convergence—for the interacting urban and economic developments that have become commonplace in the contemporary food distribution system.

Chapters 2 and 3 focus on infrastructural exclusion as a unique type of urban and economic inequality. As infrastructural interdependencies extended into new suburban territories, they also excluded areas, leaving behind urban neighborhoods and inner-ring suburbs that were dependent on older models of food distribution and market coordination. These chapters investigate the changing historical relationship between fresh produce, grocery market development, and broader transitions in population, land-use, organizational, and transportation connections.

Chapter 2 examines the rise and fall of the central fresh food wholesale system, as changing distribution connections disrupted industry conventions. At the turn of the twentieth century, policy and business leaders, including produce wholesalers, reached out beyond the local environment to increase food supplies for large city centers. They pieced together precarious supply chains and distribution channels for handling perishable objects. These market-makers in the urban center faced recurring problems adjusting to changing retail, storage, and transportation, leading to their marginalization. By the 1950s, a new distribution infrastructure crystallized profit-making conventions around a different land-use array of residence, industry, and transportation. Downtown wholesale markets were labeled as "business slums" and were eventually razed.

The conflicts surrounding wholesale markets were also related to the expansion of vertically integrated supermarkets. Chapter 3 explains how the pervasive urban grocery chains of the early 1900s were disrupted by the rise of the suburban supermarket distribution infrastructure. In the early 1900s, retail grocers established nimble ways to extend supply chains from downtown wholesale districts into dispersed urban neighborhoods and into inner-ring suburbs. In search of competitive advantages, some corporations replaced storage facilities in the urban center with regional distribution centers. The realignment of the retail food system around the movement of higher volumes and more varieties to more places heightened competition and led to wide-ranging economic mistakes and bankruptcies. The urban grocery system—along with the downtown wholesale districts—became economically obsolete and constrained urban food access in this period of infrastructural exclusion.

Chapters 4 and 5 explain how the implementation of new information technologies and logistical methods into the food distribution system changed supply chains and retail merchandising. Chapter 4 examines how digital technologies and information management tools transformed the movements of material objects. Manufacturing industries entered the age of automation, but the retailing side continued to face profitability issues as a high-volume but low-tech sector. In the 1970s, manufacturing and retailing were interactive but not compatible. Because of the supermarket's high-volume and low-margin merchandising platform, different arms of the food industry negotiated new shared uses of technical devices, such as bar codes, optical laser scanners, and computer data processors.

The infrastructural transformation integrated information management with new distribution competencies built for the supermarket age. The new sociotechnical machinery eventually transcended the supermarket by spreading the information management tools into corporate discount retailers and pharmacies. Wal-Mart's implementation of the bar code and computer logistics systems—and eventually its own satellite system—solidified the company's success in small towns. Wal-Mart sent a signal to retailers that mass-merchandising markets filled with the same stuff could open up in unpredictable places. This new age of product mobility broke down boundaries between territories, merged the supermarket with the general discount store, and forced supermarkets into another round of profitability constraints.

These constraints led to a period of corporate mimicry and widespread mergers. Throughout the 1980s and 1990s, supermarkets increasingly handled more products and were owned by fewer corporations. The system also reassembled supply chains. Chapter 5 develops the case of infrastructural isomorphism, in which supply chains around perishable products adjusted to the retailing industry's organizational, technical, and economic constraints. This chapter explains how markets defeated seasons by turning the produce aisle into a year-round high-volume and high-variety "fresh" produce department. The distribution system finally went cold as interdependent, long-distance, refrigerated transportation chains developed to serve more and more perishable commodities. Food arrived into regions from far and wide. Shipping ports, cold storage operations, and logistics services—that is, "logistics clusters"—made the perishable durable.[62]

The mass-merchandising system promoted standards and tools to hold the fresh stuff for longer periods, but not everything fit. Chapters 6 and 7 explain how organizations and distribution sectors created something new out of rejected stuff and older places. Chapter 6 shows how locational expertise gave rise to the management, assessment, and valuation of object qualities excluded from the supermarket model. Three local distribution channels became pervasive. The first is older wholesale terminals repurposing supermarket rejections for alternative markets. The second is the food banking sector turning mass-market excess into new tools for responding to food insecurity. The third is the transformation of local food from a market process outside of corporate standards into a consumer status category and moral economy unto its own.

While it may be that the urban center does not hold, it can, with the reconfiguration of investments and distribution connections, take on different roles and rise again. Although the center lost its position as the primary node in the flexible distribution system, it regained a prominent "place-making" symbolic status. Chapter 7 untangles how the convergence between planners, activists, politicians, public health experts, industry executives, and social scientists redefined the problem of urban food access and, with it, made some neighborhoods part of the distribution network. Food deserts first emerged in the 1970s, but more than 20 years later, the gentrification of food and place brought together intersections between public health, social science, and market sectors into new ways of evaluating and confronting inequalities in food access.

The final chapter revisits the core issues surrounding infrastructural transformations and their consequences. It asks: how does this infrastructural approach to the transformation of a complex system force us to reconsider how we think about feeding cities, solving social problems, and addressing inequalities in health outcomes? It argues that explanations of the urban order require closer attention to infrastructure as the social and material basis of abundance, convenience, and inequality. The key to mitigating long-term urban, environmental, and public health problems is to address the mundane interdependencies and the disruptions that flow out of them.

TWO

The Rise and Fall of the Urban Middlemen

Urban centers were rapidly growing at the end of the nineteenth century. The distance between farmers and the largest concentrations of consumers created one of the major problems related to urbanization: building interactive and compatible infrastructural interdependencies to reassemble resources to nourish increasing numbers of people.[1] The storage, standardization, and shipping of grains were already commonplace by the middle of the nineteenth century, making surpluses possible and opening up urban wholesaling opportunities.[2] Additionally, processed commodities like sugar, flour, and salt, as well as other bulk commodities like coffee and tea, were widely available by the end of the century.[3] Market actors handled these durable items without disrupting their expected qualities.

Perishable foods, in contrast, created unique infrastructural problems.[4] Different fruits and vegetables, for instance, were dependent on climate, soil, water, and land-use characteristics of particular regions, and this was especially the case for agricultural sectors trying to advance the circulation of high-volume supplies beyond local markets. Agriculture was never a purely natural process, not even for the foods now deemed most "natural." High-volume agricultural production was dependent on innovations in irrigation; plant and biochemical sciences; organizational methods; and harvesting, packing, and transit techniques. In particular, turning perishable objects into high-volume market commodities for feeding cities was an experimental and trial-and-error sociotechnical process.[5]

Market actors at all stages of production, storage, and distribution had to learn how decomposing objects interacted with and responded to changing and varied environmental conditions. Once the commodity was harvested, different actors competed over how to stabilize the organizational and technical applications and align them with consumer demands. Different fruits and vegetables had autonomous lifecycles even after they were separated from the plants. Each commodity had a different rhythm and rate of decomposition, which led shippers to try out various methods to secure the transit conditions.[6]

In 1900, inhabitants of large cities like Philadelphia mostly relied on fruits and vegetables grown in close proximity. Fruits and vegetables were seasonal products. Some were considered delicacies in the off-season because of the combination of their material characteristics and difficulties for transport.[7] Others were even deemed exotic and high class. Department stores, like Macy's, took pride in carrying "rare tropical fruits and vegetables irrespective of season."[8] These varieties of fresh foods were luxury goods for a few, not necessities for everyone.

Turning fruits and vegetables into health necessities has partly been a matter of education and taste. Public health experts have shown that learning about and trying different food textures and flavors, including exposure at a very young age, is important for developing a palate that remains open to variety.[9] However, exposure and taste are dependent on access, and that means facilitating the conditions that make exposure routine. And in the early 1900s, exposing the public to new tastes and expanding the nutrient variety by making different kinds of food products available was a matter of moving beyond localism.

"Today," the economist Arthur Barto Adams wrote in 1916, "more than fifty per cent of our population is centered in towns and cities, many of which are so large that they are unable to get their perishable food from the immediate territory surrounding them, but are compelled to depend on farms hundreds of miles away."[10] A survey of fruit and vegetable shippers conducted by a joint commission of shipping and wholesaling industries in 1922 found that "the nature of the commodities, the variation in seasons, the location and development of producing districts, and the centers of population and demand emphasize the vital importance of transportation."[11] Feeding northeastern cities like Philadelphia was a challenge of overcoming time and space between diverse regions of production and the largest population centers.

The rise of urban industrial capitalism is often told as the story of improving efficiency through new mechanized techniques of mass production, storage, and distribution. But there were also conflicts over how mechanization should be applied, what should count as the most efficient methods and tools, and who would benefit from such industry efforts.[12] Such was the case in the rise and dominance of food processing industries that positioned mass production in relation to agriculture. Debates and negotiations—and the eventual dominance of processing industries and their branded products—shaped the widespread dissemination of breakfast cereals, canned goods, and packaged flour, sugar, and grains in the first half of the 1900s.

The conflicts over the "pursuit of efficiency" were maybe even more pronounced and enduring in the production, storage, and distribution of perishable fruits and vegetables. Gradually, farmers, engineers, and scientists grew more interdependent, converting fields into orderly and mechanized growing "factories."[13] Urban wholesalers emerged as the middlemen in this distribution system. They mediated the relationships between farmers and consumers as city centers gained consumer power.

Yet aligning the supply and demand dynamics around perishable goods was also filled with uncertainty. Urban inhabitants were accustomed to direct farm-to-market exchanges, especially with perishable goods. Food market development of the eighteenth and early nineteenth centuries existed as a public trust, much like the rise of regional and state water authorities. Even in cities with increasing population sizes, like New York and Philadelphia, public marketplaces were set aside by state authorities for farmers and other producers to display and sell their products.[14] In Pennsylvania, public markets were heavily regulated. It was illegal to broker exchanges between farmers and consumers.[15]

The realignment of distribution infrastructures altered public expectations around exchange relationships. It integrated the logic of the "pursuit of efficiency" into the perishable food system. As public health and nutritional experts advised the public to eat more food varieties, politicians and agricultural societies promoted agricultural efficiencies in surrounding farm regions. In the early 1800s, state and federal agencies and civic and scientific associations like the Philadelphia Society for Promoting Agriculture encouraged farmers to increase yields to meet the demands of towns and cities. However, the direct farm-to-market system increased the demands on farmers. In addition to working the fields, they were pressured to learn new scientifically supported production techniques to improve volumes and qualities of fruits and vegetables, and they expended additional time and resources at the marketplace.[16]

Marketing agents in growing cities gained leverage in the shifting exchange dynamics. City-based market actors fought legal regulations on brokering supplies. Wholesalers, street hucksters, and other middlemen began carving out new roles in the food supply system to complement the time-intensive agricultural labor.[17] An elongating chain of distribution governed the supply of fresh fruits and vegetables. The public grew more dependent on the complex market process, shifting consumer expectations about availability. In Raymond Williams's terms, the urban provisioning system turned "users" into "consumers"; the former had more direct knowledge of objects and their applications while the latter depended on "an external and autonomous system" for presenting more "abstract" products and varieties to the public.[18]

Conflicts arose between different marketing positions, especially as urban and suburban development extended consumer demand beyond the large city centers. Changing transportation, food preservation methods, and population settlement patterns posed difficulties for downtown urban wholesalers. Even though wholesalers were crucial in the development of the market-based provisioning system, they were also place-based connectors. They procured and distributed foods for a specific territory. They assembled goods arriving on ship, rail, and truck from multiple regions into downtown market districts. They then sold them off to smaller-scale vendors, brokers, and retailers who connected the supplies to neighborhoods and nearby towns beyond downtown. Urban wholesalers faced industry, institutional, and infrastructural challenges that over time constrained their place-based exchange relationships.

The urban fresh produce wholesale districts—from Philadelphia to Chicago, New York to St. Louis—were trapped in declining urban centers after the 1950s. As central cities lost their economic leverage, place-based growth machines turned against these downtown markets. Politicians and business leaders viewed downtown wholesale locations as obsolete nodes amid more flexible mobility platforms, regional distribution projects, and changing economies of scale. Urban boosters took up a new battle over how to value and promote profits in the urban center. In that conflict, they associated wholesalers with urban decline. They labeled them as "business slums," sites of infrastructural inefficiency and decay. The disinvestment and demolition of downtown wholesale market districts became an important part of the urban renewal strategy.[19] Wholesalers were forced to reinvent their role, this time in a decentering food supply system.

The Rise of the Urban Supply System

By the end of the 1800s, produce wholesalers established a bustling market district in Philadelphia's oldest downtown area on Dock Street, between Front and Second Streets, adjacent to the Delaware River—an area called Society Hill. Other wholesalers, like the meat and poultry houses and some additional fresh produce vendors, relocated a mile north to Callowhill

Street to access more space. Initially, the produce wholesalers relied on relationships with New Jersey farmers.

New Jersey produce, coming from across the Delaware River, provided variety when it was in season, dating back to the colonial-era "Jersey Market," a public market shed at the foot of the river.[20] Wholesalers took on more central distribution responsibilities in the provisioning system. They expanded beyond the single location but still maintained ties to New Jersey growers during peak months when farmers consolidated products at the South Jersey docks and loaded them onto boats.

Even the close proximity of New Jersey farms was no guarantee of standardization in quality, quantity, and price of fresh produce. Because of the precarious nature of the objects themselves and the limited techniques available to preserve and secure them in transit, traveling from just across the river could lead to damages and fluctuating supplies. A reporter in September 1885 observed that eight to ten small sailboats traveled from South Jersey loaded with about 100 baskets of fruits and vegetables each. This food arrived into Philadelphia at 2:00 a.m. Then at 10:00 a.m., two steamships originating from the New Jersey ports of Billingston and Bridgeton docked at the Arch Street Wharf. They carried an additional 1,500 to 2,000 baskets. Finally, at 4:00 p.m., dozens of additional small boats holding 600 to 800 baskets each arrived at Dock Street, along with cartloads crossing bridges from various parts of Southern New Jersey.[21]

The produce was transported in open baskets on the open decks of small boats and ships. The uncertainty of arrival times, volumes, and quality—not to mention unpredictable transit methods—translated into unstable prices throughout the day depending on what was available at any given moment. "There is nothing that fluctuates so much in price as fruit and produce," said one Dock Street dealer later that month in 1885. "It is impossible to estimate one day's prices with another." Even within the same day, the prices of fruits and vegetables could ebb and flow. The Dock Street vendor remarked, "I have come here at four o'clock in the morning and sold peaches at $1.50 per basket and at noon offered the same quality of fruit at $1 per basket. Strange, you say, nothing strange about it. In the morning, the peaches would be scarce and high, but by noon the market would be supplied to the extent of five or six additional carloads of the fruit. This applies to all that is sold in this vicinity."[22]

There were multiple reasons wholesalers wanted to incorporate products grown in other regions. In addition to unpredictable quantities and quality, consumer demand was increasing, and local growing seasons were volatile—an early frost, a drought, an insect invasion, or other unforeseeable threats could easily wipe out a crop in any region.[23] Most important to wholesale entrepreneurs was the additional economic prospect of expanding the market. Steam engines, rail networks, and emerging preservation methods changed the possibilities of shipping over longer distances. They brought new profit-making possibilities, but no guarantees, given the fragile composition of products and the unclear transport connections between distant sites of production and the final site of consumption—in this case, Philadelphia.

Building the infrastructural interdependencies was key to the political-economic growth competitions in both agricultural and urban locales.[24] Different commodities were tied to different places and regions, which meant there was ongoing work to assemble transport networks linking production sites to cities. In the early 1900s, citrus fruits were grown in parts of California and Florida; celery and lettuce came from California, Florida, and New York; potatoes, onions, and cabbage were grown around the Great Lakes region; spinach grew in areas of Texas; cantaloupe production concentrated in California's Imperial Valley; strawberries and peas were found in Maryland, Delaware, and Virginia; and peaches grew in Georgia.[25]

Railroad networks knitted together distant places.[26] The Southern Pacific Railroad was an economic engine in the California growth machine. It turned the state into the nation's premier fruit and vegetable production system. According to Douglas Sackman, the railroad "transformed California from a terra incognita with a wide variety of soils and microclimates into a known landscape ripe for a new system of control and cultivation."[27] Citrus fruit, in particular, was lucrative. With the use of new cooling methods in rail cars, the products—typically unripe "green fruit" in the early days—traveled from California all the way to the Northeast. Sunkist, which would eventually become the largest fruit-growing cooperative in the world, started shipping oranges from California to the Northeast in refrigerated railcars as early as the 1880s.[28]

Another profit-making angle for Dock Street wholesalers was linked to global supplies. Although tropical fruits remained luxuries for decades, some commodities like bananas became more commonplace at the end of the nineteenth century. Like oranges, bananas had a protective skin and could be shipped in their green, unripe state. They were the earliest global fresh commodity available to United States consumers in large quantities.[29] Some wholesalers specialized in handling banana shipments from bigger companies like the United Fruit Company as well as smaller competitors like the Atlantic Fruit Company.

Michael Levin, for example, was a Jewish immigrant from Lithuania who moved to Philadelphia in 1906 and started selling bananas by building relationships with shippers. Ships would dock in the Philadelphia ports looking to offload their supplies. Levin, initially a street huckster, loaded small quantities of bananas still fastened to the stem onto a horse-drawn wagon and carted them into neighborhoods around the city. He eventually made enough money to build a wholesale business on Dock Street in a basement unit with two rooms.

Levin used his new storage space, including a heated basement room, to ripen bananas on the stems. He and his sons sold them to immigrant vendors looking to make a start in the city. The peddlers found Levin because of his hand-painted wooden sign hanging at the street level—*Michael Levin, Bananas Downstairs*. Over the next 20 years, Levin continued to buy bananas in even larger quantities and expanded the size of his storage space and operation. By the 1920s, he was a major supplier for the Atlantic Fruit Company, running one of the largest banana middleman operations on the East Coast, redirecting bananas to many retail locations.[30]

Philadelphia's market district on Dock Street was the primary point of convergence for fresh produce coming into the city. The density of businesses made it a major market district, even as the city expanded geographically. Downtown market districts provided easy access for the range of buyers coming from surrounding Philadelphia neighborhoods, and from surrounding suburban towns, who would make their purchases from wholesale sellers before heading back to meet the needs of their own customers.

Wholesalers gained power in the supply system by taking on the risk of larger quantities. They employed procurement and storage skills to mediate between shippers and smaller-scale market-makers. Bananas and oranges were good travelers. If packed, stored, and cooled properly, they could maintain their expected quality for the duration of the trip and easily convert into a stable market product. Wholesalers, however, wanted to add more varieties into this networked system, which meant learning to deal with products that were less durable and coming from additional untapped regions.

Mike Amato, a third-generation Philadelphia produce wholesaler, said his Italian grandfather initially worked on Dock Street loading and unloading supplies for other produce men.[31] He eventually formed his own wholesaling business by hooking up with growers from a variety of growing regions. He explained how his grandfather connected to different suppliers:

> There were lots of people who had families that were growing, particularly in South Jersey. They were all from Southern Italy and had farms. He knew some of those people. He met farmers in the produce market and built up personal relationships. But my grandfather also traveled a lot. He would go

as far down as Florida. He would go around little southern towns and ask, who's got peaches, who's got peppers, who's got eggplants. He had stuff from the Carolinas and Maryland. It would come up by rail line.

Wholesaling was a system of uncertainty. Amato says that his grandfather was pressured to invest in agricultural production, advancing money to farmers and taking on some of the supply risk. At one point, Amato's grandfather made major investments in Florida eggplants. "He would go down there, give a guy $5,000 to plant a crop and expect two loads a week, and then 'Gee, there's only one.' And if the weather got a little bad and the product got tight, 'Gee, I don't have anything this week.' So, at the end of the season, [if you're an investor,] maybe you got your money back, maybe you didn't."

A major part of the problem in the early 1900s was the patchwork of regional interests that accumulated into a convoluted network of distribution. The rail and shipping infrastructure in the early 1900s did not fluidly and directly connect point A to point B. Moving the food between regions required shippers and wholesalers to patch together a mobility network between transaction points. For example, arduous journeys by way of multiple forms of transit between southern states and northeastern cities damaged products before they reached the final destinations. One investigative reporter in 1900 described the disjointed process of piecing together steamships and railroads to reach Philadelphia's Dock Street Market:

> From Florida fruit shipments are made by rail to Savannah and Charleston. To these two cities come heavy consignments of potatoes and cabbage from Young's Island [South Carolina], asparagus and potatoes from Mt. Pleasant [South Carolina], crates of tomatoes and other vegetables from other sections, all of which are loaded on the docks. They are transferred to steamers [steamships] and taken to New York or Baltimore. Again they are carried from the steamer to the docks, then to the railway stations, from whence they are shipped to this city. By the time they reach the consignee [in Philadelphia], after this series of transfers, many, many crates are damaged; hours if not days have been lost and the cost of transportation is much higher than by a direct water communication.[32]

Wholesalers in New York, Chicago, Boston, St. Louis, and Philadelphia faced comparable difficulties in procuring fresh food supplies during the early part of the 1900s.[33] Between 1889 and 1919, the increase in the total volume of fruits and vegetables transported on rail across the United States increased from 4.5 million to 20 million tons.[34] The rail infrastructure grew into a more comprehensive network as well, which would seemingly resolve the above dilemmas. But it did not.

The material qualities of products were an independent factor. The USDA reported that 20 to 30 percent of perishable products decayed before making it to the marketplace. Artho Barto Adams, an economist, went on to investigate the problems across the country. He found in his 1916 report that an additional 25 percent of the product rotted by the time it arrived at the wholesale markets. "It is not an over-estimate," he concluded, "that between 30 and 40 per cent of the perishables which are raised on the farms are never consumed at all."[35]

Distance required preservation, so it was no surprise that food processing industries gained so much power and influence in the food system through the sheer will of product shelf life. In terms of shipping fruits and vegetables, there was nothing similar. Rail cooling was inadequate for the job. Refrigerated rail cars were first introduced in the 1850s and were quite common in the movement of California fruit and vegetables by the end of the century. Yet in 1920—on the verge of the automobile revolution—they were still working out technical difficulties in building a reliable fresh food rail system connecting different regions. The implementation of refrigeration into distinct rail lines and around diverse products happened at different times. Some products, like unripe oranges and iceberg lettuce—products viewed as "virtually indestructible"—were known to travel better than others over long distances.[36]

Before mechanical refrigeration made its way into transportation systems, the railroads relied on ice, insulation, and air circulation to chill the cars. Engineers and policy-makers from the Department of Agriculture, the United States Railroad Administration, the Agricultural Conference, and the Joint Commission of Agricultural Inquiry all suggested the need for "standardized refrigerated cars" to solve long-distance shipping problems. The railroad companies, however, disagreed about which "standard" characteristics to integrate into the rail cars. The recommendations included improvements in basket ice bunkers to store the ice underneath the car, solid insulated bulkheads to protect the product from outside elements, and floor racks to enable better air circulation.[37]

In 1920, only a small percentage of the 85,000 railroad cars surveyed by the joint commission met the minimum standard requirements. According to the Interstate Commerce Commission, "There can be little doubt . . . that many of those cars, judged by modern practices, cannot be operated with efficiency and economy." Different parts of the supply system contested the control of supplies, the meaning of efficiency, and the value of quality standards. The National Poultry, Butter, and Egg Association found that shippers loaded products with the "presumption" of being "modern and efficient" only to find when the products arrived at the destination that the railroad companies were using "old cars freshly painted and with exterior repairs, but with obsolete and inefficient insulation."[38]

Although urban markets were increasing volumes and varieties of fruits and vegetables, consumers continued to complain about price fluctuations. The spatial distances and regional varieties between production and consumption were constants, but various interest positions in the system—growers, shippers, packers, dockworkers, railroad companies, wholesalers, and retailers—contested how to construct the link between profit, quality, and efficiency and who was responsible for building and maintaining the relationships on the way to reaching consumers.

The elongated infrastructural system was growing into a reification machine that dismantled previous exchange dynamics in food marketplaces. Consumers could no longer recognize where the products originated; and sellers could no longer guarantee it. The wholesale markets converted perishable products into anonymous and abstract commodities, open to multiple interpretations about their value. The news dailies reported on the wholesale market's vibrant abundancies but continuing inefficiencies. The proximity and visibility of the wholesale market itself—and the distancing and invisibility of the elongated supply chains—made the wholesalers a prominent target of local ridicule.

The various actors in the supply chains tried to separate out their independent roles from the interdependent system of uncertainty by placing blame on others. An editorial in *Railway Age* read, "In addition to continuing their efforts to enrich themselves by paying producers as little as possible for their products and charging consumers as much as possible for them, [wholesalers] are now trying to force down freight rates by a campaign of falsification [that improper handling by railroads is responsible for price fluctuations]."[39] The American Farm Bureau Federation, looking to call attention to the discrepancies in profits between farmers and the market middlemen, regularly advertised in newspapers across the country about the black box of profit-making between production and consumption by asking: "What happens in the dark?" (see fig. 1). It turned out, on closer scrutiny, that wholesalers and farmers took home only a small fraction of the profit, with most of the money going to shippers and rail lines.[40]

The uncertainties of managing the distribution system were crystallizing in the context of an industrial era celebrating the pursuit of efficiency:

What Happens in the Dark?

1 American Farm Bureau Federation. Advertisement in
the *New York Times*, January 22, 1920, p. 14.

the spread of mass production, product standardization across industries, and chain grocers experimenting with new economies of scale. A narrative about consumer convenience and cheaper food was on the rise. Urban consumers visiting their neighborhood grocers expected the standard replication of commodities, as well as stable prices or even decreasing prices. That was the case for goods like grains, cereals, tea, coffee, sugar, and salt.[41] Nonetheless, fresh produce remained unique in this regard: infrastructural interdependencies—not any single position in the supply chain—elevated the rates of damage and waste in the movement of fruits and vegetables. It locked in a convoluted distribution system for decades and pushed political and economic actors into increasing concerns and conflicts about how to manage market uncertainty.

Splitting the City's Distribution System

City leaders and businessmen tried to solve the wholesale efficiency problems, but the meaning of "efficiency" was a moving target. The commitment to certain ways of doing business became sunk into the costs of maintaining the built structure and their interdependencies.[42] Yet urbanization, market-making, and mobility methods were not—and are not—static relationships. The wholesalers were entrenched in an iterative and cumulative process of expanding the boundaries of cities through population growth, annexation, patterns of development, and transit interconnections.

Philadelphia, like so many of the major cities in the United States in the first half of the 1900s, did not commit to the complex urban and regional planning strategies necessary to make sense of these changes, let alone find ways to manage them. Philadelphia did not establish a formal city planning committee until 1942, finally addressing changing infrastructural, economic, and spatial development relationships as collective problems to be solved. And even then, as James Scott has demonstrated, centralized state planning did not necessarily produce the most rational and effective outcomes.[43]

The infrastructure of urbanism and consumerism shifted expectations around food marketing in large cities. As the suburbs grew in the first half of the twentieth century, changing transportation methods and market connections altered how food was delivered and how people shopped for it. Economic and urban planning, although commonly thought of as strategic ventures, were embedded in complex and multilevel system interdependencies that constrained decision-making geared toward place-related problems. The distribution system was a constant work in progress between multiple actors and levels: city, state, and national politicians, state and federal food and agricultural agencies, wholesalers, shippers, grocery chains, farmers, and processing industries.

Millions of consumers relied on Philadelphia's downtown marketing arrangement for fresh produce. Although the railroad network advanced the quantity of supplies coming *into* Philadelphia, the city also faced transportation disruptions *within* the city. The railroad tracks did not come directly into the Dock Street market district, which meant that there was an extra step of connecting the rail terminals with the marketplace.

In addition, railroad shippers wanted to build more modern warehousing, but the central wholesale district was overcrowded. Railroad companies constructed new storage and marketing facilities several miles away in South Philadelphia. Splitting up the transportation and wholesale market system within the city boundaries—Dock Street Market in Center City, Callowhill Market a mile north in North Philadelphia, and then two disjointed railroad wholesale terminals in South Philadelphia (see the map in fig. 2)—increased distribution and transaction costs and complicated the relationship between wholesalers and the many retail enterprises dependent on them.

In 1926, the Baltimore and Ohio (B&O) Railroad Company and the Reading Railroad Company jointly constructed a new storage and sales depot between Delaware and Weccacoe Avenues and Jackson and Ritner Streets in South Philadelphia. The Pennsylvania Railroad Company followed by building a produce terminal to the immediate south of their rivals. These new buildings, located over two miles south of the central wholesale district, operated as hubs for the storage and sale of fresh produce coming into the region by way of railroad. With a more modern and unified structure

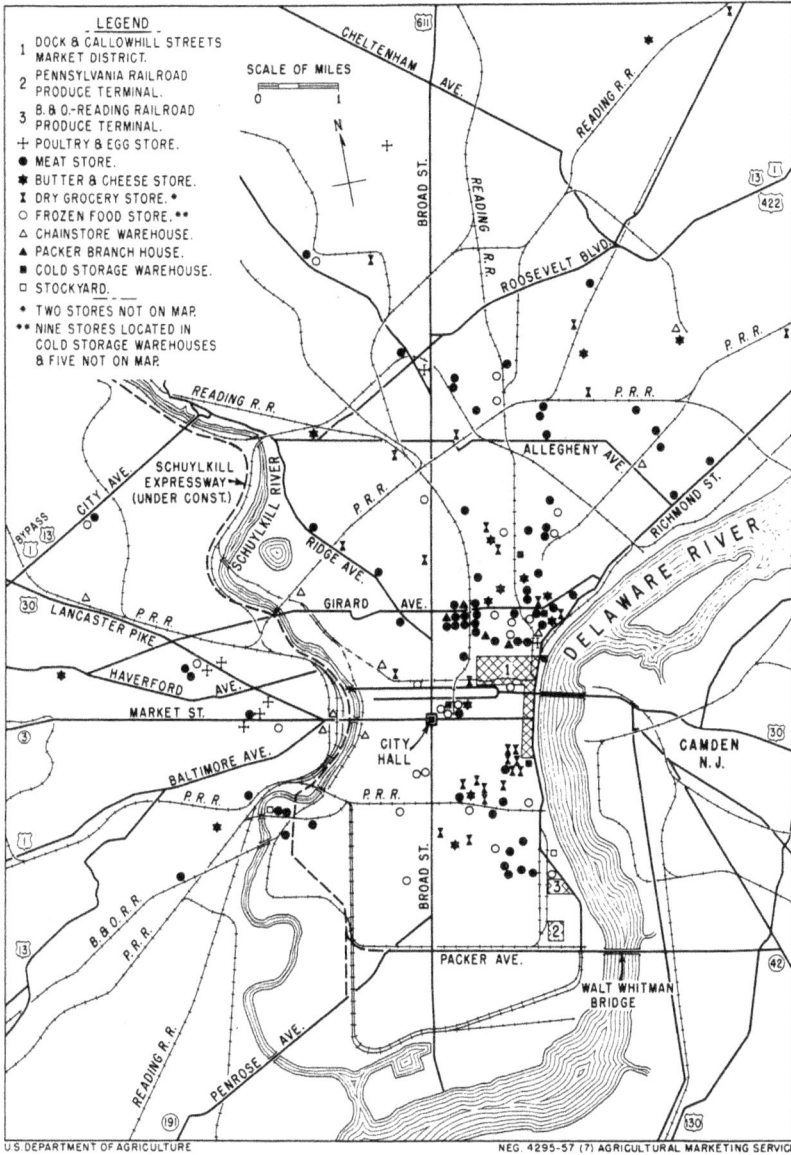

2 Map of the wholesale market system in Philadelphia, 1954. Source: Agricultural Transportation and Facilities Branch, Marketing Research Division, Agricultural Marketing Services, US Department of Agriculture, Washington, DC. Marketing Research Report no. 201.

located directly along the tracks, marketing agents unloaded fresh produce off of train cars, stored it in refrigerated warehouses, and sold the produce to a range of consumers at auction.[44]

The new B&O/Reading Terminal had a different storage and selling structure. It housed an auction room seating 250 people—various types of wholesalers, brokers, and retailers—who bid on the incoming product. It also included 1.3 million cubic feet of cold storage in seven stories, divided into rooms of different temperatures to preserve perishables of different classes.[45] Dock Street, in contrast, lacked any refrigeration whatsoever. The wholesalers continued their long-standing transaction principle of procuring and selling products on the same day.

Each day, the sales manager at the new railroad terminals produced a catalog of the different lots. Samples were set up for people to observe before they made their purchases. In the auction room, buyers bid on the products. After taking ownership, customers loaded them onto their carts or into their trucks and took them to their warehouses and stores. Mike Amato, the third-generation wholesale trader, said his grandfather, and his father thereafter, bought fresh commodities from the railroad terminals for their Dock Street business.

> There would be a guy there that had onions and two sizes of Idaho potatoes. Another guy has lettuce and celery. And another guy has lettuce and broccoli. They would put a couple of boxes of each next to a podium. At a certain time of day, all the buyers would rush in and buy product from these people and load their trucks. The fruit auction was the same thing. They could have 100 to 200 cars of fruit on the track. They would roll the cars in, and the product would be unloaded onto the platform and sold at auction. Typically, the people were buying for somebody else. So, if you were from Scranton or from Atlantic City, you would call your guy up and say, "I need 400 or 500 88 size Valencia oranges today. Is there anything there?" And he would say, "Well, there's a car due, if it makes it, I'll let you know." I might call up and say, "You know, I need 500 peaches. I need the best peaches." Or "I need 500 peaches, but I don't want to pay too much." So, he would go into the sales room and he'd wait for that lot to come and then he'd bid on it. You would tell him what you wanted to pay, but a guy like that might more than likely know more than you. He'd call and say, "I bought you 200 extra 88 Valencias because there's not going to be any here the rest of the week."

The Dock Street wholesalers, as regular buyers, were interdependent with the rail terminals. Yet this setup meant that market-makers moved products between multiple storage and selling locations in the city before reaching the final customer. In 1936, the Bureau of Agricultural Economics conducted a study in conjunction with Penn State College and New Jersey College of Agriculture. They found that having multiple points of exchange required more cross-hauling through the city and strained the market system. The report suggested that consolidation of the markets and better co-ordination between various forms of transportation would save time and money. According to the report, "To buy wholesale quantities it is necessary for larger buyers to visit two or three markets in widely separated parts of the city. This situation results in too many evils." These "evils" were about internal contestations and constraints of an increasingly complex system: difficulties collecting information on supply, demand, and prices; lack of regulation of hours between markets; increased handling costs; and price fluctuations.[46]

Changes in the modes of transportation aggravated existing problems. The newer South Philadelphia terminals were positioned as the central markets for produce coming by way of rail, while the older Dock Street district—located in the more congested downtown with narrower streets—came to rely on trucking. Even when Dock Street vendors arranged for the movement of produce into the city from another part of the country by way of railroad, they still had to transport the product from the rail terminals to their downtown market district.[47]

A survey of urban wholesale districts in the United States conducted by the Bureau of Agricultural Economics found that evolving transportation trends impeded fresh food delivery. Just a decade after the construction of the multimillion-dollar modernized rail terminals in South Philadelphia, rail receipts steadily declined while trucking receipts rapidly increased. Marketing agents were aware they were positioned in the middle of this historic transformation, but they did not know how to manage the challenges. The Philadelphia *Evening Bulletin* wrote about the situation in terms of the constraint on the collective pursuit of profitability and efficiency:

> There are ample facilities for shipments that have been declining in volume and insufficient arrangements for those on the increase. It is noted that a buyer from out-of-town who begins at Dock Street at nine in the evening of one day will finish buying a complete line of fruits and vegetables in the summer months, somewhere in the maze of markets around noon of the following day. The ramification of obstacles to easy buying renders the present condition, dividing the wholesale business among the two railroad produce terminals and the two markets on Dock and Callowhill streets, unsatisfactory

for the efficient operation of large buyers and for wholesalers and the markets themselves. The conditions are no better suited to the needs of local retailers and hucksters nor to requirements of growers and shippers.[48]

During two weeks in the middle of July of the same year, the Bureau of Agricultural Economics traced how many cars of fresh produce came into Philadelphia, to which distribution center they arrived, and to what types of retailers the fresh produce ultimately moved. Of the nearly 5,500 total cars, more than 3,000 went to the Dock Street market district and about 1,000 went to the Callowhill Market. After cross-hauling between the railroad and wholesale settings, products were then redirected to different retailers who sold them off to their customers. Of the total incoming supply, 1,900 eventually went to out-of-town stores; more than 3,000 went to independent Philadelphia dealers; and more than 500 landed in Philadelphia-area chain stores. In the 1930s, most of the supply coming into Philadelphia still went to Philadelphia markets, and Dock Street wholesalers remained the primary market node. However, a substantial sum, almost 35 percent of the fresh food supply, came into the city of Philadelphia only to immediately move to areas beyond its boundaries.[49]

The infrastructural incompatibility and unsteady prices opened another round of criticisms of the system as "inefficient." Wendell Calhoun, an agricultural economist for the USDA, reported in 1940 that the split-market system inflated the prices of fruits and vegetables by more than $35 per load. He found that the rail terminals and the central wholesale district hardly coordinated at all: different hours of operation at Dock Street Market and the Oregon Avenue rail terminals meant that produce was held an extra day before it was delivered, often sitting in crates and baskets in "the street and gutters of Dock Street." He described the relationship between the different parties as a "cart-before-the-horse order of selling." "In most markets," Calhoun explained, "the order of sale is from the grower to the wholesaler to the jobber [middleman distributer] to the retailer. Here, because of the two markets, it is from the jobber to the wholesaler to the retailer."[50]

Vital parts of the food distribution system, such as growers, shippers, and truckers, adapted to the changing transporting demands. The central wholesale markets—their building stocks, road infrastructures, and technological capacities (especially those related to modern refrigeration)—were being left behind in the evolving supply chain.[51] According to the *Pennsylvania Farmer*, a journal dedicated to investigating the state's agricultural conditions, Philadelphia's wholesale produce business was losing $1.5 million annually because of its infrastructure. As early as 1939, farmers in the sur-rounding regions of Pennsylvania, New Jersey, Delaware, Maryland, and Virginia, so concerned about the decline of one of their most important market centers, organized the Growers' Committee for Improving the Phila-delphia Market. One temporary solution involved establishing a trucking platform at the Pennsylvania Railroad Terminal in South Philadelphia. Ac-cording to Leon M. Van Hekle, the manager of the rail terminal, "Growers who move their stuff by truck can get in and out of this market in a fraction of the time required to do business in Dock Street. Furthermore, the ease of doing business here attracted many out-of-town buyers who have de-serted the Philadelphia [Dock Street] market because conditions have been so unsatisfactory."[52]

By 1950, multiple interest groups with a stake in the urban supply chain had become aware of the infrastructural mismatch between transportation and wholesale market locations. The mayor's office reported in 1951 that Dock Street's location near the river made no sense, as boat shipments, which were once central to the market growth in the nineteenth century, had disintegrated. Joseph Enarson, the executive assistant to Philadelphia mayor Joseph Clark, wrote to the city's director of commerce, "To feed to-day's population requires huge shipments of perishable produce: 180 car-lots [a measurement equivalent to an entire train car load] of fresh fruits and vegetables each day, or a total of 66,000 a year. Boat shipments have disappeared; a trifling 22 carlots came in by boat for the whole of 1951. Yet Philadelphia's principle wholesale market is still at Dock Street near the river, which it no longer needs, and away from the railroads, which it badly needs."[53]

The split market was a continuing problem of interactive but incompat-ible components of a system without a coherent strategy between the vari-ous parties for managing changes in mobility and storage. The *Economics Business Bulletin* reported in 1952, "The wholesale fruit and vegetable mar-ket in Philadelphia grew up in a piecemeal fashion without the aid of any planning whatsoever—the city government did not coordinate activities of the various groups for the benefit of all concerned whenever new facilities were added."[54] Studies by the USDA and the Urban Land Institute started in 1936 and continued steadily through the 1950s. They all found the same thing: the market system did not "naturally" find solutions to the private and public problems. The split-distribution system was both an economic problem for businesses invested in the system and a vital infrastructural problem for feeding millions of people.

Infrastructural Inefficiency to Infrastructural Decay

Following the Great Depression, political and business leaders in major urban centers found it difficult to manage the severe financial setbacks. Complicating matters, federal programs provided support after World War II to move people—almost exclusively the white and middle classes—to new suburbs by funding the mass production of single-family houses and supporting the rapid construction of highways and roads.[55] The development of shopping centers and malls beyond the central city contributed to the process of urban decentering across the nation. The result was that a huge proportion of the public no longer relied on the historic urban centers for access to highly demanded commodities. (See fig. 3.)

Wholesalers were stuck in the middle of large industrial-era cities at a time when those cities' populations and infrastructures were eroding.[56] Urban wholesalers were small business owners and community traditionalists. The wholesale market district consisted almost exclusively of family businesses passed down from generation to generation. Being market middlemen in this model was about bridging *their* local community to resources beyond the reach of its citizens. These businessmen, many of them first- and second-generation Italian, Irish, and Jewish immigrants, valued their ties to the local economy and affiliations to local ethnic and religious groups. Paradoxically, as the city's growth machine came to view Philadelphia as falling apart, the urban wholesalers emerged as emblems of the city's decline.

The Greater Philadelphia Movement, an organization of 150 business leaders formed in 1948, sought to solve problems related to Philadelphia's weakening economic position. Both the city and the food system were framed as market and infrastructural problems. They argued that as existing businesses hastily departed, few new ones replaced them in this once-strong manufacturing city. According to them, Philadelphia was "going to hell on a one-way toboggan." Philadelphia business leaders enlisted the help of major corporate executives, both from the region and from around the country, revealing shifting public-private alliances in the future of urban business development.[57]

A series of lengthy reports put out in the 1950s, including one by the Greater Philadelphia Movement, observed a wholesale market system out of date in relation to changing modes of food delivery. In 1931, more than two-thirds of all fruits and vegetables arrived into Philadelphia by rail. By 1949, trucking surpassed rail as the largest source of produce delivery into the city. In 1953, trucks accounted for 55 percent of the traffic into the wholesale market district. Even when trucks were not the source of direct delivery

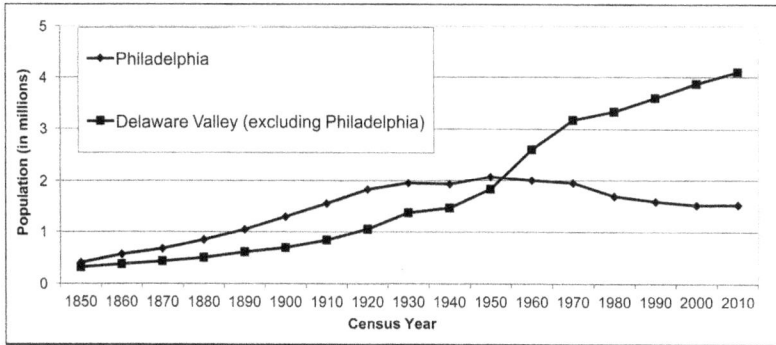

3 Demographic changes in Philadelphia and surrounding nine-county area. Sources: US Censuses, 1850–2010.

between the site of production and the marketplace, trucks were still used within the city to connect Dock Street and the Delaware River ports and South Philadelphia railroad terminals. The growing numbers of trucks, and the increasing size of them between the 1930s and 1950s, overcrowded the streets in and around the wholesale district.[58] (See figs. 4, 5, and 6.)

The Dock Street produce market was not built for tractor-trailer trucks. The area was made up of narrow cobblestone streets, which constrained easy passage through the market neighborhood. A report by the Greater Philadelphia Movement found that a trucker "must inch his way through streets jammed curb to curb with traffic." The streets of the Dock Street Market, only 30 feet wide, resembled "a solid mass of motor vehicles." A retailer would "pay bribes" in order to "reach a curbside parking place" near their pickup location, running around the city for hours on end, from market to market, putting in "an exhausting day's work even before he can get his purchases home to sell to customers." Truck drivers, unable to park at a wholesaler's doorstep, unloaded their supplies 25 to 35 feet away, in the middle of surrounding streets, blocking passageways and creating obstacles for efficient movement from the trucks to the storage spaces.[59]

The city's development patterns also compromised the ability to fluidly connect rail and trucking. Tracks were ultimately laid down so that freight could travel alongside the Delaware River from South Philadelphia rail terminals to a point closer to the wholesale district. Freight trains carrying produce crawled through "streets in the very heart of the city," where "darting pedestrians and tangles of trucks" blocked their movement. But with such overcrowding, there was no way to build access points for the rail cars into

4 Trucks parked at Dock Street wholesale market, 1928; Philadelphia *Evening Bulletin* Photographs (Copyright: TU Libraries). Credit: Special Collections Research Center, Temple University Libraries, Philadelphia, PA.

the market itself. The rail transaction point was still a few streets away from the wholesale market district, requiring cart services to move the supplies to the actual market houses.[60]

Large chain retailers started bypassing the produce wholesale markets as early as the 1930s by vertically integrating fresh produce supply chains into their high-volume merchandising operations. In this era of suburban supermarket expansion, only 25 percent of the Philadelphia wholesale market business went to chain stores.[61] Dock Street wholesale markets were mostly servicing independent grocers, green grocers, street hucksters, restaurants, and other small businesses. Yet increasingly, retailers of all types started to avoid the produce market district, including hundreds of one-store operations. For example, Harrisburg businessmen stopped buying from the Philadelphia market, and businesses in Wilkes Barre, Pennsylvania, and Trenton, New Jersey, traveled the longer route to New York City to purchase produce for their stores. Highways made a range of wholesale options in different cities more accessible in the 1950s, creating competition between them. Harry Batten, an advertising executive and chairman of the Greater Philadelphia Movement, believed the problem of Philadelphia's inefficiencies was endemic: "Several years ago a federal food marketing authority told Philadelphia city planners that sellers and buyers preferred to use the New York market rather than endure what he called the discomforts of doing business in Philadelphia."[62]

In 1953 the market district handled only 88 percent of the produce sold in 1931. Business leaders and the merchants themselves were troubled by this fact. For one, the metropolitan region grew by almost one million people during that period, a clear sign that other avenues of distribution were forming to connect fresh produce to the suburbs. Secondly, in the decades following World War II, the nation's median disposable income level rose, and the amount of money people spent on consumer items increased accordingly.[63] Thirdly, by then most houses had refrigerators and freezers,

5 Trucks parked at Dock Street wholesale market, 1947. Philadelphia *Evening Bulletin* Photographs (Copyright: TU Libraries). Credit: Special Collections Research Center, Temple University Libraries, Philadelphia, PA.

6 Large tractor trailer trucks crowding Dock Street, 1950s. Housing Association
of the Delaware Valley Photographs (Copyright: TU Libraries). Credit: Special
Collections Research Center, Temple University Libraries, Philadelphia, PA.

which benefited the fresh food industries overall. In fact, the total quantity
of fruit and vegetable consumption increased even as sales in the downtown
wholesale markets declined.[64]

The tense relationship between the central cities and growing suburbs
crystallized an anti-urban sentiment across the country, and downtown
wholesalers were caught in the webs of the changing conditions. Many organizations and actors—the Greater Philadelphia Movement, the USDA,
Philadelphia politicians, and local journalists—connected their previous
concerns about infrastructural inefficiency with mounting public anxieties
about urban decline. The Dock Street Market buildings were over 100 years
old and unstable. They ranged in size from one to four stories high. None
had proper elevator facilities to move products between levels. They had no
truck-level platforms in the front or rear of the buildings to facilitate moving
products in and out. Most of the businesses lacked any back entrances whatsoever, which meant the loading and unloading of supplies required access
to the front door. Large semitrailer trucks lined up by the dozens, limited by

the lack of back-door loading, unable to squeeze in and out of the parking area. As the trucks increased in size, the infrastructural mismatch between transportation and market delivery grew more extreme. The delays caused financial problems for retailers, who often incurred significant losses of perishable goods.[65]

Tim Cooley, a partner at a produce wholesaling firm, described to me the debilitating Dock Street Market conditions when his father was a produce dealer there: "There were elevators in the building, but they were still taking potatoes up the stairs because the elevator was in the basement. They had to walk down the steps to get to the elevator to take it to the top. There was no use for it. That was a rundown building. You'd go through holes in the walls to get to other buildings. And nobody had refrigerators back then. Back then it was like, 'If it comes in today, sell it today, you'll have more tomorrow.'"

The Dock Street wholesale district was not an isolated example. Downtown wholesale districts across the country were built for the infrastructural regime of feeding cities. Dock Street wholesalers lacked refrigeration of any kind, let alone refrigerated rooms differentiating temperatures for different classes of fruits and vegetables. In fact, many of the businesses lacked appropriate storage space altogether. Truckers unloaded fresh produce onto the sidewalks and in the middle of alleys and streets, where it remained in direct sunlight for hours, never entering protected inside units while it awaited pickup by various jobbers and retailers. The Agricultural and Transportation Branch of the USDA described the sidewalks as "cluttered with many food items, sometimes intact but many times dumped or tumbled, along with debris of broken boxes, chicken coops, and egg crates."[66]

The wholesale district was labeled a public nuisance. Harold L. Enarson, the mayor's executive assistant, concluded in a conversation with Walter Philips, the city's director of commerce, that "Dock Street is out of date by at least a century. The Dock Street Market is old, dirty, cramped, and congested—a recurrent target of cleanup campaigns. The market is a source of unending frustration to truckers, to local retailers who do business there, to the city authorities who must regulate its health and sanitation, and to the city planners who see land of high value and strategic location occupied by one and two-story ancient fire traps."[67]

The label of Dock Street as inefficient had been around for decades, due to the convoluted infrastructural relationships that increased rates of food spoilage and waste. The label of infrastructural decline added to the concerns. Complaints surfaced about unsanitary conditions and contributed to the city's disinvestment in the market district. Many of the buildings had no restrooms or washrooms for truckers delayed for hours trying to get in

7   Run-down street conditions of Dock Street, 1950s. Philadelphia *Evening Bulletin* Photographs (Copyright: TU Libraries). Credit: Special Collections Research Center, Temple University Libraries, Philadelphia, PA.

and out of the market. Without other options, people urinated in the public streets or in the back alleyways, intensifying public health concerns. Writing for the *Evening Bulletin*, Raymond C. Brecht referred to the market as "primitive," as food is "stacked on sidewalks or dumped there like so much garbage." He wrote, "Food heaped on sidewalks collects dirt and germs. There are no public toilets and quite often, not even toilets within market buildings. Loading platforms, public streets, alleys and vacant lots fill this need."[68] Daniel Langan of the *Philadelphia Inquirer* described it like this: "The pleasant aroma of fresh fruit clashed with the stench of decaying garbage piled high from the dilapidated buildings occupied by merchants."[69] (See fig. 7.)

Just as the blame about middleman inefficiency and corruption in prior decades was situated between multiple sides of the distribution infrastructure, concerns about unsanitary conditions also had multiple points of view. But this time, the conflicts were not only about consumer prices and business profitability. They also tapped into concerns about responsibilities for managing public health and maintaining food safety standards. Was it the responsibility of public or private interests? The city blamed wholesalers for their own predicament and argued that wholesalers should invest in improving their storage capacity so food crates were not exposed to the elements. They wanted merchants to install toilets for truckers and laborers so as not to worsen already unsanitary conditions. The merchants, on the other hand, argued that the city was required to clean up the excrement and waste in the public spaces surrounding the buildings.[70]

The Association of Wholesale Fruit and Vegetable Distributors, representing 55 Dock Street merchants, complained that the city's failure to improve the market district was a form of public disinvestment that furthered the market decay and endangered public health. Previously, the city had cleaned the market daily, but it had cut that service down to once a week. The association wrote, "The Dock Street produce market sells about one-half of the fresh fruits and vegetables consumed by the citizens of Philadelphia. The people of Philadelphia are entitled to the most sanitary conditions possible in such a market. The City is not doing its part in maintaining the cleanliness of this area. . . . Any garbage, filth, or debris that accumulates there during the week remains there for up to 6 days until the following Saturday."[71]

As urban abandonment and population decline continued and the city's poverty rates surged, the wholesale district became tied to the narrative of urban deterioration. The players in urban growth machines changed as well, and wholesalers were pushed aside. The Greater Philadelphia Movement, representing the new growth machine, described the wholesale district as part of the "old Tenderloin and Skid Row," an area that was "regarded by the police as one of the worst breeding areas for crime in the whole city." They labeled it a "business slum" with "their dirt and disease, their bums and drifters, and their shabby old buildings, and the hazard of fire which they create."[72] The people living in the vicinity and handling the food amplified the image of declining health standards. "Some of the markets draw labor for loading and unloading from adjacent slums, from the underworld and from the floaters who drift from city to city. Such laborers work an hour or so, earn enough for a bottle of cheap liquor, and sleep on the streets or in corners of the very buildings from which food is distributed. There can be no training or physical examinations for such workers, and it is impossible to have proper health standards."[73]

Planners and developers believed solving the city's economic problems required a major effort of urban revitalization. In the 1950s, special hearings started in Philadelphia to deal with the city's problems. Philadelphia already had tens of thousands of abandoned houses, and job prospects in the city were evaporating. Some residents raised concerns about safety, but city leaders were primarily concerned about the aesthetics and infrastructure of abandonment and its impact on the city's ability to attract new economic activity. In some areas of the city, garbage was strewn about on streets, and empty lots and yards were overgrown and unkempt. Political and economic leaders described the bridges into the city as introducing visitors to neglected sections with squatters living in abandoned homes and warehouses and empty dumping grounds. The Philadelphia Redevelopment Authority, with the assistance of business-led organizations like the Greater Philadelphia Movement, started an urban renewal campaign to find ways to eliminate urban blight and remake Philadelphia into a thriving economic center. The demolition and relocation of the wholesale district fit into the new model of planning symbiosis that focused on improving Philadelphia's downtown and developing regional economies of market agglomeration.

Planning Symbiosis and Regional Integration

City leaders and developers viewed Philadelphia's downtown—Center City—with new eyes. To bridge housing and business development, they broke up the city into districts with different economic and service-based functions. It was a strategic approach that would eventually become a key factor in the postindustrial consumer culture. The city reorganized its outdated and dreary commuter transportation system accordingly, knocking down the massive above-ground rail tracks, commonly referred to as the "Chinese Wall" for the way they physically divided Center City. Plans followed to develop one of these districts, Penn Center, as a financial and commercial hub with a range of new skyscrapers, financial businesses, and related services.

The Center City renewal effort included cleaning up existing parks and squares. Federal, state, and city agencies financed new grassy malls and parks surrounding Independence Hall, the site of the signing of the Declaration of Independence. The city also marked the East Washington Square area of Society Hill for renewal. This area, close to the Delaware River and Independence Hall, has unique historical value, with the nation's largest number of original colonial-era residences, some of which were homes to members of the Continental Congress.

Society Hill was also the location of the Dock Street market district. City leaders and developers, under the guise of the Philadelphia Redevelopment Authority aimed to remake Society Hill, including the Dock Street Wholesale District, into an upscale locale and tourist attraction. As a result, the wholesale fresh food businesses were in the middle of two disruptions: one, the changing conventions of food distribution and prospects of profitability; the other, the changing valuation of centralized city land uses in the context of suburbanization.

Across the country—and eventually across Europe, including in London, Paris, and Berlin—wholesale markets were moving out of urban downtowns to access more space and enable distribution via new transportation networks.[74] In Philadelphia, the relocation of the wholesale district was a form of planning symbiosis that brought together solutions for urban renewal, urban abandonment, transportation network access, and the evolving food industry. By relocating the wholesale food market, the city was able to redevelop the land in this downtown area while also building a new food wholesale center on an abandoned parcel in South Philadelphia, an area with no proposed alternatives for renewal.

This shift to a tourism and service economy in Center City was an early iteration of what would eventually be seen as a robust movement toward postindustrial economic change related to tourism and residential life. Wholesalers, of course, are not explicitly "industrial" enterprises—they do not manufacture goods. More precisely, the produce wholesalers that occupied Center City were a remnant of the infrastructural regime of feeding cities. The rise of the postindustrial urban era—although typically analyzed in the historic "urban center"—was actually intertwined with the decentralization of urbanization and consumption and the infrastructural regime of feeding regions.

The struggling wholesale market system, as part of the behind-the-scenes structure that made everyday food access possible, was seen, in the 1950s, as anathema to the growth machine's new strategies.[75] The north end of the grassy mall around Independence Hall and the Liberty Bell stopped less than 500 yards from the old Callowhill Market, while the park's east end directly bordered the Dock Street market district. Business leaders believed that the millions of dollars in investments in revitalizing Independence Hall as a public spectacle would be undermined by the proximity of the declining wholesale infrastructure.[76]

In the context of Center City renewal, the Dock Street market district was now perceived as a reinvigorated site of economic value. The Philadelphia Redevelopment Authority pushed for the relocation of the wholesale district to allow for new housing construction for the middle and upper classes. They reported, "Too many gracious homes [in Society Hill] had been converted to apartments, cheap rooming houses, taprooms, warehouses, and stores. A key 15 acres in the most historic section was occupied by a 150-year-old wholesale food market district centered around Dock Street, which spread traffic, congestion, dirt, and noise over a wide area." The demolition and relocation of the Dock Street Market would make room for Society Hill renovations, as the space for new residential, commercial, and tourism developments.[77]

A dual city model of urban renewal was crystallizing. Huge investments in Center City starkly contrasted with continuing abandonment plaguing South, West, and North Philadelphia. Political-economic interests perceived the construction of a new regional food distribution terminal on deserted tracts of South Philadelphia as a win-win situation. It would remove the outdated market from the higher-valued center, improve the wholesale merchants' economic potential of building transit connections to the broader region, and assist Philadelphia's image by redesigning another blighted zone with new economic activity. Observers described South Philadelphia, near east Municipal Stadium, the former home of the Phillies, and below the Oregon Avenue rail terminals, in stark terms: "acres and acres of burning dumps" occupied by "squatters' shacks" that "wear a perpetual blanket of rubbish" giving off a "hovering haze of smoke."[78] (See fig. 8.)

The movement of the fresh food wholesale district to an abandoned dump was considered a public function. The Pennsylvania Redevelopment Act funded the elimination of "blighted areas," which it viewed as "economic or social liabilities, harmful to the social and economic well-being of the entire community."[79] According to the Philadelphia Department of Commerce, new market development on this blighted area would improve the overall appearance of Philadelphia and make it more appealing to visitors, no longer exposing them to some of the most derelict sections when they entered the city.[80] As the business leaders of the Greater Philadelphia Movement cautioned, "Coming into Philadelphia over the Delaware River Bridge [eventually renamed the Benjamin Franklin Bridge] the city shows its worst side to people, with a Skid Row which is actually part of the present wholesale food market [at Dock Street]. The new Packer Avenue Bridge [eventually named the Walt Whitman Bridge] over the Delaware would, if this [Wholesale Distribution] Center was not built, lead people into the city through another blighted area. No city can hope to grow and flourish if it greets people with a display of dirt and disease and ugliness."[81]

The city's internal economic ecology was changing in relationship to shifting political-economic strategies built upon the zero-sum growth machine agendas. Cities and industries were forced to compete on a broader scale for businesses, residents, and consumers. Food businesses, for one, rapidly altered their methods of distribution and profitability by taking

8 Aerial view of the new food distribution center site, 1957. Philadelphia
Evening Bulletin Photographs (Copyright: TU Libraries). Credit: Special
Collections Research Center, Temple University Libraries, Philadelphia, PA.

regional economies of scale into account. This was especially true of the
growing supermarket industry, which had a direct effect on wholesalers.[82]

Regionalism, and the logic of business and service agglomeration, grew
into a common political-economic language concerning efficiencies and
transaction costs. The USDA and the Urban Land Institute found that the
relocation of certain markets into a new regional distribution platform dramatically cut costs. St. Louis, for instance, was among the earliest to align
their wholesale market infrastructure with the changing highway system to
great financial success.[83] Following findings from these studies, the United
States Congress sought to help fund the movement of urban wholesale districts to more peripheral locations, making them part of a broader regional
market apparatus that configured trucking and railroad routes. The House
of Representatives proposed a bill to allocate $100 million guaranteeing
85 percent of the loans used for the construction of new "terminal markets."[84]

Even though the House attempted to reform the marketing system, competitions between interest groups stalled implementation in Philadelphia.
As Harold L. Enarson, the mayor's executive assistant, described, "Farmers

and consumers, railroads and truckers, carlot receivers, large wholesalers, commission merchants, and local receivers all have a stake in the market." The wholesalers were ready to sign the new agreement, but the banks refused to finance the move, uncertain about whether different parts of the urban food market system would cooperate and achieve a profitable arrangement. Although the House passed the bill, the stalemate between market middlemen and financiers concerned senators who opposed it because of "banker distrust of such cooperative ventures."[85]

The construction of a regional food distribution center was delayed, but that did not stop the food supply chain from continuing to shift to a higher-volume model that rapidly proliferated into the suburbs. The largest supermarket chains operating in Philadelphia saw benefits in a regional food distribution center, labeling the proposed project "welcome and necessary." Paul Cupp, then vice president of American Stores Company (Acme Markets), among the oldest and largest food retailers in the region, wrote to Philadelphia Mayor Joseph S. Clark Jr. He said that as the large-scale supermarkets purchased in higher volumes, they had circumvented the outdated wholesale markets in recent years. The link between profitability and efficiency was fundamental to their concerns.

> Our Company by virtue of its size is less dependent on a Terminal Market than most buyers, and of course we are not typical. There seems no doubt that in the interest of the great majority of the distributing trade, as a help to more efficient distribution, and therefore in the public interest, that few serious questions can arise on its desirability and advantage. We believe that the few very larger buyers would avail themselves somewhat more of the services of a modern market, than they could possibly do of the present outmoded facilities.[86]

Industry leaders advocated for an organizational complex of sellers and services that could contribute to regional, rather than place-based, distribution. The aim was to establish Philadelphia as a "market basket" for the region. Samuel Cooke, the president and CEO of Penn Fruit, a grocery chain started in Philadelphia, advocated for the changing design and improved regional integration:

> Today's market handles every food commodity under one room, making it extremely difficult for the buyer to assemble his goods from a scattered distribution system. Present day food retailing must be matched by modern, integrated wholesale facilities. Failure to do this is resulting in a tremendous

annual loss of business activity for Philadelphia. The new integrated food terminal I visualize would embrace all types of food handling and food storage facilities. It would serve an area with a radius of 150 miles, extending to the shoreline on the east and as far north, west and south as a truck could go and return in approximately one workday. Philadelphia is a natural setting for such a terminal because of its geographic position—the confluence of great highways, including the Pennsylvania and New Jersey Turnpikes and the bridges across the Delaware, a fine inland harbor, and a highly developed network of railroad facilities—Pennsylvania, Reading and B&O. No large city in the area I have mentioned has the geographical position or the varied ingress or egress to make it capable of matching Philadelphia as a mass food distribution center.[87]

The USDA also invested in understanding regional advantages in food distribution. St. Louis's terminal market was part of that city's growth potential. It seized business from centralized markets in Chicago, Kansas City, and Memphis. USDA officials believed a Philadelphia terminal market was primed to do the same thing, given its proximity to Baltimore, Washington, DC, and New York City.[88] Moreover, Philadelphia's rapidly updating transportation infrastructure made building a regional food distribution center possible. The *Evening Bulletin* reported in 1954, "Other cities have fine airports and new downtown business developments, but no city in the United States or in the world will have anything to match the food distribution center. No other city can offer the location and the giant network of transportation which Philadelphia's food distribution center will have."[89]

The redesign of the decentered urban transportation network in the 1950s created a new site of convergence in South Philadelphia. In the early 1950s, a $91 million Walt Whitman Bridge was proposed over the Delaware River to connect South Philadelphia's Packer Avenue to the New Jersey Turnpike. The railroads, coming from north, south, and west, already had networks of sidings in the vicinity of the proposed market site to allow freight cars to move directly into the proposed market location. South Philadelphia connected to Delaware, Maryland, and Southeastern Pennsylvania by way of the Industrial Highway and the recently constructed Penrose Ferry Bridge. The city planned for an extension of the Schuylkill Expressway to connect the area around the proposed distribution site with the Pennsylvania Turnpike to the west of Philadelphia. As part of the Federal Aid Highway Act of 1956, the federal government funded an extension of Interstate 95, the new Delaware Expressway, running alongside the Delaware River, which brought traffic directly to the site of the new food terminal. The planning commission had workers clean and repave Delaware Avenue, the widest street in the city, so that traffic could more easily access the market district. A combination of city and state agencies, along with private firms, eventually updated shipping ports in very close proximity. Moreover, land in this new market setting was free of other uses, which meant that unlike the overcrowded Dock Street location, wholesalers had ample room to expand.[90]

Wholesalers saw possible benefits in this new infrastructural configuration, too. In 1953, $1 billion worth of fresh fruits and vegetables moved through the city's central wholesale facilities. They received 159,100 carlot equivalents per year, which amounted to 436 per day. Almost 200 wholesale produce businesses brought hundreds of different products into the city, ranging from packages of cauliflower and celery arriving by rail from California to loads of cabbage shipped from Florida. Fresh foods were coming to Philadelphia from almost every region of the United States, and wholesalers, losing ground to the prospering supermarket distribution structure, redirected their supplies, not only to Philadelphia marketplaces but also to profitable exchange partners throughout the region. They brought in products that reached a purchasing population of anywhere between five and six million people at a time when Philadelphia's population was about two million.[91]

The Philadelphia Department of Commerce expected the new intersection to link millions more to Philadelphia, at once providing jobs, attracting new business opportunities, and improving Philadelphians' access to inexpensive food options.[92] Unlike the original Dock Street location and the subsequent "split market," this new regional food terminal was identified as a coherent and strategic cluster to address the relationship between population resettlement, transportation infrastructure, and food marketing industries. Walter M. Philips, speaking before the city council, said:

> A Food Distribution Center is a specialized type of modern market for one particular type of commodity. To establish such a center is in line with modern developments by which different types of commodities or services are clustered around the same part of the city. But while in the past this happened as part of the crowding process in unplanned loft buildings [in the trapped Center City], the new approach is to plan such concentrations way ahead and give them enough space for expansion and for the convenience of customers.[93]

The economy of agglomeration was about financing business clusters that positioned the value of the city in relation to the region. "Additional facilities in a new market," the real estate broker Emerson Custis wrote, "would include farmers' and truckers' sheds, rail connections to stores and team tracks, offices for the market superintendent, brokers and others, buildings for related services, parking space, and streets. There would also be need for space for such related operations as a public refrigerated warehouse, a public garage, and service station."[94]

In 1954, the City Planning Commission voted to qualify the South Philadelphia site as a redevelopment area. Edmund N. Bacon, the executive director of the commission, said it qualified because of "unsafe, unsanitary buildings" and "undesirable land use." The proposed food center cost an estimated $100 million.[95] The City of Philadelphia paid $15 million to condemn the land and acquire the dump, then filled it in and graded it. The city provided water, sewers, wider streets, and lighting. The Greater Philadelphia Movement campaigned and raised an additional $85 million in private funds.[96] The plan included 55 buildings on 420 acres of land south of Oregon Avenue between the Delaware River and the baseball stadium to replace the Dock Street Market. Operating as an integrated food distribution center and matching the new supermarket logic of "all-in-one" distribution, the area housed facilities for the storage and sale of fresh meats, seafood, fruits and vegetables, dry groceries, frozen foods, butter, eggs, and poultry.[97]

In October 1959, the doors swung open at the new South Philadelphia site while a wrecking ball knocked down the abandoned structures on Dock Street. Within four years, the city almost completed the Society Hill revitalization project around Dock Street. A partnership between the City Redevelopment Authority, the Greater Philadelphia Movement, and the Old Philadelphia Development Corporation funded the demolition of the downtown wholesale district, the revitalization of a number of older buildings, and new construction. Three sleek 31-story towers designed by architect I. M. Pei stood in the center of a grassy area and commercial shopping district, all surrounded by historic cobblestone streets.[98] (See figs. 9 and 10.)

The media celebrated the food distribution environment in South Philadelphia. William Forsythe of the *Evening Bulletin* wrote, "The center is buzzing with activity at nighttime. But it's an organized activity, not the kind of tangled mess that characterized old Dock St. The tourists who made special trips to Dock Street to see how apples, tomatoes, onions, grapes and other foods were tossed around would see a sharp contrast in food handling on a nighttime visit to the center."[99] Food moved quickly through the new terminal market, reducing spoilage and waste. Unlike the narrow cobblestone streets downtown, wide passages encircled the Packer Avenue site. Hundreds of feet of parking space separated market buildings, each fitted with loading docks matching the height of freight trucks to facilitate loading and unloading. Massive open areas at the end of the streets left enough room for tractor-trailers to maneuver into and out of the docks, and the market houses were all equipped with working bathrooms. The intersection of

9 Aerial view of Dock Street before Society Hill Towers, 1950s. Philadelphia *Evening Bulletin* Photographs (Copyright: TU Libraries). Credit: Special Collections Research Center, Temple University Libraries, Philadelphia, PA.

10 Aerial view of Dock Street with Society Hill Towers, 1965. Philadelphia
Evening Bulletin Photographs (Copyright: TU Libraries). Credit: Special
Collections Research Center, Temple University Libraries, Philadelphia, PA.

major transportation routes attracted related services, such as a truck port,
a 32-bed motel, truck repair facilities, a late-night restaurant, a post office, a
gas station, a bank, and even a physician nearby.[100] (See fig. 11.)

By 1964, five years after the distribution center's opening, 158 food-
related firms and services settled into 18 buildings. Philadelphia Mayor
James Tate described the public-private initiative as "symbolic of what cooperation among city government, public-spirited citizens and business can
achieve. The center has been spectacularly effective in bringing new industry
and employment into Philadelphia and putting wasteland to productive
use. It has permitted elimination of the crowded, dirty Dock Street food
area, opening the way for important mid-city renewal."[101] The symbiosis
between Central City redevelopment, new economies of agglomeration, urban abandonment, and the transformation of the food distribution system
repositioned the city as part of a regional competition for business and was
viewed as a great public benefit. However, in turn, this infrastructural process repositioned the middlemen and the value of central cities, and that
would have repercussions for decades to come.

11 Photograph of new market with ample parking facilities. Photograph courtesy of PhillyHistory.org, a project of the Philadelphia Department of Records.

Repositioning the Middlemen and the Urban Core

The wholesale middlemen initially established their market houses near the Delaware River in an infrastructural regime of feeding cities. As the city and region changed around them, the fundamental logic of food distribution also shifted. It was no longer just consumers in the "center" who were dependent on an evolving supply system. The centralized wholesale apparatus was stuck in a geographically decentering system of suppliers, distributors, retailers, population settlement patterns, and new regional planning goals. The market relationship between urbanism and consumerism started in the center, but it was spreading well beyond it.

Organizational interests that were seemingly disconnected were pushed together into an interdependent social, spatial, and economic infrastructural system. Uncertainty arose around every new organizational and technical iteration. Previous investments in organizational routines along with transportation and marketing infrastructures constrained options for moving forward. New conflicts emerged about markets and distribution on one hand, as well as the value and future of the urban core on the other hand. The Dock Street market district was an emblem of a changing system fit with power struggles over the relationship between profitability and efficiency and which positions in the interdependent system had the most leverage.

At various points in history, city planners, developers, federal government agents, and market-makers tried to fix the central market apparatus, but they were unable to simply replace the established system with new structures, connections, and public and private relationships. They had to figure out how to deal with previous organizational investments, existing physical structures, and the dense built environment. The reorganization of the system was not only about replacing "inefficiencies" with "efficiencies" in an upgrading evolution. Efficiency and value are cultural concepts situated in the context of institutional and infrastructural interdependencies—that is, they become embedded in the distinct infrastructural regimes. The eventual repositioning of the wholesale system required different growth machine initiatives and determinations around economic and spatial development: building demolitions, design and development of new buildings, moving entire business districts to new areas, renovation and preservation of historical national landmarks, revival of parks and public spaces, modification of transportation routes, and attraction of new neighborhood services and amenities.

City leaders strategically worked to reimagine and revalue Center City to fit into an emerging "postindustrial" service climate of financial, tourist, and status-based consumer industries. In the effort to rebrand Philadelphia's downtown, peripheral neighborhoods were ignored—many faced housing abandonment, structural decay, and population decline. The entanglement of regional growth, urban renewal, and abandonment led to the relocation of wholesaling to a formerly abandoned tract in South Philadelphia. Decentering the urban landscape was becoming the order of the day. The city's economic approach in the face of decline was to reposition different zones to compete with other cities and towns—a zero-sum logic of industry agglomeration and interdependency.

The chain grocery markets, in contrast to the wholesale system, adopted a different set of distribution concerns and competencies from their earliest organizational iterations at the end of the nineteenth century. Even though grocery chains did not carry fruits and vegetables at first, the grocery system was built upon more flexible and nimble distribution arrangements and market skills that allowed them to more easily integrate new products and locations. Still, this infrastructural system built around the logic of "pursuing profits and efficiencies" generated its own uncertainties, constraints, and consequences in response to broader changes in the environment. In this case, it led to the rise of food deserts through a process of infrastructural exclusion.

THREE

Infrastructural Exclusion

Philadelphia's earliest housing and food market booms extended out from the Delaware River in western, northern, and southern directions. The wholesalers established market positions near the river, but retailers built up different priorities and obligations. Retail grocers extended food provisioning to neighborhoods beyond downtown by delivering a range of staple products. If downtown produce wholesalers became defined by their "inefficient" position in the changing food system, then the grocery retailers became defined by their frontier framework of geographic flexibility, nimble handling techniques, and strategic organizational goals to connect incoming food products to urban consumers in multiple locations.

In the urban division of distribution in the early 1900s, grocery businesses handled easier-to-manage bulk commodities. As new employment opportunities attracted more people into urban municipalities, not only did processed and branded food products increase the range of food items available to more places, but they also created the surplus conditions for retailers to challenge the boundaries between business sectors and their distinct forms of expertise. First, chain retailers replaced independent neighborhood grocers by establishing new forms of procurement, storage, standardization, and cost-cutting methods. Second, they usurped the role of wholesalers by building direct relationships with producers and shippers. They gained organizational and technical competencies for handling higher volumes of more kinds of products, and that eventually included perishable products too.

The spread of chain neighborhood grocers in the first half of the 1900s was about the pursuit of economies of scale for feeding cities. Yet the strategic pursuit of profit-making was contingent on changing contextual factors, environmental conditions, and infrastructural interdependencies. There was no single trajectory through which market-makers reached for "efficiency."

Grocery retailers, once defined by their relationships with urban neighborhoods, created multiple organizational prototypes for handling higher-volume and higher-variety supplies, saw profitability opportunities in both urban and suburban locations, and came to participate in a fiercely competitive low-margin industry.

It would not have been obvious when supermarkets first arrived on the scene in the 1920s that the suburban supermarket model would become paradigmatic. The spread of the supermarket system into the suburbs between the 1930s and 1950s was gradual. As the infrastructural connections changed, market and development decentralization grew evermore commonplace between the 1950s and 1970s. The industry's conventions for pursuing efficiency and profitability became embedded into regional distribution arrangements.

Even though the largest food retailing companies had opened supermarkets in central cities, they faced difficulties sustaining them, leading some into bankruptcy and others completely out of business. Companies closed down dozens of outlets at the same time, creating a new period of consumer anxiety about food access. Urban grocery stores experienced a major period of decline well before the term "food desert" grew out of United Kingdom policy circles in the 1990s. The origins of the food desert came about in the 1970s as infrastructural exclusion—the "reorganization of spatial and material interdependence" that "separates resources from those reliant on them."[1] Reorganizing distribution networks gradually extended membership to new groups and places, while in turn marginalizing others.[2]

Infrastructural exclusion is different than organizational and malicious intent. There was no centrally coordinated plan to extract populations, businesses, employment opportunities, and food supplies from cities. Heterogeneous political and economic processes, taking place in multiple industries and locations, generated cumulative patterns of spatial development. Latent organizational, institutional, and technical interdependencies generated unintended consequences.[3] For instance, real estate redlining was a strategic political and economic project to encode racial categories into housing markets, but it also occurred alongside multiple phases of suburban development, urban renewal, and white flight. These processes accumulated into a mutually reinforcing system of residential segregation.

Certain food retailers also had suspect histories in black urban neighborhoods. They exercised explicitly racist hiring practices and unfair pricing schemes that led to widespread protests.[4] However, the actual closing down of urban-based stores in the 1970s was not a by-product of malicious intent. During the 1950s and 1960s, the largest food retailers opened stores in segregated black neighborhoods, and some companies even became seen as community partners during the major period of urban political unrest, suburban expansion, and white flight.

The rise of food deserts demonstrated a more-subtle process embedded in the transformation of the secular distribution system that, even without collective and centralized coordination, still reinforced race and class exclusion. Retailers made big mistakes along the way. It was not just consumers who experienced new difficulties. Some of the largest food retailing companies were crushed by the infrastructural changes as well. The rise of the urban food desert represents a case of infrastructural exclusion as a unique form of urban inequality.

The Convenience of Chain Grocery Stores

In the early 1900s, thousands of food sellers coexisted with grocery stores in Philadelphia: butchers, delicatessens, variety stores, department stores selling food, market halls like the Reading Terminal Market, and street corner and pushcart fruit and vegetable vendors. Philadelphia alone, not including its surrounding suburbs, housed over 9,500 concrete locations where residents could purchase some type of food product. Grocery retailers slowly carved out a unique role in everyday neighborhood consumption as places of ritual market exchange, neighborhood interaction, and consistent sources of food staples through the first half of the 1900s. By 1915, there were already 5,300 grocery stores in the Philadelphia region—in both the city's municipal boundaries and its radiating suburbs. Yet only one-sixth of them were chain outlets.[5]

The expansion of the chain retail system, in particular, reconfigured the relationship between neighborhoods and the culture of convenience. The grocery business grew at an astounding rate, reflecting both a new consumer need and an economic opportunity. The growth and influence of the chain grocer gradually accumulated in this age of entrepreneurialism. The Great Atlantic & Pacific Tea Company (A&P), which became the most dominant national chain of any type, was a New York–based firm. It moved into different cities and towns, including Philadelphia. In 1875, it had already opened stores in 16 different cities and had a mail-order catalog.[6]

Although A&P was the most famous chain store in the United States, it was not the only one in operation. Philadelphia had five major chains beside A&P in the early 1900s. Each one started out as a single store, just a few hundred square feet, and grew into a powerful supplier to the city and its surrounding region. Immigrants, many of them the pushers of the carts, were also strong actors in the corporatization of retail food.

Thomas P. Hunter founded the Acme Tea Company in the 1880s and was later celebrated as "the father of the modern chain grocery" in Philadelphia.[7] He first learned the grocery business as a young boy in Ireland, and when he came to the United States at eight years old, he began working in a local store, where he saved his money for five years and opened up his own store at 1644 Germantown Avenue, beyond the downtown core, near 5th Street in North Philadelphia.[8] He began his operation with $500 of working capital and grew outward from this location to other parts of the city. Upon his untimely death in 1915, he had expanded his business into the largest chain operation in the Philadelphia region, with over 420 stores. His company motto was, "No resident of Philadelphia or Camden could live more than three blocks from an Acme store."[9]

A feedback pattern was emplaced: economic success enabled expansion that led to the buying out of competitors. Robert H. Crawford worked as a grocery clerk upon his arrival to the United States from Northern Ireland. When his friend Samuel Robinson came over in 1888, Crawford helped him gain employment in one of the city's local stores. In 1891, Robinson and Crawford together opened up their first grocery store called The House that Quality Built at Second and Fernon Streets in South Philadelphia, an area quickly becoming packed with Irish and Italian immigrants. In ensuing years, each had a sibling move into the city, and between the four of them, they slowly grew the number of stores, changing the name to the Robinson & Crawford grocery chain. In 1893, they had three stores; during the next decade, they opened up a new outlet each year.[10] In 1915, they purchased the William Butler Company of South Philadelphia, and by 1917, they owned and operated a total of 186 stores. (See fig. 12.)

Chain grocery stores generated new possibilities to pursue cost-cutting methods by mimicking the established grocery wholesale system. Independent grocers had already started cooperative buying before the turn of the twentieth century, purchasing from manufacturers as a group and "earning for themselves a part of the charges formerly paid to wholesalers."[11] Chain grocers, with centralized executive authority, secured bulk-pricing benefits on their own, without the cooperation of other businesses. Companies with large concentrations in a single city maintained their own warehouse operations to store dry goods purchased in bulk and had their own trucking fleets—at that time, an important advantage—to distribute products to their many corner stores.[12]

12 William Butler corner grocery store, early 1900s. Photograph courtesy of PhillyHistory.org, a project of the Philadelphia Department of Records.

Successive mergers within the same region allowed companies to synchronize resources. The five largest chains in the Philadelphia region—Robinson & Crawford, Bell Company, Childs Grocery Company, George M. Dunlap Company, and Acme Tea Company—consisted of over 1,200 stores. They merged in 1917 into the American Stores Company, which later also used the banner of the largest of the five chains—Acme.[13] Each chain in the merger had a set of vehicles "traveling from five widely separated warehouses to the stores." The newly formed American Stores Company shut down targeted warehouses and stores where too much of an immediate overlap in territory existed. They closed over a quarter of their more than 1,200 stores after the merger, but they opened up scores of new stores where further profit potential was determined, trying to mark their dominant place in Philadelphia and nearby cities and towns.[14]

Wholesalers were often portrayed as corrupt middlemen during the early 1900s, but in contrast, the managers and employees of chain grocers built up personal relationships with their customers. The American Stores Company capitalized on those relationships. They linked the pursuit of efficiency and expansion to a narrative about the "public good" as a way of gaining the loyalty and support of the average working family. They combined rhetoric about improving food quality and decreasing prices, the two main concerns for consumers.

The first president of American Stores Company, Samuel Robinson, said that the "chain store in the past has been a boon to the people of Philadelphia, Camden, and all of the many other places in which this modern and effective system of food distribution has been established." He believed that the merger of the five largest Philadelphia chains would provide even more benefits to the public by intertwining quality, efficiency, and geographic expansion into new consumer standards. Robinson said,

> The motto of the American Stores Company will be that in foods, quality is of most importance. To this end, thoroughly experienced men will be placed at the helm of each buying department, which will prevent unknown qualities from falling into our stock, while because of the tremendous turn-over the housewife will be able to purchase the freshest and best qualities of foodstuffs at any of our stores at all times. . . . Where thought advisable, the company will open additional stores, which will afford the public greater shopping convenience. As far as is possible, the stores will be standardized, and all will be brought immediately to the highest point of efficiency. . . . There need be no fear on the part of the employes [sic] of the present companies that they are in danger of losing their positions through the consolidation, as it will be the policy of the company to continue increasing the number of stores and extending the territory, which will mean the need of an even larger number of employes [sic] than at present.[15]

Urban grocers celebrated their efficiency innovations, but they still ran a relatively primitive business by today's conventions. Stores supplied mostly bulk items and did not yet incorporate specific brands. Economic historian Marc Levinson writes, "Almost all food shops offered a very limited

13 Example of a curb market in North Philadelphia. This one was on Marshall Street in Northern Liberties, circa 1925. Photograph courtesy of PhillyHistory.org, a project of the Philadelphia Department of Records.

selection of merchandise, rarely more than a couple hundred items, most of them purchased from wholesalers in 100-pound sacks and wood barrels and then doled out to individual customers."[16] Grocers rarely incorporated precarious commodities like fresh fruits and vegetables, offering only the most durable fresh objects like potatoes and cabbage at first, because they better maintained their qualities without refrigeration.[17]

Residents of newer peripheral neighborhoods still desired a consistent variety of fruits and vegetables, however. As neighborhoods were developed miles from downtown, residents raised concerns about their accessibility to the wider variety of foods, most of which were only available in the markets and neighborhoods closer to the Dock Street district. In 1912, the Philadelphia Department of Public Works began to encourage curb markets in neighborhoods with limited food supplies. Some emerging neighborhoods were located over 10 miles from the major market districts, such as West Philadelphia on the other side of the Schuylkill River, Frankford in the northeast section, and Chestnut Hill located northwest of the center.[18] (See fig. 13.)

Attracting street vendors was not a farm-to-market movement like we would think of it today. While city officials reached out directly to farmers in nearby counties, they also developed exclusive neighborhood market spaces for "truck men," vendors buying from the downtown wholesale district and trucking fresh produce to these distant neighborhoods. The director of the Department of Public Works said that the curb markets served as temporary interventions with the simple goal to add more products and reduce prices. He added that this was especially a problem of limited mobility, as the electric rail lines did not yet reach into these neighborhoods and provide routes to downtown.[19]

The fresh food distribution infrastructure was further convoluted in the first quarter of the twentieth century by the extending territories of development and settlement. Yet corner grocery stores continued to grow in number and geographic coverage. They also looked to capitalize on new methods of market coordination. Similar to other large retailers of the time like department stores, food retailers started to purchase supplies from wholesalers in larger quantities. In some cases, they completely bypassed wholesalers. The National Salt Company started selling directly to retailers in the early 1900s.[20] Large-scale food processors including Domino Sugar, Campbell's canning company, and the cereal companies Kellogg's and Post contributed to a new era of uniform packaging, making it easier for grocers to build direct shipping relationships with manufacturers.[21]

The increasing number of packaged items provided large grocery chains with a unique advantage. Dry goods wholesalers were handling products that were easy to store, and the grocery retailers realized that with the combination of packaged and branded products and stable dry goods, they could handle higher volumes of more varieties in their own warehouses. As consumer demand of branded products grew more consistent and predictable, the chain grocers eroded the boundaries between wholesaling and retailing. The *Quarterly Journal of Economics* published a report in 1912 finding that "nearly every industry" had started to cut down on "the number of successive steps in distribution."[22] Wholesalers were losing ground. A study of the changing grocery wholesale industry less than a decade later in 1920 noted that grocery chain companies negotiated directly with manufacturers and suppliers of breakfast foods, canned goods, and gift objects that offered "reduced prices to all who buy in quantity, whether or not they are legitimate wholesalers."[23]

The grocery industry reaped rewards of the improved mechanization and standardization in the production and distribution of staple commodities and branded products and that contributed to increased volumes and varieties in stores. Processed foods were becoming more like other industrial-era products: mass produced, easily replicated, associated with clearly identified packaging, and easily stored and distributed. The fresh food market infrastructure remained an anomaly, however. It stood out by the 1920s, becoming labeled as an infrastructure of inefficiency. The power dynamics of food distribution were shifting as the infrastructural regime changed. The burgeoning and more flexible chain retailers started to look for ways to incorporate perishable products too.

Managing the Chain Store "Threat"

Agricultural production, food processing, chain retailing, and urban decentralization were all influenced by mass production, mechanization, and new transportation methods in the first half of the 1900s. The infrastructural regime was changing through new organizational and technical interdependencies, but it was not yet clear in what direction it was moving. There were multiple iterations of innovation and implementation that gradually built on one another.

With greater mechanization, the number of American farms decreased along with the number of employees used per farm. The average farm size increased in acreage, and the total output per acre multiplied.[24] Food processing firms like Heinz and Campbell's built fortunes off of agricultural surpluses, at a time when continuous-process manufacturing in canning and bottling allowed for higher output of branded products. Henry John Heinz even negotiated exclusive contracts with farms employing 20,000 people on 16,000 acres to produce fruits and vegetables for his bottling plants and branded goods.[25] Large retail chains, including A&P and the American Stores Company, pursued their own production mechanization, opening up manufacturing and processing plants. They created their own coffee blends, bottled milk products, and bakeries, all with the aim of configuring supply and demand and cutting down on transaction costs.[26]

In the first half of the 1900s, central cities were still growing too, but there was a gradual shift underway: population settlement and mobility networks were spreading out in ways that observers did not yet identify as a clear pattern. As shown in figure 3 (in chapter 2), Philadelphia's population growth began to slow down, but suburban growth gained momentum. Mass-produced cheap materials, refrigeration, and trucking made suburban expansion more likely. Inexpensive materials became available for housing and commercial construction. Automobiles and trucking grew more important in the nation's transportation network. And home refrigeration allowed for a range of new products that could be kept stable for longer periods.

The combination and accumulation of these changes led to interdependencies between agricultural production and urban consumption, but it also increased symbolic distance between them. Small agricultural towns worried about the spreading consumer culture they were feeding. Although agricultural production was at the whim of changing economic conditions, including industrial processing and high-volume retailers, residents in small agricultural towns and the politicians representing them distrusted the big businesses.

In the 1930s, federal and state governments imposed new taxes to protect farms and small towns. The Agricultural Adjustment Act of 1933 taxed industrial processors profiting from overproduction. This new federal law restricted agricultural surpluses and created artificial periods of commodity scarcity. It was a way to protect farmers, not consumers. Farmers raised their prices during this difficult economic time. During this same period, United States Congressmen began labeling chains, like A&P, as monopolies. Twenty-seven states passed tax legislation to impose higher taxes on chains and rein in their influence and the urban consumer culture they promoted. Rather than seeing them as mutually reinforcing and interdependent in a "necessary" provisioning system, state actors pitted urban against rural as different interest groups.[27]

Congressman Wright Patman of Texas, who led the charge, claimed that "the day of the independent merchant is gone unless something is done and done quickly. He cannot possibly survive under that system." The option was seen in binary terms: either "turn the food and grocery business . . . over to a few corporate chains" or create laws that protect people's chances to make a fair living.[28] Patman proposed a bill in which A&P would be responsible for $524 million in taxes, even though the company's net income in that same year was only $9 million. Basically, Patman wanted to tax chains like A&P out of business by exceeding their net worth.[29]

That bill never came to fruition. By the end of the 1930s, food processing, grocery chains, and suburbanization continued their dominance. The taxes on industrial processing were proven unconstitutional, and the Agricultural Adjustment Act was amended to privilege market mechanisms that "naturally" weighed the competing interests of urban consumers and agricultural producers. President Roosevelt proclaimed, "We are agreed that the real and lasting progress of the people of farm and city alike will come, not from the old familiar cycle of glut and scarcity, not from the succession of boom and collapse, but from the steady and sustained increases in production and fair exchange of things that human beings need."[30]

The idea of stabilizing "cheap food" as a "necessity" took a more central position in the national discussion. Renewed emphasis on unregulated free trade at the end of the 1930s once again allowed for farm surpluses, which benefited industrial food processers like Pillsbury, General Mills, Kellogg's, Post, Campbell's, and Heinz. They increased their numbers of canned, bottled, and packaged goods over the ensuing decades, filling up grocery store aisles with standardized branded products.[31]

Likewise, the National Chain Store Association organized an influential pro-chain movement in the 1930s. They built new alliances that helped them to win over public support. The first major alliance was with labor unions, putting the food retailing industry at the forefront of the progressive labor movement. The second alliance was with agricultural fruit and vegetable cooperatives to help manage their surpluses now that they no longer benefited from a weighted system. Volume, variety, and the pursuit of efficiency as free market profitability were pushed further together.[32]

Grocery chains also built alliances with farmers to handle more fresh commodities, but this partnership was not an instant success. Grocery chain stores rarely handled perishable products and continued to rely on the downtown produce wholesalers for the few fruit and vegetable items in their stores. To move into the fruit and vegetable supply trade, for instance, grocers had to build up relationships over years with supply chain after supply chain. They had to establish trust, and that first came by purchasing surplus fruit supplies for canning and processing.

In 1936, for example, the large national food retailing companies purchased the vast surplus of peaches to be used for canning, which enabled farmers to then sell canning companies their new crops at a greater profit. H. C. Merritt Jr., the chairman of the California Canning Peach Stabilization Committee, wrote to the National Association of Food Chains, "We believe you have not only been instrumental in averting a disastrous situation but have effectively demonstrated how helpful chain store methods of distribution can be to producers."[33]

George Travis, a former leader of the Federal Farm Board, came to work with the National Association of Food Chains to facilitate interdependencies between grocery chains and fruit and vegetable cooperatives. He said the retailing chains wanted political leverage to stop tax initiatives against them and alleviate public concerns about their economic status and dominance. They "took the minimum margin" on farm produce, "increased store volume by attracting customers," and "went out of their way to make these relationships with the farm groups and farm leaders, who were political leaders in their states." One chain executive recalled that they successively built relationships with "the grapefruit grower, the potato grower, the apple grower, the peach grower, by saying, 'Here, we've got the facilities. If you've got a surplus, a problem, tell us. Let us see if we can do something about it.'"[34]

The transition to more branded products and then integrating more fresh foods into grocery stores gradually built up between 1920 and 1940. By the end of the 1930s, new alliances between chain food retailers, agricultural cooperatives, and labor unions had a major impact on state governments. According to Paul Ingram and Hayagreeva Rao, chain stores like A&P targeted organized cooperative growing initiatives in states where anti-chain sentiment was high. They helped to avert a number of surplus crises, and in turn, those farm cooperatives grew their political support of chain operations. Those states repealed more of the chain taxes than they enacted, representing a shifting tide in the reception of chain retailers' role in the national economy.[35]

Over a period of decades, firms learned, with the help of USDA Agricultural Marketing Services, to implement a high-volume and high-variety system by improving competencies for handling a wider range of goods. Building interdependence was not just about getting a good price and developing fair exchange between partners, although that was clearly a concern at the time. The Perishable Agricultural Commodity Act of 1930 helped to alleviate concerns about fraud and distrust between trade partners.

Employees gained expertise in new supply chains, learned how to interpret the different qualities of different fruits and vegetables to understand fair exchange, helped to establish a grading system that was agreed upon by different sectors, and fit various kinds of commodities into established merchandising systems. This all occurred in the days before business partners routinely sent digital images by phone to demonstrate visible qualities of perishable products. Grocery firms sent representatives to agricultural regions to learn about these sectors, held training sessions with USDA officials, and slowly developed understandings of growing seasons and commodity evaluations. By the 1940s, the grading standards had evolved into an industry-wide system of agreed upon market qualities for perishable goods. The aim of these government actions was not regulation, per se, but the "orderly flow of perishable agricultural commodities in interstate and foreign commerce."[36]

The movement into a high-volume, high-variety market system was not unilaterally supported by consumers. It took some work on the part of retailers to convince consumers of new marketing approaches and to sell the "necessity" of higher-volume and higher-variety chain retailing. George Hartford, the CEO of A&P, wrote to the Philadelphia public in 1938 to convince them that this high-volume marketing arrangement was not simply about corporate greed, countering the prominent messaging from members of Congress during previous years. He reiterated the message from the earlier period of reconfiguring supply systems: it was a mutually beneficial search for efficiency through volume, quality, and price point.

A&P sold over $881 million of food at a mere 1 percent profit on sales. Hartford described the interdependencies between sectors as necessary for the nation's economy. He wrote that if families "were denied the opportunity to buy at these lower prices" then "millions of homes" would "have to leave meat off the table another day a week, eat less fresh fruits and vegetables, give their growing child one bottle of milk less every week or stint on butter, cheese, poultry, eggs, and many other nourishing foods." Likewise, Hartford argued that farm surpluses were a problem for farmers who often find that it is "literally cheaper . . . to let his apples or his peaches rot on the ground than to expend the labor costs necessary to pack and ship them."[37]

Building infrastructural interdependencies between sectors was the central response to the political critique of industrial food processors and chain stores after the Great Depression. Yet food retailing executives continued to disagree over how to pursue efficiency and build these interdependencies into a coherent and profitable system of cheap food. The high-volume mass-merchandising supermarket eventually became a forceful part of that equation. Nonetheless, the supermarket was not instantly received as the conventional approach for linking efficiency and profitability. The dominance of higher-volume procurement—initially through the chain grocery retail system—led to new organizational uncertainties and increased competitions over how to embed profit-making conventions into shifting methods of distribution.

Investing in Supermarkets or Not?

Chain store companies chased higher-volume distribution, but the supermarket was not a chain store innovation. It was an independent venture challenging the chain system. A key question facing grocery executives in the 1930s and 1940s was whether or not to adopt the supermarket approach. Supermarkets became the dominant market platform after the 1950s, but for 20 years before, there was uncertainty around this new market type. Two different organizational models were developed in response to the Great Depression. The first was the chain *combination store*, building on the

14 The produce section of a grocery combination store, in which shoppers
still depended on clerks to weigh perishable merchandise for them, 1955.
Philadelphia *Evening Bulletin* Photographs (Copyright: TU Libraries). Credit: Special
Collections Research Center, Temple University Libraries, Philadelphia, PA.

previous chain corner store model. The second was the *supermarket*, a distinct entrepreneurial venture that combined higher-volume merchandising with another idea that was spreading—self-service marketing.

In the 1920s, chain grocers first introduced the combination store, which offered more food varieties while retaining the clerk service of pulling products from shelves for customers. It was a slight break from the corner store retail system. It allowed chain stores to build on their existing networks and forms of expertise. Only one out of three chain outlets was a combination store in 1929. The proportion grew to 50 percent by 1939 and 60 percent by 1946, at which point 15 percent of sales came from fresh produce.[38] (See fig. 14.)

The chains had a major advantage in incorporating more varieties. Because chains had so many outlets, they could handle larger volumes of products. A&P, for example, had 16,000 stores in the United States in the 1930s. As a comparison point, Wal-Mart—today, the world's largest retailer—operates more than 11,000 stores in 28 countries. Of course, the sizes of typical A&P and Wal-Mart stores are incomparable, the latter building on technologies and information systems that did not yet exist in the 1930s. A&P and Wal-Mart, however, are similar in that they gained dominance through expertise in managing the relationship between expansion and standardization, using the available tools at their disposal. This frontier framework was so familiar to A&P executives that they commonly opened up stores within a week of signing their leases.[39] As chains like A&P and the American Stores Company moved to this combination store model, they extended their economies of scale by incorporating more branded goods and more perishable products into stores in many locations at the same time.

These combination outlets were not nearly the size of another innovation of that period: the "super market." At first, "super" was an adjective, but over time, as more companies adopted the platform, it turned into a closed compound, the "supermarket." Larger all-in-one self-service markets opened in multiple locations, emphasizing higher volumes, more brand names, and lower prices. Self-service was a key organizational innovation, but it first arose independent of the supermarket. In 1916, Clarence Saunders, a former factory worker and salesman for a grocery wholesaler, opened the first self-service grocery store, Piggly Wiggly, in Memphis, Tennessee. Saunders applied "basic principles of standardization and simplification found in industrial management books" to increase gross sales and decrease the overall costs of operation. He reorganized his store layout into aisles so that customers could pull products off shelves without assistance; he provided hand baskets for them to carry selections; he sold more packaged brands to differentiate the supply; and he implemented multiple checkout lanes. He grew his number of stores quickly, and purveyors in several regions integrated and expanded the self-service approach into the new supermarket model.[40]

In the late 1920s, Ralph's grocery chain in Southern California was among the first to address changing shopping methods for the coming automobile era, integrating more "national brands" and "respected local brands," customer self-service, checkout lanes, standardized supplies across stores, increased storage space to deal with turnover, and locations beyond walking neighborhoods. It is not surprising that Los Angeles, which developed as the premier decentered urban municipality rather than as a centralized urban core like New York or Philadelphia, contributed so forcefully to auto-centered retailing. The Southern California environment allowed companies like Ralph's to seek out profitable opportunities based on their proximity to major agricultural growing regions. For all intents and purposes, Ralph's stores were the first supermarkets, even if they did not call their market platform by that name.[41]

In 1930, King Kullen opened in Jamaica, Queens, rather than in one of the dense Manhattan neighborhoods. In fact, King Kullen was not a neighborhood store at all. Michael Cullen, a former executive for Kroger, the Midwestern grocery chain, tried to convince his bosses to move to a higher-volume merchandising approach. When they refused, he went out on his own. Cullen believed the California markets were too glamorous for the troubling economic times, and he insisted on a simpler approach. His first store was in an abandoned garage, providing more space for dry groceries, meat, baked goods, and dairy. He leased remaining space to purveyors of produce, paint, hardware, and auto accessories. He created a shopping atmosphere with "no partitions, crude floors, bare ceilings, unpainted fixtures, glaring lights, gaudy signs, and merchandise piled everywhere." He opened additional stores in abandoned warehouses, former department stores, and empty factories.[42]

Cullen described his super-sized marketing approach as "the world's greatest price wrecker." He followed the logic of "pile it high and sell it cheap."[43] Industry experts described King Kullen stores as "cheapy markets," and soon, others followed Cullen's lead. Big Bear, founded in 1933 by former merchandising and wholesaling executives, expanded these principles into a 50,000-square-foot abandoned auto plant in Elizabeth, New Jersey. The store's high sales volumes and profits awed competitors. Big Bear grossed $30,000 in its first three days and netted $165,000 in its first year.[44] It took 100 A&P stores in the surrounding area to match this single store's sales volume.[45]

The self-service warehouse-style "cheapy market" gained traction and was gradually institutionalized into a distinct market-form—the "super market." A trade publication *Super Market Merchandising*, founded in 1936, provided management tips for new business owners wanting to replicate the format. The Super Market Institute, a trade association, created "a degree of unity" in the industry.[46] In 1936, 1,200 supermarkets operated in 32 states. Within the next year, the total almost tripled to more than 3,000 stores operating in 47 states.[47] Introducing new economies of scale—through both combination stores and supermarkets—reduced the percentage of disposable income Americans spent on food from 21 percent in 1930 to 16 percent in 1940.[48] "Cheap food" had arrived.

The expectation of cheap food was part of the infrastructural system even as retailers remained divided over whether to invest in supermarkets or combination stores. There was no clear consensus. There were four major chains in Philadelphia during this period. Newer chains like Food Fair and Penn Fruit, without national market infrastructures to convert, quickly invested in the supermarket approach. The older companies like A&P and American Stores Company were much slower to adopt the new model and continued with combination stores.

Food Fair started as a single corner store on Manhattan's Lower East Side in the early 1900s. It completely converted to self-service supermarkets by 1935 and relocated its headquarters to Philadelphia. The early transition enabled the company to succeed in a crowded market field.[49] In 1933, the Friedland brothers owned and operated 25 Food Fair combination stores. They observed changing market trends and began experimentation. In Harrisburg, Pennsylvania, they opened a 10,000-square-foot garage that warehoused more varieties and quantities than was typical of that era. They grossed $15,000 in the first week, and quickly opened another in Reading, Pennsylvania. Their two self-service supermarkets sold a higher volume than the rest of their 25 stores combined. They closed their smaller stores, moved their headquarters to Philadelphia, and began building supermarkets in that territory.[50]

Companies like Food Fair and Penn Fruit, the latter a Philadelphia-based green grocer turned supermarket chain, entered the industry at a historical juncture when trial and error around organizational innovations reaped major rewards. The profits and skills they accrued for building supermarkets enabled them to advance into new suburbs—where there was initially less competition—over the next decade. The Friedland brothers opened 100 more supermarkets by 1948. They further increased the rate of growth the following decade, leading the *New York Times* to label Food Fair the "fastest growing chain" in the grocery industry. Between 1950 and 1955, Food Fair opened an additional 100 outlets, and then 100 more in the two following years. By the end of the 1950s, Food Fair totaled 367 supermarkets in nine states, from Connecticut to Florida, with sales over $600 million a year. Just like the national chains, they developed multistate economies of scale, except at a much higher volume per store (see table 1).[51]

Executives studied demographic trends and consumer preferences to find new profit-making options. George Friedland, the president of Food Fair, wrote in 1953 that retail growth beyond the urban core was necessary due to high birth rate, low death rate, immigration, and a 2 percent total increase in the nation's population. He established a store control and research department to prepare statistical reports on all dimensions of the industry: sales, profits, and expenses; consumer habits; and demographic and geographic

Table 1. Food Fair, Inc. Sales Figures 1951 to 1970

Year	Sales in Millions	Net Profits in Millions	Profit Margins in cents on the dollar
1951	225	4.9	2.18
1952	282	4.0	1.43
1953	318	4.8	1.51
1954	376	6.1	1.61
1955	444	7.7	1.74
1956	517	8.9	1.73
1957	592	9.0	1.52
1958	655	10.1	1.55
1959	734	10.4	1.42
1960	771	11.4	1.48
1961	840	11.9	1.41
1962	923	11.1	1.20
1963	1,003	10.4	1.03
1964	1,105	10.0	0.91
1965	1,120	9.2	0.82
1966	1,205	12.5	1.04
1967	1,297	12.0	0.93
1968	1,372	10.8	0.79
1969	1,555	12.0	0.78
1970	1,762	10.6	0.60

Source: Food Fair Annual Reports, Archives of the Hagley Library.

reports on the changing population distribution.[52] He noticed changes in where consumers bought food and in what they ate. The supermarket, he noted, was becoming integral to US consumption.

The bread and potato eaters of the '30's have become . . . the steak and vegetable eaters of today. Plenty of food and a growing demand indicate further increase in retail food sales and further gains in supermarket sales in particular. The supermarket, which has grown from comparative insignificance in the past quarter-century, now accounts for the major portion of total retail sales.[53]

Friedland turned to venture capitalists. He found a Wall Street firm to underwrite a growth program that transformed the company into a retail innovator.[54] In 1955, Food Fair established a separate real estate company to develop and manage shopping centers within and beyond city limits. Food Fair Properties purchased land, constructed commercial centers, leased spaces to different merchants, and positioned their own stores as anchors in these shopping hubs. Within the first year of operation, Food Fair planned to build 23 shopping centers in dispersed areas and developed a distribution infrastructure to continuously stock high-volume supermarkets in all of them.[55]

A&P and the American Stores Company, two of the nation's four largest food retailers, did not pursue the supermarket model at first. In 1936, national chains only cautiously experimented with it. They delayed, constrained by established organizational routines and prior investments in infrastructure. Initially, they converted dry grocery departments with packaged goods to self-service, because they believed consumers could handle branded products. Slowly, they introduced self-service into produce, dairy, baked goods, and other departments. As they opened new stores, they integrated the self-service philosophy into every department.[56] Changing spatial and income dynamics of US population settlement caused them to convert, but they were too late.

The American Stores Company (often operating under the Acme banner) had been the largest chain in Philadelphia since the merger of the city's five major grocers in 1917. It grew into the fourth largest chain in the nation. In 1947, however, the majority of its stores still had clerks pulling products from shelves. Only 37 percent of its nearly 2,000 stores were self-service supermarkets.[57] American Stores fell behind in profit margins too. The company started to switch over to building supermarkets in 1941, but during the next two decades, it still had not completed the transformation. By 1957, it finally moved full force, shrinking the number of stores from almost 2,000 to about 900, with 88 percent self-service.[58]

Similar to Food Fair's earlier conversion, American Stores' sales figures doubled despite the striking reduction in total number of outlets (see tables 1 and 2). Yet reorganizing its infrastructure was expensive. In 1958, 95 percent of its stores were self-service supermarkets and the company reported its highest sales figures in history, but due to incurred costs in building the new distribution infrastructure it slipped to ninth in profit margins out of the nation's 12 largest grocery chains. In this competitive industry, cents on the dollar constrained economic success. In 1946, American Stores netted almost 2 cents on the dollar; by 1958, it earned only 1.25 cents per dollar. Paul Cupp, then the company president, raised concerns about the remaining clerk-service stores and costs associated with reorganization. "We're not content with being ninth in profit margins," he said. "We have more obsolescence than we should have in our stores." He described plans to eliminate clerk-service stores by the end of the decade. "Ultimately only a few of our stores will not be self-service—in small, isolated communities where the old-fashioned store is profitable and desired by our customers."[59]

As firms moved toward the supermarket system, they faced another equally complicated question: where should we build supermarkets?

Table 2. American Stores Company Sales Figures 1949–1969 (excludes 1958–1960; 1962–1965; 1967)

Year	Sales in Millions	Net Profits in Millions	Profit Margins in cents on the dollar
1949	417	6.7	1.6
1950	470	7.1	1.5
1951	521	5.1	.97
1952	542	5.1	.94
1953	604	7.5	1.2
1954	625	7.0	1.1
1955	655	8.3	1.26
1956	780	9.7	1.24
1957	837	10.5	1.25
1961	1011	10.76	1.06
1966	1200	10.45	.87
1968	1293	8.33	.64
1969	1479	10.7	.72

Source: *Evening Bulletin* clippings and Annual Reports of American Stores Company, Temple Urban Archives.

Between 1930 and 1950, the suburbs were steadily growing. Business leaders already recognized the consumer opportunities and opened profitable stores there. Although decentralization was part of the shifting infrastructural regime of urban and economic development, it was not yet convincing to retailers that the distribution paradigm was changing. Grocery executives were stuck in the middle of this transformation: tied to historic urban centers but aware of the economic potential of market growth in new suburbs.

Urban or Suburban Supermarkets?

Studies of suburbanization identify how changing transportation infrastructures influenced decentralized commercial growth. They show how public and private investments precipitated a new "drive-in culture" built upon highways, automobiles, parking lots, and shopping centers.[60] Yet a suburban commercial culture—built on the logic of moving more and more products to more places—did not initially cohere as a distinct infrastructural regime with interactive and compatible components. The chain grocery store was an urban neighborhood innovation, but companies gradually transformed in response to the shifting suburban infrastructure.

Between 1950 and 1970 the nation's total disposable income more than tripled from $206.9 billion to $629.7 billion.[61] Companies sought to profit from the largest concentration of consumers with the highest disposable

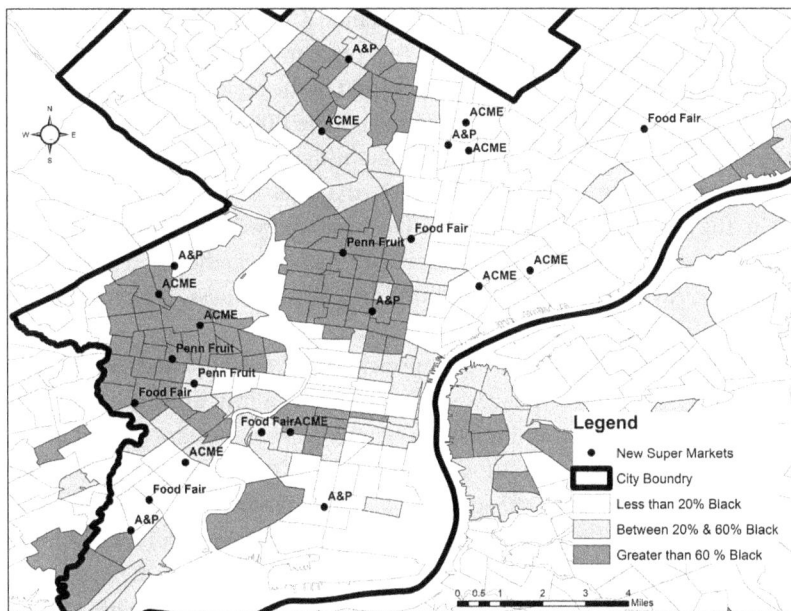

15 Sample of openings of Acme, A&P, Food Fair, and Penn Fruit supermarkets in Philadelphia, 1956 to 1976, in the context of neighborhood by percent black. Sources: Basemap provided by ESRI; census tract data from Geolytics Neighborhood Change Database; supermarket openings from Temple Urban Archives, *Evening Bulletin* clippings.

incomes—those residing in the suburbs. Mass consumption, automobile and trucking mobility, interstate highway development, and suburbanization were mutually reinforcing. The more flexible highway-bound trucking economy replaced rail distribution. Trucking was less regulated, more adaptable to changing trends of supply and demand, and better equipped to directly haul goods from "loading dock to unloading dock."[62]

During this period, companies built supermarkets in both cities and suburbs, not strategically avoiding urban centers at first—and this was true even for the prescient expanders like Food Fair and Penn Fruit. The map in figure 15 shows that Philadelphia's four largest grocery companies built new supermarkets in the city between 1956 and 1976, including stores in majority black neighborhoods. Even as suburbs grew, executives believed urban markets were still profitable.

Food Fair, for instance, demolished the Surpass Leather Company factory at 9th and Allegheny in North Philadelphia, constructing a large supermarket in its stead. It then opened a 27,000-square-foot supermarket in

West Philadelphia in a new shopping center. The company started a trend of building new urban supermarkets to replace multiple smaller stores, even developing a new distribution center as part of the regional terminal wholesale market system in South Philadelphia. The 800,000-square-foot warehouse was accessible to new highway and bridge connections, could handle 115 tractor-trailers at a time, and serviced 150 stores in the region. Louis Stein, the company president, said, "We think we owe something to the city. We came to Philadelphia 22 years ago with a small warehouse at 58th Street and Grays Avenue . . . doing a $6 million a year business. We expect to do $800 million in 1959."[63]

Penn Fruit followed Food Fair's model.[64] Penn Fruit opened its first store in 1927 at 52nd and Market Street, operating as a fruit and vegetable vendor servicing this West Philadelphia neighborhood. Besides special attention to produce, the store's founders, Samuel Cooke and Morris Kaplan, experimented with a 16,000-square-foot supermarket in 1932 at Broad and Grange Streets, claiming the first self-service supermarket in Philadelphia's city limits. Adding to the fresh produce, they offered seafood, meat, poultry, a delicatessen department, a bakery, and grocery departments with a broad assortment of packaged goods.[65]

Penn Fruit's first supermarket was also uniquely "urban." With no parking lot, it differed from suburban supermarkets, strategically fitting into this North Philadelphia neighborhood.[66] Penn Fruit expanded on this approach. In 1941, the company opened at the intersection of 19th and Market Streets in the city's business district—again without a parking lot. Still, Cooke and Kaplan developed an information infrastructure for high-volume distribution. The company studied transportation statistics in relation to necessary sales volumes, determining that 170,000 trolley passengers and 18,000 automobiles came through this intersection daily. Penn Fruit converted this former wholesale warehouse into a 46,700-square-foot supermarket.[67]

Penn Fruit and Food Fair were not alone in developing the urban model—all the other stores did it too. But the model itself gradually became outdated. Samuel Cooke shifted his problem-solving framework in response to suburban development, changing modes of transportation, and recognition of the necessity of increasing consumer volume to match increasing product variety. Cooke observed "the great resettlement of the population, increasing use of the automobile, greater emphasis on home living, an increase in the number of children per family, the home freezer, and a more casual way of life." He argued that food executives must recognize "the full significance of automobile shopping" by providing more parking facilities to handle more people "converging from greater distance" and thereby operate as a "one-stop shop" for more types of merchandise.[68] The company started building supermarkets in urban and suburban locations *with* parking lots.

By 1956, Penn Fruit had 41 stores and grew to more than 70 stores over the next two decades. The company expanded into the suburbs and as far away as Delaware and Maryland, but it also opened new stores in Philadelphia, such as stores in majority black neighborhoods at 22nd and Lehigh Streets in North Philadelphia and 48th and Pine Streets in West Philadelphia. Penn Fruit also transformed its first store at 52nd and Market Street to rival Food Fair's new market, even as the neighborhood demographics changed around the store from white to black and the location stood at the cross-section of many black-owned businesses.[69]

The national chains followed the smaller local and regional companies, as changing population settlements solidified economic prospects, including the profitable expansions into California and the West. The American Stores Company acquired the California chain Alpha Beta, but it also opened Acme markets in suburban Pennsylvania and on Lehigh Avenue in the Kensington section of North Philadelphia—already considered one of the poorest and most racially segregated neighborhoods in the city—with 11,435 square feet of selling area, 10 checkout booths, 102 feet of frozen food cases, and a parking lot for 83 cars. It opened up additional markets in other sections of the city too: Northeast Philadelphia and South Philadelphia, including one in a working-class neighborhood on 25th Street, between Reed and Wharton Streets, where 85,000 square feet allowed for 16,800 square feet of shopping space and a parking lot for 155 automobiles.[70]

A&P sought to regain its market position by investing in cities and suburbs too. A&P introduced a giant regional market in the Springfield Shopping Center servicing residents of upper-income suburbs like Springfield, Media, Drexel Hill, and Haverford. The company also remodeled an outdated store in the black majority North Philadelphia Olney neighborhood, converting it to a 100 percent self-service market, adding air conditioning, new flooring, a new meat department, additional dairy cases, grocery tables, fresh produce, and new checkout services.[71]

A decade later, at the height of the civil rights movement, A&P partnered with Reverend Leon Sullivan. Sullivan, a local religious and political leader, initiated his "10-36 plan" to overcome abandonment and poverty in black neighborhoods. Congregants from his Zion Baptist Church contributed $10 for 36 months to finance new developments such as an apartment complex and shopping centers.[72] By 1967, 650 congregants contributed to finance Progress Plaza in North Philadelphia. The 186,600-square-foot shopping center had parking facilities for 300 cars and negotiated leases with

16 Progress Plaza in North Philadelphia, 1969. Philadelphia *Evening Bulletin* Photographs (Copyright: TU Libraries). Credit: Special Collections Research Center, Temple University Libraries, Philadelphia, PA.

commercial tenants, including A&P.[73] Sullivan described this as the first partnership between a national food chain and a black-owned shopping center.[74] In the context of redlining, white flight, housing abandonment, and losses in manufacturing industries, many Philadelphia neighborhoods were desperate for new services and job opportunities. Supermarket companies initially opened new outlets in cities, including in black neighborhoods. (See fig. 16.)

Not every Philadelphia neighborhood embraced supermarkets. Some neighborhoods, especially poorer areas outside of Center City, built alliances with large supermarket companies. But urban renewal programs also brought about a different tension over the aesthetics of markets and the "fit" with neighborhoods. Urban renewal heightened the symbolic distance between Center City and more peripheral neighborhoods in North, West, and South Philadelphia. As the city poured millions of dollars into Center City revitalization efforts, middle- and upper-class residents opposed commercial market developments out of fear they would "cheapen" their "refurbished" neighborhoods.

In this changing context, A&P continued to seek out new opportunities to develop supermarkets and capture this part of the changing urban public. The company wanted to open a store in an abandoned taxi depot on Panama Street, between 22nd and 23rd Streets, in the recently refurbished Fitler Square area that runs from 20th Street to the Schuylkill River, between Walnut and South Streets. The empty taxi depot was an anomaly in the upscaling residential neighborhood, as it was zoned for commercial uses. Yet the Center City Residents Association voted to oppose the development out of fear that "there would not be enough trade in the neighborhood to support the supermarket," and the store would therefore "have to draw from other neighborhoods." Its concern was for neighborhood exclusivity and aesthetic design. Dr. Richard Caplin, who had a coveted nearby Delancey Place address, said at one meeting that he would "look with horror on tripping over wire baskets found as far as two or three blocks from markets."[75] The financial editor of the *Evening Bulletin*, J. A. Livingston, was also a Fitler Square resident. Livingston urged A&P executives to think not just about their own corporate bottom line but also about residential aesthetics, urban design, and commercial street use. He wrote,

> Rundown, slum-type houses have been torn down or redone. Whole blocks have been redeveloped. . . . Should executives put urban design ahead of their own profit-and-loss possibilities? The automobile has changed the character of cities, and, as people in the cities—who love the short walk to work, the parks, and the convenience to theater, music, and restaurant—fight back, it is important that corporations fight with them, not against them. Business officials must not only examine sites as businessmen (will they be profitable?), but also as urban planners: Will our entry here impede the revitalization of the section and interfere with the aspirations of the neighborhood and the long-term recrudescence of the city?

A range of circumstances outside of any single firm's control—the Great Depression, suburban growth, and changing transportation systems—influenced the initial movement toward the suburban supermarket system. Yet companies did not immediately close down urban access or view the historic centers as an economic problem. Initially, not all food retailers were sold on the idea of the supermarket, and in the age of urban renewal, not all consumers wanted them in their neighborhoods either. There was no agreed upon framework for understanding the supermarket as the taken-for-granted source of convenient food shopping we have today.

Suburban Supermarkets as a Feedback Loop

Between 1950 and 1970, the conventions of retail profitability became more fully embedded into decentered and regional distribution arrangements. The industry sold $40 billion worth of goods in 1952. By 1969, industry sales exceeded $62 billion.[76] Suburbs and supermarkets grew together into new infrastructural interdependencies in ways that reframed the meaning of "the center" from the point of view of retail profitability and managing market risk. Historic cities and downtowns began losing their hold on population and economic growth, and the distribution center—a mundane commercial architectural form—came to occupy key transport functions. Events and organized actions slowly became inscribed into a new "sociotechnical ensemble."[77]

Firms incrementally invested in an interdependent system made up of bureaucratic organizations, distribution warehouses, logistical technologies, trucking fleets, shopping centers anchored by supermarkets, and employee training in new technologies and product standards. They used demographic knowledge about where to build their stores and warehouses, and they gained technical proficiency at procuring, consolidating, and moving thousands of commodities to hundreds of stores in multiple locations at the same time. The distribution center occupied a node in the middle of a network of hundreds of stores, locking in profit-making conventions that forced firms into precarious economic positions.[78]

A&P executives described the company's distribution system as its "heartbeat" and "intelligence center," which could "assemble goods from all over the world" and "anticipate" stores' needs in many locations. A&P's 1962 annual report stated: "All suppliers obviously can't deliver their wares to each A&P super market directly for a very simple reason: the hundreds of delivery trucks involved would surround every store with a monumental traffic jam. So, instead, suppliers ship their products to A&P's warehouse . . . combining these items and re-shipping them to individual stores in the swiftest and most economical way. The company's warehouses are strategically located close to the center of specific distribution areas to reduce this secondary transportation cost to a minimum, and they are also equipped to check all goods to ascertain that they meet our demands for high standards of quality."[79]

The language of pursuing quality and efficiency remained from the prior era, but its meaning was now caught in different sociotechnical relationships. Distribution centers were slowly turning into higher-tech enterprises through the 1960s. Food Fair's large distribution center in South Philadelphia as part of the regional food terminal replaced smaller warehouses in

Northeast Philadelphia, one for dry goods and another for fresh produce. The $7.5 million investment was 650,000 square feet and handled all products except seafood, which was housed in an additional $300,000 refrigerated warehouse directly next door. The entire complex had temperature- and humidity-controlled refrigerators for perishables. Its accessibility to air, water, and rail transit, as well as new interstate highways, enabled Food Fair to consolidate products from all over the nation and then service 150 supermarkets in Pennsylvania, New Jersey, Delaware, Maryland, and Virginia.[80]

By 1970, Food Fair's CEO Louis Stein described the company's distribution centers as coordinated information and intelligence networks that were focused on improving the control of time and space. Computers were beginning to change the ordering process. He wrote, "Stores today can relay merchandise orders by telephone to data centers, where they are printed and transmitted to distribution centers. These orders are filled and delivered within 24 hours. Cutting 'lead time' from order to delivery permits better inventory control, requires less store warehouse space, and helps reduce the number of out-of-stock items." Stein viewed these new technical advances as having the potential to route trucks to stores and evaluate the profitability of locations of stores around the distribution center itself.[81]

New techniques for handling more varieties also allowed companies to augment store sizes. Stores multiplied from 10,000 to 15,000 to more than 30,000 square feet in less than a decade. Stein noted in 1970, "Another trend that will continue . . . is the increased size of the supermarket. The sales area of tomorrow's supermarket may be 30,000 to 35,000 square feet, more than double the present-day store." Larger stores allowed for more experimentation in developing and manufacturing new products. Stein said Food Fair will carry 8,000 items, "half of which were not available 10 years ago."[82] John Park, American Stores president, concurred. "Today's market contains about 8,000 items, tomorrow's will likely have twice that."[83] Stores already incorporated many food varieties, but new categories like "convenience foods" opened space for products designed for quick and easy preparation, including "prepacked" meats and produce.[84] Nonfood commodities also spread: "health and beauty" aisles became highly profitable, and "hardware" sections incorporated paint and electrical home goods such as light bulbs.[85]

The high-volume and high-variety retail system cemented low profit margins. Tables 1 and 2 show how Food Fair and American Stores—a regional chain and a national chain—continuously increased sales volumes. However, when net profits stabilized in the mid-1960s, profit margins sunk to less than 1 percent. Capturing higher sales volumes became critical to profit maximization with decreasing profit margins. Companies tried to stand out through experimentation, but they also had to imitate successful innovations so as not to fall behind.

Faulty decisions and advancing positions by competitors easily led to losses in this infrastructural system. The supermarket distribution infrastructure was expensive to maintain. Savings from high-volume purchases did not offset operational costs in certain types of stores and locations. The scale of distribution grew in direct tension with the costs to maintain profitability in aging markets.

The Origins of the Food Desert

The center of food distribution was repositioned from urban downtowns to the dispersed distribution centers themselves. An iterative reconfiguration of infrastructural interdependencies reshaped the profit-making conventions. Company decision-makers, aware of the environmental shifts, tried to capture new advantages. Changes in the conditions of opportunity opened up a new era of cutthroat competition between companies. Three types of situations represent how the reorganization of infrastructure contributed to mass closings and the origins of the food desert: localization of price wars; innovations that failed to fit into the profit-making conventions of the time; and intra-organizational turmoil of companies trying to compete in multiple types of locations at the same time.

Price wars became localized, with extreme inter-organizational competition in cities like Philadelphia. In particular, larger companies put pressure on smaller companies. Penn Fruit, the smallest of the four chains, went bankrupt in 1975 after suffering losses from a two-year price war. Some businesses cut product prices to increase store foot traffic. A&P, for example, slashed its prices in the most competitive locations like Philadelphia. The company developed loss leaders, which sold below cost, making up profits through higher margins on other products and from more profitable stores in less competitive regions. For example, A&P paid 12.5 cents per tomato soup can, but then sold each one for 9 cents. Still trying to find a model that could fit into the old city centers, A&P converted some stores into a "warehouse economy model," displaying canned goods and groceries in shipping cartons and selling produce from crates in order to further cut down on labor costs.[86]

Penn Fruit, with less access to reserves, struggled to maintain profitable sales volumes, losing customers to lower priced competitors and more aggressive companies like A&P. James Cooke, the company chairman, said in 1975:

17 Penn Fruit supermarket closing, 1972. Philadelphia *Evening Bulletin*
Photographs (Copyright: TU Libraries). Credit: Special Collections
Research Center, Temple University Libraries, Philadelphia, PA.

Penn Fruit, which operated profitably for many decades, suffered severe losses
because of a supermarket price war in Philadelphia that lasted for two years.
Unlike our major chain competitors, the great bulk of our stores are in the
Philadelphia area and we could not draw on profits from other sections of
the country not affected by the severe local competitive conditions. Since the
price war, Penn Fruit has not had the available cash resources to restore sales
volume lost during that period of unprecedented competition.[87]

Penn Fruit was stuck between two poles. It needed to invest in infrastructural expansion to match the buying power and sales volumes of larger companies. Yet it faced aggressive pressures from larger chains, which augmented
risks of such investments. The company could not get ahead. It closed almost
half of its stores in 1975 after losing $32.2 million in that year.[88] By 1976,
Penn Fruit could no longer afford to stock its shelves and closed down its
remaining 35 supermarkets and its warehouse facilities. Within the year, it
sold 17 stores to Food Fair. Eleven were in the city of Philadelphia, reflecting
some executives' continued belief that the density of smaller outlets in the
city could support a profitable volume of goods.[89] (See fig. 17.)

The changing infrastructure opened up opportunities for some companies to pursue profit-making conventions through multiscale and national networks. Part of this reconfiguration was about trying to develop innovative methods for handling higher volumes. Food Fair tried to merge food and nonfood industries into a new market type. The company was decades ahead of the mounting trend of the 1990s when Wal-Mart opened "Supercenters" that integrated supermarkets and discount stores. Food Fair never mastered the distribution infrastructure supporting this model, and the company faltered.

In 1958, Food Fair supermarkets carried 20 percent nonfood commodities. Executives experimented with increasing the proportion. The *Evening Bulletin* reported, "Food and non-food lines will be interspersed with each other so that a woman hunting lettuce will find herself looking at dresses and slips. If it's ketchup she's after, she may find herself walking through sweaters, shirts, stockings, summer furniture, irons, mixers, and other household items." Food Fair executives justified the approach, claiming that the goal of super-marketing is "high sales volume under one roof" and carrying a nonfood line of "disposable" products with "high turnover" is "an extension of the idea."[90]

Not all agreed that this innovation was prudent. Cupp, the American Stores president, said, "From all the talk you hear . . . you'd think selling nonfood items is a great, expanding deal. It isn't that at all. Selling these items requires different talents, besides investment in inventories, space, and fixtures."[91] In other words, Food Fair needed sound organizational and technical methods to build and manage the infrastructural interdependencies between manufacturers, distributors, and consumers. In 1961, Food Fair further invested in this infrastructure by purchasing J. M. Fields, a 79-unit discount department store chain. Over the next decade, the company worked to connect supermarkets and discount stores into a new retail model. Yet between 1975 and 1977, in the face of continuing price wars, Food Fair lost $33.4 million. Executives tried pouring an additional $100 million from the more profitable food sector into renovations of this new merchandising approach to no avail.[92]

Food Fair closed down smaller less profitable stores to make up for its losses. In North Jersey, it closed 26 supermarkets without the volume needed to cover expenses. It closed 50 more stores in Long Island. Profits from 250 stores in central Pennsylvania, Maryland, Virginia, Florida, Georgia, and South Carolina helped offset financial problems and stabilize stores in Philadelphia, the pride-filled location of its corporate headquarters. Food Fair purchased Penn Fruit, hoping to strengthen its local position.[93] Just two years later, however, Food Fair filed for bankruptcy. Philadelphia's largest nonfinancial corporation, the nation's sixteenth largest retailer, and the employer of 30,000 workers in Greater Philadelphia declined in net worth from $140 million in 1974 to $25 million in 1979.[94]

Only half of Food Fair's 88 Philadelphia outlets remained profitable. In its bankruptcy reorganization, Food Fair could not effectively rearrange its current distribution infrastructure designed for a larger multistate network into a lower-volume model for its 44 remaining stores. Executives closed Philadelphia outlets and distribution centers. The company relocated its headquarters to Florida, prioritizing growth in the less competitive region.[95]

Large national chains also fell behind, facing obsolescence in relation to the changing distribution infrastructure. Many companies competed at the national scale over buying power to maximize sales volumes and at the local scale for higher proportion of consumer dollars. This multiscale approach forced regular adaptations and innovations.[96] Yet converting to higher sales volumes and standardized stores created problems in old urban centers. Square footage cost more in the densely developed cities than it did in the suburbs. Building codes and the established built environment also made renovations and expansions difficult.

Following a multidecade effort to renovate its distribution infrastructure, A&P reduced its number of stores from a high of 16,000 to 2,000 by 1980. A&P was the most prosperous innovator of urban grocery stores, but the suburban supermarket system challenged its profit-making formula. In 1975, it closed over 1,000 stores, including 17 in the Philadelphia area and 9 in the city itself. Jonathan Scott, chairman and CEO said in 1975, "There is no longer any way we can support the burden of so many old stores. In recent years, we have tried very hard against heavy odds to continue to serve local areas in many cities and towns. Now we must move ahead to complete the transition we started long ago."[97] A&P's roots as an urban-based corporation constrained its ability to adapt. Cornell agricultural economist Willard Hunt said in 1979 that A&P "was too late moving to the suburbs. When the company did move, the competition already was there."[98] Facing decades of financial turmoil, A&P executives sold majority ownership to a German supermarket corporation.[99]

American Stores faced a similar scenario. Ida E. Brown, a resident of Philadelphia's Germantown section, owned 900 shares of company stock. At the annual shareholders meeting, she contested the closing of a store in her neighborhood. She said it caused "great inconvenience" to seniors, as the nearest remaining supermarket was too far to walk. John R. Park, chairman and president, responded, "There is no quick and easy solution to problems created for the elderly and poor by the closing of city supermarkets. I wish I could promise you a solution." A spokesperson for American Stores said the 15,000-square-foot store in Germantown "wasn't big enough to generate the volume necessary to make a profit under Acme's price-discounting policy set up three years ago." They planned to open 39 stores in the range of 25,000 to 30,000 square feet during the fiscal year and close an additional 20 smaller stores. Profit-making conventions embedded into infrastructural interdependencies compelled them to open larger supermarkets in areas with more secure sales volumes while closing less profitable outlets.[100]

Infrastructural Exclusion as a Social Problem

The above example of the elderly woman from Germantown exemplifies a unique form of deprivation. The poor, the elderly, and those with limited mobility faced hardships when the supply system was disrupted. Areas once housing multiple markets were left with none, solidifying a period of consumer vulnerability. For example, a West Philadelphia neighborhood around Baltimore Avenue lost its Pantry Pride (a banner of Food Fair), Acme (a banner of American Stores Company), and Penn Fruit, all by the end of the 1970s. Only smaller higher-priced stores remained. Convenience store companies like 7-Eleven wanted to move into the neighborhood, but as Bennie Swans, president of the Baltimore Avenue Business and Community Association, rejecting the convenience store, said in 1979, "What the residents need in this area is another supermarket where they can purchase items at discount rates."[101] (See fig. 18.)

Consumers, activists, and politicians witnessing and experiencing this infrastructural exclusion viewed it as a public problem without necessarily understanding its deeper roots. The immediacy of vulnerability masked how sociotechnical interdependencies created deeply entrenched profit-making difficulties. Public officials accused declining companies of strategically excluding poor neighborhoods. State Senator Freeman Hankins, representative of the Seventh District, discussed a senate investigation into closing supermarkets:

> I have an interest in eliminating some basic problems that face my constituents who find themselves without the services of food markets with competitive prices beneficial to them. . . . The fact is that there is money in those places which people think are impoverished and negligible in terms of income potential, and that the state might be able to develop some plans to assure that people in West Philadelphia, Germantown and North Philly will

18 Abandoned grocery store in Philadelphia neighborhood, 1972. This one is in South Philadelphia. Philadelphia *Evening Bulletin* Photographs (Copyright: TU Libraries). Credit: Special Collections Research Center, Temple University Libraries, Philadelphia, PA.

be respected for the profit business people can make dealing with them. It is important that people cease having to walk a proverbial "mile" just for a loaf of bread.[102]

Hankins pointed out that people in poor neighborhoods still spent money on food. Yet he missed the broader infrastructural context. Without public investment in equitable distribution, private firms sunk costs into organizational and technical interdependencies. New taken-for-granted organizational strategies and profit-making pursuits became embedded into the high-volume and low-margin distribution system. Following the period of market decline, executives started to assume urban market development was less viable. A vital infrastructure had become entrenched with concerns for managing market risk.

Corporate mergers once again gained traction following this period of collapse. Decision-makers in centralized corporate headquarters were increasingly separated from local consumer markets. Executives determined volume, advertising, sourcing, pricing, and distribution, which reduced the autonomy of in-store managers. Competing in multiple states and developing new logistical technologies further compelled standardized commodity lines and store layouts to maintain profitability. Infrastructural exclusion became a pervasive form of urban deprivation.

The Changing Means and Ends of Pursuing Efficiency

The chain grocery retail system was initially set up for urban neighborhood convenience, but businesses developed the frontier framework of flexibility and standardization. The initial profit-making goals also solved early food access problems for large urban population settlements. Suburbanization, changing mobility networks, and the Great Depression gave rise to new organizational uncertainties and fierce competition. The logic of "feeding cities" was eventually replaced with the logic of "feeding regions." The urban downtown lost its structural position as a central node between sites of production and sites of consumption. The retail distribution center—a mundane space of assembling—replaced it. This flexible site of supply coordination enabled firms to restock stores in multiple states, hundreds of miles apart, with the same products.

These changes might all seem like inevitable outcomes of efficiency-driven and profit-seeking efforts. But from the perspective of given corporations, even very large ones, control was uneven. Judgment calls were made and risks were taken. Sometimes, it led to ruinous results for the companies involved and not just for the neighborhoods where they operated.

A&P—once the largest corporation in the nation—grew to prominence in the previous era as an urban grocery store. It failed to read the industry's movement toward a suburban supermarket profit structure. Not only did it lose its dominant position, but it also set in motion a course of economic demise that continued for decades. In contrast, Food Fair heavily invested in infrastructural innovations. As one of the first supermarket chains on the East Coast, the company gained ground on older players through its pursuit of higher-volume regional distribution. But Food Fair went too far beyond the industry conventions of the time. Its executives tried to combine multiple merchandising approaches—the discount department store and the supermarket—into one organizational platform over a decade before Wal-Mart mastered it. Being ahead of the curve had equally devastating consequences as being behind it.

The infrastructural system of feeding regions crystallized as a semi-autonomous force that constrained corporate decision-making. When industry conventions became embedded into the vital distribution system, they overwhelmed corporate intent and strategy. It was not easy to match up the supply system, market prototypes, and the industry's profit-making conventions. Many companies got it wrong. Some companies went completely out of business, unable to make the necessary adjustments. Others filed for bankruptcy and restructured corporate goals around newer industry priorities. The four major food chains in Philadelphia closed down dozens of stores at a time, following a period of opening stores in urban neighborhoods and suburbs at the same time.

Chain expansion was not initially a zero-sum process of pitting suburbs against cities. The transformation of the retail system was a recursive process through which the pursuit of linking organizational efficiencies to profit-making opportunities became embedded into infrastructural interdependencies that over time grew less adaptable to older cities and inner-ring suburbs. Infrastructure was a reinforcing mechanism of race and class exclusion, knocking down companies and leaving behind innocent bystanders at the same time.

On the consumer side, residents of large cities had become accustomed over a period of decades to the idea that grocery stores were part of the infrastructure of abundance and convenience. The closing of stores disrupted the "daily round"—people's routines embedded into the spatial environment.[103] Urban consumers now had to build new shopping habits in the context of sparse retail options. The origins of the food desert gave rise to a unique kind of urban inequality at a time when mass consumption had become fundamental to American culture.

The suburban supermarket system was not the end of the transformation of the American food system. Decentralization continued as an iterative and cumulative process filled with unpredictable turns and consequences. The next chapter underscores the continuing expansion of flexibility through new uses of information technology. Even though the high-volume and high-variety suburban supermarket was deemed the most profitable food retail model, its limited automation posed problems for the manufacturing industries supplying them. New information technologies reshaped food distribution by refocusing the industry on managing the relationship between products, mobility, and new forms of data. It led to new organizational adaptations, competitions, corporate consolidations, and even more precise mechanisms for managing market risk and controlling time and space.

FOUR

The Bar Code:
A Micro-technical Force of Change

The rise of the suburban supermarket system was part of a political-economic transformation that included the development of roads, highways, suburban towns, shopping centers, retail stores, and distribution centers. It was also a collective and cumulative process of rearranging the macro-level interdependencies between production and consumption—a transformation of the infrastructural regime from feeding cities to feeding regions. The distribution center replaced the urban downtown as the key node of connection between retail stores in multiple states.

This chapter explains how the micro-production of a technical component developed into its own autonomous force that once again reconfigured economic decision-making and broke open the path toward the infrastructural regime of feeding the nation. The bar code—the mundane design now found on millions of market products—was part of an information and communication network that changed the conventions of pursuing profitability in food distribution. Roads and highways were fixed physical connecting chords. The bar code slowly but powerfully enabled corporations to tighten control over those chords and locate new forms of economic value in supply coordination.

The supermarket system changed public expectations about convenience. Nonetheless, a core tension materialized between supermarket companies' precarious profit structure and powerful manufacturing firms stocking stores with thousands of different products. Companies like Heinz, General Mills, Kellogg's, Pillsbury, Kraft, General Foods, and Coca-Cola invested billions of dollars to sell wide-ranging mass-produced food products—from ketchup to soda to corn flakes—through the supermarket platform. As the manufacturing side of the supply system implemented new forms of mechanization and automation to cut costs and boost profits, the retailing side remained a high-volume but low-tech sector.

In the beginning of the 1970s, executives and technical advisors from different manufacturing, distribution, and information technology companies came together to discuss the idea of a product code system to create interactive compatibility. This technical apparatus eventually enabled firms to turn millions of products into sources of information. New product-tracking methods signaled to retailers the need to invest in supply chain management and logistical operations.[1]

The bar code was a micro-technical force setting off another competitive search to reconfigure the means and ends of pursuing efficiency and profitability. Retailing sectors once categorized as distinct—supermarkets, pharmacies, and discount stores, for example—competed over cost-saving techniques, overlapping products, and consumer foot traffic. Companies experimented with new product combinations and aisle arrangements, inventory management protocols in distribution centers, different store sizes, and new types of retail locations.

Creating compatibility between manufacturers and retailers was an iterative and uncertain process. It was marked as much by historical timing as it was by corporate strategy and inter-industry negotiations.[2] Before the bar code system became embedded into the distribution arrangements, certain companies like Food Fair failed to integrate the discount store and the supermarket into one-stop shopping. Two decades later, Wal-Mart—once a small discount chain in the South—was on its way to becoming the most successful food retailer in the world.[3] Employing data-processing and logistical expertise, Wal-Mart challenged the industry-wide principle that concentrated population density was necessary for high-volume distribution.

Wal-Mart proved that the same stuff could be assembled and sold in highly profitable formats in places industry experts once thought impossible.[4] The bar code system prompted another industry realignment and created new constraints on supermarkets. Just as grocery chains were forced to follow competitors into the suburban supermarket project or risk bankruptcy, supermarkets were now forced to mimic Wal-Mart's supply chain management successes or face another round of decline.

Searching for Retail Automation

The introduction of the product code was initially about fixing the retail side of the infrastructural system. Manufacturing firms had steadily integrated new forms of mechanization since the early 1900s, pushing the logic of mass production into the food system. Retailers, in contrast, lacked in-store tools and resources to sustain the high-volume and high-variety scale of operation—and it showed in their profit margins. Supermarkets had almost no mechanization, and a period of economic inflation, beginning in 1965, exacerbated the problems. Manufacturers of cheap processed foods found additional ways to cut costs. The retail side of consumerism remained interactive with the machine-heavy production sector, but it was not compatible with it.

Before 1970, supermarkets were both low-tech and locally managed. Retail stores determined their own prices, and supermarket employees hand-applied price stickers on almost every single product in stores and warehouses. Meanwhile, the cashier tabulated customer purchases using a cash register that was basically a large calculator. It had automatic receipt functions to tally customer totals and change, but it lacked computing capabilities and automated connections to other parts of the system. All accounting and inventory assessments were managed at the store level without centralized control. Despite efforts to build research departments to help with locational analysis and sales volumes, retail companies had limited information about the "invisible" spaces between production and consumption.

As early as the 1940s, grocery executives visited engineering colleges to encourage faculty and students to explore technical methods to offset the most obvious points of retail inefficiency—price marking and checkout lines.[5] Retailers wondered whether engineers could devise time-saving mechanical methods for stores. Norman Woodland, an engineering graduate student at Drexel University in Philadelphia, came up with an early symbol-based classifying system. Woodland saw an analogy in Morse Code. He tried to create a visual representation as a series of dots and dashes. He realized that the key to reducing time in stores was to introduce a flexible symbol that machinery could read and decode from any direction so as not to delay transactions.[6]

Woodland, along with another Drexel engineering student, Bernard Silver, came up with a bullseye design as an omnidirectional symbol. They received a patent for it in 1952.[7] In their patent application, they wrote that the "classifying apparatus and method" would involve "photo-response to lines and/or colors which constitute classification instructions and which have been attached to, imprinted upon, or caused to represent the things being classified." It would allow for "different identifying combinations within a fixed pattern area" so as to represent "different articles."[8] Their product symbol would require optical scanning equipment to read the line, space, or color variations in the symbol that represented distinct products. It is no surprise that when a product symbol mechanism was finally implemented

Oct. 7, 1952   N. J. WOODLAND ET AL   2,612,994

CLASSIFYING APPARATUS AND METHOD

Filed Oct. 20, 1949   3 Sheets–Sheet 1

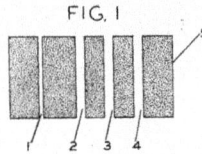

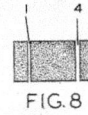

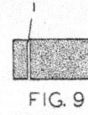

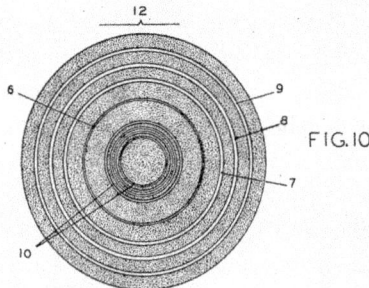

FIG. 1

FIG. 2   FIG. 3   FIG. 4   FIG. 5

FIG. 6   FIG. 7   FIG. 8   FIG. 9

FIG. 10

NOTE: LINES 6, 7, 8, AND 9 ARE LESS
REFLECTIVE THAN LINES 10.

INVENTORS:
NORMAN J. WOODLAND
BERNARD SILVER
BY THEIR ATTORNEYS
Howson &
Howson

19 Woodland and Silver's Classifying Apparatus and Method,
October 7, 1952. Patent #: US002612994.
Source: United States Patent and Trademark Office.

in stores decades later—as the bar code, and not the bullseye—it was part of a "co-diffusion" of technology. That is, the product code symbol and optical scanner were each unremarkable without the other.[9] (See fig. 19.)

Yet when Woodland and Silver patented their bullseye product symbol and classifying method in 1952, the technology needed to build the interactive retail apparatus was in its infancy. In fact, the various technologies that would be integrated into store operations had different origins with different intended applications. They required strategic engineering, manufacturing, and retailing industry efforts to bring them together into an interactive market ecosystem. In the 1950s, no one knew whether the bullseye product symbol would work or even what the right kinds of questions were about how to integrate this classifying apparatus with technical equipment as a business platform. Woodland began working for International Business Machines (IBM) on these and related issues after graduation. IBM made Woodland and Silver an offer to purchase the patent, but Philco Corporation, another electronics company that specialized in manufacturing transistor radios, made them a better offer.[10]

The technology needed to integrate the code symbol into working equipment was either too expensive or unavailable in those early years. The first optical scanning approaches relied on high-energy technology, including 500-watt lighting, which was too expensive to routinely run in stores. Lasers, which eventually became the cost-effective mechanism, were not available until about a decade later, first used by defense and aeronautics engineers. "Laser" technology—i.e., light amplification by stimulated emission of radiation—was invented in the early 1960s but not with optical scanning in mind. In fact, engineers described lasers as a "solution looking for a problem."[11] Lasers eventually became a core element of optical scanning equipment because of the efficient energy and pointed accuracy of infrared lighting. Woodland's early tests of lasers at IBM in the 1960s, when they became more widely available, operated at .0004 watts, a major energy reduction compared to the first photo-response scanners.[12]

If these complications were not enough, no one knew how to successfully print the bullseye product symbol in the 1950s. Clear, affordable, and accurate printing devices without the ink smearing on the labels were not readily available. Had the printing tools been deemed efficient and the optical scanning been proved accurate, retailing companies in the 1950s still might not have immediately implemented the technologies across multiple checkout lanes and thousands of stores due to expensive and time-intensive applications. They would still have to train employees in their uses, disrupting established work habits and rhythms. The early idea was that the individual stores would print and label symbol stickers on products matched to the company's inventory system.[13] The idea of a product symbol mechanism existed, but the range of technical expertise for industry-wide implementation remained abstract over the next decade.

By 1960, new forms of mechanization—eventually known as "automation"—were widespread in manufacturing industries. The term "automation" came from the word "automaton," which referred to the machine operation of a series of sequences. Henry Ford was among the first to establish an automation department, moving beyond simple applications of machines to assembly lines. Automation involved machine integration between subsequent steps that eliminated segments of human work. It was built on complex technical recipes—it took a series of difficult steps, worked out obstacles in their relationships, and then created reproducible operations, techniques, and work competencies that could be applied to various situations.[14] According to President Kennedy's Secretary of Labor, Arthur Goldberg, automation would become central to industries that "refine oil, make artillery shells, bake cakes, process chemicals, generate electric power, cast engine blocks, dig coal, produce atomic materials, and perform thousands of other jobs."[15]

The logic of automation spread through food manufacturing industries, and many on the retailing side heard about a growing interest in automating retail. But hearing about a phenomenon and understanding its potential applications or how to implement them are different. Technical engineers saw the complex physical realities of the infrastructure in unique ways—in terms of problem-solving and technical knowledge, or what Bowker and Star refer to as "infrastructural work."[16] For others, including retail executives looking to cut costs, they were immersed in industry conventions and everyday organizational routines that made them cautious about new technology.

In the 1960s, it was difficult for retailing executives to conceptualize the relationship between the new information technology and retail practice. The Markem Corporation of Keene, New Hampshire, a company specializing in the design of product identification, began doing preliminary research on grocers' perceptions of retail automation. The company's researchers found that executives of the seven largest supermarket chains in the Northeast and Midwest could not imagine what retail automation would look like. Executives of Hannaford Brothers, a chain in Portland, Maine, told them that stores did their own pricing and an industry-wide technical fix would never work. Giant Eagle in Pittsburgh reported that automation was a "gimmick." A&P executives were among the few that actually liked the idea of automation, but they feared accusations of collusion if they talked to manufacturers about product-pricing.[17] An inter-industry alliance and improved supply chain integration was considered unlikely at best and corrupt and illegal at worst.

Ben Nelson worked for Markem during that period. He recalled that it was conventional for each retail company to control its own pricing. In fact, different stores often "charged different prices for the same item." Even though price marking and checkout were regarded as store inefficiencies, there was no conversation about manufacturers "source marking" prices and product information for retail use. Moreover, price marking was still a core unionized job. Supermarket employees opened cartons and stamped each product unit with a wheeled ink stamper that had rotating numbers that employees manually lined up to affix the right price for each product. Often the cartons were two to three layers deep, which meant employees took the objects out and repacked them. Because stores offered price reductions on weekends, this recurring process throughout the week was extra paid work. Employees put the reduced prices on products for the weekend and then replaced the old prices for the coming weekdays.[18] (See fig. 20.)

IBM did not own the product code patent, but its technical engineers, including Woodland, did not stop exploring the knowledge ecosystem that surrounded it. Woodland continued his research on the project, studying the feasibility of optical scanning equipment in the 1960s and helping to develop point of sale (POS) technologies and inventory software. He advised IBM executives in a report in 1962 that a standardized code system and symbol was the primary solution to established retail inefficiencies, because scanning equipment required uniform marking dimensions to work effectively. As he studied scanning, he thought it would be difficult to make efficient scanners that read variations in brand labels of different sizes, colors, and fonts. He pushed IBM into research on technical solutions to optical scanning around standardized symbols.[19]

IBM was not the only information technology company with an interest in retail automation. During the 1960s, dozens of companies invested in research on computers, data-processing software, optical scanning technology, laser applications, printing methods, and telecommunication networks. The information age was on the horizon. Engineers and contractors working for aeronautics, space, and defense industries spilled over into other sectors. The laser was first invented in Hughes Research Laboratories in California, with subsequent innovations developed in Bell Laboratories in Princeton and then by engineers at GE and IBM.[20] Engineers eventually started to find fresh ways to apply the laser technology to industry-related problems, from medicine to banking.[21] Likewise, research on data-processing computers and telecommunication networks started in government and defense organizations and slowly spread beyond them.

During the 1960s, a wide range of sectors, from banks to retailers to manufacturers, were consulting with information technology and equipment manufacturers on how to apply computing and optical scanning to their accounting, inventory, and efficiency problems by identifying untapped areas of market value and risk management. Meanwhile, information technology

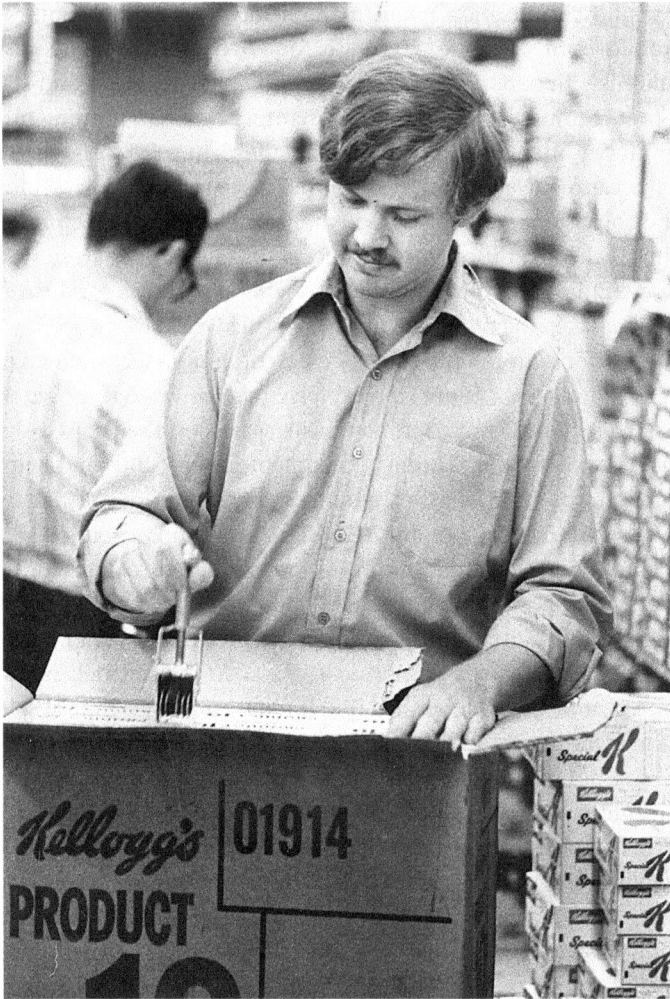

20 Supermarket employee stamping products with prices prior to UPC code, 1973. Philadelphia *Evening Bulletin* Photographs (Copyright: TU Libraries). Credit: Special Collections Research Center, Temple University Libraries, Philadelphia, PA.

firms consulted with telecommunications companies about how to build networks between multiple locations so that the scanning technology, product code symbols, and computer software could share information instantaneously without human intervention, that is, to automate the communication process.[22]

Both the Super Market Institute (representing supermarket retailers) and the Grocery Manufacturing Association (representing grocery manufacturers) gained interest in the product code and symbol idea at the same time, but as autonomous projects. They were not unified toward supply chain integration and shared value-added efficiencies. In 1963, the Philco Corporation partnered with the American Stores Company (Acme) to set up an in-store test on the bullseye symbol. However, the test never materialized because of printing setbacks. They could not accurately and routinely print the symbols.[23] In 1964, Oscar Mayer, the processed meat manufacturer, started looking for ways to mark its cartons on conveyor lines to better manage its inventory. Once again, the project never materialized.[24]

The technology companies also faced constraints. The Ford Motor Company purchased the struggling Philco Corporation and eventually shut down its supermarket project. Meanwhile, executives from the Kroger Company, an Ohio-based firm and the nation's third largest supermarket company at the time (now the largest supermarket company and second only to Wal-Mart in food retailing), also started to inquire about automation. They eventually contacted the Radio Corporation of America (RCA) about implementing product scanning. RCA took up where Philco left off, purchasing the bullseye symbol patent.

RCA was already working on manufacturing mainframe and industrial computers, semiconductors, lasers, scanning equipment, and retail displays. It was among a select group of companies in which engineers mixed and matched forms of expertise and specialization. RCA was at the forefront of building the retail ecosystem, strategically combining technical forms of knowledge that previously existed in separate spheres.[25] Its engineers had the strategic mindset of building interdependencies between components into a retail store system. RCA now owned the product symbol patent and worked closely with Kroger on transforming one of its Cincinnati stores into a computerized network.

Francis X. Beck Jr. was the technical director at RCA Princeton Laboratory developing the bullseye supermarket system. From the point of view of engineers, the technology was becoming actionable. He writes, "There was little doubt about the availability of physical resources to design and manufacture a product to automate a supermarket's front end."[26] Opening the line of communication between various technical sectors and supermarket firms started to move the food distribution system toward acceptance of automation. It marked a shift in collective perception, if not yet a coherent technical recipe, of the specifications needed to implement it. RCA was converting localized in-store problems into actionable hypotheses about general technical solutions.

RCA remained cautious, however. The company did not want to reproduce the technical setbacks Philco had experienced with Acme. RCA turned to Avery, a label company, to run tests on routine accuracy of printing the bullseye product symbol. RCA's team worked with technical advisors from Sylvania to better understand different possibilities with scanning. RCA engineers then worked closely with Kroger executives and employees to develop and test a range of in-store operations—trying out product code printing equipment and copying protocols, as well as different scanning techniques and checkout station arrangements. They also worked with AT&T on communication networks that integrated scanning and price look-up through a backroom computer. The goal was to have near instantaneous information between scanning, product look-up, and price tabulation. They successfully created a working protocol.[27]

Between 1960 and 1970, a confluence of circumstances shifted the tide of collective understanding. The first was that information technology engineers put together previously separate innovations into an interactive "sociotechnical ensemble."[28] Another factor contributing to this change was the "Great Inflation." Gas prices tripled and even quadrupled in some places, which affected manufacturing and shipping rates. Energy costs also multiplied, creating operational problem for retailers heavily dependent on air conditioning, lighting, and refrigeration.[29] Supermarket firms had no available solutions for managing rising costs. In addition, supermarket unions sustained a well-paid workforce at a time historians often describe as the beginning of the decline of unions in the United States. Supermarkets were labor intensive, and checkout clerks and baggers made up a quarter of gross margins. Yet breaking union contracts was not an option. Industry consultants advised retailing executives that automation was the primary time and cost-saving solution.[30]

In the 1930s, the Great Depression, along with suburbanization and changing transportation methods, opened up the possibility for a new trajectory of organizational innovation and competition—it led to the rise and spread of supermarkets. Similarly, this period of inflation in the 1960s and early 1970s exacerbated economic problems that, along with new information and communication possibilities, pushed the industry into another strategic direction of system reconfiguration. The industry shifted from focusing on identifying and patching up retail inefficiencies toward searching for interactive compatibility between manufacturing, distribution, and retailing.

Searching for System Integration

In 1970, the Uniform Grocery Product Code Council (UGPCC) was formed. Manufacturers, retailers, wholesalers, information technology engineers, and industry consultants came together to study the idea of system integration. Participants included executives from grocery manufacturing firms like General Foods, H. J. Heinz, and General Mills; pharmaceutical manufacturers like Bristol Myers; corporate wholesalers like SuperValu, which represented large chain wholesale operations; and supermarket companies like A&P and Kroger.[31] Industry consultants from McKinsey & Company, along with more than a dozen information technology and equipment company representatives, were also involved in creating a standard product code system. Together, they applied techniques of printing, scanning, and computer integration, and studied the cost-benefits of implementation. With top executives and technical advisors and consultants from major firms involved, the committee pushed forward an agenda about converting the physical infrastructure of the supply system into a corresponding information and communication network.[32]

Even though executives of big corporations were involved, the implementation of a product code system was not an outcome of the domination of the power-elite. The decisions that were made and how they were carried out and put into practice were not simply about imposing power from the top down or from the center of a network. In reconfiguring complex systems, the old hegemons fall away, because coordination is about getting the details right—and working out the organizational and technical details is extraordinarily difficult in practice. Negotiating the implementation of complex sociotechnical relationships produces effects and new power centers that cannot be predicted.

Decision-makers in different sectors had distinct forms of expertise that forced compromises between them. Early questions were related to defining the parameters of implementation. It required agreement on the functions and applications of a product code system, including how to create a numerical classification apparatus and represent it visually as a product symbol linked to manufacturer and product information. Different sides also had to gain a better understanding of the technical equipment and cost-benefits associated with adopting it. Every organization in the supply system would require new hardware and software in order for the new applications to reach their cost-saving potential. More than a decade after the formation of the committee, various manufacturing and distribution arms agreed that automation techniques were the key components of an interactive and compatible infrastructure. It took yet another decade before the collective project became embedded into the coordination and distribution arrangements, which then put new constraints on the various organizational relationships and profit-making opportunities.

Early conversations in the UGPCC moved the industry toward source marking (rather than store marking) the product code symbol. Yet the previous decade of building the equipment focused on in-store methods, which immediately placed limits on how manufacturing companies translated the existing technology into a different kind of project. Technical engineers designed the optical scanning machines to interface with a standard symbol. RCA, Sylvania, and Avery made clear in their work with Kroger that an in-store standard code was actionable. Moving to a source marking agenda meant translating a decade of work around the retail ecosystem to a much larger scale of production while also integrating the particularities of the distinct manufacturing operations for every company and product.[33] R. Burt Gookin, the president of Heinz and the first chairman of the UGPCC, wrote, "To get an idea of the complexity of this problem, just consider the number of different products sold in supermarkets, the number of printing processes currently in use, the number of different materials being printed on, and the number of different coatings and overwraps being applied over the printing."[34]

It was one kind of problem to print a product code symbol on adhesive paper in a store and stick it somewhere on the manufactured items going onto the shelves. It was another kind of problem to fit a standard symbol into the limits of different kinds of manufacturing settings, materials, and brand designs before products arrived at the stores. Industry consultants from McKinsey & Company were charged with studying and supervising the feasibility of the translation project. They viewed system integration as a symbiotic process. Most significantly, early projections found that for retailers to experience any cost-saving benefits, manufacturers had to standardize the product code. However, if retailers resisted investing in scanning equipment to read the symbols in their stores, then manufacturers were wasting time and money by incorporating symbol markings into packaging, design, and printing operations.[35]

The committee started outreach to make the industry more familiar with the idea. In the first year, members of the committee, along with consultants, met with executives of over 300 manufacturing and supermarket companies. They also addressed audiences of thousands more at industry trade association meetings. The committee raised $1 million in its first year, most of it from the top 20 supermarket chains, which pledged $20 for every

$1 million of sales. The UGPCC used the money to pay McKinsey & Company for its research and consultation as well as to finance the beginning stages of the rollout.[36]

The idea of a product code system now circulated beyond the small group of committee members. Participants in the UGPCC deemed code standardization an important aspect of building organizational and industry compatibility. Yet they also understood that building a system of interactive compatibility did not mean creating uniformity. It meant integrating flexibility into the standard protocol so that individual companies could incorporate the agreed upon methods into their established organizational routines.[37]

Corporations already connected the high-volume and high-variety market system to complex bureaucratic methods of classification, accounting, and inventory management. Manufacturers, wholesalers, and retailers alike had distinct operational and organizational methods for differentiating brands, types of products, and retail aisles as procurement divisions, and monitoring profitable and unprofitable products. They managed overstock and understock of hundreds of thousands of different units at a time. They decided what new types of products to introduce and how many of each type. On top of it, retailers had to keep stores fluidly moving with products and customers, which meant keeping tabs on what other companies did, printing coupons to increase foot traffic, and monitoring successes and failures of weekly advertised specials.

A symbol standardization subcommittee started working with technical advisors and information technology companies on guidelines for bridging a numerical code system with the representative product code symbols so that companies could tie together information classification and material goods. Five members of the subcommittee came from the manufacturing side and five from the distribution side. Executives of five additional supermarket companies agreed to hold equipment tests in their stores and serve as consultants on feasibility measures and evaluating cost-benefits of the different symbol and equipment options.[38]

The UGPCC invited information technology equipment companies to come up with a standard symbol. The symbol's utility cannot be understated, but it is important to note that the symbol was the visible mechanism of a deeply structured industry reorganization effort. The UGPCC had to figure out what the symbol represented; how an industry standardized a symbol on all products; how to link it to corporate and store classification structures; how to distribute new codes and symbols for new businesses and for new products so as not to deter innovations; and how the industry would keep track of all of this information.

The subcommittee initially came up with a 10-digit code structure that would correspond with the product code symbol, thinking that it would allow enough space for a wide range of companies and products that wanted inclusion. Each manufacturer—H. J. Heinz, for example—would get a manufacturers' number as the first half of the digits on all of its products. Then, each particular item within the company's profile—for Heinz that could be products like baked beans, ketchup, or vinegar—would have distinct product codes as the second half of the digits. The distribution of code symbols would eventually integrate these numbers into subtle space and color variations in the standard product code. The decoding equipment would read the symbol variations and link it together with stored information about product types, prices, unit quantities, and accounting information, and even potentially create and automatically analyze inventory and product-tracking data.[39]

The committee initially contracted with Distribution Codes Inc., a subsidiary of the National Association of Wholesalers, to oversee the designation of the numerical codes to manufacturers. Distribution Codes Inc. already had experience with a coding system in the wholesaling industry and worked with many of the same manufacturers. This nonprofit organization could apply its former methods to the larger endeavor. Distribution Codes Inc. worked with the various trade associations to access member lists and contacts so as to assign manufacturing numbers without duplication. The information storage conditions of the time required a hard filing system. They created a physical number bank, with sequential tear-off numbers that they affixed to membership certificates. They then photocopied the certificates into a master file of all the distributed codes.[40]

UGPCC still described a chicken or egg problem: Who was going to be the first to invest in the collective project of interactive compatibility between sectors? Continued outreach was necessary to get mutual adoption to inch the project forward toward interdependency—and it was inches at first, not feet. Kroger executives sent letters to all of its manufacturing partners about the benefits of product code standardization. Others like SuperValu followed suit.[41]

The UGPCC worked on these problems for more than a year. The committee studied the process, evaluated early surveys and tests, and came up with new projections on cost-saving benefits. It sent out information newsletters, which included updated guidelines, procedures, and recommendations for moving forward, including how to apply to Distribution Codes Inc. for numerical product codes. The committee outreach materials described the need for compromise between interacting parties to reach for the benefits of "total system efficiency." One document suggested that to build momentum, companies could take small steps: manufacturers could start using "standard invoices" while distributors could start using "standard purchase orders" with the universal numerical system. The committee wrote, "Like donkeys straining at opposite ends of the same tether, neither party benefits until both parties give a little. Giving a little means adopting and using the industry standard."[42]

The delays were multifaceted. Part of the delay was about the difficulties of economic compromise across different profit-seeking interests. But also, the practical side posed its own dilemmas. Companies had to figure out how to fit the classifying logic of the numerical code into mundane operations. They had to integrate it onto labels on shipping cartons, invoices, purchase orders, and accounts payable reports, and the most daunting of them all, convert previously written inventory systems to automated methods. Companies like General Mills, the manufacturer of Cheerios, applied the codes to their products before the symbol was available. The company printed the numbers without a product code symbol on its product boxes and phased out its previous inventory and accounting methods. Other companies like Del Monte, a leader in canned fruit, built on existing company code structures. Del Monte integrated its existing four-digit product codes (it had no existing "manufacturing number") into the new 10-digit structure. Del Monte was assigned a five-digit manufacturing number and then simply added "0" to its four-digit product codes as its fifth digit for each of its existing products.[43]

Fitting the classification structure to routine applications was a necessary precursor to purchasing information technology equipment. Yet there were further delays due to skepticism. It was both expensive and time consuming to implement radical technical changes to daily employee operations in such a low-margin field. And the reports demonstrated projections, not concrete evidence that the symbol system would have cost-saving advantages.

As the numerical code structure circulated, the UGPCC had not yet selected a corresponding symbol. In the early 1970s, Woodland's bullseye symbol, now the RCA model, was the most established. Thirteen other technology equipment companies saw the potential in the retail ecosystem and wanted a chance to make their cases to the UGPCC. These companies proposed product code symbols, each with different features, but all adopting the 10-digit code structure along with required size limits, printing requirements, and other committee-designated standards. Eventually, seven companies presented full proposals.[44] For example, Litton Inc., which was largely a defense electronics and technology company, introduced a

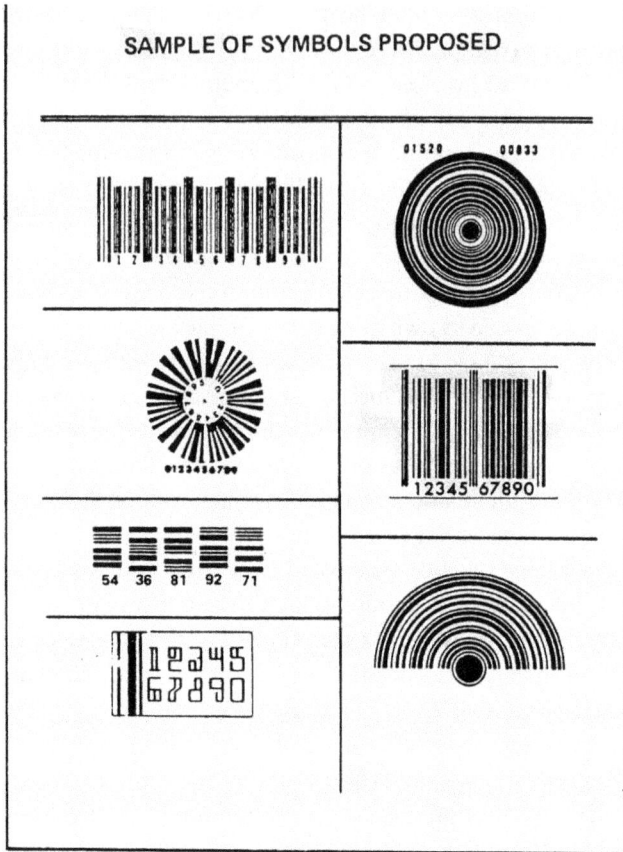

SAMPLE OF SYMBOLS PROPOSED

21 Sample of proposed product code symbols. Source: UPC '72:
Executive Summary of Timely Information about the Universal Product
Code, October 10, 1972. ID History Museum, IDHistory.com.

half-circle model. IBM, in contrast, proposed a bar code representation.[45]
(See fig. 21.)

The UGPCC required store tests, lab tests, and proposals from each of the
technology firms so that the committee could comparatively evaluate them
along the same dimensions. They tested price and effectiveness of checkout equipment; efficiency of cashiers handling the equipment at checkout;
costs of printing the code; capacity of the scanners to read many different
code variations; workability of the symbol in a truncated cross-section form;
applicability to different kinds of scanning equipment such as handheld
wands and slot scanning on the base of the checkout station; ability to scan

symbols through different kinds of label wrapping; accuracy of information through scans; adaptability to changes in the code structure, such as adding more numbers if more products made it necessary; size specifications of the symbol to maximize accuracy; and symbol location specifications where it scanned best. The committee and consultants believed that establishing accuracy, flexibility, and fluidity of the process and equipment in the beginning by such a detailed comparative evaluation would allow them to eliminate future blind spots.[46]

The RCA and IBM symbols were the two finalists—they enabled the most information variations in the least amount of space with the most flexibility for adaptation to different kinds of industries, packaging materials, and product shapes and sizes. In earlier years, Woodland and his team of IBM engineers worked on building a retail ecosystem that supported the RCA symbol. They believed, throughout the 1960s and even into the early 1970s, that the bullseye symbol was the state of the art and could not be improved upon. But one colleague at IBM, a senior engineer named George J. Laurer, started working on another proposal. He suggested a rectangular box housing a series of black and white straight lines, which like Woodland's bullseye, could still scan in any direction.[47]

Laurer convinced the IBM team of its superior qualities and, based on IBM's proposals, lab tests, and store tests, ultimately convinced the UGPCC. Laurer and his colleagues argued that manufacturers would face difficulties printing RCA's larger design on a range of packages. The bar code was smaller and more flexible. According to Laurer, the other proposal "would have prevented applying the U.P.C. Symbol to many items, such as soda cans, bottles, [and] wax cartons." The committee accepted a version of the IBM bar code.[48]

At the end of 1973, the various committees of the UGPCC established a product code structure, they demonstrated near-perfect accuracy of the optical scanning equipment, they selected the bar code symbol, they established printing precision of the symbol on a range of materials, and they ran in-store tests showing that computers and telecommunication networks could integrate all of the technical components into a fluid checkout system. At the end of the year, manufacturers began printing bar codes on their products and supermarkets started to scan them. A cashier at Marsh Supermarket in Troy, Ohio, scanned the very first bar code on a multipack of Wrigley Juicy Fruit gum.[49]

When sociotechnical interdependencies materialize, they can enforce convergences between various actors and interests, such that they become necessary. Such interdependencies create what Michel Callon calls an "obligatory passage point." The sociotechnical entanglements themselves become "performative," making them fluidly integrated and difficult to reverse.[50] Yet that was not immediately the case with the bar code system. As Andrew Pickering points out, technical implementation is different than technical innovation.[51] Even as the apparatus was secure and technology engineers and industry consultants believed it was fundamental to the future of retailing profitability, implementation continued as a push and pull between different interests and investments to move this working apparatus toward system integration.

A full year after the first scanned items, only 40 different stores—not 40 companies, but 40 physical store locations—had used the bar code and scanning technology.[52] The UGPCC governing committee reported that the main challenge of wide-scale implementation was motivating "total cooperation between the product manufacturer, the printer/converter, the engraver, the package designer, the wholesaler, the retailer, and in the end, the customer." It required different firms adapting different organizational routines into specified conventions of "package design, symbol location, container size, [and] color schemes."[53] The slow rollout reaffirmed the UGPCC's earlier concerns about adoption. Industry experts believed that the scanning systems would provide cost-saving advantages only if 70 to 85 percent of products in stores incorporated the bar code.[54]

The Micro-technical Gains Autonomy

During the first half of the 1970s, retailers focused on how to implement new time-saving methods into the checkout process. Manufacturers, in contrast, concerned themselves with product code compatibility with other retailing sectors beyond the supermarket industry. Most executives on either side still did not understand the nuances offered by different technology companies about related data-processing projects. These different spheres—retailing, manufacturing, and information technology industries—had different ways of conceptualizing and enacting routine work and problem-solving. As the Universal Product Code (UPC) system spread, various arms of the industry gradually converged around a shared goal of information management. Retailers extracted integrated inventory data from different stores as a shared company and market research platform, while manufacturers located distribution as a unique space with its own potential for cost-saving efficiencies.

Manufacturers had two main priorities during the early transition to the UPC system. One was investing in new printing and design methods that could reproduce the standard symbol and code design on their products. Another was making the classifying system as inclusive as possible, so that the UPC was not specific to grocery manufacturers and supermarkets. Manufacturing executives wanted the code standards to integrate other industry classification projects: the National Drug Code, the Canadian Grocery Code, and the Distribution Industry Codes of the National Association of Wholesalers. At that time, the National Merchants Retail Association, which included general discount merchandisers, department stores, and clothing stores, did not have a standard code system.[55]

In March 1974, the National Bureau of Standards organized a conference in Gaithersburg, Maryland, that addressed "Automation in the Retail Industry." The National Bureau of Standards, now the National Institute of Standards and Technology, is a government agency started in the early 1900s to study and facilitate relationships between different industries in the name of the public benefits of innovation and efficiency.[56] At the conference, retailing and manufacturing executives and technology engineers leading the UGPCC efforts shared their stories, setbacks, and innovations. Some companies, like Marsh Supermarkets, had already successfully moved into retail automation and experienced cost-saving benefits. Alan Marsh, the firm's president, reported that the technology was easy to use and enabled a 12 percent increase of product throughput in the checkout process with only 58 percent of the store's products coded. As the company increased its percentage of marked products in the next year, he expected even greater benefits.[57]

The conference facilitated a conversation between different industries whose supply chains were historically different but were increasingly overlapping.[58] Months later in November, the UGPCC board of governors approved the integration of drug, general merchandise, and discount outlets and manufacturers into their product code council membership. The organization removed "grocery" from its name as a symbolic gesture. The organization was renamed the Uniform Product Code Council (UPCC).[59]

As an independent nonprofit organization, UPCC took over responsibilities from Distribution Codes Inc. for assigning numerical codes and bar codes. It eventually increased the number of digits in the code to make it more amenable to thousands of additional manufacturers servicing various retail sectors. The UPCC saw the potential of benefits across the board for all kinds of companies: supermarkets, of course, but also chain pharmacies like Walgreens, general merchandising outlets like Kmart and Wal-Mart, and a wide range of manufacturers, not just of food, but of pharmaceuticals, soaps, shampoos, cleaning supplies, and so much more.

Fred Butler was the vice president of operations at the pharmaceutical company Bristol Myers and the chairman of the UPCC drug product code subcommittee. In 1974, he described the growing convergence between retail sectors. He said that grocery stores were adding more and more non-grocery items while other kinds of "retail complexes" sold everything from "groceries and prescription drugs to lawn mowers and home furnishings." He believed that "versatility" across "different classes of products" was fundamental to the mass-merchandising project. Butler described the same balancing act that plagued the system-building project from its inception. "In order for UPC to become a successful working reality and to support retailers who are investing large sums for UPC checkout systems, it is vital that all manufacturers who sell their products through grocery outlets to source-mark those products with the appropriate code and symbol."[60]

Grocery manufacturers increasingly source-marked codes onto their products, but the spread to other manufacturing industries was almost nonexistent in the 1970s. By 1977, 5,300 manufacturers were members of the UPCC, and 83 percent of packaged goods on supermarket shelves were marked with symbols. However, in 1978, only 1 percent of grocery retailers had adopted the scanning systems—not exactly the profound success that earlier members of the UGPCC had envisioned. Supermarket executives continued to worry about the costs and benefits of investing in automation equipment.[61]

A significant piece of the puzzle was overcoming the epistemic differences between information technology companies, manufacturers, and retailing companies. They did not have the same taken-for-granted knowledge and industry language about what the system could and should accomplish. Periods of infrastructural transformation are inherently confusing. They do not just make visible different strategic visions. These sociotechnical ruptures bring to light completely different taken-for-granted knowledge competencies and routines.[62]

In the 1970s, the UPCC sent out various information manuals and newsletters to get over this hurdle. Distribution Inc. put out monthly newsletters that explained the technology. It incorporated a section called "Scanning the Symbol" to discuss the inner workings of scanning and the range of practical problems retail employees might experience, from how fast the symbol moves through the scanner to managing wrinkled or torn codes on the package.[63] Some manuals addressed the "definitions of the terms," which focused on "important to understand words that are not only explained but illustrated in the context of their use" so that "technical and nontechnical people" alike could understand the innovations.[64] The manuals had

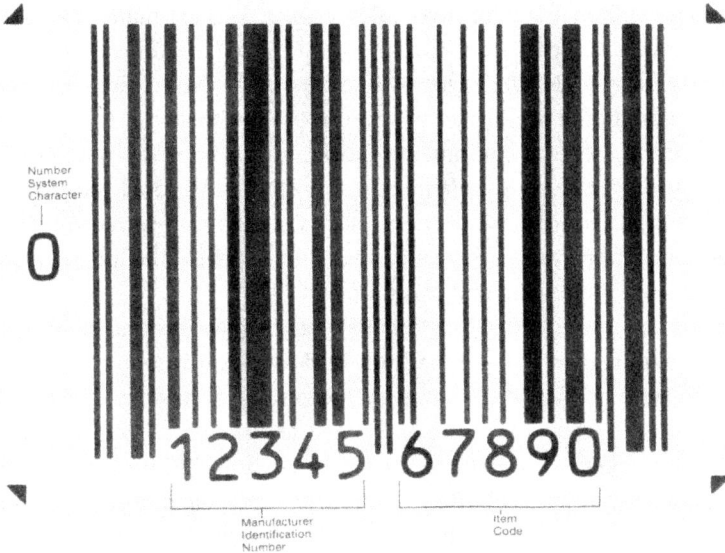

Number
System
Character

0

12345 67890

Manufacturer
Identification
Number

Item
Code

22 Bar code with explanation of numbers, from *Universal Product Code: A Guide to Manufacturers*. Uniform Product Code Council, Inc. Dayton, OH, 1980. Artifact 93, ID History Museum, IDHistory.com.

pictures to support the definitions and alleviate confusions. In one manual, the heading "Nomenclature and Definitions for UPC Code" was followed with definitions for new technical words like "code," "identification," "manufacturing ID," and "item ID."[65] (See fig. 22.)

Even as the symbol was more widely applied on manufacturing items by the end of the 1970s, many in the retailing industry still did not understand the various potential uses built into the technology. IBM won the competition over the product code symbol, but IBM engineers' vision for the technology went well beyond in-store applications. IBM's salesmen had a hard time convincing retailers about the benefits of computing technology and data-processing. IBM had a data center, a distribution industry division, and training centers to teach retail and manufacturing companies how to use its new computer equipment and varied information and analysis services to make the most of the new code system.

The competing interpretations of the technology represented a fundamental tension of system reconfiguration. Advanced "system-building" companies like IBM had to compete with consumer-friendly technical equipment companies like National Cash Register, Memorex, Datachecker, and Data Terminal Systems over sales territory in supermarkets and other retail outlets. IBM engineers and salesmen believed they offered retail firms more value in data-processing and analysis, yet these other equipment companies offered user-friendly checkout options that were less expensive. Much of the checkout equipment of these other companies was geared toward tackling in-store problems related to the transitional moment. The computer and telecommunication systems, in contrast, would fundamentally change how corporations measured and evaluated the interdependencies between production and consumption.[66]

Retail executives had a difficult time imagining an integrated system that could do more than just automatically read codes, calculate prices, and help with in-store accounting—that is, see beyond local in-store efficiency operations. Bill Selmeier was one of the lead salesmen for IBM working with the supermarket sector at the time of the spreading UPC project. He writes, "The whole concept of building a centralized integrated system to manage a business was so far from their day to day experience, it took a while for them to fully get the scope." Selmeier pointed out that once they invested in less sophisticated checkout options they no longer wanted to, nor could they afford to, invest in another round of equipment for up to seven years.[67]

Many of the equipment options available to retailers matched in-store conventions. For instance, most checkout machines had "key-only" systems and no scanning equipment, such that cashiers could type in the product codes or prices. These machines could integrate a scanner if the retail company wanted.[68] IBM had a different approach that did not fit with the precise conditions of the transitional moment. IBM's first supermarket model in the early part of the 1970s, even before most manufacturers adopted the bar code, was more expensive and had no key entry. It was ahead of the curve, and most retailers were not ready for it.[69]

Some of the supermarket firms invested in optical scanning machines, but they still focused on a simpler strategic goal of getting technical applications on the front end to work properly. In other words, they had to integrate human movement with the new technology. It is hard to imagine people in the United States not understanding what to do at a retail checkout station dependent on scanning products. Retailers have now installed self-checkout lanes, betting on the idea that ordinary consumers have the dexterity and know-how to manage the equipment themselves. Children at supermarkets can even slide bar codes over laser scanners as the beep registers successful interactions with the checkout machine.

There was a time in the 1970s and even into the 1980s when handling the technology was considered foreign for employees and consumers alike. The connection between laser scanners and product codes was indisputable. They had to go together if they were used at all. But it was not always clear how to make them fit together as a routine checkout operation. If IBM wanted to dominate the market for retail system-building, they had to learn to compete with user-friendly companies focused on the liminal moment between established and incoming methods. IBM incorporated flexible key entry options into its supermarket checkout system to complement the scanner and worked closely with retailers to choreograph a checkout process.

The sociotechnical implementation was a work in progress. IBM equipment was initially not stationed at the right height for cashiers, making it difficult for them to maneuver the parts together. The early equipment did not accurately integrate the sound and information. The scanner was supposed to beep when it captured the information. While there was no actual delay in information transmission, there was a sound delay. Cashiers waited for the beep before they moved to the next item, which slowed them down. Supermarket executives at Kroger, who installed some of the IBM equipment, could not figure out why their checkout throughput was not becoming faster with the implementation of new equipment. IBM videotaped the checkout process and figured out the range of human-technical interaction problems, and then its engineers worked alongside the supermarket companies to fix them.[70]

At the same time, information technology companies like IBM and RCA continued to hold information sessions at their research facilities for supermarket companies, other retailing industry executives, and manufacturing executives. Just as making check out into workable stations was an iterative process, so was shifting the collective perception among retailing and manufacturing decision-makers about data-processing and information integration. IBM was heavily invested in the supermarket system, but the company also worked on another project for general merchandising firms that they called the "retail system."[71]

General merchandising was a rapidly growing retail field in the 1970s, and IBM was at the forefront of helping firms think about their potential. One IBM advertising brochure stated that the new integrated "retail system" would eliminate "the stand-alone cash register, the handset ticket maker, the batch process computer and the telephone credit checker." It "will not only control these functions, but will integrate and interrelate the information to provide tools which will assist the retailer in much more effective management of his store." The "point of sale" is the "tip of the iceberg."

The system will control the "back-room functions" that include "payments, purchase order entry, receipts, personnel and payroll records, administrative messages, adjustments, returns, transfers, and merchandise ticket and credit card preparation." It will provide an accurate "inventory control system."[72]

The supermarket and the general merchandising sectors were entering into a new competition, although, again, it was not fully comprehensible to them. The different retailing industries increasingly contracted with many of the same manufacturing companies, opening up an isomorphic relationship through mutual adaptation.[73] Supermarkets were carrying more and more nonfood items, and general merchandisers carried many packaged food items. The supermarket sector moved into the UPC system and some companies like Kroger of Ohio and Giant in Washington, DC, moved into computerization. Likewise, general merchandising companies like Kmart and Wal-Mart invested in similar computing operations to manage stores and inventory. In 1975, Wal-Mart had 125 stores, but Sam Walton, the company's founder and CEO, leased an IBM computer system to better account for distribution in warehouses. He adopted electronic cash registers in 100 stores that automatically recorded sales information. Two years later, Wal-Mart built its first company-wide computer network and was starting to construct a new information system for working with its suppliers.[74]

IBM viewed the UPC and POS systems as components of a broader interactive ecosystem. As the early adopters turned the human-technical interactions in retail stores into routine checkout processes, they also benefited by using the UPC/POS interactions as an information system to externalize and study physical inventory. In other words, they could observe and manage the inventory and sales processes on a computer screen. They started to explore the potential to capture, correlate, and analyze data, which became a fundamental area of market competition in ensuing years.

Fred Butler, the pharmaceutical executive at Bristol Meyers, made a pitch to manufacturers and retailers still on the fence about system-building technology. He argued that immediately available information will shift the focus to "movement of all merchandise" from manufacturer to consumer. Retailers will "be in a position to furnish manufacturers with current information about the movement of their stock" in order to "avoid stock-outs" and "assure manufacturers of continued shelf distribution of their merchandise." The technology will facilitate a more complex yet easier to use "reordering process" as companies learn how to analyze the entirety of the process based on "what goes on at the checkout counter." He summarized his argument like this: "Gone will be the days of continual inventory counts and buyers' guestimates about how much to buy." The information system would allow for new analytical and predictive capabilities to forecast and configure supply and demand.[75]

By the end of the 1970s, the projections of the UPCC and information technology firms were becoming a reality. Market research firms were running studies that used the new sociotechnical system. The supermarket industry had long established market research protocols through consumer panel data linking demographic information to purchasing behavior into longitudinal research design. Historically, however, this market research was conducted by telephone, through mail, by enrolling and reminding customers to complete purchase diaries, or by face-to-face interviews with customers in stores. The UPC and POS systems changed the nature of market research and opened up new practical applications that had clear cost-saving benefits.[76]

Valerie Demuro was a special projects manager at Selling Areas-Marketing Inc. (SAMI), a market research subsidiary of Time Inc. She wrote in 1977 that these new tools were creating new kinds of "automatically captured purchase data." Market researchers still approached customers the same way to conduct initial demographic background interviews, but once the basic enrollment occurred, they systematically tracked them through "coded identification cards" used in the "test stores." The UPC and POS systems then automatically recorded item-by-item purchase information matched to demographic data, transmitted the information to store computers, and then transmitted the cumulative information to SAMI headquarters in Chicago. There, analysts correlated and evaluated the data to come up with applied organizational and marketing strategies. They now collected information about how consumers' income influenced their product purchases, whether shoppers continued purchasing the same products over periods of time (brand loyalty), how often they purchased competitive products in the same stores, whether new products competed with other items in the manufacturers' profile (cannibalization), and how promotions worked in relation to purchasing behavior.[77]

Data analysis was emerging on the retail side. Peter Andrews, an advisory programmer for IBM, pointed out a major infrastructural realignment taking place behind the scenes. Historically, computers were kept in a "glass house," a restricted location accessible only to authorized specialists. It was seen as a sacred space. Everything in the restricted location—the mainframes, the printers, and the storage devices—was large and imposing. The control center was a visible location where the computing machines were placed on "raised floors" to allow for the complex power and communication wiring and cables. Some of the old computers demanded so much electrical energy and circuitry that they needed water pipe systems to cool them down. The computer infrastructure was in the background of the store, but it was not discreet.[78]

The new computer systems were different. The customer interacted with the cashier in almost the exact same mundane way as before. Certainly, the cashiers were increasingly scanning items, but employees were learning how to fluidly integrate scanning processes by the end of the 1970s. And the connections between cash registers, scanners, and price displays were accurate and easy to read for customers. As the choreographed market interface turned into a sociotechnical routine, it also became part of an invisible decentralizing operation of a "fully programmed computer system."[79]

The checkout stage tabulated and sent information to a control computer station in a small backroom office where managers dissected their stores as a subsystem in a larger network. They analyzed what products were selling, what aisles and products needed restocking, and what products needed reordering. The manager then sent this information from the store to "the host," an offsite location where regional managers assessed "data for a group of stores." Andrews said that the "back end" was where the real savings and efficiency opportunities opened up. The checkout machines were no longer simply large calculators used to "manage inventory and sales, measure performance of individual cashiers, change prices and add and delete items." They now had analytic functions that measured effectiveness of the entirety of the store inventory, company-wide ordering, and marketing processes, from how well a single advertisement worked to assessing the best-selling items and most lucrative values in the stores.[80]

For manufacturers, it meant they could use the "automated data capture" methods to target their own unobserved "inefficiencies." The push and the pull between manufacturers and retailers tuned up the system. The manufacturing side first automated the process of production, which increased the number and variety of products and instigated the search for retail automation. Then manufacturers moved toward source-printing the UPC bar code to facilitate the intersection between high-volume and high-variety products and a new framework of retail efficiency. Once retailers routinized the checkout process, they turned to the more complex automated data-processing project to locate new sources of economic value. Manufacturing sectors took notice. Robert Peterson, the director of contract administration for Distribution Codes Inc., wrote that manufacturers began to examine the relationship between "their own internal processes" and "their customers' distribution systems."[81]

We tend to think of "traceability" today as the monitoring of distribution information along a supply chain, but the term was first used in the manufacturing and assembling industries in reference to quality control and productivity in the manufacturing process. Peterson pointed out that manufacturers from a range of industries, including food, drug, candy, and tobacco companies, started to encode information that kept track of the time and date of manufacturing, the specific product line, the manufacturing shift number, as well as raw materials going into the products. They used "automated identification techniques" to maintain accountability and liability of the process, especially in product assembling industries using dangerous raw materials. In the pharmaceutical manufacturing industries, for instance, the automated process kept track of production count, batch and lot identification, as well as label control with a bar code that was scanned to match product and label accuracy. Some manufacturers used new data capturing methods to mark the stage of production, such that a new bar code was printed each time the product passed a certain key point or was moved between different facilities.[82]

The automated data capture through the bar code mechanism had organizational and management applications outside of the checkout aisle. Peterson pointed out that these information and analysis methods through traceability had great potential in wholesale operations and distribution centers. He wrote in 1977, "Productivity enhancement and reduction in the rate of error are of critical concern to the wholesaler. For example, a very large wholesaler . . . may inventory some 15,000 items. . . . In such an operation the greatest majority of errors occurs in the receiving function and in order picking and assembly and after potential cost-effective applications for automatic data capture in checking receipts, in order assembly, and in verification of orders prior to shipment." Nonetheless, at the time of Peterson's assessment, only one wholesaler and not a single retail distribution center had put these applications into practice.[83] While data capture took off on the retail side and the manufacturing side, companies had yet to tap into the economic potential of applying traceability techniques to the movement and handling of goods in the spaces between production and consumption.

The Logistics Signal

Technology companies made advancements on the bar code, as well as in computing and data storage capabilities. New bar code models encoded more information, which allowed inclusion of more manufacturers and products into the system. It also opened up new organizational traceability methods on raw materials, shipping containers, and pallets. It facilitated the relationship between assembling and shipping products by creating geographic interdependencies, especially between international manufacturing sites and United States–based retailing.[84]

Firms also integrated new bar code techniques in their distribution centers. Combining the scanning methods in multiple parts of the system opened up the additional movement into electronic data interchange of shared information management between retailers, wholesalers, and manufacturers. The UPC system, initially developed to solve the supermarket problem of low profit margins, grew into autonomous technical recipes that could be applied in a wide range of organizational situations. Between 1975 and 1985, the supermarket sector used the UPC system to redefine the checkout process. Between 1985 and 1995, different organizations applied this sociotechnical ensemble to identify time- and cost-saving possibilities in the spaces of distribution between manufacturing and retailing.

The bar code emerged as a micro-technical force remaking the food system into a logistics system. It set up the conditions for three interrelated organizational and technical adaptations. The first is that Kmart and Wal-Mart, the two largest discount merchandising companies by the mid-1980s, officially adopted the UPC system. The second is that product traceability and inter-industry communication networks were decentralization mechanisms that reconfigured market measurement and forecasting principles. The physical mobility of products created information that analysts could study in locations separate from products in transit. The third factor is that supermarket companies were forced into another isomorphic process. When Wal-Mart fully entered the grocery industry at the end of the 1980s, the new interdependencies constrained supermarket profitability and led to a period of organizational mimicry and corporate mergers.

Between 1975 and 1985, the UPC system continued to spread throughout the supermarket industry. In 1977, only 200 stores regularly scanned bar codes, but 5,300 manufacturers were members of the UPCC, 83 percent of packaged goods on supermarket shelves were marked with bar codes, and the industry collectively printed bar codes on 9.5 million product units per month.[85] Throughout the first half of the 1980s, the large supermarket chains had finally come around. The total number of grocery stores implementing scanning systems increased to 10 percent in 1981, representing widespread implementation by the largest firms.[86] By 1985, more than 15,000 stores across the country had scanning equipment.[87]

In this first round of diffusion, the UPC system was clearly a grocery industry project, even as other industries moved into computing and communication technologies. The economist John Dunlop noted that in 1975 more than 64 percent of manufacturers registering for product codes were in the food and beverage industries. A smaller group of manufacturers in the housewares and beauty industries made up an additional 8 percent. By 1994, the field of registration had completely shifted. Food and beverage manufacturers constituted only 28 percent of total UPC registrants.[88]

The adoption of the UPC system in general merchandising was the definitive factor in this transformation—especially Kmart's and Wal-Mart's move into the system. The discount general merchandising industry was positioned between retailing industries since its inception in the early 1960s. General merchandising stores were neither department stores nor grocery stores, thus creating categorical confusions in terms of building inter-industry alliances and standards. The general discount merchandisers started their own association called the National Mass Retail Institute in the late 1960s, which operated with a shared research agenda to advance the discount sector. But they were also affiliated with the National Merchants Retail Association, led by department stores, which pushed a different code and scanning option that was dependent on a hand wand to scan in-store product codes and labeling methods. That checkout system lacked the capacity to scan from multiple angles. It worked well for department stores' needs at the time, and the residual technology remained for decades.[89]

In the 1960s, general merchandising was part of a market shift in the field of discount retailing. In fact, Kmart, Target, Woolco, and Wal-Mart all opened up their first stores in the same year—1962. Both Woolco and Kmart were tied to prominent five-and-dime variety store corporations. Woolco was Woolworth's general merchandising arm and Kmart was an outgrowth of the S. S. Kresge Company, an earlier discount retail giant. John Geisse, who worked for the Dayton Company, a prominent Minnesota department store, partnered with the Dayton family to create Target, an "upscale" discount store that differentiated itself from the field's leader, Kmart. Wal-Mart also had its roots in the old five-and-dime era. Sam Walton's first attempts at discount marketing came as a franchisee of the Ben Franklin chain of five-and-dimes before he eventually founded Wal-Mart.

The expansion of chains has always been dependent on bridging territorial development, population density, and commodity replenishment. Like the development programs of supermarkets, the general merchandising companies opened up as anchors of shopping centers and malls in the suburbs. Executives and entrepreneurs looked to Kmart as the model through the 1970s and into the early 1980s. In 1979, Kmart was far and away the leader of discount retailing with almost 2,000 stores that were unbelievably profitable—the company averaged over $7 million per store. Management experts of the time attributed Kmart's success to economies of scale, but as Wal-Mart eventually demonstrated, it was not solely about scale.[90]

In the early 1980s, Kmart and Wal-Mart both implemented scanning equipment into some of their stores as test runs. In 1985, the companies fully embraced the UPC system. Their executives liked that the UPC system used both handheld devices and slot scanners that cashiers could slide through at any angle. By this point, these companies were organized more like supermarkets than department stores in terms of their aisle arrangements, checkout lanes, overlapping products, and distribution centers. More nonfood manufacturers were moving into the UPC system and printing bar codes on their packages. Joseph Thomas, the executive vice president and chief administrative officer at Kmart, said that his company was looking to follow the lead of supermarkets and discontinue the process of employees price marking goods in stores. "The grocery industry uses UPC and a lot of items we carry are also carried by groceries—and you don't see them marking merchandise because the goods are already marked."[91]

It was one thing to adopt the UPC system like supermarkets to manage the checkout process. It was another thing altogether to develop novel organizational and technical strategies that could link the physical distribution of millions of objects to complex information systems. Kmart and Wal-Mart were in the same field, but throughout the 1980s, they demonstrated distinct strategies for using and employing data. Sam Walton admits to regularly visiting Kmart stores to observe how they worked in order to learn about discount retailing.[92] In the early 1980s, when Kmart had clear dominance, Wal-Mart was a relatively small company with only 229 stores, with half the revenue per store of Kmart. Wal-Mart did not overtake Kmart by mimicking its store sizes and distribution volumes—that is, through economies of scale. Wal-Mart gained ground by capturing unique advantages made available by emerging organizational and technical interdependencies. Wal-Mart better managed and analyzed the invisible spaces of distribution, which led to cost savings and available capital needed to encroach on Kmart's territory and then the supermarket territory.[93]

Small towns were historically resistant to chain stores in the era of A&P's expansion. As urbanization and suburbanization spread out across the United States, the reverse happened: retail chains became resistant to small towns. No company took the risk of opening high-volume merchandising stores in low density areas. Sam Walton did something radical by turning what was generally conceived of as a constraint into a major advantage. Walton writes, "We were forced to be ahead of our time in distribution and in communication because our stores were sitting out there in tiny little towns and we had to stay in touch and keep them supplied."[94]

It took Wal-Mart years to build up the distribution apparatus that could replenish store after store. The contingencies of sociotechnical change were once again at work. Abe Marks was the president of Hartfield Zody's, a California-based discount chain, and the first president of the National Mass Retail Institute. He first met Sam Walton at the IBM School, an applied computer technology training school for executives. Walton was learning how to incorporate computers and information technology into his business. Marks had never heard of Sam Walton or Wal-Mart at the time of their first encounter, but he invited the young entrepreneur to join the National Mass Retail Institute. Marks taught Walton about the concept of logistics, and especially about the relationship between information and inventory control under "absentee landlord" situations. Marks writes that Walton came to understand that "the more you turn your inventory, the less capital is required."[95]

Walton and his team of technical managers pursued an integrated systems approach to distribution based on timing, constant communication with partner organizations, and better pricing for consumers. The company built up a coherent store and distribution center development program. The economist Thomas Holmes describes it as a "radial pattern." Since the construction of Wal-Mart's first store in 1962 in Bentonville, Arkansas, the company followed a consistent growth program by determining the locations of new stores on the basis of already established stores. Sam Walton and his team came up with an idea of greater store density in the same regions, growing one region at a time. This radial pattern around central distribution hubs facilitated an easier store replenishment process that could cut costs and basically undersell competitors.[96]

Economists Paul Ellickson and Paul Grieco point out that it was a strategy that drew small-town shoppers out of their local consumption areas by creating "economies of density" between the supply and selling locations. This method worked really well in areas that "lacked the population density to support a rich diversity of specialized outlets." Wal-Mart's distribution approach "created the shopping density of a city" in small towns. The distribution centers contained more items than typical distribution centers, because of the constant need to replenish the multiple stores around the distribution hub. Once they mastered the profitability of radial growth through trial and error, one store at a time, they then applied it to another territory, one region at a time. It was a slow and meticulous expansion process.[97] It was almost like they were building the infrastructure of small cities over and over again.

It was not just development and growth that facilitated Wal-Mart's success, however. It was also the integration of organizational methods, information technology, and new architectural spaces all in the service of logistics.[98] Throughout the 1980s, Kmart and Wal-Mart encouraged manufacturers to adopt the UPC system, and a decade later, these companies became even more forceful, mandating that suppliers adopt the bar code standards.[99] Wal-Mart established a highly advanced distribution program that used the data capture capacity and integrated it with its trucking lines and its own massive computer and satellite systems. Wal-Mart isolated spaces of inefficiency that others had not even begun to study. Each addition of technology opened up the possibility of another innovative insight, a constant tune-up of their organizational methods.

In the early 1980s, Wal-Mart experimented with the scanning technology in its stores. By the mid-1980s, it implemented scanning systems in its distribution warehouses. The scanning systems provided new data, but as Sam Walton says, the data was so voluminous that communicating over phone lines between stores and the corporate home was too slow to keep a constant management over the supply and demand relationships. Moreover, the company's computer system did not have enough storage. Wal-Mart built its own computer and satellite system, a $700 million investment that became the largest civilian-owned computer and satellite network in the world. The system's storage simultaneously held a great deal of historical information while rapidly exchanging information between the system's different parts.[100]

This information network opened up the possibility to locate new time and cost-saving technical solutions. For instance, when shippers did not want to invest in moving masses of products to small towns, Wal-Mart executives decided to develop a corporate trucking fleet into the largest in the country. Integrating stores, distribution centers, and transportation gave them great insight into managing transit networks and the constraints between sites of production and consumption. In contrast, companies like Kmart and Target relied on third-party trucking companies.[101]

Wal-Mart kept a centralized "rolling history" of the exact specifications of every single item: how many its stores currently have, how many were bought over time, and how many were sold. This information was kept at every level, including company, region, district, and store.[102] The information also allowed Wal-Mart to merge unique tracking methods with physical structures. For instance, the company made great use of cross-docking, for which it became famous. Cross-docking was the continuous mobility process through which products rarely lay idle in Wal-Mart's warehouses. The company timed the movement such that "goods just cross from one loading dock to another in 48 hours or less."[103] Its distribution centers were run with miles of automated conveyor belts, which were linked to lasers that automatically scanned bar codes. As pallets were unloaded from trucks on one side of the distribution center, they were automatically synched with the loading docks on the other side of the distribution center, where they met outgoing trucks.

Throughout the 1980s, grocery retailers and general merchandise retailers started to consider inter-industry communication standards, but Wal-Mart, with its complex approach to information and data analysis, was already expanding its shared data and logistics program. Bob L. Martin, who was the chief information officer of Wal-Mart and eventually became the chief executive officer, said that the UPC system was the most important information producing mechanism. It underlay the entire enterprise of automated data sharing between firms. He wrote that the UPC system was the basis of "Collaborative Forecasting and Replenishment," the system that enabled improved "merchandise planning and availability." The new systems gave them analytic insights into how to work with manufacturers and also how to predict the pace of movement in the various steps along supply chains. Martin writes, "Information about when the customers shop and what they buy ties back to what began with the U.P.C., which is now driving the system paradigms between retailers and manufacturers farther than was ever imagined."[104]

By the end of the 1980s, Wal-Mart became the most influential retail company of its time. It was the organizational vessel that most profitably bridged the relationship between physical and information infrastructures. Wal-Mart started the decade with total sales of $1.2 billion in 276 stores and ended the decade with sales of $25.8 billion in 1,500 stores. By mid-decade, Wal-Mart started experimenting with other retail formats as well, further blurring the categorical distinctions between retail sectors. Sam's Club, the company's warehouse membership platform, was so successful that it opened 125 more within a few years.[105]

Yet maybe even more significant than the success of Sam's Club was the failure of Wal-Mart's "Hypermarket," a 200,000-square-foot building that combined general merchandising and the supermarket. Just like Food Fair a decade earlier, Wal-Mart could not make a profit from the model. However, company executives learned a lot about working with the food distribution system—they learned how to better manage the relationship between different kinds of supply chains. The Hypermarket was the precursor for the Super Center, a more "modest" combination of the discount store and supermarket that opened in 1988 with 125,000 square feet of market space.[106]

The Super Center's success led to Wal-Mart's continuous investment in the model. By the end of the 1980s, the supermarket industry was reeling over how to best address not just the high volumes of Wal-Mart stores but also the sociotechnical applications. The trade magazine *Chain Store Age* described the 1980s as the "big-box decade."[107] Ken Wagar, a former supermarket vice president and then-industry consultant, wrote in *Supermarket Business* that the supermarket industry was filled with confusion over the basic conceptions and applications that companies like Wal-Mart used to great success, such as "cross-docking" and "flow-through logistics." The rapid mobility and exchange relations were important factors in their "26 percent lower prices." The larger returns gave Wal-Mart the necessary capital to continue developing new stores and trying new models. It was becoming necessary for retailers of all kinds to "re-engineer" their distribution and inventory systems to incorporate automated ordering, electronic data interchange between retail and manufacturing companies, and continuous replenishment methods. All of these new infrastructural interdependencies involved an organizational learning curve for building the new bridge between physical and information infrastructures.[108]

Complex systems are built and transformed through a logic of mutual adaptation. General merchandising firms initially followed the supermarkets into the UPC system, but Wal-Mart's entrance into the food system compelled supermarket companies to go in the other direction—to follow the lead of general merchandising. Wal-Mart's move into new towns had an immediate impact on grocery retailers. When the company opened a Super Center in Batesville, Arkansas, in 1992, all the nearby supermarkets—even Kroger, the largest supermarket company in the nation by that time—were forced to immediately lower prices on milk, a loaf of bread, and other everyday items. They had to learn to "compete without going broke."[109]

The profit-making capacity of Wal-Mart's logistics system was highly constraining on other companies. Robert Messenger noted in *Prepared Foods Magazine* that a new cutthroat instant success model was prevailing: "If a product, through scanning data, does not show significant early results, it can end up discontinued. Given more time to compete, it might succeed."[110] By the mid-1990s, the interactive and compatible relations further constrained manufacturers and distributors, now forced to invest in these new sociotechnical interdependencies. Wal-Mart, for example, pushed Procter & Gamble (P&G), the conglomerate that manufactured everything from paper towels to toothpaste to shampoo, into a product traceability system. Once P&G invested in that information apparatus, they then wanted to employ the same tools of "upgraded electronic communications and other logistical capabilities" in their relationships with other distributors. They partnered with SuperValu in "Streamlined Logistics." A year later, Kraft, the massive food product manufacturer, was engaging in the same project—developing "cross functional teams" that met regularly via video conferencing to figure out cost-saving factors across "all supply and distribution activities."[111]

The shift was having physical infrastructural effects in the supermarkets themselves, as companies adopted the "supersized" format. In 1980, supermarket companies averaged 14,145 products per store. By 1994 the average grocery retailer had increased the number of products it carried to 21,949. In 2004, grocery retailers were on average selling over 30,000 different products at the same time.[112] By the end of the 1990s, Wal-Mart was not just a temporary shock to the system. The corporation was the second largest grocery operator in the nation. One headline compared Wal-Mart to the early A&P, wondering if it reflected the organizational moment that would break the food system. Another asked, "Is the supermarket era at an end?"[113]

Since 2002, Wal-Mart has outperformed Kroger as the largest food retailer in the nation.[114] Across the United States, Wal-Mart has 40 distribution centers that exclusively handle food products, and more than 40 additional regional distribution facilities for other types of commodities like clothing and other merchandise. The corporation's food distribution centers service more than 4,000 stores for its Wal-Mart and Sam's Club banners. Wal-Mart builds on the flexibility of 2,000 trucks, 5,000 refrigerated trailers, and 51,000 dry van trailers moving from farms and shipping ports to distribution centers and stores. Each truck driver in Wal-Mart's fleet drives 100,000 miles annually, or as Wal-Mart boasts, "that's like driving around the world 4 times!"[115]

Kroger is the second largest food retailer. The company has also assembled a national model with 34 distribution centers servicing thousands of stores, including more than 2,400 supermarkets in 31 states. With 2,770 trucks and 10,500 trailers, Kroger's fleet makes 3,300 deliveries daily, which in 2012, equated to almost 304 million miles of traveling to facilities around the country.[116] However, Kroger, like other major supermarket companies, has built its expansion on mergers and acquisitions of various regional chains to match the national infrastructure of Wal-Mart. This pattern of merging or acquiring regional chains leaves behind a landscape dotted by regional banner distinctions and a historical mythology of localism.

Behind the scenes, Kroger looks more and more like Wal-Mart, although it took them a while to get to that point. As late as 2009, *Modern Materials*

Handling reported that the days of "labor intensive" distribution centers were gone, having been replaced by "bar code scanning and voice technology" that automate materials handling. The traceability tools that were emerging at the end of the 1970s found additional applications in automatic coordination and sequencing of building distribution center pallets, putting materials into reserve, replenishment of products, and picking and packing for store orders.[117]

The reorganization of national corporate retail infrastructures has forced the food wholesaling industries to also grapple with the changing distribution landscape. A range of corporate wholesalers emerged in direct relationship to the spreading higher-volume retail infrastructure by handling many kinds of products at the same time. Corporations like SuperValu and Fleming, which both started in the Midwest, and C&S, which first opened in the Northeast, developed into the three largest food wholesaling corporations in the country and evolved into major components of the national food distribution system.

SuperValu, the largest of them, initially operated distribution centers for independent supermarkets in the Midwest, first opening in Minneapolis and then expanding into new territories through subsequent mergers.[118] Over time, SuperValu merged with wholesalers in various regions, but then the company began developing its own chain retail locations, working as a wholesaler for its own stores as well as the distribution arm of regional chains and independent stores. This gradual move toward vertical integration shifted the company's focus. By the end of the 1980s, SuperValu had 900 trucks and 1,800 trailers traveling 55 million miles each year and serving 3,100 retail stores in 32 states. A decade later, by the end of the 1990s, SuperValu managed 15 percent of the American food supply. In 2006, SuperValu merged with Albertson's, originally from Idaho but by then one of the nation's largest food retail outfits. Albertson's was the parent company of banners in many regions, including the American Stores Company, once a Philadelphia-based chain, which it purchased in 1998. As of 2012, SuperValu is the nation's second largest wholesaler and the third largest grocery retailer, with a distribution network spanning 21 warehouses servicing 4,000 stores in 47 states, including such banners as Sav-A-Lot, Acme, and Albertson's, as well as regional chains and independent stores.[119]

The New Infrastructural Regime

Executives from various industries once perceived the retail store profit margins as the most pressing food market problem. The solution to that problem came by way of a search for new automation methods. Multiple industries came together and gradually implemented organizational and technical components that were historically developed separately: numerical code systems, bar code symbology, optical scanners, laser technology, computers, telecommunication networks, as well as the human practical competencies needed to fluidly work alongside the machinery. Strategic problem-solving interests brought them together into an interdependent ensemble and fluid market and consumer ecosystem.

The sociotechnical system surrounding material products turned the objects themselves into sources of information to measure and manage distribution. This information system was not an instant success by any means—in fact, there was a great deal of resistance among manufacturers, retailers, and consumers alike about how to implement new product monitoring systems into exchange relationships and mundane consumer experiences. Once implemented, data analysts, consultants, and corporate decision-makers were able to observe and name patterns, sequences, and spaces that were previously invisible. Engineers then worked on solving "new inefficiencies" in order to cut time and costs in configuring supply and demand.

Reconfiguring the sociotechnical system was a recursive process, which speaks to the central constraint on organizations in their efforts to identify and manage problems. Decision-makers can only seek solutions to patterns they can identify and analyze as "problems." The implementation of technical fixes creates new material conditions and the potential for new visible information and hence new visible inefficiencies previously unobserved. Some of the sociotechnical solutions get implemented, but many do not. Firms engage in a process of innovation, implementation, routinization, and elimination. If new routines develop into cost-saving and time-saving benefits, then competing firms and supply chain partners are forced to respond to the "efficiency and effectiveness" signals to maintain their own competitiveness.

The bar code system was a micro-technical force that became autonomous. Firms applied similar technical recipes to various kinds of situations in the supply system. They produced new information about parts of their businesses that enabled new profit-making capabilities. In this case, the search for a standard product code system disrupted established boundaries: new organizational formats disrupted the boundaries between distinct industries; new methods of sharing information disrupted the boundaries between distinct firms; and new logistical capacities disrupted the boundaries between distinct exchange partners and the geographic territories of production and consumption.

The UGPCC in the early 1970s never foresaw the range of possibilities of the bar code system. Their initial approximation that 6,000 grocery manufacturers would register products was not exactly an oversight.[120] It represents the difficulty—dare I say impossibility—of predicting the trajectory of infrastructural and economic development. In 1994, about 20 years after the first bar code was scanned, 110,000 manufacturers had registered products in the system. Three years later, the number increased to 177,000.[121] Since 2005, the standardization efforts have become global in their reach, merging with the European Article Number system into GS1—the "global standard." GS1 now has oversight committees in countries spanning every continent. In the United States alone, GS1 reports 300,000 different manufacturers in 25 different industries managing 10 million different items with distinct product codes. Across the globe, two million companies participate in this complex information system. More than five billion bar codes—that means five billion different objects—are scanned every single day.[122]

The shift in the infrastructural regime altered the taken-for-granted expectations about consumption. The spread of the supermarket distribution logic was a change from feeding cities to feeding regions. It altered the concept of the "center" from urban downtowns to the distribution centers themselves. The UPC system became the decentralization agent par excellence. It turned the distribution network—and the very products in transit—into an analytic information infrastructure. The products themselves became sources of data capture independent of any geographic location. Standardizing information on products in transit meant that distribution centers were still important, of course, but now companies could create new micro-level information and pursue profit-making potential in previously invisible distribution relationships. The very idea of the "global value chain"—rather than the "supply chain"—was born from an interconnected supply system identifying measurable "value-added" potential.[123]

Wal-Mart's success was the most visible signal of this infrastructural shift, but Sam Walton and Wal-Mart were not the direct causes of the system transformation. Institutional isomorphism is an ongoing and iterative collective process of mutual adaptation that crystallizes some sociotechnical methods through the design and implementation of interactive compatibility. The process signals organizational information about cost- and time-saving methods throughout the industry. New interdependencies and value opportunities then constrain future organizational and profit-making options.[124]

Yet just like previous eras of infrastructural change, the perishable industries—especially the fruit and vegetable supply chains—lagged behind processed and packaged goods. The standardization of decomposing materials remains difficult to control. The iterative process of turning fresh produce into mass merchandising requires organizations to account for the distinct material and aesthetic qualities of decaying objects. The next chapter addresses the issue of defeating seasons. The fresh produce aisle was turned into an interactive and compatible distribution system to reassemble standard qualities of high volumes and high varieties of constantly decomposing objects.

FIVE

Defeating Seasons:
Reassembling the Produce Aisle

Dozens of forklifts whiz past us. Their humming engines echo as we walk through the 160,000- square-foot refrigerated warehouse. Rob Simms, the owner of the business, tugs on my yellow iridescent vest that he made me wear over my jacket, along with a matching hardhat. He points to the beehive-like zigzag movements of forklifts in and out of aisles and yells above the roaring machinery, "Things move quickly in here, so pay attention!" I nod in acknowledgment.[1]

The movements through the facility are fast but well-orchestrated. Forklift operators unload pallets stacked with boxes of fruits and vegetables from trucks and move them into numbered warehouse slots, piling them about eight feet high. At the same time, other forklift operators pull pallets from numbered locations around the facility and load them onto refrigerated trailers hitched to trucks parked outside. The tail ends of the trailers are open and securely fit into the warehouse so as not to disrupt the refrigerated cold chain. As they reorganize the space, they pull out older products ready to move to the next destination and load newer arrivals into their spots. Laser scanners affixed to forklifts flash bar codes on the plastic-wrapped pallets. Each scan links the product to a remote computer in the back office, where employees monitor millions of dollars of fruits and vegetables in real-time, connecting company ownership, storage location, and transporting information.

"Do you have any sense of how much food moves through here?" I ask Simms.

"We put through here about 200,000 pallets of product in a given year," he says. "If you put it into poundage, you multiply that by about 2,000 pounds a pallet. That comes to 400 million pounds per year at least."

It is an enormous undertaking. I try to comprehend all of the moving parts: growers, shippers, importers, receivers, brokers, truckers, wholesalers, retailers, and consumers. To illustrate the complexity, Simms walks over to some of the pallets stacked near us. They are awaiting forklifts to move them to refrigerated zones set to temperatures to optimize their distinct shelf lives. "These are pears, pomegranates, garlic—these are Argentinean," he tells me. "The blueberries are from Chile. The mangoes are from—." He moves closer to get a better view of the labels on the boxes. "Those are out of Peru."

Refrigerated Storage Inc. is a global city of fruits and vegetables. The products have arrived from Chile, Peru, Argentina, Mexico, Guatemala, Canada, Spain, Morocco, England, South Africa, Australia, and New Zealand. They get assembled alongside fruits and vegetables coming from the western, southwestern, and southern United States. Much of the food comes to the facility by way of ships docking in the ports of the Delaware River: Wilmington, Delaware; Philadelphia, Pennsylvania; and Camden and Gloucester, New Jersey. Refrigerated semitrailer trucks, incoming at all hours of the day through the night and into the morning, deliver loads picked up at those locations.

Maintaining the cold chain has become fundamental to how fruit and vegetable distributors match rapidly decaying products to the broader food market system's logic of efficiency. As Simms reminds me, "The minute it's harvested, it's dying. It doesn't get better with age. It's not wine." He owns the machinery to sort, code, pack, preserve, and rejuvenate the quality and economic value of fresh products before they move to their next destination, such as supermarket distribution centers or wholesale terminals as nearby as miles down the road to hundreds of miles away. His business is part of the service and logistics infrastructure that economic sociologists refer to as the "economy of qualities" set up to "finely tune supply and demand." Such businesses evaluate and qualify the physical characteristics of products so that they fit into subsequent exchange relationships.[2] The critical infrastructural issue for reassembling the produce aisle is just that: how to fit objects that change with time into a system that demands they arrive "just in time."

Simms does not own a single product in the warehouse. Inside, his team manages commodities owned by dozens of different companies. Some of the largest food distribution, retail, and shipping corporations and cooperatives use his services to manage supplies and surplus. Not everything is sold when it arrives. Exporting, receiving, and brokerage firms representing growing and shipping companies—some of them as far off as Spain, South Africa, and Chile—hire cold storage companies to hold their products as they work the phones trying to move supplies to downstream retailers and wholesalers.

Walking around the facility, we are inundated by click-clacking sounds of swarming forklifts and steel contraptions weighing and packing fruits and vegetables into netted and plastic bags and punnets. Buzzing computer monitors and omniscient security cameras are all around us. We are not touring a warehouse in Philadelphia, Chicago, or New York, where prior to the 1950s, we would have found the most hectic nodes of product consolidation and coordination for such a capital-intensive endeavor for feeding cities. Instead, this cold storage warehouse is in a small New Jersey town about 50 miles outside of Philadelphia. Yet as I came to understand the inner workings of the food system, I realized that this facility also sits in one of the densest population corridors in the world. It is within hours driving distance from Washington, DC, Baltimore, Philadelphia, New York, all the way up to Boston, and includes all of the high-density sprawling settlements in the middle of these large cities.

The market system bridging information technology, material objects, and distribution centers has configured around a logic of "just-in-time" product mobility. Fresh produce, however, has lagged behind, only recently catching up. The history of food distribution is filled with similar periods of industry-wide organizational and institutional adaptations followed by lagging fresh supply infrastructures. The aim of this chapter is to better understand this lag, along with the organizational and technical efforts to turn fresh commodities into a routine mass-merchandising enterprise.

Defeating seasons was an invisible process of adjustment and technical accumulation, starting one commodity at time. The cumulative project shifted from actors carving out new trajectories for growing, moving, storing, and selling perishable goods into reinforcing complex multiscale relationships. Perishable foods are now locked into a complex system that demands high volumes and more varieties. An infrastructure for reassembling the produce aisle has enabled hundreds of millions of people in towns and cities all over the United States to have access to dozens of varieties of fresh fruits and vegetables that retailers restock as seemingly uniform objects.

One Object at a Time: The Rise of an Out-of-Season Market Infrastructure

The supermarket produce aisle we have today was a long time in the making. It required building and configuring the growing, storage, distribution, and market infrastructures to control time and space, an outcome of what Steven Shapin calls "invisible science." Scientific and technical work built up into new market relationships, one perishable object at a time. Each product— apples, lettuce, and oranges, for instance—was gradually integrated into a system of reassembling year-round supplies and everyday consumerism.[3]

Improvements in refrigeration and storage were important components of the fresh market equation, but they were not sufficient. Each product required a distinct market and mobility ecosystem, fit with distinct handling and packing methods that could be integrated across transaction settings in the supply chain. At the end of the nineteenth century, the Reading Terminal Market in Philadelphia was an innovator in cold storage. Located in the space below the Reading Railroad station, the market installed 200,000 cubic feet of refrigerated space in its basement, initially broken up into 26 rooms that were further divided by different meat and produce dealers. The entire space was cooled by 125 miles of refrigeration pipes running through the rooms in three different series, which made it possible for dealers to regulate different partitions at different temperatures. It helped the city's food businesses—from market vendors to restaurants—manage diverse products.[4]

Market refrigeration was an important component of defeating seasons, but getting the products to the markets remained difficult. A process of technical problem-solving existed around each perishable product. The unique qualities of perishable objects, and the infrastructural limitations for sustaining their market qualities over long-distance transit, made it difficult for industries to reliably transcend seasons as a blanket market endeavor. California orange shippers were among the first to send products across the country in the late nineteenth century through the transcontinental railroad network. Oranges could hold market qualities for over a month, able to attract consumer demand in the Midwest and Northeast. Even then, despite the stability of oranges as "well-kept travelers," the citrus market was available to urban wholesalers only in the winter.[5]

Lettuce, a fragile backyard garden product, was an unlikely target for an early national fresh commodity without seasons. Farmers and shippers entered into the lettuce growing business at the right historical moment. They transformed a single variety called crisphead lettuce into a nationwide fresh product. Bruce Church, a farmer in California's Salinas Valley, saw the potential of the local shipping infrastructure. Prior to 1920, Church was one of six farmers in the area with the proper equipment, including tractors and listers, to mechanize seed planting and harvesting into higher yields. An industrial shipping infrastructure had already developed in Salinas Valley around beet production because farmers tried to replace imported cane sugar with domestic beet sugar.[6]

Church had the foresight to advance lettuce-packing methods to fit the existing rail system for cross-country travel. He packed the new crisp lettuce variety in protective wooden crates and covered each head with crushed ice, resembling icebergs, a name that eventually caught on. Moreover, because

Salinas Valley had such a unique vegetable growing climate, he and others could grow the product—eventually labeled "iceberg lettuce"—almost all year long. As early as 1925, California's icebergs were the only lettuce products available between fall and spring to urban consumers in the northeast. While Church's "top icing" method was a major improvement on previous shipping techniques, it was far from perfect. It commonly froze or bruised the outer layers. As the ice melted, it hastened decomposition en route to other states.[7]

The spread of refrigerated trucks in the 1930s and 1940s challenged rail distribution methods by allowing shippers to better maintain products between locations. Objects could more directly travel from specific farm to specific market. Improved air compressors and condensers on the units allowed truckers to manipulate the flow of air to regulate the relationship between internal trailer temperatures and external air temperatures, which then enabled more precise control and specialized care of each type of commodity—meat, fish, poultry, fruits, vegetables, eggs, dairy, and various frozen products—over longer distances. Truck refrigeration was viewed as an important device to preserve fresh commodities in transport, but it did not have the pressure to rapidly decrease the internal temperatures of higher-volume commodities packed in boxes, which was also needed to ensure longer shelf lives for the budding supermarket system.[8]

In the 1940s, Rex Brunsing invented vacuum cooling, also known as "flash cooling," as a response to cross-country shipping problems. Brunsing found that flash cooling significantly decreased the amount of time it took to bring down internal temperatures of lettuce from more than 24 hours to 25 minutes. By holding the lettuce in a tube at 33 degrees and evaporating the moisture, Salinas Valley growers and shippers could more evenly preserve the entire product, cooling the inside and outside simultaneously.[9] Likewise, fiberboard cartons—that is, corrugated cardboard boxes—could be used alongside flash cooling to make the harvesting and packing methods more flexible. Field hands harvested, cooled, and then packed the lettuce into the durable dry boxes right in the fields.[10]

Lester Antle and his son Bud assembled these different techniques into a routine harvesting and shipping method. Antle moved his family to California in the 1930s, where he and Bud worked as lettuce packers. They learned the inner workings of the industry and about new investment opportunities. They purchased farm property in Salinas Valley, and during the next two decades, they modified the truck distribution infrastructure that made iceberg lettuce available in more places, building greater interdependencies with supermarket retailers.[11]

During the 1950s, adjustable shipping methods extended the growing operations to new locations in the region and increased the supply for the national market. The editors of the *Packer*, the fresh produce trade magazine, described how farmers challenged production locations in ways that influenced distribution boundaries. "Suddenly, large lettuce acreages were produced in previously unheard of districts. Vacuum cooling tubes could be moved in to accommodate short deals in out of the way places. Huge crews of field packers could be temporarily moved into these new districts, and it was not unusual for shipments to suddenly jump by as much as 100 carlot equivalents per day."[12] According to a USDA report in 1955, changing the packing technique from ice cooling in wooden crates to flash cooling and dry packing in fiberboard cartons also decreased the loss of the product in cross-country travel.[13] This "dry pack method" eliminated water soaking, diminished discoloration and bruising, maintained crispness, and resulted in easier handling for exchange partners.[14]

Iceberg lettuce, with its unique distribution ecosystem, became a favorite commodity of large retail companies. By the 1950s, Salinas Valley, touted as "America's Salad Bowl," was responsible for producing half of the lettuce supplied to American markets, reaching 46 out of 48 states. Commercial farmers like Church and Antle continued to advance their growing, shipping, and innovation infrastructures and marketing ambitions. They helped Salinas Valley integrate carrots, artichokes, celery, cauliflower, and dozens of other vegetables into an existing nationwide growing and shipping infrastructure for much of the year—although not in the winter for many products, a problem that market actors would try to overcome years later.[15]

The apple industry was another early example of how mutual adaptations changed the interdependencies between farming technology, storage capacity, and high-volume retailing in ways that manipulated time and space and created new conventional means of distribution. Different varieties of apples were once available to local consumers during confined seasons. Regional climates produced different flavor profiles and material varieties, and local orchards used established methods of shipping to nearby markets. Although the number of supermarkets was growing, independent entrepreneurs and regional corporations still owned and operated most of them.[16] Creating an apple industry without seasons was different than in the lettuce industry. It initially entailed storage and preservation methods that slowed down respiration.

Since the 1800s, scientists in the United States and throughout Europe experimented with modifying gases and temperatures to prolong the duration of "freshness" for fruits and vegetables. Yet it was not until the 1940s in the United States—the formative era of suburbanization, supermarket expansion, and refrigerated trucks—that scientists systematically linked new preservation techniques with commercial markets. The changing environmental and consumer conditions created new economic opportunities. Robert Smock, a plant scientist from the University of California, Davis, and then Cornell University in New York, coined the term "controlled-atmosphere storage" for the manipulation of temperatures and gases to preserve apples in larger quantities.[17]

Apples are breathing entities. Smock and his colleagues engaged in the trial-and-error process to find the right series of steps to reduce respiration.[18] After years of experimenting with New York McIntosh apples, they worked out a series of steps—a sociotechnical recipe—that could be routinely applied to apple storage and distribution. They added nitrogen gas to reduce oxygen levels; maintained refrigerated temperatures in the range of 32 to 40 degrees depending on the volume of the supply; controlled for humidity; and manipulated carbon dioxide levels.[19]

During this period, chain grocers took on more produce in search of expanding the link between volume, variety, and profitability. They prized fresh objects like iceberg lettuce and certain apples that were more uniform in size and color and had the volume they wanted.[20] New York's McIntosh apples and Washington's Delicious apples consistently met these standards and these two regions competed for the national market. Both states heavily invested in out-of-state shipping infrastructures while moving toward production of fewer varieties.[21]

Controlled-atmosphere storage heightened the interstate competition. Smock's successful tests allowed New York growers to move McIntosh apples into the "late season" market of November and December, which directly challenged Washington state's prime season for their Delicious varieties. As orchards improved production methods and yields during this period, they faced additional questions about whether they could strategically control surplus to extend the seasons. New York farmers and scientists believed they could overcome low prices during periods of market glut by building new marketing opportunities between April and June, when the nation's apple supply was scarce.[22]

The early success in New York led to a slow diffusion of controlled-atmosphere storage to other parts of the country. Smock's students carried the sociotechnical recipe into new locations. Building relationships with university agricultural centers, they established controlled-atmosphere storage and testing sites in New York, Massachusetts, New Jersey, Virginia, and Michigan. The state of Washington, despite its vibrant apple growing and shipping system, was slower to adopt the innovation. Washington had different epistemic assumptions about how to create markets. Competing science, agricultural, and distribution interest groups debated the utility of controlled-atmosphere storage.

Smock's early tests in New York proved conclusive with McIntosh apples but it was less clear if his findings translated to other varieties. In fact, USDA scientists pressured Washington orchards to maintain their own established sociotechnical recipe: timing the harvest, carefully packing supplies, monitoring existing temperature-controlled storage, and making the product available to shippers to categorize and track the products.[23] These techniques worked well for decades, leading to one of the nation's largest out-of-state shipping infrastructures. The Yakima Valley Grower-Shipper Association had been assembling, organizing, and tracking the state's apple supplies since the early 1900s.[24]

In the 1950s, Smock and others had completed experiments in Virginia, Michigan, New York, and Massachusetts, where they recommended extending the sociotechnical operation to different varieties. During that time, one of Smock's students, Washington native Archie Van Doren, left Cornell to become the superintendent of the Washington State University Tree Fruit Research Laboratory. Van Doren was able to leverage new evidence to convince a pioneering group of Washington apple growers to invest in the controlled-atmosphere approach. By 1960, commercial quantities of Delicious apples were held in a mylar tent in a cold storage warehouse in Yakima Valley. By 1964, 2.5 million boxes of Delicious apples from controlled-atmosphere storage were made available for off-season commercial distribution.[25]

The process of transposing the sociotechnical apparatus from one state to another, and then from orchard to orchard, was gradual and iterative. Successful storage ventures of the 1960s eventually reinforced Washington's prominent position in the apple supply chain. It was a feedback loop: the economic benefits led to further investment in controlled-atmosphere storage; it then created new national consumer expectations for Delicious varieties, which motivated programs to invest in cold storage, limit other apple types, and increase the density of the state's apple production.[26] Between 1952 and 1961, the number of apple trees in Washington increased by 64 percent. The density of trees per acre multiplied over subsequent decades, from 100 trees per acre in 1961 to close to 400 in 2001.[27]

Although 27 states currently grow apples for the national commercial system, the impact of this supply ecosystem created market expectations and conventionality in apple consumption. Changing consumer expectations pushed apple growers across the country to convert their production to the

23 Supermarket produce departments in 1975 were just two sides of a single lane. Philadelphia *Evening Bulletin* Photographs (Copyright: TU Libraries). Credit: Special Collections Research Center, Temple University Libraries, Philadelphia, PA.

three most popular varieties of the time: Red Delicious, Golden Delicious, and McIntosh apples. For decades, most supermarkets consistently carried the same small number of apple varieties, only changing more recently to incorporate newer types.[28]

These early organizational and technical projects did not instantly create a produce aisle without seasons. Certain products like iceberg lettuce and Delicious apples became more widely available beyond local production conditions. Each fresh commodity required similar trial-and-error methods to build the routine market competencies and sociotechnical apparatus that crystallized into national distribution. Technical innovations in production and distribution helped to extend the seasons, but not all objects could fit the high-volume market infrastructure.

By the middle of the 1970s, supermarket produce aisles had expanded the number of year-round products, but they still retained a seasonal stock for most perishable products. The typical produce aisle itself was small in comparison to today's standard marketplace (see fig. 23). Certain objects were simply a better fit than others for creating year-round supplies. That did not stop scientists and industry leaders from searching for new ways to defeat seasons.

Place Infrastructure Meets the Global Political Economy

I interviewed dozens of produce industry veterans: cold storage operators, produce managers, supermarket buyers, growers and shippers, port managers, and wholesale and distribution center managers and executives. I always asked them about significant industry changes that they had witnessed during their careers. Without fail, the topic of produce aisles transcending seasons came up in every single conversation.

Bill Monk, a produce manager at a national supermarket chain in a New Jersey town outside of Philadelphia, started working in produce departments in the 1980s. There were still regular gaps in availability at that time, as corporate supermarket buyers cobbled together fresh produce aisles. It was always a work in progress with a great deal of uncertainty about which items would be available. Having worked his way up to being a store produce manager, Monk now places orders with the retailer's distribution center. He consistently refills any fresh item all year long. "The line has been blurred," he says. "Right now [in January] I'm still getting peaches, plums, nectarines, grapes, but they're coming from Chile. We have a smaller display of it compared to the summertime, but we still have it. The displays change throughout the season, but the varieties pretty much stay the same. There might be a gap for a month or two in some varieties, but overall we have everything almost all the time." (See fig. 24.)

By 1970, supermarkets housed over 10,000 different products. The period leading up to it also saw refrigeration extend its reaches. The home refrigerator and freezer industry took off after the Great Depression, and with it came an explosion of the frozen packaged food industry. Clarence Birdseye worked with the DuPont Chemical Company to develop new ways to process and package frozen foods. Between 1949 and 1959, this processing industry provided convenient prepared meal options and more frozen fruits and vegetables, growing by 2,700 percent and giving rise to a multibillion-dollar industry.[29] One of the advantages of frozen fruits and vegetables was year-round economic consistency in different commodities from corn to peas to spinach.

Commercial agricultural interests also began expanding production into new states to increase yields and break down seasonal constraints for objects that did not grow all year long—trying to further match the conventional market logic of creating the "same stuff everywhere." Tomato growers, for instance, developed a massive agricultural and agrochemical complex in Florida, in association with the University of Florida. As Barry Estabrook explains, despite Florida's humid and sandy conditions that seemed

24 Much larger produce section in 2010s. Credit: Rasysonho@Open
Grid Scheduler/Grid Engine/Wikimedia Commons. https://commons
.wikimedia.org/wiki/File:EmpressWalkLoblaws-Vivid.jpg.

incongruous to tomato cultivation, the industry wanted to meet the largest
off-season consumer demand. He writes, "Florida growers have to wage what
amounts to a total war against the elements. . . . We're talking about chemical, biological, and scorched-earth warfare against the forces of nature." Estabrook describes Florida as just warm enough and close enough to provide
year-round tomato supplies—despite their sometimes-maligned quality—
for millions of Midwestern, Mid-Atlantic, and Northeastern consumers.[30]

In ensuing decades, between the 1970s and 1990s, companies sought
new growing locations to integrate even more fresh commodities. A key part
of this project was finding and nurturing global complementarity between
regional production sites to create year-round formulas. Transforming regional conditions can work especially well for adaptable commodities, such
as bell peppers, cucumbers, squash, and eggplant. The North American Free
Trade Agreement—especially advancing new interdependencies with Mexican agricultural sectors—stabilized the availability of these products. In the
1990s, Florida and Mexico supplied 95 percent of vegetables during winter
months when California production was not possible.[31]

Mexican growers, especially in Culiacan, Sinaloa, where many vegetables
are grown for United States export, fostered relationships with United States

shippers. Nogales, Mexico, and Nogales, Arizona, share a border, located about 450 miles from the agricultural growing region. These towns contain the storage, customs, and standardization facilities. Refrigerated and temperature-controlled trucks travel 12 to 18 hours to the border. According to agricultural economists Linda Calvin and Veronica Barrios, a series of steps was transformed into a routine economic project. "As soon as the truck leaves the packinghouse, information is sent electronically to Nogales to the customs brokers and the distributor who begins selling the product, often even before it has actually arrived. After clearing Mexican and United States customs, the trucks deliver their loads to Nogales, Arizona, distributors." From there, distribution is set up for the national market.[32]

Florida and Mexico provide conveniences, but a lot of commodities are less adaptable, requiring particular growing and shipping conditions. Market actors have navigated environmental, social, and political contingencies to discover appropriate growing regions, trading alliances, and technical innovations to stabilize interdependencies between production and consumption around more and more varieties.

In the 1970s, following a decade of stringent controls over profitability on agricultural land, Chilean dictator Augusto Pinochet opened up Chilean agriculture to global trade, precipitating a major transformation of the nation's fruit growing infrastructure and wine industry. California's agricultural and shipping industries that dominated the lucrative grape supply in the United States sought to build a year-round inventory. Chilean and California industries nurtured new interdependencies. Much of the infrastructural development in Chile resulted from United States technology, and in particular, dependency on California seed innovations and patents. Chilean landowners even sent their children to the United States to study agronomy and business.[33]

As the amount of agricultural land increased under Pinochet's rule, most of the production was geared toward export industries, three-quarters of which went to the United States. Historian Heidi Tinsman describes it as "competitive collaboration." The orchards and vineyards were owned and operated by Chilean families, as were many of the packing plants and storage facilities. However, United States–based growing and shipping companies, including the largest transnational agro-industry corporations, like Dole and Standard Fruit Company, invested in additional packing plants and cold storage operations. American shipping interests educated their Chilean partners on the basic requirements for entering the United States consumer market. According to one marketing representative for a large California grape-growing company, "They didn't know what a shipping pallet was. They didn't understand what pre-cooling was. We had to go through all the steps."[34]

Over the next decade, the Chilean industry integrated much of the technology that was already available in California, converting it into another recipe of recurring distribution. Chile first connected to United States consumers through grapes, but once the shipping interdependencies materialized, Chilean growers expanded their United States exports to stone fruit. This mutually reinforcing global trade relationship created year-round United States market access to peaches, nectarines, and plums.

Fred Mankoff, a shipping receiver of Chilean produce coming to the United States, has been working with Chilean growers for decades. He advises them on how and when to get their fruit into the American market system. He also directly advertises and sells their products. His company designs packaging and carves out the connections to supermarkets. He believes that the commodities and the infrastructure that sustains their qualities in storage and shipping are the most important features for stabilizing the geographic interdependencies. He says,

> The characteristic of the Chilean investment was unlike most of the South American countries at the time. . . . Everything is packed in packinghouses and it's refrigerated. In California, they pack in the fields in wagons, and so Chile became more modern than California. Over the years, we developed an advertising program to publicize their endeavors. And the fruit is excellent. So the best ambassador really is the commodity. It's a live commodity and there are many possible qualities, and maintaining the quality of the fruit has been instrumental in creating a great market.

Businesses invest years—sometimes even decades—scouring the planet for the right climate and soil conditions, as well as figuring out the local social, economic, and political supports for high-volume distribution. Mike Ellison is an executive of a growing and shipping corporation. He saw the potential of expanding different products beyond the summer months. He says that consumers were historically forced in the winter to "eat apples because those are commodities that could be stored under controlled-atmosphere and distributed year-round." He and his partners started to explore growing and shipping options to advance new varieties. He explains that melons grow in the desert, and they looked for places that mimicked the Arizona climate. He and his partners found places in Zacapa, Guatemala, and Choluteca, Honduras. He says,

> It took 20 years to build the business and the relationships, and now we're one of the largest producers and shippers worldwide. Usually in the spring,

we determine what kind of planting schedule we're going to put together and once we do that, we start acquiring fertilizer, doing land preparation, and so forth. And then we start planting in Guatemala around September . . . and then we start seeing production usually in mid-November, and the cycle will continue with the volumes producing all the way through May.

To make the global distribution system work as a fresh market without seasons, United States sites of receiving and distribution are also set up to connect and coordinate the movements of products to retail and whole-sale sites all over the country. Port infrastructures build together the storage and mobility relationships that service the global commodities.[35] Political-economic collaborations have built up port zones over decades into key niches for strategic economic growth, especially since the 1970s when bar codes, logistical strategies, shipping containers, and global trading opportunities spread mass merchandising throughout the United States.

The Los Angeles port system emerged as the foremost container port for apparel, electronics, and other commodities coming from China. The containers could be discharged from ships and quickly attached to trucks en route to corporate distribution centers.[36] Houston has an importing infrastructure to support petroleum-based products for the oil industries housed in Texas. The New York and New Jersey Port Authority is a web of infrastructural and support services, just like its vast and heterogeneous region. It mixes together a carport, container port, and "break bulk" fresh food shipping in which fruit is directly loaded into the refrigerated hulls of the ships without containers.

The Delaware River ports are similar to New York's port infrastructure in terms of offering varying services. Although they operate on a smaller scale, they have strategically grown as sites of global fruit importing, directly competing with New York. Frank Camp, a marketing representative for the Philadelphia Regional Port Authority at the time of the interview, said that the location of the Delaware River ports coupled with less dense and varied users of their services, allowed for strategic growth in the fresh food industries. The ports of Philadelphia, Pennsylvania, Wilmington, Delaware, and Gloucester and Camden, New Jersey, became central points of discharge for Chilean grapes that companies then transport to many locations in the United States and Canada. He says,

If you go to the supermarket right now [in the winter], any grapes that you see, red or green, they're all going to be from Chile. And they all came through the

Delaware River. From this point, Chilean grapes are distributed up to Eastern Canada, to Indiana, and it may go as far as Chicago, as far south as the Tennessee area. Once the cargo comes in, it has to be quickly handled here at the port. We've got a large network of refrigerated truckers and warehousing in the three states that can handle the cargo. Because of our success in handling the Chilean fruit, our reputation grew and we branched off into Brazilian fruit, Ecuadorian fruit, Peruvian fruit, and Colombian fruit.

As political and business alliances dissolved geographic trade barriers through interdependent economic ventures, more objects from more locations were compiled into strategic regions. This convergence and accumulation of interests and infrastructures crystallized regional economic ties and developed into "logistics clusters."[37] These regional clusters brought together investment capital, political alliances, transporting intersections, storage capacity, and high-volume objects. They were not set up simply to meet the demands of consumers in that location. Different shipping companies carried them away from the region to meet consumer demand all over the country. This global political-economic endeavor fit into the infrastructural regime of feeding the nation.

The process created another feedback loop: crossing geographic boundaries allowed business and political actors to assemble a connecting infrastructure and negotiate more directly with each other and strengthen the global interdependencies. For example, Nogales, Arizona, and Nogales, Mexico, functioned as "one city divided by an international border."[38] These interdependencies solidified as routine alliances and mutually reinforcing interactions between interest groups that make Mexican agricultural products so easily available to so many supermarkets in the United States. Similarly, marketing directors of the Delaware River ports now network with representatives of foreign governments, nurture relationships with major transnational shipping corporations like Del Monte, Dole, and Chiquita, and strengthen local ties to labor unions and trucking, logistics, shipping, receiving, and storage and customs support services. These entanglements altered the governance structure of global supply chains and the framework of seeking value-added efficiencies.[39]

It is a multiscale endeavor: the global network enables localized political-economic growth machines to build port and service infrastructures that support the national market system. Over the past two decades, nongovernmental trade and policy organizations have played an important role in securing public/private alliances. Founded in 1988, the Chilean and American

Chamber of Commerce works with government officials in Chilean growing and shipping regions and the cities and states along the Delaware River, along with almost 400 different private companies, to improve the relationships between parties invested in these spatially separated locations.

I attended several of the chamber's events, including a conference about fresh produce, where I was struck by the diversity of participants. I was surrounded by USDA officials, congressional representatives from various local districts, staff members of the Philadelphia mayor's office, staff of the Pennsylvania governor, government representatives of major Chilean growing states, owners of Chilean growing and packing companies, local port marketing directors, representatives of US-based family-owned shipping companies, executives of transnational corporations, regional and national retail and wholesale executives, as well as local leaders representing the interests of port operations, brokers, labor unions, cold storage businesses, and logistics experts.

The interests spanned locations both far from and near to Philadelphia. However, they shared the framework that multiscale organizational and infrastructural connections supporting fresh food distribution was mutually beneficial for sustaining the placement of Chilean products in the United States merchandising system. Ricardo Maldonado, the director of the Chilean American Chamber of Commerce, says that these interdependencies maintain the credibility of "Chile" as a fresh produce brand. He says,

> We push for the right infrastructure to keep the whole process very healthy, very clean, and very fast, because it's a perishable product that we need to protect from the farm to the table, and it's a long process when it comes from Chile. There are many parties involved from different countries, to the middle of the sea, to when it gets here. The different steps of logistics from the fumigation process to the distribution process to the inspection process to the warehouse to the supermarket. At the end of the day, once it gets to the supermarket the label says "Chile." We want to protect that brand, because it only takes one fruit to be in bad condition to ruin the whole perception American consumers have of the product.

Different interests from various countries configured seasonal production, shipping infrastructures, and port cold storage into year-round United States commercial markets. As the global political-economic relationships solidified into routine market availability, the organizational logic filtered back down into local adaptations.

Local Adaptations to Global Political Economy

The global political economy converges and accumulates into localized techno-political artifacts, such as importing and cold storage systems. The Port of Wilmington, for instance, is now the central import location for bananas consumed in the United States. The port directors rent space to Chiquita and Dole, the two largest banana shippers, as well as smaller competitors. All of these companies have relationships with different kinds of retailing, whole-saling, and institutional food service corporations, ranging from Wal-Mart to Starbucks to US Foods to various supermarkets and wholesale terminals. They truck their products from Wilmington to dozens of states.

With 800,000 square feet of cold storage, the Port of Wilmington now houses the largest square footage of port cold storage in the United States. The South Jersey port of Camden is now the primary import location for Del Monte, the world's largest pineapple grower and shipper. Delaware River ports in total—in Wilmington, Philadelphia, and New Jersey—are the central importing hub for Chilean grapes and other Chilean produce, a major discharge center for Central and South American produce generally, as well as primary importing sites for Spanish and Moroccan clementines.

These accumulating relationships enable and constrain entrepreneurial activity. Some local companies find benefits in investing in new opportunities, while others become deeply constrained by the system reconfigurations. It is a contextual and trial-and-error process of resituating organizational priorities amid changing political-economic relationships.

Rob Simms, for example, started his cold storage business by chance. After graduating college, Simms went into his family's local farming business. He hired a truck driver to haul his family's supplies to various markets. The trucker also worked for a large multinational importing company and he told Simms that the company was looking for cold storage to house its increasing volume of Chilean imports. Simms saw an economic opportunity. New Jersey peach and apple farmers hardly used their cold storage in the winter, so Simms went around the area and rented many of them. He continued to expand as the demand increased. In 1985, he added 400 pallet positions, and then in 1986, 1,000 more, while still renting many of the other cold storage units in the area. He then rented another building with 2,000 pallet positions, and then opened up a much larger 4,000 pallet facility. He continued to expand to over 10,000 pallet positions.

In the infrastructural regime of feeding the nation, the aim is not to move the commodities to any specific location. Rather, organizations manage and reproduce the cold chain interdependencies by creating value niches in the national and global distribution system. Simms fit his business into that framework, but not all businesses match the changing infrastructural dynamics. The wholesale produce terminal markets that once thrived as place-based dealers for central cities were pushed to the periphery of cities to match the regional distribution system.

The South Philadelphia terminal market on Galloway Street was a success when it opened in the 1960s, replacing the downtown Dock Street Market. Yet over the next two decades, the national and global political economy shifted the distribution logic again. According to Don Marcus, a Philadelphia wholesaler, most of the small family wholesaling businesses did not foresee the system changing around them. The Galloway terminal market had key weaknesses that made it incompatible with the global trends. Most significantly, refrigeration in the small businesses was limited. Marcus says, the market was designed for trucks to "unload in the back, put the stuff in the store, and sell it out the front to customers" in the same day (see fig. 11 in chapter 2). As a result, certain products like strawberries and mushrooms posed problems. In the summer, Marcus explained, if you did not quickly sell out of strawberries, then the business owner had to dump them. Some of the wholesalers started to install refrigerated coolers to handle these products, but the coolers were not big enough. They put in larger diesel-fueled refrigerated trailers in the back, but the diesel was expensive and the trailers blocked the unloading process.

Marcus says, "We made it as inconvenient as possible for our customers to come in and buy. We thought with the fruit auction and vegetable depot [of the old rail distribution system] gone, we were a seller's market. But guess what? The customers fooled us and they found other ways to find produce. We made it inconvenient enough that through the '70s and early '80s, we wondered, 'Where's the future for us?' "

The system relationships and profit-making priorities shifted around national and global supplies and many of the wholesale terminal markets were being left behind. Certainly, Hunts Point in the Bronx remained viable because of its unique connection to the largest city in the nation. But many of the terminal markets closed down. In Philadelphia, the wholesalers went in another direction, relocating again, and this time, connecting with the broader infrastructural logic of the refrigerated "cold chain." The new Philadelphia Produce Wholesale Market, which opened in 2011, is a 680,000-square-foot refrigerated building with more than 200 loading docks. It has more than 20 produce businesses with different specialties and scales of operation.

The storefronts are lined up next to each other down a central path of the large warehouse kept at a stable temperature of 50 degrees. Unlike New York's Hunts Point or Philadelphia's previous Galloway Street market, this newer space has no open-air exchange. Rather, it is set up to maintain refrigeration throughout all of the exchange dynamics. In the front stage, the 20 businesses display what they have on offer for small business customers who peruse the stock. The backstage holds the bulk of the supply, leading to a maze of refrigerated rooms at different temperatures and connections to the loading docks. (See fig. 25.)

In addition to servicing local small food businesses, the new wholesale produce market operates as "fill-in" to the corporate retailers—an adaptation to the new infrastructural regime of feeding the nation. Tad Thompson was the marketing director of the Philadelphia Wholesale Market when I spoke to him in 2011. He said that the power of the new wholesale market is its refrigerated infrastructure and its number of businesses in one spot. He said that the wholesale businesses are not exclusively tied to the local area; they are also selling to large supermarket buyers like Publix in Florida and other large chains all along the East Coast and up into Canada as a "fill-in" operation.

Dave Rogers has been involved in the produce industry for decades. He is a sales director for a large growing and shipping company and formerly a buyer for a national retailer. He describes the current role of the wholesale terminal market as a "forwarding house." He says, "Chains are under a lot of pressure to keep their inventory tight. They don't want a lot of inventory. As a [retail] buyer, you say, 'Look. I'm going on ad for strawberries.' I'm going to need 25 trailer loads and I'll probably buy 20. You tell them [the wholesaler] that you may need 2 to 5 loads, and they work with the retailer to carry that inventory." Rogers says there is always the chance that large retailers run out of the supply, because of the contingency of the environmental and shipping conditions. The terminal market adopted a fill-in position as an extension of the mass-merchandising operation. If a supermarket runs out of cucumbers and needs 20 boxes, a family wholesale business can fill in to maintain the supply's continuity.

The spread of the cold chain was about mutual adaptations between national and global supply systems and shifting distribution expectations—a transformation from feeding cities to feeding regions to feeding the nation. In 1921, the United States had 544 million cubic feet of cold storage throughout the country. By 1957, as highways, trucks, supermarkets, frozen food industries, and suburban consumers became interdependent, the total cold storage capacity increased to over 900 million cubic feet. In 1973, with

25 Central path of Philadelphia produce wholesale market
with different storefronts. Photograph by author.

mass merchandising an established distribution model and supermarkets aggressively increasing square footage, the quantity of cold storage capacity reached over 1.5 billion cubic feet. The amount has continued to grow as retail stores increased their volumes of supplies and incorporated more frozen and perishable products. In 2013, the total cold storage capacity in the United States was over 4.6 billion cubic feet, by far the world's largest refrigerated infrastructure.[40]

New infrastructural interdependencies around product preservation and mobility reframed the web of sociotechnical connections into recurring modes of distribution. It helped to dissolve global, national, and regional boundaries. However, the fresh market system continues to mimic other mass-merchandising approaches. Not only does it defeat seasons by stabilizing high-volume supplies as year-round products, but it also introduces "new and improved" varieties to fit into the market's ongoing search for product diversity and novelty.

"New" Fruits and Vegetables

Fruits and vegetables are caught up in overlapping histories of science and technology and urban and economic development. They are not "natural" objects—that is, objects produced without human intervention in "the wild." Scientists and product engineers strategically, and often times accidentally, created hybrid varieties by tuning up the commodities and their qualities since the earliest iterations of agricultural production. As horticulturist Noel Kingsbury puts it, hybridization is a process of conversion and domestication. The products that result are often "more appetizing" than their "wild ancestors," as well as "more productive, easier to grow, and very often more nutritious."[41]

In the contemporary market environment, this scientific and technical process is linked up with the infrastructural dynamics of the high-volume, high-variety system of distribution. An example is Japanese researchers combining two apple varieties—the Rall's Janet and the Red Delicious—into its offspring, the Fuji apple. Over a period of decades, scientific experimentation and consumer feedback led to the Fuji's crisp texture, sweet flavor composition, and consistently round and uniform market qualities that made it one of the most popular apple varieties for United States supermarkets.[42]

Whether it is an entirely "new" object or something that has simply not yet been introduced to the supermarket system, the process of integrating it is similar. Introducing new fresh fruits and vegetables is as much about implementation as it is about innovation. Marketing actors introduce commodities, packaging methods, and entire commodity categories. Only after trial and error, do some of them become widely adopted in ways that change the look and feel of produce aisles. As new market objects are established into mutually reinforcing production, storage, and distribution relationships, actors tune up the interdependencies between them.

Companies and organizations search the globe for existing products not yet meeting market potential and especially those that do not yet reach the United States, which houses the world's largest consumer market for fruits and vegetables—and most things, generally. Certain business arms are anthropological in focus. They work with farmers and scientists, getting to know the flavor profiles, textures, colors, preparations, and applications of objects not yet familiar to United States consumers. Marketing agents in the fruit and vegetable industries are skilled at seeing and understanding the potential of cultural translation. They explore the techniques of preparation and consumption, evaluate material characteristics, and study the possibilities of introducing them to new market and cultural contexts. Some objects are initially perceived as too foreign for United States mass consumption. Mike Ellison, the growing and shipping executive, says,

> When you see what people eat around the world you realize, "Wow, I didn't even know that existed." And it's hard to predict what's next. I remember years ago tasting a rambutan, which is like a lychee nut. It was just growing on one of our farmer's properties. It's a fuzzy round object, and you break it open and it has this white, fleshy meat that is very sweet and then inside the meat, there's a big seed. He asked me, "Is there a market for it?" At the time, I said, "Geez, I don't know!" I thought with the appearance alone it wouldn't work. But now it has made it to a few stores.

In today's consumer space of niche marketing, it is possible to bridge previously unknown commodities with adventurous consumers willing to take a chance on purchasing it. Marketing actors face an entirely different set of constraints to infiltrate the high-volume retail and wholesale market space. Don Marcus, the Philadelphia wholesaler, says that he has tried to introduce a range of products into the United States marketplace over his multidecade career. He helped establish a red pepper supply by connecting retailers to Dutch and Israeli greenhouse growers several decades before Mexican production took off, which then shifted consumer expectations around the year-round red (and then yellow and orange) pepper supply. He says, "At that time, there were no red peppers on the market." Green peppers were an established retail category, and so it was not a huge leap for consumers to commit to a color variation of an already familiar object. Not all "new" commodities take off like red peppers. Marcus says,

> There are a handful of radicchio items [a red bitter lettuce] that we bring from Italy and they're extremely popular in Northern Italy and in other parts of Europe. The problem is it's expensive to bring from overseas and it's a niche item. It's a question of identifying the market, bringing the product in, promoting it, and putting it in the hands of the people who want it. It's a great product and everyone I give it to loves it. But the operative word is "give." When it comes time to buy it, they're not as interested, because the price just doesn't meet their budget.

A major trend in expanding fresh variety is to identify commodities that are already popular elsewhere and figure out how to overcome their unknown characteristics in the United States. Certain fresh products have been widely consumed around the world for decades—even centuries—but have not taken off in the United States as commercial products. The Cavendish banana is famously the only banana—out of a thousand different varieties—consumed in the United States. It is the most popularly consumed fruit in the country. Yet the mango is the world's most popular fruit. Native to India, Pakistan, Bangladesh, and the Philippines, the mango has traveled widely across Europe but never reached the same level of popularity in the United States. In fact, just several decades ago, in the early 1990s, chain supermarkets rarely sold mangoes. When I was growing up in the New Jersey suburbs in the 1980s, my local supermarket did not carry them in its produce aisle. I remember buying one for the first time when I was in college, at the end of the 1990s, trying to figure out with little success how to cut and eat the fruit with its thick inedible skin and giant seed in the center.

A national commodity board emerged around the mango to promote it and dissolve the barriers. Commodity boards advocate on behalf of objects, rather than any specific profit-making firms. They do not sell anything. They are funded by growers invested in the commercial market to frame the specific object for consumers. Wendy McManus, a former marketing director for the National Mango Board, says that the organization's goal is to "grease the wheels" and "move mangoes through the system." She says, "In general, we try to fill demand and break down barriers or obstacles." One way is managing the "pull effect" of bringing mangoes to the "minds of consumers" in subtle ways. Through public relations efforts, she and her staff provided mango-based recipes to food and cooking magazines and posted videos on the internet about how to cut mangoes. McManus says,

"We wanted to give the customer the confidence to go into a supermarket and buy a mango."

The mango commodity board also invested in "push" based marketing. McManus and her staff worked with supermarket buyers and category managers, helping them to set up promotions and displays, and train employees. The commodity board used its funding to educate retailers and consumers. She and her team tried mango display contests to motivate larger in-store displays and pushed mango recipes into weekly advertisement circulars. They also educated retailers and produce staff to better understand the characteristics of mangoes. McManus explains,

> A customer could walk up to [an employee] and say, "I want to buy a mango. Which one of these is good?" And if the store employee says, "I don't know," we probably lost a sale. We want the employee to say, "Oh here's how you chop it, and don't worry about the color." People think it's not ripe if it's green, but color doesn't matter. It's how it feels. We want him to say, "Do you want to eat it tonight? Let's find one that's got a little bit of a give to it." They squeeze the mango and find a good one and now you've made a sale.

Marketing fresh fruits and vegetables requires a multitiered education process in the cultural competencies of handling and tasting the objects to make people comfortable with them. Very few people in the United States, at this historical juncture, fail to understand how to eat an apple or a navel (seedless) orange. We know what they taste like, what the textures should be, and what parts we are supposed to eat. We also know to avoid the apple core and its seeds and discard the orange's peel. It sounds absurd to even raise the possibility of cultural confusion around these fruits, but anyone with children will recognize that this taken-for-granted knowledge is actually learned over time until it becomes obvious. Once a commodity is established, it becomes easier to introduce a variety on the theme, which is why there are often multiple variations of the same objects. Like bananas, there are thousands of mango varieties. Initially supermarkets tried the greenish-red Tommy Atkins, and when that was established, they added the smaller yellow Ataulfo "champagne" mango to the market. In 2018, mangoes made it onto the list of the 20 best-selling fruits in the United States for the first time, at number 19.[43]

A seedless and easily peeled variety of mandarin orange—the clementine—serves as one of the more interesting historical examples of turning a once-confusing market item into one of the most popular commodities. When Dave Rogers was a produce buyer for a national retailing chain in the 1980s, he saw the introduction of the clementine. He says, "You couldn't give them away. They came from Spain. They didn't know how to ship them. They came in a 40-pound bulk box. Half of them would be bad when you would get them, and some of them might taste good, but you couldn't get an acceptable arrival." The clementine is part of a growing line of "new" fruit varieties, like the Chinese gooseberry (i.e., the kiwi), the mango, or the new apple varieties like the Fuji, the Honeycrisp, and the Pink Lady.

Clementines had to be framed for the American consumer through new marketing agendas and shipping infrastructures. Supermarkets needed to know how to store them, present them, and sell them, while customers had to learn how to eat them, how to peel them, and what to expect from their textures and flavors. Alvaro Boda is a consultant in the global clementine trade. He mediates relationships between Spanish cooperative packinghouses that assemble fruit from over 1,000 Spanish citrus farms, the shipper who transports the product to the United States, and the American receiver of the Spanish product who works to move the materials to the market.

Boda refers to himself as "the connecting guy." Representing the object itself allows him special expertise in seeing multiple sides of the supply chain. He explains, "It's hard for people to understand who I am because many people think I represent [the receiving company], which is true, and some people say I'm with one of the packinghouses [in Spain] because they have my photo up. I'm neither one and I'm both. I get the product they need. The quality they need. The supply in time. You can call it an operations guy, but I'm involved in the marketing, involved in the sales indirectly, involved in pricing, and I'm the one who knows what's there [in Spain] that they can use here [in the United States]."

Boda helped to create the mass-merchandising appeal for this misunderstood commodity. In the early 1980s, when clementines entered into the United States market system, consumers were confused about how it differed from other types of mandarin orange varieties, like tangerines, which looked similar but had seeds. One of Boda's major initiatives was to translate and reframe this popular Spanish and Moroccan commodity for American consumers. He and his partners put clementines into five-pound wooden crates and allowed customers to peel them and taste them in supermarkets. Customers were quickly drawn to the sweet and seedless "easy peeler," and the supermarkets liked that the shippers packaged them—it moved them in bulk.

Many people in the industry whom I interviewed credited the clementine market as influencing current trends of seedless and packaged fruit and vegetables, both of which have become quite common. Clementines emerged as one of the most lucrative and highly demanded fresh fruits for supermarkets, often given their own valuable island space in the front of the produce department. Boda says, "We didn't invent the clementine market but we developed it. We made them to go to the supermarkets. In the first year, we did close to 50 [shipping] containers in the whole season. Then 250, then almost 700, and then we jumped to entire ships [full of clementines]." Jim Bazzano, a supermarket fresh produce executive at a large national chain, remembers,

> Everybody was selling in [bulk supply] kilos and the markets were selling them by the piece. They were labeling them as 99 cents per piece, but then they were labeling the tangerine as 49 cents per piece. As a consumer, you don't know the difference. You buy the one that's 49 cents. Why pay 99 cents? That was slowing the growth of the clementine market. When they decided to do it with packaging, supermarkets liked it, because it moved a lot of weight and they didn't have to do anything. It's got a barcode at the bottom and it goes through. It multiplied, because the supermarkets were making money. Supermarkets are like that. We're not there to sell apples. We're there to sell what consumers want.

The mediating process between supply and demand is where the feedback dynamic emerges. Consumers decide what they "want" based on what is made available to them. Exchange partners then develop the corresponding infrastructures through back and forth negotiations. Dave Rogers, the fruit company sales director, says that now that freshness transcends seasonality, producers no longer dictate the market. Instead, marketing arms like commodity boards, marketing consultants, and cooperative and corporate brands themselves manage the relationships between the market's push and pull. He says,

> Our biggest growth has been in new varieties. We look for products with different flavor profiles, durability profiles, and we have to introduce them to the marketplace. One variety that has really exploded in the citrus industry is Cara Cara oranges. It's a navel orange that's pink in the middle. It's higher in lycopene. It's more nutritious than the regular navel orange, and it's got a little bit of a different flavor to it. Now we have to educate the buyers, educate the consumers, let them taste it. We do a lot of demos and heavy advertising. We do produce shows. We have to bring something to the table. The fruit has to have some attribute to it to be introduced that's different from what's out there. We have to give the [retail] customer a reason to cut in a new SKU [stock keeping unit].

The infrastructural change happens slowly over time. Creating the new physical market space and electronic inventory category is key, but companies also have to educate growers about what retailers report in their sales trends. For instance, California citrus growers did not initially foresee the potential of the clementine trade. In fact, some even stalled in planting seedless navel orange varieties, remaining stuck in an older trend of Valencia oranges, which are less popular, in part, because they have seeds. Growers have to learn about new consumer trends and invest in them as part of this gradual tune-up of the market ecosystem. Rogers says,

> You don't throw seeds in the ground and the next year pick the fruit. It takes five years for the average tree to produce in ways that's paying and worthwhile. . . . If you're the guy looking at Valencia orange trees that your great-grandfather planted, you have to change. The market doesn't want a seeded orange in the wintertime. They want easy peelers like clementines. I have to show them the numbers, the trends, educate them about what's going on in the marketplace. It's the law of diminishing returns. Every year the demand is getting lower and lower. But then you've got progressive guys that are picking mandarins right now or Cara Caras. The demand is high and we're able to give more money to that grower. Then his neighbor sees that he's making a lot of money so he starts planting, and then the guy next to him starts, and sooner or later you get to a point where now it's over-produced. You have to constantly manage it.

Ellison, the shipping company executive, is always on the hunt for new produce that fits the existing United States consumer profile. He talks with seed companies and farmers in different parts of the world, and then if he likes something in his field research, he tries to convince his company to "take the plunge." Ellison says that during any season the global shipping company for which he works may test 100 to 150 different varieties of melons hoping to find one or two that demand further testing to match consistent qualities with high-volume production. He says, "If you have a beautiful piece of fruit but you only get one piece of it on the plant, your cost is so high you obviously can't make money. No one is going to pay $25 for a melon, even if it's the most perfect melon you ever saw."

One kind that paid off for the industry was the "harper" melon, a hybrid cousin of the honeydew. When a seed company introduced it to Ellison, others in his company did not want to take the risk because honeydews are seen as secondary melons. He says, consumers often look for color and flavor variations in relationship to the more popular cantaloupe and watermelon. The Harper variety, with its light orange flesh, looks and tastes more like a cantaloupe than a honeydew but it can stay on the shelves longer and maintain consistent quality.

Ellison's company spent eight years conducting tests on the melon before marketing it as a Harper cantaloupe. He says, "It might be a honeydew, but if it looks like a cantaloupe, it's a cantaloupe. The consumers welcomed it. So we converted entire farms into producing this variety and it was lucky for us, during a year that the weather affected the production of standard melons. We were standing there with this new melon but we were the only ones with *any* melons. And we had the quantity as well as the best quality." The balance of strategic planning, established growing infrastructures, and contingent market circumstances created an opening moment that allowed them to successfully introduce another variation into the commercial retailing system, in this case another fruit that resembled an established commodity.

Produce marketing associations have for decades exposed people to "new and improved" fresh products. The United Fresh Produce Association, the Produce Marketing Association's "Fresh Summit," and more recently, regional produce shows like the New York Produce Show, have helped new and old businesses introduce products, technologies, sales ventures, and marketing plans. It is a collective industry project to facilitate exposure and educate retail and wholesale buyers on a company's expertise and product lines.

At the New York Produce Show, I walked from booth to booth talking with marketing and sales agents about their companies' agendas, reading marketing materials, and trying "new" products. Companies gave away thousands of samples. Large brands like Chiquita, Dole, Green Giant, and Sunkist positioned themselves next to national commodity boards, wholesale companies, trade associations representing strawberries, blueberries, and mangoes, and risk-taking entrepreneurs showcasing new ideas, technologies, and products.

One large company gave away samples of the Cavendish bananas, but wrapped them in a plastic film, which the sales representative told me was designed to delay ripening. Another handed out brochures about its ventures into the brussels sprouts category, with new varieties building on technologies for making them sweeter than competitors. An innovative horticulture firm handed out samples of "micro-vegetables." Its founder travels widely to locate edible plants with powerful flavor profiles. These edible flowers, micro greens, and herbs enable cutting edge culinary aesthetics and flavors, from "micro mustard red" that tastes like "Dijon mustard" to "micro tangerine" that looks like a little clover growing on the side of the road but tastes like "fresh picked citrus flavor."

Produce aisles evolve slowly, product by product. They reconfigure consumer expectations over time by updating the collective aesthetics of the marketplace. Jim Bazzano, the supermarket fresh produce executive, discusses the evolution of the produce aisle over the past 20 years. He points to the rise of bagged and packaged salads and new tomato varieties as significant. The produce aisle used to have more space for regular greens. He says, "You had lots of Romaine and 15 to 20 feet of fresh greens." The "value-added packaged salads" changed the proportion and configuration of the aisle itself. The updates can be subtle. He says, field tomatoes used to dominate the category, but now hothouse tomatoes and grape tomatoes do. He explains, "It changes our buying patterns, where we look to get our stuff, the way we organize our space, and how we advertise. It doesn't happen fast. We continually look at our setup to see where our sales trends are going and what we need more of."

The mass-merchandising culture of "new and improved" varieties has spread into fresh produce industries. Marketing agents establish space for new object varieties, and if the demand is there, they entice other companies and regions of the world to invest in higher-volume supply infrastructures to support that commodity, expand the category, and directly compete in the global fresh market. Regardless of where it comes from and what variety it is, once a fruit or vegetable gets established in the market—clementines, mangoes, Fuji apples, bagged lettuce, or grape tomatoes, all of which did not exist in my supermarket as a child—it develops into a complex connecting system of interdependent distribution agents. These interdependent agents coordinate a reliable market without seasons, but they still have to manage the contingencies of high-volume supply and demand for rapidly decomposing objects.

Configuring Supply and Demand

Trying to manipulate and preserve objects that change qualities over time and are easily damaged is difficult enough. Trying to scale these same changing objects into a "just-in-time" system for tens of thousands of markets across the country is another issue altogether. The supply systems for decomposing fresh objects have distinct types of contingencies, and understanding and managing them is key to the collective pursuit. Patterned social, economic, and environmental conditions enable and constrain the active management of perishable commodity qualities.

The parameters of uncertainty are patterned in ways that allow market actors to prepare for certain kinds of disruptions around each kind of commodity. Dave Rogers, the fruit company sales director, describes the industry's supply uncertainty around strawberries like this: "You load strawberries in California, and it takes five days to get to Philadelphia, and you've got thousands and thousands of dollars worth of product on a truck, and you've got a trucker you're depending on to get it there, and the market's changing as it's coming across the country."

Mike Ellison, the growing and shipping executive, describes a fruit and vegetable market that "fluctuates, depending on weather, delays through customs, and demand." The relationship between supply and demand is not a constant force, but something that needs to be actively managed. He says, "We may have product coming into Florida. It might be 80 degrees there, but if you have winter storms in the Northeast, people aren't going to the supermarkets and everything slows down. But the cycle continues. I have product on the road, there's product being received at the customer's distribution center, there's product being received at my distribution center, there's product on the ocean, there's product being packed in the packing shed, and there's product in the fields."

Even as the fresh market without seasons extended around different varieties, companies still worked to introduce a "just-in-time" market logic for perishable goods. Companies became more interested in inter-organizational information and communication measures for fresh produce in the wake of industry-wide scares around product contamination during the 1990s and early 2000s. Tainted spinach, cantaloupe, and other fresh commodities shut down the supply system, resulting in billions of dollars of losses. An entire season of production can be decimated even when investigators attribute the problems to a small number of farms. Customers will refuse to buy products without clear confidence in their safety.

Traceability is a critical aspect of the solution. It allows firms to pinpoint the exact origin and handling components of the product, in the effort to build market resiliency, which in this case became interwoven with public health resiliency. Market resiliency refers to the adaptive organizational and infrastructural process to better prepare for the profit-loss contingencies from the agricultural field to the marketplace. At each stage of handling, physical commodities are matched with organizational and technical methods to prepare for the transfer across exchange locations. Information and communication technologies get married to established cultural competencies of material handling in specific settings.

George Goodwin is an IT expert who develops information systems to trace commodities from agricultural production to supermarket retail. He describes the bridge between physical locations and information technologies. He says that he and his team spent five years figuring out how to collect data from places all over the planet and integrate them into a central database. "We're tracking billions of items from thousands of end points all over the world, and they're being funneled into a massive data center." Collecting the information requires implementing new techniques at all the physical points of contact. For instance, a team labels the product in the fields—Mexico to Guatemala, California to Florida. He explains,

> They have big rolls of labels and hand apply them at phenomenal speeds. Then they stick the label on a form. If five people label bananas, they've got five rolls of labels being used. At the top of the form they check boxes for the date, the variety, the field that those bananas came from. It's literally like filling in a multiple-choice exam. There's only a limited set of values. We know where this packing shed gets their bananas from, and at the end of the day this form gets faxed into us. Our software reads the form, looks at the checkboxes, and reads the barcodes on the labels stuck to the form. From that information, we can figure out all of the labels that were used that day by that farm and assign all that harvest information.

Each setting along the supply chain uses information and communication technologies to reinforce the fluid mobility system. They collectively build traceability files that get implemented as different organizational applications to manage contingencies. Customs clearance and brokerage firms service the supply chain, facilitating the physical and information relationship to dissolve national borders. Joe Bonilla is an assistant vice president of import operations and a licensed customs broker at a third-party logistics company. His company conducts private freight forwarding services to manage commodities through customs. Bonilla manages the ins and outs of the legal requirements for hundreds of different commodities moving across national borders and translates the physical shipments into shareable information files to ease the exchange process. He says, "We don't physically see the cargo. We marry the logistics information with the commercial invoice information and provide that to US Customs."

These logistics arms work behind the scenes. They take the commercial invoice and locate the shipper's name, importer's name, product type, product value, its weight, and a range of other information pertinent to transcending national borders. Each product that is brought into the United States gets assigned a tariff number found in a 99-chapter book. Bonilla says, "We present the documents to Customs and FDA. That information gets transmitted via computer to Washington. It runs through Customs and FDA edits. And then the response comes back through the local customs office in Philadelphia or New York, or another FDA office. Those results determine whether Customs or FDA wants to look at the product."

Information and communication technology is becoming part of the collective process of exchange and mobility for perishable goods. When I visit the Port of Wilmington in Delaware, I stand on the port deck in the shadows of a giant refrigerated cargo ship—a "reefer ship." Along with John Haroldson, the port's manager of international trade, I watch as longshore-man unload pallets of grapes and stone fruit originating from the Chilean ports of Valparaiso, Coquimbo, and Caldera.

Haroldson explains that reefer ships carry four to five decks filled with 7,000 to 8,000 pallets, which is approximately 14 to 16 million pounds of fruit. As with most ships from Chile, the product is sent in "break bulk" decks, which are distinct from shipping containers used with most other kinds of international trade. When growing and shipping companies spon-sor an entire shipload of product, they stack wooden pallets filled with cardboard boxes of fruit directly into the ship's holds, which maximizes space and refrigeration energy use. Each deck on the ship is set to a specified temperature to match the product held in that deck. At the port of origin, shippers stack boxes of fruit on pallets and they "pre-sling" them, that is, they wrap rope-like chains around the pallets in order to anticipate rapid movements of materials out of the ships into refrigerated warehouses or onto refrigerated trucks once they arrive in the United States. (See fig. 26.)

These sociotechnical features are set up for timing interdependent mo-bility and exchange across locations and platforms. Haroldson and I watch the ongoing coordination of movements between the ship, information management, and the next handling stage. Laborers open the central hatch in the middle of the ship's top deck and begin unloading. Operators of large cranes mechanically insert hooks into the slings, pulling the pallets out of the center and onto land. To reach the pallets in the narrow lengthwise wings of the ship, cranes hoist forklifts into the central hatch, where driv-ers then move the pallets from the wings to the center, enabling the cranes to pull them out onto land. They move through the same process for each deck. Forklift operators scan the pallets as they proceed, recording informa-tion about the transition from the ship to the next organizational stage, simultaneously integrating information, physical commodities, and distinct

26 Break bulk vessel at Tioga Marine Terminal in Philadelphia unloading South American fruit, June 2007. Photograph credit: Philadelphia Regional Port Authority.

organizational platforms with their own software, tracking equipment, and techniques of storage management and distribution.

Timing is crucial, because the qualities of perishable objects are always changing. The infrastructure linking mobility, quality, and economic value exists as another sociotechnical recipe of worked-out steps. The technical coordination around fumigation sheds light on how organizational actors turn a chain of events into a routine operation. The USDA requires some products, such as Chilean grapes, one of the highest-selling imported fruit commodities, to be fumigated before they enter the United States market. Fumigation guarantees that microscopic organisms foreign to United States soil do not contaminate agricultural production. The process is not just about spraying products with chemicals. It involves a series of carefully worked-out steps built into the routine distribution apparatus.

Haroldson walks me through the port's 150,000-square-foot fumigation warehouse and describes the temporal coordination between shipping and fumigation. He says, "Normally grapes are held at 32 degrees. The problem is you've got to fumigate them tonight to get them out the door tomorrow, but the fumigant doesn't work unless the grapes are 40 degrees. In the ship, you've got all this packaging around huge amounts of product, and you've got 32 degrees in the middle of the ship. In a couple hours, you need the grapes at 40 degrees or you're screwed because it doesn't get fumigated that night because the temperature isn't right. Now you're losing a whole day."

The technical complexity surrounding temperature, movement, and product materiality has to be accurately managed to sustain the fluid relationships of the supply system. The ship's crew gradually raises the temperature while out at sea. They do it slowly. As Haroldson says, "You don't want to shock it." When the grapes arrive at the port, they are primed at 40 degrees. Then the company hired to conduct the fumigation at the Port of Wilmington works in conjunction with USDA agents and shippers, receivers, longshoreman, stevedores, and other port operators to prepare the fumigation warehouse for the specifics of the product. Arlene Stametz is an executive of a port fumigation company. She says, "Ports need fumigation capacity just to be competitive. They can't be involved in international trade and even in certain domestic trade, unless they can get commodities treated, which is why historically, they've allowed fumigation on port property. It was a good way to get customers." She says, "It's a huge logistical exercise, every single time."

The fumigation company is given a schedule of all the ships leaving Chile that is updated via the internet. It lets them know at what port the ship will dock. For Delaware River ports, it might be the Port of Wilmington, the Holt Terminal in Gloucester, New Jersey, or the Tioga port in North Philadelphia. Stametz says that fumigation companies receive constant updates, but the most important update comes when ships pass through the Panama Canal. The timing between the canal and the final destination becomes more accurate. To prepare, the company is given an electronic manifest of every single ship, so that it can pinpoint the exact location of the product in transit. The fumigation team works with the receivers to start figuring out where they are going to put the product in the warehouse. She says, "The warehouse has lanes painted on the floor with numbers, because every pallet carries a barcode and it gets scanned as it comes in the door. They say, 'This goes in lane such and such.'"

Depending on the progress of the ship, the fumigation company prepares the warehouse for different volumes and varieties of products. When the ship arrives, forklift operators unloading the ship quickly set up stacks of pallets. They install a large metal framing device around the pallets, and a tent is lowered over the frames to cover the stacks. Before they apply the chemical vapor, methyl bromide, they install a ventilation system to quickly remove the chemical fumigant from the air due to its toxic effects. Once the fumigation is completed, warehouse operators use a rapid cooling system through which high fan rates propel chilled air into the stacked pallets and return the bulk of material to its optimal preservation temperature of 32 degrees. Laborers then disassemble the arrangement with forklifts. They flash the bar codes on pallets to maintain information tracking and move the product to the next organizational platform. They load materials onto refrigerated trucks or into nearby refrigerated storage warehouses at the port, depending on previous agreements.

Timing the integration is important, given the contingent dynamics of the market system. Not everything is sold when it arrives into the port. Samuel Montross, a shipping consultant, says, "When we pack [in the country of origin] do we know if it is sold? No. Maybe when it arrives. We're unloading a ship now. Some is sold, some not." As a result, companies that own and market the products often draw upon the expertise of cold storage facilities.

Rob Simms, the cold storage operator, handles fresh fruits and vegetables from all over the world for major retail chains. He manages "less than trailer load lots," that is, "LTL lots." It requires configuring the inbound product arrivals with the outbound deliveries. He describes this ongoing practical accomplishment as "a daily transactional business." In the morning, when Simms arrives, he knows only about 20 percent of the product in his warehouse that is going to move out that day. "The phone starts ringing in the morning and the information starts flowing. We start making the calls, start moving trucks. We'll say, 'You go to Holt Pier [in Gloucester, New Jersey] and pick up six pallets.' And while you're there, we might get another call and have you pick up two more pallets. And then we will have a truck going out to Wilmington's port."

The process is always contingent on managing the information coming in to assemble the truckloads. As the trucks arrive at the cold storage facility, Simms's team has to figure where all of the products go next. They make lists from compiled electronic data records that allow them to know the next step. He says, "This truck might have stuff going to Boston on it. Another might have stuff going to Florida on it. They come back and then we already know when we unload it where it's going. They are all barcoded. We have compiled all the information and we stage everything in certain slots. As soon as [a truck] unloads, he might be the truck going to Florida. Then all the other guys that had little bits and pieces for Florida, their stuff gets reloaded on his truck and then off he goes."

Firms have to manage unsold items and distribute purchased items. Operations managers work with their teams to configure storage systems in pursuit of sequences that offset the contingent conditions and preserve commodity value. It is an important component of just-in-time freshness for preparing, organizing, and sustaining the qualities of perishable objects.

Just-in-Time Freshness

In 1939, the USDA developed its Agricultural Marketing Services. One central aim was to create certified commodity grades to facilitate fair and efficient marketing of agricultural products.[44] Although these grades reflected particular quality attributes, they were also meant to serve as practical guidelines. A USDA Marketing Services report, written in the 1970s, asserted that the standards "are meant to be used." Developing and revising standards required expertise in the variability of material qualities, because specialists had to know the range of qualities of each object as it relates to the most common characteristics of the total supply. The report stated, "It would hardly be practical to set standards for the top grade of any product so high that they would represent an ideal rather than an actuality." The goal was to use the standards in real situations in which the "grader must judge the product, weighing in his mind how it compares with the standards."[45]

There are grades for hundreds of agricultural commodities, including a wide range of fruits and vegetables. For example, the common supermarket product "US No. 1 greenhouse tomatoes" must "consist of similar varietal characteristics which are mature but not overripe or soft, clean, fairly well formed; which are free from decay, sunscald, and freezing injury, and free from damage caused by bruises, cuts, shriveling, puffiness, catfaces [cavities on the blossom end], growth cracks, scars, disease, insects, moldy stems, skin checks, or other means."[46] Each commodity standard allows for specified size, color, and defect tolerances, up to a certain percentage.

The standards create relational criteria through which industry actors interpret quality across contexts. Evaluators must manage the unique tension between the qualities of the particular objects in front of them and characteristics of the total supply. In the perishable industries, the properties of objects are changing over time, but large retailing companies want everything to look similar. The primary goal of this top grade—Grade 1 supermarket quality—is to reproduce just-in-time freshness in terms of the conventional look and feel of the objects.

For one, quality inspections are built into commodity circulation alongside the technical information and communication arrangements to minimize deviations from the supermarket standard. Evan Kramer, a vice president of a multinational growing and shipping corporation, says, "Quality inspections happen throughout the production, packaging, and distribution

27 A checker inspecting and registering pallets of clementines.
Photograph credit: Philadelphia Regional Port Authority.

chain. You have various quality inspections happening in the field to establish whether the product is progressing normally. You have inspections happening at the reception of the product from the field into the packinghouse, where you identify if there are any products that do not meet your specifications, at which point you determine whether it will be packed at all. And then upon arrival you have another inspection to ensure that they meet all the standards and the quality was maintained during transport. And upon arrival at the distribution center again you would have another level of inspection." (See fig. 27.)

Quality evaluation is so central to the fresh produce system that the USDA, along with the lead trade association, United Fresh, sponsors hands-on training courses. Companies can have their employees learn practical handling competencies to determine the relationship between object characteristics and standard information. Each retail company has field buyers, nicknamed "bird dogs," placed at points of transference to put this object quality expertise into practice, touching and observing samples of bulk commodities and evaluating their conditions. An invisible process maintains the visible aesthetics of the high quantity of decomposing objects.

Dave Rogers says that when he was a buyer for a national supermarket corporation, he had people in Salinas, California, watching over the vegetables and the strawberries; in Fresno, California, managing the citrus; in Yakima, Washington, keeping tabs on the apples; and down in Florida for the range of products grown there. The company also had import offices that would take care of grapes, bananas, and imported citrus. He says, "They were bird-dogging the fruit, getting eyes on it. And I would call them, and say, 'Okay, what are you seeing?'" Long distance does not eliminate the importance of building trust in markets. He says that digital photography now bolsters trust levels in long-distance exchange dynamics. "A quick snap, and we can see what was harvested today and we know what to expect."

Technical controls diminish the amount of time humans spend handling the materials. Maintaining the cold chain throughout circulation keeps distinct objects at optimal preservation temperatures and stalls decomposition. Most shipping companies now maintain the cold chain from the point of packaging the product in Chile, Peru, Brazil, or California all the way to New Jersey or Pennsylvania cold storage facilities and even to the supermarkets themselves. They can track the cold chain through digital thermometers that automatically record temperature information in transit so exchange partners can monitor temperature stability. Because certain products require particular conditions for maximal preservation, trading partners use the temperature readings to confirm that each part of the supply chain meets its responsibilities before exchanging materials.

Different storage and distribution companies have installed "temperature zones" in their facilities. Louis Myers, a sales director of Green Market, a produce wholesaler in a small agricultural town in Pennsylvania, walks me through the refrigerated warehouse. We weave in and out of temperature-controlled rooms and experience instantly changing climate conditions in adjacent spaces. We feel the temperature decrease from 50 degrees in the main receiving warehouse to 33 degrees as we enter the "wet room," where boxes of vegetables are packed with ice. Cardboard boxes are stacked on metal shelving units in aisles.

Myers opens a box of brussels sprouts packed tight with crushed ice, slowly dripping from the bottom. He explains, "It takes specialized knowledge, specialized resources. You need to have storage that's at the right temperature, the right humidity. You need to have the equipment to store it, to transport it, and good connections with the growers. In this room [the wet room], we have sprayers [automatically] spraying a disinfectant across the open doorway [between different temperature-controlled rooms] every five minutes. When the forklifts roll through they spread the disinfectant so we don't have bacteria growing on the floor."

On some occasions, the shipping company recognizes that the product is losing its grade, and they call upon service agents to bring commodities back to standard. This process prolongs the time that the product holds market value. For example, asparagus may come into the Northeast wilted, unsellable in large retail markets in its current condition. Rob Simms, the cold storage operator, has machinery that returns it to mass-market quality.

In a spacious refrigerated room, hundreds of asparagus boxes are stacked on pallets. Simms yells over the booming drone of high-powered fans, "Here we have asparagus and we are pre-cooling it." The product came by airfreight and, he explains, there is not good refrigeration on airplanes. "It came in a little warm and we're trying to bring it down to 34 degrees as quickly as possible to increase the shelf life. What we are doing is pulling air in." He points to a high-powered fan, and says, "If you put your hand up in there [I put my hand between the boxes], you'll feel air going through the boxes." The fans propel the cool air through the bottom of the pallets and boxes, which pushes out the heat and decreases the temperature.

These techniques stall the aging process and extend time and value. Other techniques encourage aging to meet the specifications of the next business platform. Bananas, tomatoes, avocados, mangoes, and a range of other fruits pass through a mechanical ripening process to integrate trading partners' expectations. Major growing and shipping companies like Dole, Del Monte, and Chiquita have ripening facilities at their ports of entry. Multistory airtight rooms in their vast warehouses hold hundreds of pallets (i.e., thousands of boxes) of bananas at a time.

Many retail distribution centers and wholesalers also have ripening facilities. Myers, the wholesale sales director, describes the coordination of qualities. He says that containers of bananas come to the warehouse in a solid green state—they are hard and starchy, more like a potato. Without triggering the ripening process, they would take weeks to ripen to a "full colored banana." It involves a controlled process of introducing warmth and ethylene gas, the same gas the fruit emits upon ripening. He points to a little box [a small gray container] that sprays a slight mist of ethylene into the air, in the enclosed ripening room. That starts turning the starches into sugars. The ripening process lasts between four and six days to bring it to the right color, but once the ripening starts, it cannot be stopped. He explains, "We sell them in different stages of color. Some stores prefer to get them greener than yellow and keep them in their back rooms and put them out as needed.

Others want them daily and want it more yellow than green." Supermarkets, for instance, might demand greener bananas, so they can stay on the shelves longer, whereas a café or coffee shop selling bananas on the same day as the arrival to the shop, may want them ready for their customers to eat.

Technicians manage the process. They place a thermometer, connected to a computer system, into the center of the banana boxes that informs the computer how warm the bananas are getting. The ripening builds up heat. Myers explains that if they leave them in this room with no air rotation, "the bananas in the middle of this palate would go from green to yellow to black, and if left unchecked, they could start a fire." The ripening rooms incorporate columns that circulate air, which allows them to "switch the rotation so that we're getting an even ripening process throughout the box." He says, "If the inside of this palate gets up to 65 degrees, we may cool the room down to 54 degrees to slow the ripening process. If we're really short on a color, we may warm the room up to 62 degrees to get things going faster. It's a constant balance to ripen them. More orders this week, we ripen faster; less orders, we keep it low."

The stabilization of qualities across platforms requires anticipating objects' transformation. Some objects, like bananas, are easier to manage because of the balance between their physical properties and sophisticated technical controls. The various fruit and vegetable industries have increasingly implemented packaging as another tool to control the perception of bulk supplies as equivalent mass-consumer products, much like buying a carton of eggs. It creates the appearance of product uniformity and limits consumer handling. Many fruit and vegetable products have packaged alternatives: lettuce, carrots, clementines, oranges, grapefruits, apples, potatoes, avocados, lemons, peppers, berries, cherries, and grapes.

Still, many fruits and vegetables are shipped in bulk supply because of their rapid rate of decomposition. Once they arrive in the marketing region, they are then processed and packaged. Packing and repacking services eliminate rotting objects from bulk circulation and put the remaining supply back together as comparable commodities. Simms shows me the high-tech machines to circulate bulk materials. Employees are trained to work alongside the machines and quickly interpret defects and pull them out. Some of the machines automatically package remaining materials by weight, creating uniform packed products for major retail chains. Walking through the sorting room, Simms describes one machine running cherries over lengthy conveyor belts. The machine electronically sorts them, by taking out the ones with decay, cuts, or splits, as another machine weighs them in little buckets and fills up plastic containers.

This qualification process gets integrated into the information systems as a first in/first out operation at every stage of distribution. Kevin Ainsworth is the logistics manager of a South American based fruit and vegetable growing and shipping corporation. He discusses how the traceability technologies are integrated into a routine sequence of steps. He says, "We take that traceability, which is a raw data file, and we set up our inventory system so that we can track which order, which product should be shipped out to which customer. And once those orders are completed and loaded onto the truck at the warehouse that same documentation is used to trigger our billing process. It also lets you know exactly which pallets were put on which truck. Our forklifts now have computers on them so people scan the cargo as they move it and give you a real live update on where it's being stored and where it's going."

When supermarket distribution centers receive the product, they work with corporate procurement executives and retail produce managers to arrange the next movements to retail stores, such as supermarkets and big box stores. Bill Regan is the operations manager at a supermarket distribution center that fills orders for chains throughout the northeast, in Boston, Philadelphia, Washington, DC, and Baltimore. He says there are built-in check points so that the selector is getting the right product for the customer. It is a process through which the computer tells the human what to do. "The selector has a headset that he wears, and the computer dumps the order in there and tells him where to go and how many cases to select out of a particular pick spot [in the warehouse]."

The enterprise is about efficiency but through a specific lens: matching products and qualities to the next stage. Regan says that the arrivals are computer dated and put into a rotation. "The computer system knows the order. If we still have lettuce in the building, it knows that the lettuce that just came in goes into the reserve location. If we didn't have any more lettuce, it would say to rotate the new product in there." The sociotechnical integration configures information and physical infrastructures as an ongoing timing of high-volume mobility. With each organization setting up a routine series of steps as a technical recipe, the system manages the contingencies to configure the qualities and maintain the high-volume supply.

Reassembling the Produce Aisle

The fresh distribution system synchronizes the qualities of high-volume, high-variety products across trading contexts. Maintaining the standard qualities of decomposing objects for a mass-merchandising system presents unique

distribution problems. Material standardization poses an ontological problem. Trading partners have to agree, not only on the prices of things, but
also on whether the objects themselves—the millions of individual units—
meet the agreed upon physical attributes in order to maintain the fluidity of
reassembling the produce aisle.[47]

The produce aisle has dramatically changed since the origins of the supermarket. It has integrated increasingly more fruits and vegetables into
year-round supplies. Defeating seasons was an accumulation of "invisible
science": multiple experimental projects, hidden from plain view, crystallized into routine technical methods and everyday consumer expectations.[48]
What this chapter has shown is that those trained to work in the supply system have developed distinct knowledge competencies alongside the complex technology. This kind of "infrastructural work" is a process of managing contingency that makes the supply chain a constant object of inquiry in
order to reassert the standard qualities.[49]

Away from the eyes of the consumer, market actors reduce the possibility
that consumers will see objects that look different. This reification project
pushes the agricultural, horticultural, and plant science interests to search
for methods that improve product consistency—firmer apples, more evenly
sized raspberries, tomatoes that ripen in transit, and storage and packaging
devices that secure the market standards. One result is that, for some commodities, the market system has come to value the aesthetic look and texture over flavor profiles. Discerning consumers express dismay over the loss
of subtle flavor notes in the plastic-like qualities of supermarket tomatoes
and sugar-like attributes of apples.

Criticisms aside, the supermarket produce aisle is remarkable: a conventional market system of fresh fruits and vegetables arrives from geographic
points of production all over the world into a standard produce aisle without seasons. It has made more fruits and vegetables available to more people than ever before in human history. The mass-merchandising system promotes extreme uniformity among fragile and decomposing objects to keep
the system moving. However, what happens to the fruits and vegetables that
do not make it into this merchandising model? The next chapter turns to
that very issue: the cracks in the system. It is out of the interstices where
exceptions, accidents, avant-garde, and altogether "nonstandard" objects
emerge as precursors to shifting distribution relationships.

SIX

Cracks in the System

Lean supply chains are set up to eliminate product variability and waste. Yet an astounding 40 percent of fruits and vegetables is wasted every year, and more than half of that amount is lost prior to home consumption.[1] Perishable foods, and fresh fruits and vegetables in particular, pose a unique challenge. Quality standardization reduces ambiguities in exchange relationships, but it does not eliminate objects with alternative properties.[2]

Some variability cannot be controlled: "weird" looking carrots, bananas ripening too early in the supply chain, or crates of sweet potatoes at a small farm unable to meet the supermarket size and packaging standards. Actors at all stages of circulation, from packing sheds to cold storage warehouses to shipping ports to supermarket aisles, manage and maintain the boundaries of market acceptability. They also try to reposition and repurpose deviating objects in order to squeeze out economic value, offset financial losses, and reduce waste. Deviations from the standard generate cracks in the system out of which new distribution interdependencies form. Wholesale operations, produce auctions, street vendors, food banks, and farmers' markets carve out local and specialized networks.

Objects traverse the chain of production, storage, distribution, and consumption—it is all part of the "biography of things."[3] The evaluations of object qualities are embedded into distinct types of interaction dynamics and exchange settings. Webb Keane labels the temporal and spatial staging of qualities as "bundling." He argues that the "qualities bundled together in any object will shift in their relative salience, value, utility, and relevance across contexts." According to Keane, "habits and intuitions" then become rooted into each setting's distinct exchange dynamics.[4]

Cracks in the system occur when decision-makers are faced with multiple interpretations of the qualities of the products.[5] The semiotic bundles do not always hold together in coherent ways. As a result, market actors seek out different kinds of exchange sequences. Unlike in the mass-merchandising system, these alternative exchange relations are not constrained by political regulations, industry standards, and legal obligations of previously contracted quantities, qualities, and prices. Instead, these distribution sequences are dependent on actors' intricate knowledge of the range of opportunities available in the local environment. These exchange dynamics are, in Clifford Geertz's terms, "grooved channels" that routinize interaction expectations among exchange partners negotiating the particular values of the physical products in front of them.[6] Actors in each evaluation context adjudicate between the available qualities of objects in order to fit them into downstream relationships until they dissolve the potential value and utility.

It has become conventional wisdom in the social sciences that food tastes are markers of class and status—a system of conspicuous consumption and distinction. Social scientists expect consumers in their everyday lives to make moral, health, and status judgments about cuisines (Japanese versus Italian), brands and markets (Whole Foods versus Wal-Mart), or even pesticide use (organic versus conventional). But behind the scenes, there is a great deal of overlooked infrastructural work to match the qualities of physical objects to differently valued consumers. Attention to the emerging cracks in the system—how alternative exchange possibilities are assembled and managed—demonstrates how the valuation of foods and the grooved distribution interdependencies reinforce a system of consumer distinctions.

Disrupting the Boundaries of Acceptability

Managing the boundaries of market acceptability is not about exact specifications. It is about negotiating the relationship between the particular material objects being exchanged and knowledge of the total supply variability. One of the jobs of the USDA Marketing Services under the Perishable Agricultural Commodity Act is to maintain the market's grading standards. The USDA grades (e.g., Grade 1, Grade 2) refer to the industry's agreed upon information and language about the qualities and conditions of commodities.

Fruit and vegetable types—from apples to zucchini—are integrated into the USDA grading framework. Industry interest groups can turn "new" objects into mass-merchandising commodities by establishing an information record of the range of qualities and conditions that the commodities should have when market actors assess them. Market actors, including USDA field agents, become educated in the expected properties, as well as their common variations and defects, that enable exchange partners to assess economic value.

According to the USDA Marketing Services, "quality defects" of perishable objects refer to characteristics that deviate from market conventions but do not change over time. These can include scars on an object's skin, a unique or unfamiliar shape that breaks from product uniformity, or simply the size of the object. When I visited one of the Delaware River shipping ports, Leonard Marcos, a shipping executive, took me on a tour through a refrigerated warehouse. He kept referring to "quality" defects as "ugly" defects. He said certain products get shipped with aesthetic problems that do not compromise the taste or texture of the commodity. In contrast, the USDA labels "condition defects" as "progressive" defects that worsen over time in the product itself. A product's firmness, its stage of ripeness, or visible mold or decay are all condition defects that accelerate decomposition.

Both quality and condition matter in carving out market channels. Market actors and USDA officials gain practical competencies through training, observing, and handling objects. Many go through produce industry and USDA training with experts to learn how to fit together the language of classification and the feel and look of the physical objects themselves. The market's reification project turns these decomposing material properties into the essence of expected market things.

Mark Krasner, a USDA field agent in the Philadelphia Produce Wholesale Market in South Philadelphia, discusses how the classification works in practice. He inspects a box of tomatoes at his station. One of his jobs is to understand "how it applies to the situation." Tomatoes, he says, change color as they ripen, which means color is conditional. Shippers must time the color for the marketplace to maintain the agreed upon valuation. He says, "It's like learning a new language. Every commodity has its own common defects. There will be some oddballs along the way, but for the most part it's pretty straightforward. Tomatoes get soft or overripe. They get sunk and discolored areas around them. They get bruised. Sometimes the stems get moldy." Krasner is holding and lightly pressing tomato samples. "I'm not finding much of anything. This is slight discoloration right here, but nothing major."

Each commodity requires its own knowledge bank. Krasner says that in contrast to tomatoes, the color of grapes is not a condition but a quality of the product. Color is a stable characteristic of the fruit itself. "Green grapes do not change into red grapes," he says.[7] In the port warehouse, Marcos and I walk past a table where a USDA agent is evaluating a shipment of green grapes that just arrived from Chile. Boxes of grapes are stacked on a metal table near the entrance of the warehouse. The inspector is standing under bright lights and scrutinizing bunches of them. Marcos pulls a small bunch off the table and hands me a few to eat. "I like them this way," he says. "See these are a bit yellow, the skin is a little soft and translucent. These are the sweet ones."

The product is clearly edible at this stage and the higher sugar composition might even be preferable to some. However, market actors must understand not just the qualities and conditions of the objects at that precise moment in the warehouse, but rather how that stage of ripeness relates to the potential economic valuation in subsequent distribution contexts. Marcos explains that certain scenarios can arise that disrupt the shared valuation system. Refrigeration in a ship may not have worked properly or there could have been mishandling in the packing house. Inspectors receiving the shipment are trained to recognize even the mildest color and texture deviations as characteristics of decomposition and economic devaluation. They label such conditions as defects. They are safe to eat, but they diminish the time remaining for the highest market value.

The mass-merchandising value chain is set up to stabilize USDA Grade 1 products. As we saw in the previous chapter, cold storage warehouses serve as value-added pockets of infrastructural work to neutralize defects. This kind of work is fundamental to the high-volume system, because many retailers—from Wal-Mart and Costco to large supermarket corporations—describe their standards as USDA Grade 1, but they often demand that shippers meet requirements exceeding the standards. According to Krasner, they have the industry influence to negotiate contracts with farmers and shippers that are more stringent in terms of allowable percentages of defects they will accept.

A major twist in understanding how market actors assert the highest market standard is that they must always determine and evaluate the aesthetic fit between the specific products in front of them and the general properties of the available supply at that precise moment in time. Even in managing Grade 1 perishable commodities, the governing standards are not static. As Stefan Timmermans and Steven Epstein put it, the "world of standards" does not produce a "standard world."[8] The process of bridging fruit and vegetable standards to economic values is elastic, because perishable material objects are not widgets. Agricultural production does not present uniform commodities from month to month and year to year.[9]

Despite stringent standards of large retailers, warehouse inspectors are sometimes forced to accept products that deviate from USDA Grade 1 criteria. Exchange partners can come to an agreement that certain defects in the available supply of a product are allowable as part of a temporary relative standard. Temporary specifications allow market actors to readjust "out-of-grade" products in order to keep them on the shelves when the total supply deviates. Dave Meeks is a distribution warehouse manager who handles perishable products for large supermarket chains in the Philadelphia region. He says that all sorts of complications can arise in fresh supply chains. USDA representatives and field buyers then put together a "temporary spec." He explains,

> It will have a dating on it, and we'll know how long we're going to keep it in there. It relaxes some of those defects. They may allow a little bit more bruising and they'll tell us what we're allowed to accept. Instead of 12 percent in the total defects, they may say, for a temporary period, you're allowed 15 percent. And that's what we would look for when we're grading. We relax our own grading to the temporary standard. With that new agreement, we aren't able to say, "Well, it failed out." If they didn't put that in, we'd be kicking everything out at the door. We don't have to accept the change, but the problem is, we wouldn't have any product to sell.

Large growing and shipping corporations are diligent in grading commodities before they ship them. They sort objects into multiple brands in their packing sheds for differently valued buyers. Many of the largest growing and shipping corporations have secondary labels that they use to sell their products with aesthetic differences to discounted markets. Evan Kramer, an executive for a multinational shipping company, says, "If we judge a commodity to be commercial quality but not necessarily our premium market quality, we'd still bring it into the market but we'd sell it to customers who are not necessarily as interested in the premium quality and brand recognition. That doesn't mean that the product is not edible. Sometimes it is just cosmetic defects that detract from branding or force us to brand it as something different. Still the product eats well."

Large growers and shippers of fruits and vegetables select qualities prior to shipping to maintain the essence of the highest quality products for supermarket chains. Consumers might recognize fresh produce brand names like Del Monte, Dole, Chiquita, and Sunkist. But large growers of apples, cucumbers, potatoes, and peppers, whose brands are less visible to consumers, also do comparable grading and valuation work. Yet once the product is out of the growers' and shippers' hands, and into the distribution and storage network, the possibilities of decomposition and loss of value continue. Because perishables are so fragile, the possibilities of declining economic value increase when fresh objects are being moved and handled.

At a distribution warehouse outside of Philadelphia that services various supermarkets in the region, Tom Lambusta, one of the company's sales executives, takes me on a tour through the refrigerated part of the facility. He shows me an area where pallets of fruits and vegetables await inspection before being moved to their proper holding location. He points out pallets of Golden Delicious apples marked with red "blush." Tom says, "It's marked here [on the box]—see Extra Fancy Grade with Blush." He explains that extra fancy means the highest quality, but blush means the apples are not uniformly golden. "Inspectors haven't gotten to it," he says, "but they might open this box and determine that this is not in the spec. Then we could decide not to keep it or ask for a price discount."

Large retailing companies, ambitious in upholding product uniformity, want the specific apples in front of them to be the agreed upon apples that match the essence of the objects that consumers expect. Lambusta says that some retailers might not want Golden Delicious apples with a reddish hue for that reason. However, he points out that the inspectors are less concerned with aesthetic defects related to color than they are with conditional defects that alter the texture, taste, and lifecycle of the product.

Bruising or mold on apples are examples. Lambusta says, "If the apples were dropped hard, it damages the cells and that becomes a bigger and bigger spot as the brown goes deeper." Another example is "bitter pit," in which a specific area of the apple has acidity coming out of it. "That will get worse over time, especially when it leaves this nice and cold 34 degrees and hits room temperature." The inspectors take percentages. "It's a calculated approach to inspecting," he explains.

In some circumstances, the firm's warehouse inspectors call in USDA agents to adjudicate between competing interpretations of the value. USDA marketing agents evaluate products at different settings along the supply chain. Mark Krasner, the USDA representative, says, "When we do inspections, for the most part, we first go over to the applicant who called it. He shows us what needs inspection. We pull our samples, and then they bring them over here to our station. This is the best place for us to work because we have the lighting, the tables, and everything."

The USDA representatives take 1 percent of the supply, picking out samples from the boxes to review. They are trained to write up reports in the language of the qualities and conditions of the commodity standards and their defects. They do not mandate a market response if the product does not fit the grade. They are not regulatory. They certify the market process as a third-party service. Then the exchange partners assess whether the USDA

certification matches the contract or whether the contract now needs rene-
gotiation to take into account a lower valuation. One of the major problems
is that some of the USDA grading standards are confusing. Krasner points to
a box of red peppers and discusses the ambiguity.

> Green peppers must be totally green. Any amount of another color is scored
> as a conditional defect. The confusion comes with red peppers, yellow pep-
> pers, orange peppers, or purple peppers. Those only have to have *any* amount
> of red, purple, orange, or yellow to be considered that color. Picture being
> a guy receiving those. "I bought yellow peppers." They open them up and
> 50 percent of the surface is green. "These aren't yellow peppers." But there's
> no defects here. The only thing I can do [in the inspection] is mention it on
> the other side of the form in the comments section. I can say the peppers have
> 50 percent of the surface green, but it's not affecting grade.

Supermarket corporations and large mass-merchandisers have the economic influence to mandate that shippers provide yellow peppers that are
uniformly yellow or Golden Delicious apples that are uniformly golden.
Some disagreements lead to legal challenges. But most exchange partners
have been working together for years or even decades. They have mutually
reinforcing relationships that require flexibility. This flexibility in quality
and condition assessments maintains the mutual trust needed for future
transactions. They renegotiate the value of the particular lot in order to
maintain the supplies in subsequent days and weeks. Dave Meeks, the distribution warehouse manager, says,

> We go for USDA number one, but not everything comes in that way. Some-
> times we have to get the USDA to come in and inspect it. And they might say,
> "This does not grade USDA number one. This lot grades USDA number two."
> Then that's up to the buyer and the vendor who you're getting it from, which
> can be a farmer or a shipper, to decide whether they will accept it. We might
> accept it as a different grade, but we'd also be looking for a cheaper price on
> that item. We're paying for the grade that we're buying. Let's just say I paid
> $15.00 for that case of grapes, but now it's grading USDA number two. I am
> not going to get charged that same price for a lesser grade.

The produce aisle of a supermarket—despite its late stage of circulation—
incorporates last ditch methods to reassert product value. They install automatic mist sprayers for green leafy vegetables kept under frigid conditions

to sustain color vibrancy and crispness. They carry more and more bagged, packaged, and cellophane-wrapped fruits and vegetables for the convenience of matching brand, quality, volume, and efficiency in restocking.

Every stage entails culling perishable products that no longer fit the standard. Supermarket employees pull out rotting objects throughout the day. They make sure the oldest ones that still fit the market's criteria are in the front or on the top of the display. The last chance for perishable objects in the supermarket produce aisle is to mark them as discounted sale items separated from the bulk supply or to cut up objects with visible defects to see if the inside quality is redeemable. Chris McBride, a produce manager of a supermarket in Philadelphia says,

> Anything that's mush or rotten we have to pull it off right away because that can spread to another piece of fruit. Mold on oranges or limes, lemons, we pull it off. If we can, we'll reduce the product at a half-price discount. We can cut it in half, rewrap it [in cellophane] and price it, and it sells really well. Now people can see what they're getting, as opposed to looking at the outside of it. "Oh, this cantaloupe is really bruised, but the inside isn't bruised." We wrap it and label it.

Long-standing produce wholesalers in the Philadelphia terminal market remember the old days when they were the primary middlemen for local supermarkets. Mike Amato, the Philadelphia wholesaler, recalls one of his first jobs was to wipe off mold in the backstage before shipping it off to retailers. Today, the people working in the backstage of the supermarket system no longer take the time to manage conditional defects on each object. If products start to grow mold before arriving at the supermarket, the warehouse handlers pull them from the supply and throw them into the dump pile out of fear that the mold will spread. Maintaining every single object is no longer deemed efficient by the mass-merchandising value system.

Mold and rot are significant conditional defects for a mass-market supply, but they are not the only reasons for market rejections. Large retailers reject portions of the supply, or even the total supply, after inspecting commodities upon arrival. The low tolerance of large corporations for product deviations opens up alternative distribution channels. The shippers and suppliers have no economic incentive to truck rejected perishable commodities back to the sources of production, for example from Philadelphia back to California. Instead, suppliers develop "grooved channels" in the local environment.

In such cases, they turn indeterminate qualities and values into another exchange dynamic unto itself. Jim Marino, a wholesaler in the Philadelphia

Wholesale Produce Market, says, "A lot of the rejected stuff comes here." The wholesale terminals are primary means through which local grooved channels are constructed, because they incorporate multiple layers of economic exchange at the same time. The previous chapter showed that many wholesalers take on responsibilities related to supermarket "fill-in." But many of the small businesses are also adept at managing local networks. The Philadelphia market has more than 20 produce businesses with different specialties and scales of operation.

Marino discusses the process of taking on rejected fresh produce, in which shippers sold the product to large retailing companies that no longer wanted them. He says in one example, a shipper sent a truck to Wal-Mart's warehouse with romaine lettuce that had 3 hearts in a bag and 12 bags in a box. There was no weight on the product, but Wal-Mart rejected them because the warehouse inspectors said the product was too light. "They sell them to us for a lot less money because it was a rejection. Wal-Mart washed their hands of it, and the grower, he's stuck, because he has to pay for the truck." He explains that a lot of the rejections that come to the wholesale terminal are perfectly edible. He says, "We had broccoli come in wrapped in cellophane. The stalk of the broccoli ripped through the plastic. The supermarket rejected it. They wanted three-inch stems and these were longer. Nothing wrong with the broccoli. 'Well, it's not our specifications.' We took it and sold it on a commission."

Taking on rejected produce is not always as simple as taking a commission and moving it to the next stage. It requires another round of assessment to learn where the product has been, who has handled it, and what potential economic value remains. Dan Ricci, another wholesaler in the terminal market, explains that not all rejections are created equal. Wholesalers inspect whether the product is good enough to move, because it will cost them to dump products that never make it into subsequent exchange relationships. "If it comes in and it's not looking good, you're like, 'I don't want this because I've got to pay to dump it.' Unless you make a deal with the shipper. He might say, 'Just take it, I'll pay the dump bill,' and you charge him for the dump bill if you can't get rid of it. He's got to get it off the truck because he needs that truck empty for his next shipment."

Customers come to the terminal produce market at all hours of the day. Different kinds of business owners and brokers arrive very early in the morning to compare the range of available products and qualities across the 20-plus wholesale storefronts. The customers choose boxes of products that fit the specifics of their businesses throughout Philadelphia and the surrounding region. The early morning market hours are the most hectic. In the back stage of this nearly 700,000-square-foot refrigerated warehouse, ship-ments are being unloaded from tractor-trailer trucks by forklifts that move them to storage locations. In the front stage, small crowds of business own-ers, brokers, and salesmen haggle over prices. Customers push handcarts piled with cardboard boxes of produce down designated footpaths from the stores to their cars, vans, and trucks in the parking lot.

Some of the wholesale businesses are well versed at matching indetermi-nate qualities with different kinds of small businesses, from family grocers to small restaurants to street vendors to green grocers handling out-of-grade commodities at discounted prices. Anthony Esposito, a salesman for one of the wholesale businesses, describes the exchange dynamic as "box by box." This channel is not the high-volume contracted truckload of agreed upon qualities and conditions. Exchange partners negotiate the value and price point on the spot. Anthony says,

> A lot of things bounce from place to place and end up here, because there are any number of cheaper types of businesses that buy their stuff here. It might be the mom and pop fruit store or a restaurant that is going to cut it up any-way, or a lot of the Asian restaurants and Korean fruit and vegetable grocers. Most of that kind of business is people picking up small orders—two boxes of this or three boxes of that.

Brokers do a lot of the buying for small businesses. They represent a variety of family operations, many of them too small to visit the whole-sale market themselves on a regular basis. Several factors determine brokers' purchasing decisions: the availability and quality of the specific products in front of them, the range and prices of products available at each of the wholesale businesses, and their anticipation of what kinds of qualities of objects their downstream customers might want.

Wholesalers and brokers describe the negotiations between them as a "friendly battle." One broker, Al Murphy, says, "Our job is to buy the stuff as cheap as we can, and their job is to sell the stuff for as high as they can." A major part of what brokers do is assess the supply and predict the remain-ing downstream value. Murphy says, "It's not a good value unless you can calculate what you're going to get out of it and if it's going to sell or not." He describes a specific purchase he recently made as an example:

> I bought ripe pears for $10.00 a box. Generally speaking, the market is like $26.00. They're already ripe, but they still eat well. They weren't *too* ripe that they would melt on the counter or if you took them home they'd be bad in

two days. I gave them to two customers for $10.00 [per box]. Most pears are $0.99 cents or $1.29 [per pound]. One of my guys put them out for $0.59, the other put them out for $0.39. It's not a bad quality but you have to move it quickly. Once the bruising starts, people won't pick them anymore, and now you're losing money if there's too much shrink in the box and they're throwing five pounds away.

Not every business needs the same qualities. Eddie Biasi, a broker who regularly visits the wholesale market, describes this dynamic.

We come down with a truck with the intention of buying whatever we can. If we find cheap grapes, we buy a pallet of grapes. If it's potatoes, we get potatoes. While we're down here, we're on the phone with our customers. I'll say, "I can buy this for this [amount]." And we have regular customers in mind, but we may not know what item it's going to be until we get here. The number twos aren't as nice looking, but not everyone needs number ones. We have a Greek customer who owns a diner. He's making home fries. He doesn't need to cut up fancy potatoes.

Some buyers will come in a little bit later in the morning, after the rush, to see what is left and if there are any deals. These buyers often represent discount markets or they own a produce truck that distributes lower-valued goods to lower-income neighborhoods in the city. Dan Ricci, the wholesaler, says, "Some of these guys come down from poorer areas that can use the stuff for $4.00 a box, $5.00 a box. There's nothing wrong with it. The people that shop at Whole Foods and Wegman's [a large private supermarket chain, mostly in the Mid-Atlantic region], they don't want to see a speck of anything on their stuff. Not everybody can afford to eat $3.99 a pound grapes. They can only afford 99 cents a pound grapes. People are buying with their eyes. They want to see what they're paying for and it might not be as good—the grapes might be soft or there's a mix [of qualities]. But there's product for everybody here, from the best to the less."

One of the common grooved channels is between wholesalers and street vendors in the Italian Market around 9th Street in South Philadelphia. There, fruit and vegetable vendors line the streets and sell fresh produce to local customers every day. The Italian Market itself has an open-air niche that makes it a unique consumer space in the city. The street is lined with vending stalls, produce stands, cheese shops, butchers, and restaurants and cafes. Some of the street vendors will purchase the lower-valued merchandise from the wholesalers. Steve Stein, one of the wholesale salesmen at

28 Discount produce market in North Philadelphia neighborhood. Photograph by author.

the terminal market, says, "A lot of the Italian Market, you go in there you don't touch any produce. I mean lettuce, they throw it in the bag for you. You don't pick and choose. A lot of the discount markets work like that. You can't pick up the fruit and inspect each piece. You get a prepackaged cellophane bag with eight apples for $2.50. And the quality might be mixed, but that's the deal." (See fig. 28.)

Richie, a produce vendor in the Italian Market, comes to the wholesale terminal looking for a variety of qualities. He says he has regular customers who anticipate the lower-quality goods. "We get something with a blemish on it or a crack or something dried out or wilted, and we'll just wrap it up, put a sticker with a low price on it. It's discounted. We'll have people coming at 9:00 a.m. every single day and if we put it out right in front of the sidewalk, they go right to that spot first. They come to me, 'Do you have any more of those soft tomatoes?' or 'Do you have any old peppers that you want to get rid of?'"

Organizational actors "bundle" material qualities for different stages of valuation.[10] It is a branching process, such that previous transaction situations have lingering effects. The institutionalized distribution network for managing indeterminacy reinforces the hierarchy for reframing the value of objects over time as part of distinct exchange contexts: from packing sheds to distribution warehouses to retail locations to wholesale terminals to brokers to those looking to offer reduced prices at their produce trucks, street carts, and other discounted green grocers. Some fresh produce never provides economic returns. The nonprofit food recovery system has developed a distinct but interdependent institutional structure of procurement and distribution with its own grooved channels.

Linking Indeterminate Qualities to Food Insecurity

Multiple food insecurity programs are supported by federal and state agencies: the Supplemental Nutritional Assistance Program (SNAP), the State Food Purchase Program, and the Emergency Food Assistance Program. These are not simply public programs. They are interwoven with the pervasive logic and infrastructure of the market. They filter federal and state resources through the tools, techniques, organizations, and institutions of the market. SNAP, for example, distributes state funds through Electronic Benefit Transfer cards, which individuals can then use like debit cards at the supermarket.

Food recovery programs, an integral part of the food insecurity solution, are also entrenched in the market-based infrastructure. Their operations are tied to food industry supply chains, and in particular, objects that exist outside of standards. Food banks and other related recovery and redistribution channels have historically focused on converting market excess into managing food insecurity.[11] As a result, they are forced to respond to changing market institutions and infrastructures; they are dependent on geographic proximity to concentrations of resources that can support the avenues between for-profit and nonprofit realms; and they employ evaluative techniques to channel, on a case-by-case basis, the bundled qualities of goods into "good enough" objects for human consumption.

Janet Poppendieck documents the rise and diffusion of food banking from "shoestring to stability," that is, from local experimental and trial-and-error efforts to complex and reproducible bureaucracies with storage warehouses and hundreds of interlinked agencies. She points out that, even with the diffusion of food banks across the country, the process remained tied to manufacturing mistakes and surplus in packaged food industries. Another avenue of rescuing perishable foods began separately, by tapping into excess and waste in the local environment. Poppendieck shows that both of these organizational avenues grew in number and influence across the country, assisted by various foundations and funding agencies, including the UPS Foundation that supported logistical and distribution-related projects.[12]

Throughout the 1990s, private firms improved their proficiency in handling dry goods and canned and packaged products with longer shelf lives. My interviews with people working in the nonprofit food sectors uncovered that, in the 20 years since Poppendieck's influential research, the market logic of pursuing efficiency has become even more constraining. Lean supply chains and improved logistical forecasting among manufacturing companies have exacerbated the challenges for nonprofit food recovery and distribution programs. In turn, they have pushed the food banking and perishable food recovery organizations closer together into shared responsibilities for managing emerging cracks in the standard system.

These two avenues of food recovery developed independent of each other, with distinct national organizational networks, but they merged in 2000. Today, the national network of food banks, Feeding America, promotes fundraising campaigns, sponsors food insecurity conferences, advocates for federal policy on behalf of hunger relief, and conducts studies to improve nonprofit efficiencies. The central organization also manages connections with large private donors, including retail companies like Wal-Mart and Kroger, as well as national and global growers and shippers. More than 200 local food banks, with at least one in every state, participate in the national network system through Feeding America.[13]

Nick Blawat, senior vice president of Feeding America at the time of our interview, says that the spread of food banking was largely an outgrowth of interdependencies between food banks and the Grocery Manufacturing Association, who had "mountains of waste and nothing to do with it." He describes the history of food banking as a "passive" endeavor, focused on procuring and storing shelf-stable excess. The mutual benefits between the for-profit and nonprofit sectors facilitated recurring relationships.

The availability of manufactured products has substantially declined, however. Blawat says, "Lean enterprise initiatives, better forecasting, and more conservative volume growth projections caused most of the manufactured product to drop off a cliff to the tune of a 25 percent drop in one year in the availability of that product." When talking with others in food recovery sectors, they often point to liquidation markets absorbing excess. Flourishing discount chain stores—from Dollar Tree, Dollar General, and Family Dollar to T. J. Maxx, Marshalls, and Big Lots—all stock nonperishable food products. The market opened up profitable spaces to absorb the excess from processed food manufacturers. One outcome was that common donations to food banks like peanut butter, pasta, and canned fruits and vegetables all diminished.

Food banks suffered. The Greater Philadelphia Food Bank was founded in 1981. Over a period of two decades, it extended its operations, receiving surplus nonperishable supplies from the national food bank network, as well as donations from markets and individuals throughout the region. Twenty years later, it faced decreasing donations that led to an operational crisis. Jo Ann Connelly, the president of the now-defunct Greater Philadelphia Food Bank, said in 2001, "We saw certain trends, such as the emergence of 'dollar stores' that are now competing for previously donated items. . . . Combine that impact with the consolidation of supermarkets and manufacturers, many of which are no longer headquartered in this region, and you have a half-empty warehouse." The food bank's 50,000-square-foot distribution center in North Philadelphia was capable of holding four million pounds of nonperishable food, but by 2001, it could no longer fill it to capacity.[14]

Philabundance, the city's fresh food recovery organization, was founded in 1984 by Pam Lawler. Like the Greater Philadelphia Food Bank, over the course of 20 years, the organization expanded its size and expertise. Lawler started the fresh food recovery organization by going around the city in a station wagon and picking up donations from country clubs, co-ops, farmers' markets, hotels, and even the food outlets at the local city zoo. She then brought the food to agencies that distributed it to people in need. Eventually, Philabundance developed greater expertise in logistics, purchased its own refrigerated warehouse, acquired a small refrigerated trucking fleet, and established broader connections to the fresh distribution system in the region.[15]

By 2005, the Greater Philadelphia Food Bank could no longer operate on its own, and it merged with Philabundance. The two Philadelphia-based nonprofit organizations integrated their resources, neighborhood agencies, and information platforms into a shared bureaucracy under the Philabundance banner. Today, like many food banks, Philabundance houses two distribution channels. Most of the dry good staples are procured through fundraising, connections with large retailers through the national Feeding America network, and bulk purchasing, rather than by donations of manufacturing industry "mistakes." The dry goods distribution functions as a more reliable and standard "pick system." Member agencies place an order through a computer network, similar to private industry integration between distribution warehouses and retail sites.

The food bank also has "push programs" that directly distribute fresh produce to individuals and agencies in need. Because fresh produce is perishable, these programs rely on quick-paced turnaround methods to "push out" whatever becomes available. The fresh food recovery and redistribution platforms remain the food bank's primary avenue for managing the cracks in the standard system. Across the country, Feeding America's network of food banks has developed organizational and technical methods to become more interactive and compatible with the fruit and vegetable production and distribution sectors.

When Nick Blawat was at Feeding America, he oversaw supply chain innovations in fresh produce. Feeding America reached its goal of supporting a network distribution of a billion pounds of fruits and vegetables, a number that continues to grow. Blawat says that at every stage of waste, market actors have the financial obligation to get rid of it. The fruit and vegetable industries have long minimized economic losses by using excess to supplement soil nutrition or to supply pig farmers, or if all else failed, by finding the most cost-effective dumping methods.

Dumping is always a last resort for growers, shippers, wholesalers, and retailers alike. Not only does it mean these businesses lose profits, but they also have to pay the added dumping costs.[16] The key for building relationships with growers is to convince them to reconfigure out-of-grade supplies into a distributable format so that food banks can handle the products. Blawat says the national food bank network can intervene at that level with large shippers. He explains that growers are often sitting on "truck load after truck load" of perishable commodities in storage that are not retail quality. The food banks have to convince growers that without a market for those products, there are other avenues that are beneficial to their bottom line and to the public good. The nonprofit sector cannot pay the grower's market rate, but it can offer variable costs. Blawat says,

> We'll pay him his variable cost for packaging and labor to get that product into a distributable format. If that means breaking bulk and packing five-pound bags of apples, great. If that means breaking bulk and getting into 40-pound case packs, great. Whatever it takes for that particular nonprofit to be able to distribute it. We'd rather the professionals do it. They have the materials handy and the efficient process for packing that material. We simply reimburse the variable cost.

Food banks have to learn how to locate excess, build the support infrastructure that can receive it, and maintain the qualities of objects for consumption. Local food banks differ in terms of the qualities and quantities of the objects they can receive and distribute. Most food banks take on what industry insiders refer to as the "hard seven": apples, oranges, potatoes, onions, sweet potatoes, cabbage, and carrots. These commodities have durable qualities that can be maintained in a single refrigerated facility with one temperature zone. Feeding America procures these commodities on a larger scale and can make them available through its auction system. Local food banks bid on them. The national organization also subsidizes transportation costs, especially for food banks in places with limited resources. The national-level organization and fundraising allows food banks in places like Kansas or Nebraska—or even Alaska—to have access to fresh commodities that are more widely available in other regions.

California's food banking system, and the San Francisco-Marin Food Bank in particular, stand out as the gold standard of nonprofit fresh produce procurement and distribution. California's nonprofit food sectors have become highly proficient at working with large-scale growers, capable of turning the high quantity of local fresh produce availability into a second circuit of grooved channels. The San Francisco-Marin Food Bank distributes almost 30 million pounds of fresh produce a year, which includes more than 50 different varieties.[17] To put that into perspective, Philabundance, which is a large operation in one of the nation's largest cities, distributes a total of 24 million pounds of food—and that includes all food and not just fresh produce.

Carving out this channel required learning how to reconfigure California's excess into routine push operations. Gary Maxworthy is the former president of a West Coast food brokerage company called Bromar. In the 1990s, after retiring, Maxworthy started working with the San Francisco Food Bank. He says, at that time, the food bank mostly dealt with "dry, shelf-stable boxes and cans" and they simply "did not have the infrastructure to handle much perishable product." When the availability of dry commodities started to decline, Maxworthy used his expertise to start an organization called Farm to Family to carve out the connections between California's agricultural producers and the state's food banks. He says,

> California grows more than 50 percent of everything in the United States. We searched for partners, but the only way it could work is to do it in a large, professional way. We had a partnership with the food bank in Fresno County, which is the largest produce-producing county in the country. He says, "Gary, I've got this board member who works for a stone fruit packer and he wants to give us a truckload. I can't do it. All I've got is a pickup. Can you help me?" Well, you can't go to a stone fruit packer with a pickup truck when he's got 15 weeks to process his whole years' crop. It's fast action. We had to go down there and see what was there. We did it with 11 different food banks. You need the trucking, the forklifts, and the refrigeration. At that time, none of us could take full trucks, so we shared.

Maxworthy's organization brought different food banks together to handle the bulk excess. San Francisco is the largest city in the region, and also has the region's largest number of people experiencing food insecurity. Being the biggest city in close proximity to the nation's most productive fruit and vegetable region also created new opportunities for the local food bank to adapt. When Maxworthy started working with the San Francisco Food Bank, it had only a small refrigerated space, the size of a small cooler room in the back of a supermarket. Years later, the food bank built a larger refrigerated warehouse with several loading docks, figured out how to accept tractor-trailer loads, and learned to manage different kinds of fruits and vegetables. He says, "These are functions of money and infrastructure. You have to move it quickly, or you're going to have a huge dump bill." When Maxworthy started working with the San Francisco Food Bank, it moved about four million pounds of food a year, but he says, "it was dumping close to a million." Today, he says, "We do more than 30 million and dump less than a million."

California's agricultural ecosystem is so vast and industrious that a great deal of excess remained. Farm to Family and the San Francisco-Marin Food Bank's innovations came from converting new connections into compatible interdependencies. It was what Ash Amin calls a "lively infrastructure" through which local organizations adapted their operations to the environmental conditions.[18] First, Farm to Family established grooved channels between farms and the Bay Area, but then it expanded the networks of distribution throughout the state.

Maxworthy worked with the California Association of Food Banks to increase the amount of out-of-grade product into consumable formats and distribution plans. The organization mirrored the framework of the for-profit sector. He says, "We went statewide, and we got 40 food banks, and hired part-time independent contractors who had produce backgrounds. They were either retired, semiretired, or farmers, and we put them in the Central Valley, another guy in the Imperial County on the Mexican border, Salinas, Ventura, Sacramento." Maxworthy says that as a result of the nonprofit sectors building up their infrastructure throughout the state, they can now distribute more than 100 million pounds of fresh produce a year to people in need.

Farm to Family also explored the possibilities of configuring California's heterogeneous fresh supply into a national program. However, handling diverse fresh fruits and vegetables is much more complex than just focusing on the "hard seven," which is where much of Feeding America's national-level energy and resources were historically aimed. It requires tuning up the compatibility of distribution and reception platforms across geographically distant relationships. Maxworthy explains the difficulties.

The first issue is managing the transportation costs to ship a truck load from California to New York. We're talking $7,000. The second is quality *will* suffer. Feeding America ships a lot in six 100-pound cardboard totes. But we're getting the second grade, so it's not perfect product to begin with and it's more susceptible to rot and damage. One possibility is to subsidize extra cooling. Another is to send it in 40 pound boxes instead of totes. But these are all extra costs. And then you still have to work with each individual food bank with different needs. They need the volunteer support to unpack it and put it into even smaller cardboard boxes. They need forklifts to unload it. Then you have to push it quickly. You have X number of days to move the stuff. In San Francisco, it's all push. A truck comes in the morning and all the produce is gone by the afternoon.

Time is even more dire when objects enter into the nonprofit realm. The products are typically at a later stage of ripening and decomposition. As a result, the local channels provide the most cost-effective possibilities for converting out-of-grade commodities into alternative opportunities for consumption. Most regional supply ecosystems are different than the one found in the Bay Area, however. Philadelphia's surrounding agricultural environment, for instance, does not compare to San Francisco in terms of combined volume and variety of fruits and vegetables available in the region. Yet Philadelphia still maintains a year-round distribution infrastructure. It combines seasonal agricultural industries in New Jersey and Pennsylvania with the Delaware River ports that bring a large quantity of off-season global fresh produce into the United States.

The Philadelphia-based food bank, just like the markets of the Northeast, works hard to defeat seasons. Lisa Hodaei is the senior manager of food acquisitions for Philabundance. She oversees food donations. She says that in the summer the organization works with "growers and repackers" to develop "gleaning programs." For New Jersey peaches, she says, "They have the items that meet their specs and stay on the line for repack. Then they have items that don't quite meet their specs but are still edible. They'll set those to the side for us in bulk bins." Most of Philabundance's fresh supply comes either from shipping related industries or the back channel of retail recovery. Melanie Cataldi, the chief operating officer of Philabundance, explains,

Chiquita brings in a load of bananas and for whatever reason, they may not want them on the market. That's usually because of a timing issue. They couldn't get it to market in time [such as bananas started to ripen on the ship]. Or they didn't want to flood the market. There's already enough bananas on the market and they don't want to drive the price down. We get a ton of that. We're really lucky to be situated where we are in a port city. We have produce that very few other food banks across the nation have.

Just as sustaining the relationships with the Grocery Manufacturing Association in the earlier food banking era was about creating mutual benefits, so is sustaining the interdependencies between food banks and growing and shipping industries. Bill Clark was the CEO of Philabundance at the time of my interview with him. He says, "We compete with waste management, not with the supermarket." Clark makes an important point, as studies of food waste repeatedly demonstrate that many products going to the landfill are perfectly safe and healthy to eat. He explains,

> They donate food that they can't sell, and it's cheaper to give it to us than to hold onto it. Because if I am sitting there with a truckload, let's say 1,500 pounds of broccoli and I can't sell it, it will cost me $60 per pallet to have the scavenger take it to the dump. They'll say, "If I can give it to Phila-bundance and they can use it, they'll take it for free." If they already recognized that they're not getting any revenue from it, then they say, "Is there any way I can save myself some costs?" That's $60 per pallet even before I talk about tax deductions. I give you five pallets, I just saved $300. We save companies tipping fees and then a tax write off.

This channel between excess and insecurity creates a unique tension. Objects deemed "not good enough" for the market must still be evaluated as "good enough" for consumption. Food banks engage in an ad hoc assessment of the products. Much like the terminal wholesale businesses evaluating foods rejected by supermarkets, food banks assess the indeterminate qualities of donations on the spot. Lisa Hodaei says, "My team coordinates with potential donors about bringing it in. But everything's evaluated on a case-by-case basis. It depends on the time of the week, the time of the day, the type of product, the amount of the product, and the lifespan of the product. All of that's going to determine how much time we have for the distribution cycle."

I volunteered several days at Philabundance's location in South Philadelphia to get a better picture of how the operation works. Dee, an employee of the food bank, directed me to the HUB, one of Philabundance's push programs. A major part of the operation is staging the product and then pushing it out. Dee gave me a tour through the facilities and pointed to different products. She says that the food bank receives donated fresh produce, evaluates the qualities, and stores them in its refrigerated warehouse, which has two temperature zones, one at 36 degrees and one at 56 degrees. I ask her how long things sit in the warehouse, and she says, "It depends. These bananas are stage two—they'll have about 10 days on them. Other times, we get stage four or five, and then they have a couple days to push those out. With managing the duration, it's just a free-for-all. It depends on what it is and what the quality is when we get it."

One of my visits is in the middle of the summer. A truck driver contacted Philabundance the night before, hoping to make a donation of watermelons. Dee and I discuss the ambiguity of the incoming supply.

DEE: This is a new donor. We've never worked with him before. I got an email from him last night and I talked to him on the phone.

ANDREW: Where is he coming from?

DEE: Not sure. A lot of times these guys get rejected [from a market] and instead of taking them right to a landfill, they'll try to bring them over to us. But an abundance of food is not always good. If it's junk, I don't want to pay to have to dispose of it.

ANDREW: He told you they were rejected?

DEE: No, he didn't give me any history on it yet. Sometimes they'll try to pull the wool over our eyes because they don't want to have to dispose of it themselves. And this is a new donor, and so we don't know him. We'll look at it and see. It could be something that's just off retail grade and we have the means to distribute it. But if they're bad, they're bad.

When the truck arrives, the driver shows Dee the paperwork. He says, "I figure I can give them away to somebody. I don't want to throw them away." He claims he just cut one in the truck and it tasted fine. As Dee looks over the paperwork, the driver tells her the watermelons were rejected for discoloration. We walk into the truck's trailer to evaluate the supply and we both notice a distinct smell—it's not an overwhelming stench, but more like a pungent sour smell that fills up the enclosed trailer space. Watermelons are piled into four large cardboard totes. Dee says, "When watermelons start to go, they smell like vinegar." She puts her hand into the boxes and presses on some of the watermelons. I do the same. Some are firm but others are soft, even mushy, easily denting and damaging the exterior of the fruit and pushing right into the inside.

Dee and I walk out of the trailer and into the acquisitions office where a small group discusses whether to take the load. Dee says, "Some of them are good, but not all of them. Most of them don't look bad. It's good weight.

I say we take them. He said he cut one in the truck and it was fine." The group agrees to take them. Dee walks back outside and tells the truck driver. The acquisitions department then does the work of setting up a donor card with the pertinent information so that the food bank can keep track of the product and the donor.

The watermelons get added to the HUB distribution program for the day. Dee says, "There's not a lot of time on these, and so we just want to push them out." The truck driver unloads the large cardboard totes and leaves them outside on the loading dock. Because of the late-stage quality of the product, the watermelons do not get stored inside. They are basically set up to be easily redirected to agencies picking up other supplies for that day's HUB distribution.

Volunteers prepare the objects for pickup by various agencies around Philadelphia. In the back stage, a group of students is pulling off browning leaves of cabbage to prepare them for distribution boxes. I help other volunteers loading hand trucks, piling banana boxes filled with different produce—carrots, apples, pears, and bananas. All of the objects are of mixed qualities. There are some that are definitely firm and blemish-free, but they are mixed in with others that are softening and scuffed. At this late stage, right before pick up, there is no time for culling the supply.

When the agencies start arriving, the hand carts are already packed with various boxes for them to take. We wheel out the carts and help them pack up the fresh produce into their vans and pickup trucks. Representatives of the agencies climb up to the loading dock to inspect watermelons in the large tote, digging through to find the best ones. One of the men, picking up for a church, puts his hand right through a soft one. "Some of these are no good," he says in a surprised tone, before finally finding a sturdier one to take with him. (See fig. 29.)

The volume and variety change from week to week, donation to donation, which is why on some weeks, the food bank "needs the weight" to bulk up the push distribution. The entirety of the food bank system runs on cobbling together the quantity of "good enough" objects and pushing out the products through its various channels. While getting enough good objects is always a concern for food banks, so is developing the very channels needed to reach consumers in time, before the perishable objects are no longer edible.

Most of the agencies that connect directly with people in need have limited storage capacity. They are small neighborhood food cupboards. While they may have recurring interactions with food banks, in terms of taking on nonperishable supplies, most of them lack compatibility with the fresh

29 Neighborhood agency pickup at the food bank. Photograph by author.

food system. Blawat, the former Feeding America executive, explains, "You get a case of fresh produce, and if it's not going to be distributed that day, now you have a new challenge. A lot of the agencies are open twice a month on Tuesday at 1:00 PM. That is not a supply chain that's conducive to fresh produce."

Most of the agencies I visited were small food pantries located in the basement of a church or in another small-scale community space. Philabundance has 350 member agencies. In order for agencies to remain partners with Philabundance, they have to distribute a minimum of 2,000 pounds of food per week. Only a limited number can handle produce. In order to make it worthwhile for Philabundance to provide a perishable food delivery, the agency has to prove that it can distribute at least 1,000 pounds of fresh produce as part of its weekly operation. It requires the methods, space, and sustained client demand.

The HUB, in contrast, operates as the excess of the excess, to push out remaining perishable food in the warehouse to small agencies, without restriction. About 35 smaller cupboards in the city use the HUB. Colleen Watts, at the time of the interview a senior manager at Philabundance, says, "With some of the really good food cupboards, we'll talk them into going to the HUB to try out distributing produce, to develop something a little bit more robust for a food cupboard at their location."

Food banks are always looking to create new branches off of the established channels to see if something can organically stabilize. Volunteers for the different food cupboards show up at the South Philadelphia warehouse with small pickup trucks and vans and take whatever is available on that day. If it works out, and their clients are happy with the added fresh supply, they might try it again the next week, turning into a more reliable interdependency. To get to the next stage of routine deliveries from the food bank, they have to demonstrate and record their consistency of becoming one of the flagged, high functioning agencies.

As a response to the difficulties of connecting perishable produce to individuals in need, many food banks created their own more reliable programs. Some of the neighborhood food cupboards were concerned about food banks stepping on their territory in the food insecurity supply system. The difficulties of handling perishable foods themselves required supplemental efforts, however. It is a tricky balance for food banks to manage. The cupboards are not set up to pursue efficiency, but fresh produce requires quick-handling push programs for the distribution to succeed.

Philabundance developed Fresh for All, which brings truckloads of supplies directly into Philadelphia neighborhoods. Even if some of the agencies do not like it, as one volunteer pointed out to me, the demand shows that hungry people do not care about inter-organizational conflicts. To make Fresh for All work, Philabundance finds and secures public locations in neighborhoods in need and establishes a weekly delivery time.

30 Fresh for All farmers' market style display. Photograph by author.

I visited several of the Fresh for All programs. One was set up in a parking lot on 49th and Spruce Streets in West Philadelphia on Wednesday from 2 to 3. It was a cold and rainy day and a long line had already surrounded the parking lot when I arrived. Somewhere between a 100 and 200 people stood waiting patiently for the distribution to start, standing with umbrellas and rain gear. The program employees went person-to-person checking off names. Anyone is welcome to receive the product, as there are no financial disclosure requirements, nor do clients need to provide identification.

Jessica Wyckoff, the director of the program, told me, "Usually we'll see 160 people and then in the summer we get up to 250 households a week. Today, we have produce, bread, and other dry products with us. And we'll set it up on both sides of the tables identically." It is set up in a "farmers' market style." When the volunteers are ready with the setup, clients walk toward the tables and choose what they want. There is a number in front of everything that serves as a guideline of how many of each item they can take: bananas, potatoes, onions, mangoes, bread, and other items. (See fig. 30.)

Philabundance, like other distribution channels, operates according to a process of elimination until everything is gone or no longer has consumable qualities. Jessica says, "Our numbers are based on how many households we see a week, and so we get 4,000 to 5,000 pounds per week, which is like 25 to 30 pounds per person. If we don't get rid of everything, we take it back to the warehouse and it goes out on another round, another Fresh for All, another agency order, or into the HUB."

The cracks in the system get converted into institutional methods of distribution, but the available materials and channels are not static. Different actors adjust to changing market conditions, and in doing so, carve out additional connections, some of which turn into interactive and compatible infrastructures. The process of reconfiguring supplies also multiplies possible valuations, as actors in different contexts reassemble distributable formats. Knowledge of the local conditions is key to this distribution process, but local food itself has gained in popularity, shifting the meaning and status of foods produced nearby.

Local Food as a Moral Economy

One counterintuitive effect of the mass-merchandising infrastructure is the rise and spread of the "local food" movement. In an earlier infrastructural regime, market-makers were concerned about increasing supplies beyond local production conditions. In the current infrastructural regime in which mass merchandising is pervasive, people have responded by raising concerns about long-distance transportation and energy consumption, the loss of flavor in fresh commodities, the disruption of culinary traditions, and the devastation of corporate farming on small family farms. Local food is now readily converted into alternative market channels, some of which are even classified as having higher status than the products found in the mass-merchandising system.

Sociologists and anthropologists point to geographic distinctions and local culture in terms of the moral politics of authenticity. On the one hand, they write about power struggles over classifying urban, regional, and national cultures and cuisines.[19] On the other hand, consumers and producers negotiate expectations about the meanings of objects, performances, and locations that reinforce the prominence of certain status categories over others.[20] Yet the politics of producing and consuming authenticity does not, in and of itself, sustain local culture. Collective interactions and organizational collaborations facilitate the political and economic distribution infrastructure between farmers and neighborhoods, restaurants, universities, hospitals, and food markets located in geographic proximity.

Local market channels in advanced capitalist nations are put into practice and sustained as both a moral repertoire and an economic process. It is what E. P. Thompson called a "moral economy." In Thompson's account of eighteenth-century food riots, he argued that although the riots were set off by "soaring prices, malpractice among dealers, or hunger," the movement itself was about the moral contestation over the legitimacy of values. The grievances of rioters in those days were about capitalists luring away agricultural producers from local consumers. A contestation emerged over the valuation of food—between market and traditional community norms.[21]

The changing dimensions of urban and economic development have created new conditions for local morality to be strategically injected into markets. It is not simply applied through the lens of traditionalism versus markets. Instead, the logic of localism has followed a circuitous trajectory by reframing it against the less personalized and decentered profit-driven dynamic of feeding the nation. Localism, as a moral category of market-making, has become a clear market signal and a mode of distinction.[22]

The avenues for supporting local foods are spreading. According to a USDA report, the United States had only 342 farmers' markets in 1970. In 2017, the number had increased to 8,687. The "farm-to-table" and "slow food" culinary movements are often attributed to Alice Waters and her Berkeley restaurant, Chez Panisse, which she opened in 1971. The "locavore" philosophy has since become a widespread culinary ideal celebrated by the National Restaurant Association and the James Beard Foundation. The "Buy Fresh, Buy Local" campaign, which was first used in Pennsylvania in the early 2000s, is now the national trademark of the local food movement. The USDA promotes programs under the banner of "know your farmer, know your food" to facilitate local economies.[23] Many supermarkets across the country even advertise "local" as one of their product categories, with different states instituting successful branding strategies to this effect, like the "Jersey Fresh" campaign.

Local food may operate as a distinct moral virtue, but it does so as a niche market category. Advocacy and policy organizations define the geographic limits of localism as the 150-mile radius around the consumer location. By that definition, local foods make up less than 2 percent of total food sales in the United States. The cultural category itself is certainly visible, but the grooved channels—and often the commodities themselves—continue to exist as part of the world outside of mass-merchandising standards.[24]

Mass-merchandising suppliers must learn to fit physical materials and organizational conventions into established sociotechnical coordinates. Local food holds a relative status. Most of the time, when people celebrate "buy local" movements, they refer to small, independent, and family-owned businesses, the ones facing the greatest difficulties communicating and operating through the parameters of the national and global market infrastructure.

Jeff Stoltzfus worked for 29 years as a Lancaster County agricultural instructor, mostly assisting small-scale Amish and Mennonite farmers. He is currently a Pennsylvania State University Extension Educator who helps Lancaster families connect their harvests to markets. Stoltzfus took me on a day-long tour through the agricultural county, where we toured four family farms growing a range of fruits and vegetables and one small dairy and artisanal ice cream maker. He explains the difficulties of integrating small-scale production methods into supermarket operations.

> Our food system is like a train running through the country. We can be sitting here and growing all the produce you want, but if we don't have a train station, we can't get on the train. For years, we have been fighting that battle. The system isn't set up to handle small growers very well. You need standardized packing. You need trailer load lots. You need a vehicle to get onto that train. Here we sit with a roadside stand with a bunch of sweet corn and onions and we can't get on. Acme has a 30-acre distribution center 5 miles up the road, but we can't get into it because it isn't packed right. So Acme gets 75 percent of the same stuff from California or Florida.

Creating the interactive compatibility is not just about mastering production quantities and qualities. If small-scale farmers want to enter the supermarket system, or even approach independent supermarkets in the area, they must collectively adjust their farming and packing techniques into the retailers' established sociotechnical criteria. In fact, that's one of the goals of the university agricultural extension programs—to provide more information, training, and methods to farmers for building the organizational and technical bridge between production and consumption.

Stoltzfus says that Lancaster farmers grow supermarket quality sweet onions, the same quality as those coming from Vidalia, Georgia, the prosperous onion-growing region 800 miles south of Philadelphia. Yet channeling farmers into a cooperative format is the difficult part. He says, "Learning the logistics is the killer." He says that Vidalia farmers can put 1,000 boxes of onions on a truck and haul them up to Philadelphia, only burning 200 gallons of gas at .2 gallons per box. "If I put 20 boxes on the back of my pickup truck, I burn 70 gallons of fuel at 3.5 gallons per box. That's just not going to work."

Stoltzfus explains that one of the problems is that retailers' computer systems already have the exact specifications of the commodity category encoded into their procurement and distribution operations. The standardized information synchronizes producers, distribution warehouses, and supermarkets toward reproducing exchange relationships. "Say I'm a supermarket buyer and I need 300 watermelons, but each store needs it in a 40-count bin. They don't want 38, they don't want 42, they want 40, and they want a lid on top. You have to be able to tailor that to what they want."

Over the course of my research, I visited 14 farms in Pennsylvania and New Jersey and talked to many local food activists and agricultural extension agents who work with farmers in both states. I heard a common refrain about the difficulties of matching small-scale farm production and distribution to supermarket expectations. South Jersey farms are not identical to Lancaster farms. Smaller than the large-scale farms in California or Florida, the farms I visited still had on average more acreage than the ones I visited in Lancaster County. The ones in New Jersey had hundreds of acres compared to the 50-to-100-acre farms I saw in the rolling hills of Pennsylvania. Some of the Jersey farmers I visited devote their largest fields to planting smaller numbers of crops, rather than diversified specialty produce of the emblematic small family farm. And yet they faced similar situations in relation to mass merchandising.

Lee Metz is the owner of a multigeneration South Jersey vegetable farm. He says that the size of his farm, at about 800 acres, is above average for the state. He strategically uses his space to grow crops in which he can maximize quantity, as he does for sweet potatoes, asparagus, squash, and melons. He also operates greenhouses on the periphery of his fields to experiment with specialty products like red leaf lettuce, herbs, and different colored peppers. When I visited his farm for the second time, Lee had just harvested sweet potatoes. He grew enough quantity of Grade 1 quality to establish a relationship with a regional supermarket company, but he tells me the weight of his boxes came up short. He says, "The buyer is saying to me, 'If I'm buying 15 trailer loads and these boxes are coming up two or three pounds short a box, and I'm selling them by the pound, I'm gonna lose my job.' Well, I don't have a scale in my packing line to weigh it, so we were eyeballing it. I'm not trying to hide it from them. That's how we do it."

The supermarket buyer asked Lee for a discount because of the light loads. He told Lee that future boxes need to fit the proper weight in the subsequent transactions or they can no longer work together. Lee, like so many farmers in the local region, does not have the resources, equipment, manpower, and packing materials to support this kind of economic compatibility. He turns to multiple marketing channels, many of which run on the localized case-by-case basis.

One institutional route for both Lancaster and South Jersey farmers is the local produce auction. Produce auctions are cooperative organizations that allow local farms to create regional economic value by attracting a diversity of buyers, similar to how regional wholesale terminals incorporate different businesses and scales into a recurring site of exchange. People can come to the auctions and bid on the products in different quantities, allowing the farmers to better standardize their value in the local context. Daymon Thatch, a Rutgers agricultural economist, explains that the Vineland Produce Auction in Vineland, New Jersey, one of the largest in the country, aims to "keep the buying process honest and out in the open" by spreading "the risk over the greatest possible number."[25]

Some auctions rely on bridging together different production scales into a common distribution format. In 2015, the Vineland Produce Auction incorporated 130 different commodities into the auction, which according to Carol DeFoor, the office manager, "were packaged and sold in approximately 363 different manners to meet the needs of the growers and brokers." The auction also now operates electronically, and cooperative members can use the 130,000 square feet of warehouse space, loading docks, and refrigerated storage to service the range of restaurants and retailers who are common buyers of their supplies.[26]

When the produce auctions connect with large buyers, they reinforce the standardized grade system. As we walk through his storage warehouse, Metz says, "A lot of times, we can't find a [market] space for what we have, and so that's how we end up with all of this." He shows me a large supply of Grade 2 sweet potatoes held in large wooden bins. The problem with the product is its size and shape. "And we don't have a way to sell it," he explains.

The produce auctions demonstrate that the concern for the value of local market channels is not actually new. The Vineland Produce Auction was started in the 1930s to preserve the value of the local harvest, while Lancaster's Leola Produce Auction started in 1985 for the same reason. What is new in recent decades is how local market channels are interwoven with moral repertoires into higher status consumption. The French anthropologist Michèle de La Pradelle describes a fundamental paradox of local street markets. She writes, "Market society has no need of its street or stallholder markets. It has developed other forms of distribution that better satisfy its demand for rational efficiency and profit." She argues that small-scale local markets persevere because of their symbolic value: they evoke consumer nostalgia and create community spaces for social interaction.[27]

Alternative market channels have stabilized local food as a category of consumer distinction. The relationship between small family farmers and densely populated cities has created unique exchange opportunities. Densely populated areas play an important role in converting small family farms into an urban consumer niche. Two major grooved channels have driven the most stylized aspects of the local food movement: farmers' markets and farm-to-restaurant relationships.

Farmers' markets are synonymous with small-scale diversified family farms, but they are very much a part of the urban condition. Converting urban public spaces into markets for small-scale farmers requires bureaucratic and logistical skills for running recurring sites of exchange. Bob Pierson has worked for decades organizing markets, first in Wisconsin in the 1970s. He started a farmers' market in Philadelphia in the early 1990s. According to Pierson, there were a handful of farmers' markets during earlier decades, but they disappeared by the time he began his work. In the early 1990s, the national local food movement was gaining traction, and he was the first to develop a farmers' market in the city.

His entrepreneurial effort brought farmers he knew together with local interest groups, holding meetings and dinners to have conversations about the added value of this relationship. He sought the advice of activists, restaurateurs, politicians, and developers. Around the same time, a developer approached Pierson about starting a farmers' market on South and Passyunk—an emerging commercial area where young professionals were moving. They formed a committee to explore the possibilities. Pierson says,

> Friends told me, all you need is a place, farmers, and people to come to it. It snapped into place when they said it that way. And those have been the three main categories. Place means all of the permitting that goes along with it. You need the right kinds of farmers who can work together and complement each other. And people means you need a promotion program and community support.

In terms of finding farmers, Pierson says that owners of large- and medium-size farms had different production priorities, contracting with supermarkets or connecting to produce auctions. He went after small-scale farmers. Pierson got to know the agriculture extension agents who supplied him with a list. He visited farmers and asked if they would come to the city for a market. He says,

> I didn't want them to have to put effort into marketing. We advertised around the neighborhood, put up fliers, signs, got the city on board with using the square. We gave them the space to sell directly. Then if there was something

we wanted to add to the market or something the community wanted more of, we would ask the farmers if they could grow it or if they knew someone else who could do it.

After the success of the first South Philadelphia market, Pierson was lured away by the Food Trust, an emerging organization trying to get farmers into low-income neighborhoods, an early approach to solving the food desert problem. In his three years working in the organization he found it difficult to get his initial three pieces—place, farmers, and customers—to fit together in ways that were beneficial to the farmers. He says, "I discovered that putting farmers' markets in low-income neighborhoods is mission impossible, because the farmers are low income, and they don't want to sell it cheap." Some food access activists dispute this idea, but it represents two distinct problems and two equally important agendas. Pierson grew more concerned with protecting farmers and their products, whereas the Food Trust took on advocacy related to urban consumers and unequal healthy food access as its central focus.

Pierson remained interested in helping farmers improve their economic value. His experience in starting farmers' markets led him to start an organization called Farm to City. The interdependencies between lower-income farmers on one hand, and higher-income urban consumers on the other, contributed to the rise of local food as a status distinction in the city. It is not an accident, says Pierson, that the most successful farmers' market in Philadelphia is the Rittenhouse Square market. It is located in an area that combines population density, the city's most vibrant public square, luxury housing, and nearby commercial streets. He says, "New York City is different than Philadelphia. Over there, they can deliver more people per square foot than we can ever do here. Except for Rittenhouse Square. That's where we went."

Farm to City does not produce or sell anything; it carves out distribution channels and finesses the relationships between local farmers and urban consumers. Farm to City recruits and advocates for small family farms, makes sure the markets reflect a diversity of products, helps farmers build a Community Supported Agriculture clientele, and supports a winter harvest buyers' club. The organization also works with Philadelphia community leaders to sustain neighborhood-level demand. To initiate a new market, Farm to City requires local groups to demonstrate commitment by providing letters of support from business organizations and from council members who have the authority to provide permits for new sites. He says, "The community has to do the groundwork, because we don't want to waste the farmers' time."

The farmers' markets in Philadelphia and cities all over the country have a market semiotics that inverts the mass-merchandising structure. The Farm to City markets require that farmers themselves show up to sell their products, and the direct exchange connections are celebrated. A few farmers hold seasonal festivals to strengthen their bonds to the urban communities, inviting Philadelphians to their farms for tours, live music, and sampling of products. In addition, the objects and the stands are styled in distinct ways. One farmer explains, "We keep the greens on everything now. When we first started, we cut them off. You go the supermarket and the carrots don't have greens. But we realized customers want to see them. You don't know how long they've been sitting around in the supermarket, but if the greens are there and they look healthy, you know the carrots are healthy."

Most of the products are not just presented as fresh from the field, but they are decisively not year-round, a direct challenge to the market without seasons. Rosa Spain, a farmer selling in Rittenhouse, says, "We bring what we have. This isn't one of those things where we pick and choose. If I have it and it's ready, I bring it." In fact, seasonality and atypical products are part of the pact between farmers and consumers. During the apple season, one farmer explains that she grows types that consumers cannot find in the supermarket. She tells me that her Ginger Gold is a hybrid between the Golden Delicious and the Pippin apple, while the Zestar is a crisp and sweet Minnesota variety with which customers are not usually familiar. On another occasion, customers are talking to a farmer about Asian eggplants, and they talk about how to cook them and what makes them distinct from "regular eggplants," besides the fact that they "look like someone had taken a normal eggplant and stretched it into a long and skinny purple cucumber."

Imperfections, while a problem for getting farm products into the supermarket, are viewed as natural and authentic in this setting. Scars on products, different sized objects, unique shapes, and unique varieties are all part the symbolic language of localism. So is the "rugged" presentation of the stand itself. James builds display benches from bushel baskets and two-by-fours, which hold wooden crates packed with produce. Milk jar vases are filled with flowers to spruce up the stand. He first spaces out the wooden crates across the display, and then piles up the produce in triangle-like displays. He says that over the years, what he has learned most is how to communicate with customers and to present his product in an appealing away. "You have to make a visual appeal and bring their eye to the product. I don't just have onions. I have different varieties with different colors."

In addition to farmers' markets, the farm-to-table ideal has spread across the country as a way of presenting and promoting the moral and stylistic status of the local food movement. Today, so many restaurants support this ideal, with some chefs and restaurateurs even having their own proprietary farms. That was not the case in 1981 when Judy Wicks opened the White Dog Café and introduced this philosophy to Philadelphia. Wicks did not have a culinary vision at the time. She opened a muffin bakery before she got the idea of starting a restaurant. She writes in her memoir, "I had never been to the trend-setting restaurants of California, nor ever heard of the food revolutionary Alice Waters."[28]

Defining her locavore ideology was an iterative process, configuring relationships between nearby farms, seasonal menus, and growing consumer demands. When she started her restaurant, her chef introduced her to a few small-scale farmers who began supplying her with higher quality produce. Those farmers introduced her to several other farmers growing more varieties. Over a period of a decade, she and her team created a culinary institution, a 200-seat restaurant with the ability, because of the stable networks of local suppliers and enthusiastic customers, to change its menu based on seasonal availability.[29]

Once the restaurant's reputation was solidified, the White Dog Café no longer had to look for farmers to support its changing menu. Local farmers started approaching them. Wicks recognized her place in the growing movement and wanted to find ways of using her position to extend the market channel. No urban organizational platform existed to configure the connections between local farms and city businesses. In 2000, Wicks approached Ann Karlen, another local food advocate, about the problem in Philadelphia. Together, they started an organization called Fair Food. The organization was dependent on a confluence of emerging circumstances that they assembled into the stable bridges between farmers and chefs. They did not start with a clear strategy, however. Karlen says,

> It started with some things popping up and us grabbing onto them. We were seeing the potential for these small farms growing specialty items that chefs were looking for. We saw a way to fill a gap. We weren't thinking of it as a system, to be honest. We already had a few growers related to the White Dog, and my job was to convince other chefs in the area to buy from those growers. If you don't have your supply already, you can forget looking for the demand. But then the demand took off. Chefs saw more and more demand coming from their customers. It was a surge. At that point, we had to find more farmers.

The culinary category of "farm to table" continued to gain market status throughout the 1990s and early 2000s. Lindsay Gilmour has been a local food system activist for more than three decades. A former chef and caterer, she helped with Fair Food's farmer outreach. She said that there is an educational and information component to stabilizing market relationships. "A small handful of suppliers already sold produce, fancy cheeses, charcuterie, but there were not farmers coming to the backdoor of restaurants. They were buying through brokers," she explains. The direct farm-to-restaurant channel was outside of the commonplace efficiency standards to which most restaurant buyers had become accustomed. Gilmour says that Fair Food reintroduced the idea of "farmers coming to the kitchen door."

Grooved channels around localism are not about creating efficiencies. They are about the symbolic and quality distinctiveness of the products and creating interpersonal ties. In this case, Gilmore says, the farm-to-restaurant method was less convenient and more expensive, which meant that they had to incorporate symbolic quality and taste value into the exchange. She started by bringing chefs to visit the farms so that they could better understand what kind of value this new market channel brought to restaurants. Chefs started to see the difficult craft-work that went into farming. They saw the growers as complementary to their own creative work, as people with skill sets associated with maximizing flavor qualities of foods picked at the peak of ripeness. Likewise, farmers continued to learn what restaurants wanted and needed, and not just in terms of the products and flavor profiles; they developed mutual understandings and lines of communication about economic expectations.

The farmers' markets and farm-to-table channels were important for stabilizing the visibility of "local food" as both a moral and status category. Yet Pierson says local food advocates also understand that these kinds of avenues "are a drop in the bucket of the total food supply in Philadelphia." Building a more substantial connection between local supplies and the city requires a better understanding of the infrastructure of distribution.

Cooperative growing ventures have a long history as a way of advancing the needs of growers in relation to the market. Sunkist, for instance, is the cooperative marketing channel of California's citrus growers, and over a century, it turned into a billion-dollar brand. This cooperative framework happens on a much smaller and localized scale, pulling different farmers together into an institutional market format that channels specialty products to higher-end markets, especially to urban-based restaurants and specialty retailers. Tuscarora Organic Growers Cooperative in central Pennsylvania is one example. Jeff, the general manager at the time of the interview, says, "We were local, seasonal and organic long before it was cool. We basically grew with the demand." When they started in 1988, seven growers sold

1,500 cases of produce to Washington, DC, retailers over five months. More than 30 years later, they grew to 50 member growers "and sell hundreds of thousands of cases every month."[30] To participate, Jeff says, "You have to do it according to the rules or we won't sell it." The cooperative organizes the process: it creates production cycles so the different farms can maximize their value and it manages the quality. There's a multipage document that specifies the distinct rules for each product. Jeff says, "Leeks have to be 20 pounds, they have to be stored at this temperature, you have to use this box, you've got to have a paper liner, and this is what it has to look like. And that is done for every crop." In other words, they have to follow the locally established standards.

This cooperative effort was geared toward higher-end markets. It is a different enterprise to convert small-scale farming into a vibrant wholesale operation, which required figuring out how to coordinate local production, especially around Grade 2 products, into a shared distribution platform that was not exclusively stylized for a market niche. An emerging farm-to-institution channel grew out of this interest, benefiting local farmers at the same time as it did large urban institutions like hospitals, universities, and schools. As with other channels, building together the market connections was an emergent and iterative process.

Tatiana Garcia-Granados and Hailey Johnston, both graduates of the University of Pennsylvania's Wharton School, live in Philadelphia's Strawberry Mansion neighborhood. Living in this low-income area, they realized that healthy food supplies simply did not make it to their neighborhood. They were doing a lot of community-level work through urban agriculture and youth nutritional education when they reached out to Bob Pierson about the possibility of starting a farmers' market. As an advocate for local farmers, Pierson knew it was easier to convince farmers to participate in more affluent areas. However, Pierson was in the process of trying to cobble together farmers for a winter market of local seasonal supplies, turning local food into an off-season marketplace. Johnston says, they shared concerns about the absence of infrastructural connections for the local food supply. He asked, "Why is it that the food system doesn't make it efficient for local suppliers to aggregate food for distribution? What's the missing link there?"

The farm-to-institution channel grew out of Philadelphia's existing organizational ecosystem around local food markets. Fair Food, for instance, got funding from the USDA and the Risk Management Agency to conduct workshops for farmers about how to sell to the wholesale marketplace. Karlen says farmers would introduce them to friends, and they built "one-to-one relationships" with new farmers. By 2007, she says, the "workshops were being attended by 40 different growers at a time." Gilmour, who helped establish the "farm to institution" program for Fair Food, says they trained them on the business aspects of the wholesale market, but one thing they learned is that most farmers "don't like to do distribution."

Gilmour, Karlen, and Pierson partnered with Granados and Johnston to find a wholesale distribution channel. On the basis of their previous work, they already knew how to reach local farmers and educate them about urban markets. They received a planning grant with the Pennsylvania Department of Community and Economic Development and conducted a feasibility study to start a nonprofit wholesale operation called the Common Market. Having and operating a warehouse proved consequential. The group secured a low-cost refrigerated warehouse space from another nonprofit food organization, SHARE, which distributes emergency food and food share packages to city agencies out of its warehouse in North Philadelphia.

These collaborative nonprofit organizations were not interested in maximizing profits. Rather, they saw a unique opportunity to improve infrastructural interdependencies at the same time that they were "driven by values that place farmer representation and fairness to producers first."[31] The Common Market saw the value-added possibility to consolidate products, provide transportation support, and make available warehouse space. Johnston says that their initial goal was to build bridges between farmers and low-income neighborhoods, but they realized in the beginning "it was going to be a whole lot harder to focus just on lower-income communities to solve this problem." They developed a "more inclusive approach to making local food accessible to different market segments as opposed to just making this food available to the richest of the rich and the poorest of the poor."

To establish their reputation and expertise, the Common Market first worked with Fair Food to access its farm connections, becoming the supplier for their local produce stand in the Reading Terminal Market in Center City. They also worked with Philadelphia restaurants that had already invested in local food. As they developed more knowledge about how to run the distribution organization, they were able to expand the wholesale operation. They turned to Philadelphia's institutional infrastructure as a possible market niche, taking what they learned about local production and scaling up the distribution. Johnston says,

> We were anticipating that as we scale, we want to have the ability to substitute farms. If you have a number two organic slicing tomato, we wanted the ability to substitute one farm's number two organic slicing tomatoes for another. We saw that as we scaled, it has become the case that it would require tomatoes

from different farms to fill all of our orders. It's kind of adjusting our operations to the scale of the farmers in our region and recognizing that we're going
to get to a place that any one farmer is not going to be able to meet all of the
market demand for any given product at any given time. And so we had to be
able to have different relationships with different farmers at different times of
the year for different products, and become a little more flexible.

As the "farm-to-school" movement proliferated, the Common Market
saw an opportunity to meet their original goals of connecting local farms
to lower-income communities as well. According to Garcia-Granados, the
Common Market connects farms to 26 charter schools through which it
reaches 14,000 children in the city. By operating as a nonprofit 501(e)3, she
says, "We're able to get grants for capital, and then we're able to tap into low-
interest or 'friendly' loans."[32]

Their skill set and economic training allowed Garcia-Granados and
Johnston to institutionalize a model "to assist farmers in building capacity
and infrastructure to meet these demands." Serving as a storage and logistical middleman between the local food movement for handling out-of-grade
objects and large urban institutions that did not need the highest quality
produce, they carved out a new public/private channel that they are repeat-
ing in new locations. Taking what they learned in Philadelphia, they are
bridging Atlanta's consumption needs with the needs of growers in rural
Georgia and Alabama.[33]

Cracks in the System as an Impetus for Infrastructural Repair

Just because something does not fit into the standard mass-merchandising
infrastructure does not mean that it is devoid of value. Complex systems are
not unidirectional or one-dimensional in terms of their inputs, outcomes,
and institutional rules. The paradigmatic market system strengthens the mi-
metic process at the same time that it generates a relational value structure.
Lean supply chains aim to reproduce a high-volume distribution system,
but they also assert barriers of entry that can create cracks in the system and
open up opportunities for new distribution interdependencies to form.

The standard and nonstandard become entangled, as organizational interactions and networks are set up for handling indeterminate qualities and
values. The spread of supermarkets between 1950 and 1980 led to so much
overflow in manufactured food products that local nonprofit and religious
organizations were able to build the distribution channel of food banking.
Changes in the mass-merchandising supply system altered the nonprofit

food recovery avenues by eliminating much of the packaged market imperfections and developing better forecasting tools. This change in the for-profit/nonprofit dynamic created an additional impetus for food banks to turn to fresh food recovery because of its more precarious nature.

The distinctions that emerge are not exclusively between for-profit and nonprofit realms, however. The contemporary local food movement arose through a channel to support farmers facing difficulties entering the supermarket system. That moral tension between supermarkets and small farms—between high-volume standards and local deviations—became part of the market innovation and infrastructural repair process. The production of authenticity, like in farmers' markets and farm-to-table restaurants, creates value through incommensurable qualities, interpersonal relationships, and public interaction spectacles, not from standardization and price point. And now many supermarkets and large corporations have turned local statuses into branded products and market categories unto themselves.

What is evident from studying the cracks in the system is that energetic and persistent organized actors form new connections, collaborations, and institutional and infrastructural interdependencies out of local production, storage, distribution, and consumption ecosystems. Actors learn from their mistakes, respond and adjust to rejections, build new relationships through shared interests and needs, and expand upon previous collective successes by using information, tools, and techniques available in the surrounding environment. They build the local grooved channels, some of which inform new system interdependencies. The next chapter addresses how emergent and contingent conditions can also mesh with the standards as part of this infrastructural repair. In the economically declining city of Philadelphia, for-profit and nonprofit partnerships led to new growth machines aiming to patch up infrastructural exclusion.

SEVEN

Food Distribution as Unfinished Infrastructure

Food distribution is unfinished infrastructure. Place-making, knowledge creation, and infrastructure-building get entangled through the search for new organizational, material, and symbolic relationships. Actors locate new exchange possibilities; they try out designs and practical techniques; they identify research questions in different fields from engineering to economics, sociology to public health; and planners, activists, politicians, and business actors work with the new information to define problems and search for solutions. Over time, and through trial and error, they implement interactive and compatible relationships that congeal into different economic scales, spatial orders, and public health campaigns.

Three sociohistorical factors converged in Philadelphia after the 1970s and created the conditions of possibility for the emergence of another public and private coalition. This time around, collective actors sought to patch up the relationship between high-volume food distribution and the urban center. First, Philadelphia's Center City experienced concentrated commercial investments. Policy-makers, real estate developers, and regional-transit planners redeveloped and reframed the city's downtown. The collective efforts were not geared toward making Philadelphia a necessary node in the changing spatial and economic arrangement. Rather, they were set up to link new residents and tourists with shifting market dynamics and consumer trends. Center City grew into one of the most populated downtowns in the nation.

And yet Philadelphia remained the poorest large city in the United States, with over a quarter of its 1.5 million inhabitants living below the poverty line.[1] Uneven development had materialized within the municipality itself. Philadelphia's vacancy problems started in the 1950s with white flight, middle-class out-migration, factory closings, and suburbanization, but the physical and economic deterioration of many neighborhoods continued over subsequent decades. Despite the intensive era of Center City redevelopment, abandonment in black and Latino neighborhoods remained a serious social and economic policy concern. Policy reports as recent as the 2010s estimated that Philadelphia had 40,000 abandoned lots, most of them in North and West Philadelphia.[2]

Secondly, food was used as a prominent symbol and tool of redevelopment. Innovative culinary trends and shifting consumer tastes became interdependent with gentrification, tourism, and remodeled transportation networks between Center City and wealthier suburbs. It was a push and pull between culinary innovations, new health and cultural trends, and changing contexts of consumer demand. "Natural," "organic," "ethnic," "local," and "specialty" foods were integral to neighborhood place-making projects. Food markets, farmers' markets, restaurants, and cafes gained traction and socially and symbolically differentiated neighborhoods and streets.

Thirdly, reframing Philadelphia's Center City through food consumption trends brought unequal distribution to light as a public health issue. The infrastructural exclusion that crystallized in the 1970s was an urban neighborhood constraint on convenience. However, a shared definition of the "food desert" as a public health problem did not become part of the dialogue until decades later. Real estate, culinary, nonprofit, and political sectors interacted around rebuilding the Reading Terminal Market as part of the downtown convention center construction. New public and private coalitions formed around the "new" public health problem of uneven food access, which was eventually reframed as the "food desert" and "grocery gap."

Large supermarket corporations, with their standard financing, centralized decision-making, and cookie-cutter stores, were not the drivers of infrastructural repair. Instead, tens of millions of dollars in public subsidies attracted local franchise owners who capitalized on the public financial support by aligning higher-volume distribution channels with local neighborhood needs. The problem-solving framework that emerged in Philadelphia spread to Pennsylvania state legislators and eventually to federal policy levels. A national movement to solve the problem of the food desert had arrived.

The changing environmental conditions of food market access across the country also led to new social science inquiries and debates. Studies challenged the problem-solving assumptions that consumer access to high-volume and high-variety marketplaces solved health problems like diabetes, obesity, and cardiovascular disease. The inequality in health outcomes continued despite new supermarkets opening in underserved neighborhoods. Repairing the infrastructural gaps reinforced the underlying weakness of the

American food system: it fosters consumer convenience but does not promote public health.

Place-Making through Food Market Design

Certain kinds of markets and cafes are seen as symbolic indicators of neighborhood change. Activists and authors have argued that Whole Foods, coffee shops, juice bars, and cafes drive gentrification.[3] Some have described a "Whole Foods Effect" tearing up the collective cultural fabric of neighborhoods.[4] However, the causes of neighborhood change rarely occur as isolated instances and causes; they are found in neither the immediate push of powerful corporations nor the pull of consumer tastes. Rearranging the relationship between neighborhoods, food distribution, and consumerism is an iterative and cumulative infrastructural and cultural process. It requires that business actors take risks based on emerging information, resources, and social and material conditions, learn from their failures and successes of matching up supply and demand into profit-making protocols, and then over time, strengthen and spread the profitability techniques into sociotechnical interdependencies.

Wal-Mart invented neither the bar code system nor the superstore format, but over time, the corporation became the most visible manifestation of that logistical setup. Likewise, Whole Foods grew into the most successful and well-known purveyor of natural and organic foods. The company gained a reputation for linking natural foods to higher-income shoppers, including those living in upper-income urban neighborhoods. Whole Foods capitalized on the changing relationships between urban development, consumer tastes, and natural and organic product lines by taking that configuration to a national scale of distribution and profitability. In doing so, it also compelled supermarkets to integrate similar product lines, adding natural and organic selections into their established formats.

Yet before natural and organic foods had such a visible presence in food distribution, many organizational prototypes existed for bringing new food products to consumers—especially those residing in large cities. In 1970, there was no established format for selling natural foods; cities did not have standardized health food stores carrying familiar organic and natural food brands. Yet the forces of food and cultural differentiation were at work. They were seen in food buying clubs and co-ops; small health, gourmet, and specialty stores; Italian, Jewish, Chinese, and other ethnic market districts; and in public market halls, like Philadelphia's Reading Terminal Market, Pike's Market in Seattle, and L.A.'s Farmers' Market in Hollywood.

It was not class and power—the hegemony of Whole Foods—that brought kale and quinoa to consumers. There were multiplying forms of organizational emergence, including countercultural food movements.[5] Diversified tastes and products were part of the urban fabric, but they were slowly absorbed by the shifting infrastructural relationships. The city center, once labeled as a dying node in a suburbanizing nation, was reinvented as an ecosystem for supporting cultural omnivores—those adventurous consumers of diverse foods, arts, and music who wanted more than the standard American supply systems. Eventually, as with so many other types of cultural dynamics, strategic market-makers saw the profit-making potential of matching up the diverse tastes with alternative food product lines.[6]

The Reading Terminal Market in Philadelphia's Center City is an example of how the decline of a local food marketplace became embedded in changing infrastructural arrangements. It represents the combination of interacting forces and events related to transit, consumption, and gentrification. Located underneath the Reading Railroad Terminal, the market hall was built for the railroad age of centralized urbanism in the late 1800s. In 1950, it was still a thriving consumer hub with more than 800 vending stalls, many of them selling fresh fruits, vegetables, dairy, meat, and seafood.

By the end of the 1970s, the market, the city, and its distribution connections had transformed: people no longer commuted by rail from the suburbs to shop for food; the Philadelphia Board of Health began cracking down on the market's countless code violations; and more than half of the vending stalls were vacant. As urban revitalization started in Center City, the Reading Terminal Market was caught in an escalating web of development. It was eventually converted into a vehicle of postindustrial cultural consumption and fostered a new social movement aimed at redefining the food desert as a public health problem.

The Reading Corporation built its wealth on transporting anthracite coal, but it experienced dwindling business in the face of manufacturing loss and the spread of automobile transportation. The company filed for bankruptcy. The city planned new rail terminals in other locations with the idea of eliminating the Reading Terminal.[7] When the Reading Company filed for bankruptcy, the Southeastern Pennsylvania Transportation Authority (SEPTA)—a regional-transit authority—purchased the tracks of five commuter lines, along with Suburban Station of Penn Central and the Reading Terminal, for $7 million.[8]

It was a period of federal investment in regional development. The Urban Mass Transit Administration, now called the Federal Transit Administration, paid 80 percent of the costs, and Philadelphia and four suburban counties paid the remaining 20 percent.[9] The project to consolidate the regional transport infrastructure grew through the 1970s, enveloped in a $307 million multiyear transportation project. The city and state negotiated a deal with the federal government for $240 million to support the overhaul. Of the remaining budget, the city paid $37 million and the state paid $30 million. The idea was to improve services between Philadelphia's suburban periphery and Center City—that is, to build on a growing trend to reimagine the core as economically and symbolically viable.[10]

In the context of changing urban and regional development, many worried about the future of the Reading Terminal Market. Planners, developers, and politicians debated over what to do with the market hall below the train station. With more than half of the market's vending stalls vacant by the mid-1970s, they wondered whether the Reading Terminal Market should "be written off to progress."[11] However, local activists fought for national landmark status, which fortified the market's symbolism, but not its physical conditions.[12]

City inspectors found wide-ranging code violations. Joseph P. Braig, the Philadelphia License and Inspections Commissioner, said, "There has been a decade of neglect over there." The market hall had 44 fire code violations, two plumbing code violations, and four building code violations, and the list of electric code and health code violations was so long that Braig said it would take several days just to type them all up.[13] In response to the landmark designation, former Philadelphia Commerce Director Harry Belinger said that the Reading Terminal Market is "as historic as an outhouse." The market survives only due to the "winking and blinking of city officials at violations of various city codes."[14]

The tensions between regional and urban planning priorities grew more visible by the end of the 1970s. It was not just transit infrastructure that was an issue. Landlords and vendors in the market hall experienced diminishing consumer demand and declining profits. Real estate entrepreneur Samuel Rappaport owned adjacent properties housing adult bookstores, porn theaters, and massage parlors. He sublet the marketplace. Rappaport did not think the vending spaces attracted the highest and best uses, and his first order of business was renegotiating all of the vending leases.[15] He compared the Reading Terminal Market to Faneuil Hall in Boston, which also started as a fresh food market hall but was being converted into a tourism shopping spectacle. He pointed out that merchants in Faneuil Hall were paying $22 per square foot while Reading Terminal merchants only paid $1.50 per square foot.[16]

Throughout the decade, Rappaport increased the rents of some merchants by as much as 6 and 7 times their previous rents and demanded six months in advance to hold in escrow.[17] Rappaport claimed that the extra money acquired from higher rents would help with the badly needed refurbishment, but the vendors viewed it as an effort to run them out.[18] Rappaport never did much in terms of revitalization, as the vending environment eroded.[19] By 1980, only 27 merchants remained.[20]

The 1980s ushered in a new era of investing in the urban center. The Reading Terminal Market was surrounded by new political and economic circumstances. After more than two decades of negotiation and planning, the SEPTA commuter rail tunnel linking the Pennsylvania suburbs with Center City was under construction. It connected up with three central locations: Thirtieth Street Station, the city's major transport hub; Market East Station, later renamed Jefferson Station, located across from the Reading Terminal; and Suburban Station in the heart of the city's business district. The project was completed in 1984, eliminating the need for the above-ground Reading Terminal stop. The new transport connections better integrated suburban passengers with the city's own mobility network of buses and subways.

Place-making lives and dies by its mobility connections. Integrating Center City with the Pennsylvania suburbs created additional opportunities for economic investment. Along with new housing developments and office spaces in Center City, expensive restaurants, boutiques, and galleries flourished in neighborhoods from Rittenhouse Square to Old City. The Reading Company fought its way out of bankruptcy and reclaimed the market space with plans to take advantage of the booming downtown redevelopment.[21]

Strategic postindustrial economic competitions were on the rise. City boosters advocated for a new convention center to compete with New York's Jacob Javits Center. The Reading Corporation negotiated to sell the train shed and other nearby real estate for the project. The city formed a series of nonprofit entities to run the convention center and the Reading Terminal Market: the Pennsylvania Convention Center Authority and the Reading Terminal Market Corporation, respectively. The convention center would be built between Arch and Race Streets between 11th and 12th Streets, adjacent to the Reading Terminal Market. [22]

The convention center took more than a decade to get off the ground. The project was filled with so much conflict around the price of the sale for the train shed, funding goals, allocations, and environmental problems that arose in the area.[23] Nonetheless, the promise of the convention center, coupled with population and economic growth and new transit connections, attracted hotel interests, real estate ventures, high-rise apartments, and planned shopping plazas.[24]

Despite its economic and material decline, the Reading Terminal Market retained its prized place-making identity through decades of turmoil. The old market hall—simply by evading demolition—sat primed for a new era of consumers searching for the budding symbolic economy. One journalist described the market hall as a "monument of endurance" that stood through "two world wars, the Depression, the decline of the American city and the failure of the railroad that gave the market a home and a name."[25]

With the construction of the convention center under way, debates re-emerged about the future of the market hall. Remaining merchants worried about rumors that the city might shut it down. The Reading Terminal Merchants' Association put forth a massive campaign and gathered 80,000 signatures of support from city residents. Not only did the city not close the market hall, but public money was allocated to the market's redesign project to sustain businesses during the construction and fix the architectural and infrastructural problems.[26]

David K. O'Neil, a senior director of public markets for the Project for Public Spaces, was hired to direct the redesign project between 1981and 1990. He also served as the market's general manager. He described the Reading Terminal Market as "a throwback, where people used to fast food can experience what it was like before America was gobbled up by chains." It was a place where "you get the ethnic diversity of Philadelphia and all the neighborhoods. You come here and people say, 'Hi, how are you?' You know the meat man." He continued, "I think, in a city, people really crave human contact—and they get it at the market."[27]

The public market project was reminiscent of William H. Whyte's suggestions about good uses of public spaces. O'Neil adopted place-making strategies of "connecting with local farmers and producers, adding public seating, rebuilding a sense of community, and adapting to site specific needs." He used the market hall's locational and architectural assets to attract a new generation of customers, including those moving into the apartment buildings of Society Hill and the converted warehouses and factories of Old City. O'Neil visited neighborhoods and sought out merchants that he thought would bring in a wide range of customers.[28]

The redesign project reflected a growing urban consumer trend of cultural omnivorousness.[29] The Reading Terminal Market incorporated lunch counters and prepared food purveyors of different ethnic groups: Chinese, Japanese, Lebanese, Mexican, Greek, Italian, and German. Small trendy cafes opened up next to old-style luncheonettes. Cheese mongers, coffee experts, craft beer aficionados, and local wine distributors sold their products next to Amish pretzel makers, a soul food restaurant, and Bassett's ice cream stand, the oldest ice cream company in the country. O'Neil met Kyu Chang Ro selling vegetables on the street and convinced him to open a produce stand in the terminal.[30] Ro's Produce Market was eventually purchased by the Iovine Brothers in the 1990s and became key to the market's claim as one of the largest redeemers of SNAP benefits in the nation.

By the end of the 1980s, new food themes were on people's minds. In Philadelphia, food consumption was reconfiguring around ethnic diversity and natural and local foods. Several co-ops, born out of the buying clubs of the 1970s, were now bustling with customers. The farm-to-table-inspired White Dog Café was a popular spot in University City. The Italian Market, the old vending stall environment along South Philadelphia's 9th Street, went through similar ups and downs as the Reading Terminal Market and, likewise, it was once again thriving. Regional health food chains and gourmet markets were on the rise throughout the Northeast. One of them, Fresh Fields, opened up stores on the northern and southern edges of Center City, on Callowhill Street near the Art Museum and on South Street. Whole Foods, in its national expansion of buying up the regional chains, purchased Fresh Fields in 1996.[31]

Designers working for these growing natural supermarkets borrowed from the public market format. They integrated place-making and local foods into their consumer motif. David O'Neil, who managed the Reading Terminal Market redesign, said, "It is interesting to note that many innovations which have proven successful at a public market—connecting with local farmers and producers, adding public seating, rebuilding a sense of community, adapting to site specific needs—are now being copied by savvy retailers such as Whole Foods."[32]

The Reading Terminal Market brought together local producers, cultural omnivores, and tourists. It became part of the new postindustrial consumption ecosystem. The convention center was completed in the 1990s. A Hard Rock Café then opened up just outside, and other large chains followed, including corporate hotel chains like Hilton and Marriott, which added thousands of new rooms for visitors.[33] Center City grew into the third most populous downtown in the nation, and then more recently as of 2010, it was second only to New York's midtown.[34]

Critics worried, however, that gentrification and tourism would change the Reading Terminal Market. Boston's Faneuil Hall became a "glorified food court" and mall with Starbucks, Crate & Barrel, and Sunglass Hut. Critics described the Boston-based market hall as a "tourist trap," a place locals disliked and avoided.[35] The Reading Terminal merchants and local

Philadelphians wanted to create a hybrid space, serving as both a touristy public spectacle and providing local functions by selling fresh produce, meat, and seafood.[36]

Rearranging the market infrastructure around local businesses and place-making priorities made it one of Philadelphia's "cosmopolitan canopies," to borrow Elijah Anderson's term. In Anderson's account, the Reading Terminal Market is a significant zone of civil interaction. There, people of different racial, ethnic, and class backgrounds test out their differences. However, as Anderson also points out, such sites are even more important when understood in the context of the city's persistent residential segregation.[37]

Recent sociological findings demonstrate that residents of black and Hispanic neighborhoods are not just spatially isolated in terms of their residential status; they are also isolated in terms of their movements. They are less likely to even visit nonpoor and white neighborhoods, which makes such cosmopolitan spaces, like the Reading Terminal Market, that much more important.[38] Located in the heart of the city's downtown, the old public market hall sits at the crossroads of multiple forms of transit and attracts shoppers from all over the city. As a place-making intersection of race and class differences, it assembles new interactions. Out of these interactions grew another public and private coalition. This time the goal was to repair the food distribution system's connections to underserved neighborhoods.

From Food Access to the Grocery Gap

The Reading Terminal Market's revitalization effort exposed the city's uneven food access. The public market hall was the birthplace of the Reading Terminal Farmers' Market Food Trust, a nonprofit organization that grew into a major state and national policy player. Eventually shortened to the Food Trust, the organization strategically focused on the relationship between nutritional education, children's health, and food access, building a new bridge between the Reading Terminal and underserved neighborhoods. Initially, the Food Trust's mission focused on addressing food access as a place-based disruption, but over time, the organization reframed its approach to repairing the market infrastructure by working with politicians and supermarket owners and executives.

The Food Trust organizers reached out to other nonprofit organizations in Philadelphia to see what kind of food-related work existed. They found a number of emergency food agencies, but little in the way of managing the problem of stable food sources for underserved neighborhoods. Visiting neighborhoods, they realized that the quality of food sold in local corner stores was inferior. By the 1990s, most poor neighborhoods were being serviced merely by small bodegas with few fresh products. The fresh produce that was being sold was often old and more expensive.[39]

The Food Trust organizers decided to work with the expertise of the Reading Terminal Market merchants and bring food directly to those neighborhoods. They partnered with housing project tenant councils.[40] The first site was the Tasker housing projects in South Philadelphia at 29th and Morris Streets, where 736 apartments housed more than 2,500 low-income residents.[41] The Food Trust purchased fruits and vegetables from the Wholesale Food Distribution Center and from the Leola Produce Auction in Lancaster County. Two produce merchants from the Reading Terminal Market helped out, trucking the produce to the Reading Terminal site, where a city truck then brought the produce to the South Philadelphia location. The goal was not to make money. The Food Trust charged neighborhood customers just a little over cost. A piece of bruised fruit cost merely a dime.[42]

Repairing an infrastructure, however, is different than solving a place-based disruption. Food access is both geographically bounded and systemic—its causes are not simply related to what is happening in local neighborhoods. The pattern of uneven distribution cuts across cities, states, and countries.[43] The Food Trust faced many of the same constraints that farmers' markets and supermarket companies previously faced. It was difficult to sustain the channels of distribution. Duane Perry, who founded the Food Trust, says, "Not only did we have to learn how to buy the produce, but we had to figure out how to sell it and do all the accounting for it, and transport it, and market it."[44] The organization extended its reach through fundraising campaigns and events to acquire the $25,000 necessary for each site to break even.[45]

The fundraising campaigns allowed the Food Trust to plan 10 new community markets within a year and a half, but as the organization expanded, the economic approach was not sustainable.[46] Perry says these efforts were successful in terms of outreach and getting food to underserved neighborhoods, but the organization could not go on forever without having constant sources of funding. "Everything that was driving us was removed from the profit motive. It didn't allow us to get mean and lean and run a good business. We were just running it like a nonprofit mission." The Food Trust purchased produce and distributed it, but its low-volume supplies, reliance on middlemen to move the food, and piecemeal organizational and distribution strategies would not maintain the neighborhood markets in the long run.

In the mid-1990s, a series of studies and policy reports in the United Kingdom and the United States started to link supermarket access to diet-related illnesses. These studies brought the idea of the "grocery gap" and the "food desert" to the public eye. Mark Epstein was the president of a nonprofit organization called Public Voice that, along with University of Connecticut agricultural economists, conducted an early study on the topic. They focused on 21 different cities, including Philadelphia. Epstein said, "The grocery store gap is triple trouble for low-income families. It increases their grocery bills, causes their diets to suffer, and can threaten the economic viability of their communities."[47]

In the study, Philadelphia had the second highest "grocery store gap." The number of "supermarkets per 10,000 residents in the poorest Philadelphia neighborhoods was less than half the number in the most affluent neighborhoods."[48] In areas with the highest proportion of residents receiving food stamps, Philadelphia had substantially fewer supermarkets. The city's gap between grocery market access for people living in poverty and those not living in poverty was the worst in the nation. Ronald W. Cotterill, the agricultural economist who headed the study, described it as "two food distribution systems"—one for people who have access to supermarkets and one for those who do not.[49]

Perry said that for the first five years, the Food Trust had "been so focused on nutrition education and farmers' markets" that it did not strategize to solve problems at the scale of infrastructure-building. Policy interests and nonprofit organizations turned their focus to these issues.[50] The Food Trust conducted its own studies and created GIS maps to better communicate the city's uneven food access to politicians. The organization worked with University of Pennsylvania urban designers to produce a report, *The Need for More Supermarkets*, which used the map-making technologies to demonstrate correlations between neighborhoods, income, supermarket access, and diet-related health outcomes. The report described the "uneven distribution" of Philadelphia supermarkets, such that poor neighborhoods had "70 too few."[51] They brought the report to the Philadelphia City Council, whose members suggested convening a task force. The task force included representatives of large supermarket corporations, franchise owners, nonprofit leaders, economic and real estate developers, executives of a community development financial institution (CDFI), and public health experts.

City, state, and federal governments all had programs for investing in industries. Public subsidies, grants, and tax breaks have been widely used to provide leverage in place-based growth initiatives: to attract high-tech businesses, hotel developers, port activity, corporate headquarters, and housing developers. It was part of the conventional zero-sum logic of place-based growth machines to see which municipality offered the best packages to attract them.[52] Retailing, and especially supermarket development, had a different investment and planning history. The conventional industry and community development wisdom was that food retailing was driven by demand. Perry says, "Community development practitioners at the time thought, 'If we build housing, the retail will follow. We don't have to worry about it.'" More housing meant increased population densities, which then would translate into more foot traffic and sales volumes.[53]

Certainly, retail needs consumer volume to maintain the necessary demand structure to stay in business. However, reconfiguring the relationship between supply and demand is where organizational and economic knowledge is less clear. It is also in this reconfiguration where the risk threshold is lower. Organizational scholars point out that it is difficult to change conventions already imprinted in everyday operations. Businesses accumulate economic benefits by sustaining profitable methods. Previous successes and failures get built into the forecasting and decision-making priorities.[54]

Market-makers sometimes defy conventional wisdom, however. That risk-taking dynamic of pushing against the boundaries of conventional supply and demand protocols is, in part, how industries change. Wal-Mart disregarded retailing common sense, not just by opening in small towns, but by figuring out, through trial and error, new development and distribution methods for thriving in them. It was difficult to profit from small-town mass merchandising, but Wal-Mart created new forms of distribution expertise that redefined the conventional wisdom—they changed the standard profit-making protocol.

Likewise, urban locations had unique obstacles for the food system's profitability structure. In the 1970s, companies faced bankruptcies and some went completely out of business. The urban situation scared many companies away. The profitability conventions constrained corporate decision-making.[55] Information systems, bar codes, mass-merchandising competitions, and corporate consolidations strengthened the low-margin and high-volume structure of suburban market development. As the issue of food access gained public attention two decades later, journalists investigating the problem found a common refrain from supermarket industry representatives. A *Philadelphia Inquirer* article in the early 2000s summarized the list of obstacles industry leaders reported: "high taxes; zoning regulations; a shortage of large, vacant and affordable parcels of land; and crime."[56]

Challenging the common sense does not mean that the common sense is wrong. Wal-Mart actually did come up against those small-town obstacles—and the company found solutions that had not previously been applied. Likewise, urban-based market obstacles are real. Jeff Brown is a fourth-generation Philadelphia grocer and president and CEO of Brown's Super Stores. He owns and operates 10 Shop Rite supermarkets in the Delaware Valley with an average store size of 60,000 square feet. He became one of the franchise owners to use the public subsidies eventually made available for supermarket development. He opened six stores in former food deserts, including several in Philadelphia.

In a presentation to the Opportunity Finance Network in 2012, Brown argued, "'Food deserts' are not self-correcting." Their operating costs are higher and their margins are lower. Usually, he said, supermarkets run on a 1 percent profit margin, but food desert stores typically have a 4 percent loss per store. Brown pointed out that food desert stores have lower sales volumes and lower gross profits. They also have lower sales in the highest margin departments: produce, deli, general merchandise, and gourmet. And they have higher costs in training, security, insurance, and building maintenance. Companies opening in food deserts need to find ways to make up for these losses. Brown argued that historically, private companies tried to fix the profitability structure with "higher pricing, lower wages, or reduced standards." These methods did not work. It led to consumer complaints and store failures. He suggested that the retailing industry needed other options—including public subsidies.[57]

Infrastructural systems do not change alone by resistance, differentiation, or managing products that cannot fit into standardized systems. Infrastructural systems change by finding ways to tune up the conventional wisdom and the commonsense practices of building interactive compatibility. The problem with supermarket development was partly about challenging the typical business approaches of supermarket operators themselves. But it was also about challenging the taken-for-granted knowledge of public policy-makers who did not historically make subsidies available for supermarket and other retail development.

Public Subsidies for a Retail System

Throughout history, public subsidies were necessary but not sufficient for building new food distribution connections. Subsidies for railroads and highways in earlier eras are prime examples. They did not create the conventions of market coordination, but they sponsored infrastructural linkages between production and consumption. They set up the conditions of possibility for market and place-making innovations. Public subsidies were once again important in reconfiguring the food distribution system in the early 2000s as a project of infrastructural repair.

The Philadelphia Food Market Task Force started the conversation between representatives of different sectors. Together, they came up with 10 recommendations, almost all based on public support for market-based goals to solve distribution problems. The recommendations were that the city and state should employ "data-driven market assessment techniques" to identify "unmet market demand in urban neighborhoods"; give special priority for land-use options to supermarket developers; lower "regulatory barriers to supermarket investment"; create a state fund for financing private supermarket development; and put together an advisory board of public and private interests to oversee and implement individual projects.[58]

The Philadelphia Food Market Task Force brought its list of recommendations to state politicians and policy-makers. In the early 2000s, Dwight Evans was a state representative from Philadelphia and the Pennsylvania House Appropriations Committee Chair. Evans already knew about the food access problems facing his constituents, who had complained for years about declining markets in their neighborhoods. Evans saw solutions to the problem from two different sides, in terms of both public health and employment opportunities. The issue was about neighborhood and community development in places long deprived of resources.

Along with Representatives Frank Oliver of Philadelphia and Jake Wheatley of Pittsburgh, Dwight Evans called for the Pennsylvania House Committee on Health and Human Services to hold hearings on the issue of the grocery gap. The report from the hearings corresponded with the Food Trust's previous findings. The report stated that the grocery gap was a statewide public health, economic health, and community health problem. The proposed solution was a new partnership between government and private industry. The Pennsylvania House of Representatives made it official with the Pennsylvania Fresh Food Financing Initiative (FFFI): for the first time, supermarket access was labeled by the state as a public problem.[59]

The Pennsylvania FFFI made an initial $10 million available in 2004 and then sponsored additional $10 million allocations in each of the next two years. It was the first program of its type in the nation. This public-private alliance was funded by the state, but the nonprofit sector, especially the Food Trust and the Reinvestment Fund, played central roles in its implementation. The Urban Affairs Coalition focused on the workforce side of the equation, convincing store managers and owners to pursue more equitable employment opportunities for lower-income and minority residents in the communities where the stores were built.[60]

The state put forth the initial $30 million, but the Reinvestment Fund, a federally certified CDFI, leveraged the resources into a $120 million fund that continued to grow.[61] The Food Trust was the main advocacy and community outreach partner. The organization conducted community research; put together GIS maps demonstrating the most significant spaces of need in the state; engaged in nutrition and public health campaigns; and worked with grocery store management to determine the eligibility of specific projects and locations.[62]

Maybe most important was the Food Trust's efforts to find supermarket companies willing to participate. The largest supermarket companies did not want to open up stores in food deserts. Corporate consolidations and shifting national investment priorities made it difficult for them to succeed outside of standard financing and centralized decision-making conventions. Representatives of large corporations participated in defining the problems, but not in fixing them. For example, an Acme executive was one of the chairs of the Philadelphia Food Market Task Force, but Acme did not apply for public subsidies to support opening new stores.

There are multiple reasons. Acme is a banner of Albertson's, the second largest supermarket corporation in the nation. The company faced local problems in Philadelphia, as well as financial problems at the national corporate level, that made it difficult to open up new stores in the city. Acme is a homegrown chain that was forced to close down dozens of stores in earlier decades. The corporation had built only a few new Philadelphia supermarkets since the 1980s. In low-income neighborhoods, in particular, it was up against uncertain conditions. In one Southwest Philadelphia neighborhood, a major event of gun violence severely handicapped the success of a new store.

On the corporate side, the Acme chain changed hands multiple times over the years. In the early 1990s, the American Stores Company, then the owner of Acme, sold some of its stores to the Penn Traffic Company. Albertson's purchased the banner in the late 1990s, but then sold the entire banner off to SuperValu in 2006. In 2013, Albertson's regained ownership. The shifting around of stores between corporate entities, from dozens to hundreds of outlets at a time, is commonplace. In the process, however, it leads to corporate consolidations and shifting investment priorities that make it difficult for large companies at the whim of stockholders to adjust to highly specific local needs.[63]

Franchise businesses and independent operators run differently than large corporate retailers. According to Perry, "They're the businesses that took advantage [of the public financing], because they are more cash poor and operate from tighter cash flows." They also have the ability to connect directly to the places where they open. For a project to financially succeed, the supermarket owners had to entangle business expertise, merchandise volume, consumer demands, and prime environmental conditions in the neighborhoods to offset the profit-making constraints. According to a report by the Reinvestment Fund, the public resources were provided to "help a store operator overcome location-dependent start-up costs," but they were not guarantees of "long-term profitability in the face of unsustainable operating expenses." The resources were a "catalyst for economic development."[64] As Representative Dwight Evans and Food Trust executive John Weidman wrote, "FFFI was designed to help launch stores that would then operate on their own. It is important to note that FFFI did not subsidize the stores' success. Success was up to the operator."[65]

Once again, although the public financing was motivating new supermarket developments, it was also bound up with the narratives of the market: entrepreneurial success, managing competition between private companies, and the pursuit of efficiency and profitability. Franchise owners served as bridges between local places and larger distribution networks. Jeff Brown's Shop Rites and Patrick Burns' Fresh Grocers, two of the franchise owners who participated in the FFFI and opened stores in Philadelphia, are both part of the Wakefern Corporation, the largest supermarket cooperative in the nation. The cooperative buying system allows franchisees to have access to the high-volume and high-variety efficiency networks in distribution that enable them to cut down on buying costs.

Yet as franchisees, they are also owner-operators of their stores, allowing them unique connections to their shoppers. Burns said that his Germantown store had requests for "goat meat, Chinese rabbit, oxtails, chicken feet, and flanken in the meat case, and collards, cactus pears and rappini" in the produce section. The store did not initially have those products, but Burns found ways to include all of them. One of Brown's ShopRite stores had a huge demand for halal meat. After hearing the requests, Brown went out of his way, against local backlash from some customers, to integrate the products into his store. One reporter wrote that "real supermarkets" opening up in urban neighborhoods are "following the formula of the old-fashioned corner store" by matching products to specific consumer tastes.[66]

The supermarket projects needed the right environmental conditions, too. Not all sites were created equal. Brown sat on a panel for a contest and reviewed planning proposals for a new supermarket in North Philadelphia. His comments to the participants revealed the kinds of decisions that business owners in food deserts needed to address. He said, "I think North Philly needs a grocery store, and should have one somewhere. But not this site. . . . We have a lot of stores in underserved areas, and we can make it work. But this site has too much, physically, going against it."[67]

Brown pointed to major physical and environmental limitations of the site. It lacked space for parking. Even if the majority of local residents did not drive, urban supermarkets still depended on high-volume distribution and needed to attract customers from other areas to increase foot traffic. The site also lacked space for high-volume delivery by large trucks and did not have direct access to the main road. Brown said, "You could have a sign on Girard Avenue" that signals to customers that a store is around the corner, but "stores do the best when you can see the store from the main road."[68] In opening his own stores, Brown was attentive to these kinds of physical and environmental conditions, as well as others like crime rates in surrounding neighborhoods and the need for bus stops in front of all of his stores to bring more customers in.[69]

Brown's attention to the intersection between infrastructure and consumer volume is similar to the suburban standard market design. However, at the same time, Brown continued to match the high-volume profit-making standards with local community needs. He said, "Before we open a store in a neighborhood, we work with community leaders . . . learn about their background, religion, where their families came from."[70] Some of his stores have community centers for residents to hold meetings. Other stores have credit unions with free checking and ATM use. They employ nutritionists and social workers. Some even house nonprofit health clinics. Brown also advocated for hiring ex-prison inmates.[71]

In these examples, there is no separation between economic development and community development, between public health and community health. Brown said that working on the community side helped with the economic side. It is not surprising that Brown was also the most visible success story of the Pennsylvania FFFI. He was recognized by the First Lady Michelle Obama, who invited him to sit with her during President Obama's State of the Union address.

The Paradox of Infrastructural Repair

By 2010, the Pennsylvania FFFI was changing the food landscape in Philadelphia neighborhoods and spreading across the state. It provided more than $73 million in loans and $12 million in grants, led to the opening of 88 retail stores, created more than 5,000 new jobs, and developed 1.67 million square feet of commercial space.[72] The Pennsylvania program served as the model for the national initiative. One of the motivations for publicly subsidizing supermarkets was the expectation that supermarkets contributed to public health. However, as supermarkets opened in food deserts, the social science and population health fields closely studied them. They raised questions about whether this high-volume and high-variety infrastructural system actually solved health disparities.

In 2009, more than a decade after the original Reading Terminal Market Food Trust was established, 39 United States Congress members identified unequal access to healthy food as a national problem.[73] To roll out the national campaign, the Food Trust and the Reinvestment Fund teamed up with Policy Link, a California-based nonprofit research and advocacy organization. They also worked with the United States Departments of Treasury, Agriculture, and Health and Human Services, along with the Office of the First Lady. The Reinvestment Fund managed the national allocation, leveraging $220 million in federal money into more than $1 billion available for sponsoring market development in underserved locations across the country.[74] Between 2011 and 2015, the program subsidized over 1,000 grocery stores in 35 states.[75]

The USDA also solidified an official definition of "food desert" as a social and public health problem. One report stated that an urban place was a food desert when at least 500 people and/or 33 percent of the census tract lived more than a mile from a supermarket. In rural areas, the distance from a supermarket was understood to be more than 10 miles. The idea of the food desert grew into a topic of national concern, taken up in policy debates and discussions by the Centers for Disease Control and Prevention (CDC), the American Nutrition Association, the National Research Council, and the Robert Wood Johnson Foundation. Thousands of newspaper articles, magazine stories, and blogs reported on the topic. By the end of 2018, over 6,000 academic articles in public health, policy, and social science journals referenced the concept of the "food desert."

The idea of the food desert fit into conventional problem-solving and social reform narratives about urban decline, neighborhood isolation, and uneven development. Yet the success of the Healthy Food Financing Initiative— building many new supermarkets in underserved neighborhoods across the country—created the environmental conditions to further study whether supermarket access solved public health problems.

Although many studies found a correlation between neighborhoods, supermarket access, and health outcomes, two distinct approaches challenged the findings. First, a series of studies pointed to "food swamps"—not food deserts—as the cause of health disparities. They found that fast food restaurants and other unhealthy options in the neighborhood environment "swamp out" healthier options.[76] A study out of the Rudd Center for Food Policy and Obesity, then at Yale University, now at the University of Connecticut, described food swamps as areas with "a high-density of establishments selling high-calorie fast food and junk food, relative to healthier food options." The authors argued that the "presence of a food swamp is a stronger predictor of obesity rates than the absence of full-service grocery stores."[77]

On the basis of this logic, it would appear that supermarkets—even if the surrounding commercial environment was different—would not necessarily change the behaviors and tastes of individual consumers. The supermarket is itself a food swamp. While supermarkets are the largest purveyors of the foods that nutritional experts deem the "healthiest," like fruits and vegetables, they are also the largest purveyors of foods deemed the "unhealthiest." They have aisles filled with soda, candy, ice cream, and other products with high contents of sugar, processed oils, and refined grains. One study out of the University of Illinois, based on a survey of 4,204 adults in the United States, found that 46.3 percent of the sample consumed sugar-sweetened beverages and high-energy, low-nutrient foods, and 52.4 percent of that subgroup purchased those foods at supermarkets.[78]

Secondly, a study by economists at New York University, Stanford University, and the University of Chicago found that the link between income and nutritional knowledge more directly causes unhealthy eating than proximity to a supermarket. The authors of this study argued that unhealthy eating is caused by neither the supply system, nor the neighborhoods (e.g., the "food swamps") in which people live. All else being equal—like availability and price of foods—poor people continue to have diets that are less healthy than wealthier people. They identified the problem in the structure of demand, that is, in the different consumer behaviors related to income and nutritional knowledge.[79]

Most significantly in this case, what started as a small local endeavor to address urban decline and practical problems in people's everyday lives, turned into a full-fledged research and policy field with overlapping discussions between scholars of public health, agricultural economics, behavioral psychology, public policy, food policy, political science, sociology, geography, and urban planning. Food access became part of a coherent debate over the variables, methods, and causes of unhealthy consumption and unequal health outcomes.

As with most fields of inquiry, the studies did not simplify the issues, they complicated them. The questions were no longer about whether health outcomes related to food consumption were unequal, but how and why. By pointing out alternative explanations, these academic debates have collectively, as a field of inquiry, raised the need to study the problem as a complex system: to assess the relationships between retail suppliers, fast food industries, large food manufacturers, neighborhood conditions, economic disparities in food spending, proximity to the marketplace from people's homes, proximity from where people work, how people travel through the city, nutritional information available to medical professionals and consumers alike, public subsidies directing economic development as health prevention, and the relative autonomy of cultural traditions and consumer tastes. These debates over who and what causes health and nutritional disparities speak to the difficulties social scientists, medical professionals, and public health scholars face studying the problems. Not only are the health interventions unclear from these studies, but the very definition of the problem remains murky.

The soda tax debates that have taken place in many cities, including in Philadelphia, represent an issue where profitability conventions have been pitted against public health concerns. Many public health scholars argue that taxing soda and other sugar-sweetened beverages, just like taxing cigarettes, would help slow certain epidemics, in this case, related to obesity, cardiovascular disease, and diabetes.

Yet Jeff Brown, the progressive supermarket operator who opened multiple stores in food deserts, was one of the strongest opponents of the soda tax. Brown argued that his shoppers were leaving the city to purchase soda, hurting his bottom line in stores already facing constraints on profit margins. In March 2019, Brown closed one of his stores located in a former food desert at 67th and Haverford in West Philadelphia. Brown said the "beverage tax" pushed the store into a $1 million deficit. He hung a banner outside his store, letting his customers know his thoughts on the cause: "Store Closing, March 14, 2019. A Result of the Philadelphia Beverage Tax."[80]

The conflict between politicians and public health advocates taxing soda versus supermarket entrepreneurs and corporations profiting from high-volume sales of soda exposes something deeply problematic about this vital infrastructure. Changing health outcomes is not simply about a single product like soda, nor is it only about proximity to supermarkets. It is about how infrastructural interdependencies, profit-making conventions, and consumer tastes have been built up and solidified over time. A profit-making infrastructure for fulfilling convenience and taste has become interwoven with the nation's public health.

Problem-Solving and Unfinished Infrastructure

The food distribution system entangles social and material components into coherent patterns. But like cities and regions, infrastructure is unfinished.[81] A central difficulty with managing a complex system is the ongoing search for clearer definitions of the problems as the infrastructural interdependencies, industry conventions, knowledge competencies, and environmental conditions change.

Researchers in the United States have been trying to find more precise research methods and explanations of inequality for over a century. Sociology's history in the United States has itself been embedded in the urban environment. Foundational studies in Philadelphia and Chicago on race, ethnicity, social class, neighborhoods, and economic development were geared toward urban social reform.[82] Social scientists have continued their interests in building healthier and more equitable communities, but so much has changed: the meanings and experiences of living in cities and suburbs; the physical transit connections and scales of organizational interdependencies; and the methods and research tools for studying and explaining social and public health problems.

Trying to bring supermarkets to underserved neighborhoods was not easy because the markets did not leave urban centers out of a conspiracy to deprive disadvantaged people of a healthy diet. Many companies tried to remain in cities before they eventually closed down their stores. Various corporate moves out of the urban center were increasingly reified through mutual adaptations between profitability conventions and secular trends in land use, transit, and consumerism.

Finding ways to attract supermarkets to underserved places has created difficult conversations among policy-makers and academics who care about solving persistent inequalities. The issue has revived one of the core debates in the social sciences. Some scholars have explained food access and health disparities in terms of the structure of demand, while others have looked to the structure of supply. Yet the link between consumerism and health is not based on an either/or dynamic between consumer knowledge and corporate power.[83]

The idea that access to information rather than access to food is the key to understanding healthy eating is itself difficult to assess, let alone resolve through policy levers. For one, it is not clear what kind of nutritional information matters for shaping healthier consumer choices about diet. Food diaries, which are prominent research tools for tracking individual-level consumption, are not always accurate. Moreover, limited medical research exists on the causal links between specific foods as "treatments" for specific diseases. Despite the seemingly endless advice on the internet about what to eat to improve health outcomes, medical and nutrition journals lack consistent findings from randomized trials about the relationships between diet and disease.[84]

The modern health care system was not set up to study and guide people's eating habits toward optimizing population health. Nor was the food system designed to convince people to buy broccoli and kale—or any specific food product in isolation from any of the others. Instead, a profit-making logic was embedded into a vital infrastructure in ways that shaped the taken-for-granted links between information, heterogeneous market objects, and consumerism. The system materialized to reward the sale of lots of stuff at the same time. It has promoted high-volume merchandising, cheap foods, and diet fads. Even policy-makers concerned about health disparities have framed solutions in terms of the infrastructure of abundance and convenience. The result is that in the world of problem-solving and policy-making, managing market risk has become inseparable from managing health risk.

EIGHT

The Problem with Feeding Cities

By the turn of the twentieth century, railroads connected sites of production and consumption, wholesale operations settled in urban downtowns, and chain grocery stores were sprouting up by the hundreds in cities across the United States. The infrastructural regime was geared toward feeding cities. But during the next century, it transformed from feeding cities to feeding regions to feeding almost the entire population of the nation.

The transformation of the food system was not just about extending the reach of the distribution connections. Nor was it simply a change in the visible semiotics of marketplaces—the sizes of stores and the range of products assembled into clearly marked aisles. It was a shift in the mutually reinforcing interdependencies between the physical connecting hardware, political, economic, and nonprofit organizations, technical competencies, conventions of coordinating and evaluating product qualities, and consumer expectations about abundance and convenience.

Food was like water and electricity in that its development as an infrastructural system required harnessing and controlling nature to create stable reserves of natural resources. The "standing reserve" made it possible for organizational actors to find and implement subsequent methods to configure supply and demand.[1] Yet food was, and remains, an unusual and paradoxical necessity. Food is necessary for human survival, but unlike water and electricity, which are deemed public goods, the food system was built upon profit-seeking priorities. Food's heterogeneity—what constituted food, how suppliers determined their value structures, and consumers' diverse tastes—influenced agricultural, manufacturing, wholesaling, storage, and retailing industries, as well as informed the science of nutrition and the methods of responding to public health problems.

In all its complexity, the food system has served as a bridge between urbanism, capitalism, and public health in the United States. The infrastructural interdependencies created taken-for-granted ways of interacting and exchanging goods and experiencing the environment. As William Cronon explains, infrastructural connections layered a "second nature" onto the landscape.[2] People inhabited the infrastructural interdependencies in terms of their time-space organizations, rhythms, and paces.

Although food is a necessity, the social and material manifestation of the complex system for fulfilling sustenance, convenience, and tastes was not necessary. The transformation of the food system was not the result of functional adaptations and the upgrading evolution of society. People did not need chain stores, supermarkets, highly processed foods, or any specific branded food products or packaging materials for nourishment and survival to occur. Howard Becker explains in his account of art worlds, "It is misleading in suggesting there is any necessity for such ways to survive exactly as they are."[3] The rise of the American food system was like the making of art worlds in that regard. It could have happened differently had different organizational priorities and environmental conditions interacted and materialized as infrastructural interdependencies between sites of production, storage, distribution, and consumption.

However, stating that the food system could have developed differently is not the same as explaining why it actually formed and transformed in the particular ways it did. The profit-driven logic of the food system did not arise out of functional necessity, but it also did not come about through hegemonic capitalist plots to impose, from the top down or from the outside in, the nexus between profits and efficiencies into a vital infrastructure. Likewise, political-economic planners did not seek to make people unhealthy—to strategically create food deserts or manufacture diabetes and obesity epidemics.

This book has explained *why* the American food distribution system materialized in the ways that it did by unraveling *how* it happened. To that end, it has complicated causation in terms of the formation, maintenance, and transformation of the food system and how it has affected the political, economic, nonprofit, and public health sectors. The key to explaining the transformation of a complex system is to trace the empirical decision-making contexts and conditions in order to locate how, when, and why new interdependencies formed, constrained organizational possibilities, and stabilized particular outcomes.

Rather than revisiting in close detail the wide-ranging examples from the previous chapters, what follows are sociological lessons abstracted from the range of examples to better understand how the food system has changed and why such changes led to collective consequences. Three interrelated themes are central: infrastructural uncertainty; permeating market technologies; and the unintended consequences of the transformation of a complex system.

Infrastructural Uncertainty

Disruptions of infrastructural interdependencies have caused wide-ranging problems: canals flooded, bridges were washed out, towns and cities experienced electrical blackouts, lead leached into drinking water, and droughts, storms, and contaminations affected food supplies. Most of us have no idea how the underlying infrastructural connections were made or how they get patched up when they fall apart. Geoffrey Bowker and Susan Leigh Star point out that focusing on the "infrastructural work" of actors repairing the connections allows researchers to investigate the knowledge and practical competencies for reinforcing the taken-for-granted sociotechnical ties.[4] Once the organizational and material components are locked into each other, infrastructural work is necessary for sustaining the interdependencies that make routine access to resources possible.

However, throughout history, certain disruptions modified the mutually reinforcing connections that underlay the infrastructural regimes. In those problem situations, decision-makers and technicians were not immediately able to repair the connections. Rather than calling forth infrastructural work to reinforce the sociotechnical order, these cracks in the system created an indeterminate context through which system transformations became possible. Infrastructural uncertainties occurred when multiple coordination and connection options were made available in the shared context; they challenged organizational decision-makers' established frameworks; and they created moments of material incompatibility between organizations and supply chains.

Historical studies can trace the shift in the underlying logics of sociotechnical relationships because, in retrospect, researchers are able to identify the patterns that have accumulated into distinct infrastructural regimes. However, just because a bird's-eye view reveals collective differentiation over time and space, does not mean that the people building and configuring the organizational and technical networks could see the direct pathways ahead. In contexts of infrastructural uncertainty, multiple options were made available and decision-makers were not yet clear how the conventions for pursuing the link between profitability, supply coordination, and physical connections would line up.

This book investigated different moments of infrastructural uncertainty. Political, economic, and nonprofit decision-makers considered questions at the heart of the changing intersections between urbanism, capitalism, and public health: how should organizations in cities, suburbs, and exurbs respond to population changes and development; what kinds of public and private organizations and technical innovations should they promote; which forms of transportation, storage, and coordination should take precedence; which relationships are deemed most profitable; where should the physical exchange intersections be located; what combinations of product volumes and varieties should be included in the distribution relationships; what product qualities are considered standard qualities; how should organizations manage foods that do not fit; what role should nutrition play in food supply chains; and how should political and economic actors reconfigure supplies and demands?

These kinds of practical questions were fundamental to the contexts of infrastructural uncertainty. For instance, in the early 1900s, political and economic decision-makers were uncertain about how to supply cities like Philadelphia by linking together emerging sites of agricultural production and urban-based consumption. Transporting perishable foods by rail and ship posed problems for feeding cities. Subsequent changes further complicated decision-making. These included major economic events, suburban sprawl, new preservation, automation, and transportation methods, increasing types of products and brands, and new marketing and distribution platforms.

Conjunctions of independent series of actions and interactions in the broader environment—in this case, in terms of land use, transportation development, and population settlement—were outside the control of any specific interest group. The changing environmental conditions, what Diane Vaughan calls "environmental uncertainty," informed these decision-making situations.[5] Yet the context itself gained endogenous characteristics through which political and economic actors engaged with and modified the system of interdependencies. Ivan Ermakoff argues that such situations shared a "structure of contingency." In the "absence" of a "preestablished script," actors reflected on the "alternative lines of conduct." The "interpretive schemes [lost] their taken-for-granted character."[6] Organizational actors, working in different parts of the system, tried to make sense of the emerging uncertainties.

Managing uncertainty is not the same as infrastructural uncertainty. Managing uncertainty is now a prominent feature of political and economic organization. Various sectors assemble evermore complex information departments to design contingency plans. Strategic actors create models and theories to simulate plausible actions coming from other organizational parts of an industry or geopolitical alignment. Yet using information to build forecasting models is a kind of infrastructural work that upholds the sociotechnical order. People study available historical content to find behavioral and discursive patterns, which they use to simulate the environmental conditions and inform preemptive strategies of system maintenance—to reproduce the system, not to transform it.

In contrast, infrastructural uncertainty occurs when decision-makers in the shared context reflect on and debate the alternative meanings and methods for evaluating and investing in the sociotechnical interdependencies themselves. Circumstances of infrastructural uncertainty give rise to what Owen Whooley calls "epistemic contests," which are oppositions over "what constitutes legitimate knowing."[7] In the history of the food system, these were not just inter-firm competitions, like Philadelphia's four largest grocery chains—A&P, American Stores Company, Food Fair, and Penn Fruit—competing for foot traffic in the same region. Instead, political and economic actors experienced infrastructural uncertainty when there were disturbances in the shared fabric of standardization, valuation, and coordination in relationship to the physical transit, communication connections, and patterns of urban and suburban development.

When these epistemic disruptions materialized, the political and economic decision-makers did not know which path would lead to the shared industry conventions of profitability. They sunk resources—or withheld making investments—into certain modes of coordination and connection instead of others. These sunk costs had repercussions for the exchange dynamics. Maybe most significant for the transformation of the food system was that these decisions pulled at the social and technical compatibility between different organizations in supply chains. The threads holding together farmers, manufacturers, wholesalers, storage operators, shippers, and retailers started to unwind. Exchange partners remained interactive over lengthy periods, but they became incompatible in their methods for pursuing profitability and efficiency.

In such situations, the tensions in the system's physical infrastructure and standards of valuation were visible in everyday life. As shippers replaced rail transport with larger tractor-trailers, the trucks no longer fit into downtown wholesale markets. The urban market spaces were built for a different era of coordination and connection. Trucking and rail shippers also battled for positionality. Cities housed multiple storage and wholesale depots— some rail-centered, others truck-dependent—which created confusions for farmers, brokers, and shippers trying to get their products to consumers in both cities and suburbs. The disruptions diffused downstream. Retail buyers traveled to multiple wholesale locations before stocking their stores in towns and cities across the region. The situation prompted retailers to rethink their relationships with farmers and wholesalers and how they calculated their own profits and losses.

Large grocery retail chains bypassed the urban wholesale operations in supply chains, but they were up against additional confusions regarding suburban development. They built stores in both cities and suburbs and designed different models. Chain combination stores were different than warehouse "cheapy markets"; and these early urban supermarkets, unlike their suburban counterparts, had no parking lots. Various kinds of distribution centers and marketplaces were built in cities and suburbs at the same time. It was not initially clear to politicians, agricultural economists, wholesalers, family businesses, shippers, or corporate retailers alike how industry profitability conventions would crystalize.

The suburban supermarket system eventually prevailed, but another situation of infrastructural uncertainty arose in the 1970s. Production sectors continued to expand volumes and varieties of supplies through mass production and automation. In contrast, retailing, shipping, and wholesaling industries had almost no automation to manage the increasing volume and range of products. Industry executives on all sides were fully aware of the low profit-margin problems of supermarkets, but they were uncertain as to what kinds of automation they could apply to retailing sectors to resolve the discrepancies. The information age was on the horizon, but for decades, the methods of coordination and connection remained incompatible between production, distribution, storage, and consumption.

Even as industries took on these problems of automation through the 1970s and into the 1980s, they found that processed shelf-stable foods fit more easily into the distribution system than perishable ones, especially fruits and vegetables. New interdependencies created new opportunities and constraints. Fruit and vegetable supply chains eventually defeated seasons and mimicked the supermarket's year-round high-volume and high-variety arrangement. This relationship between nonperishable and perishable supply chains was reconfigured through mutual adaptations, which then created additional downstream repercussions for nonprofit food banks. Lean supply chains for shelf-stable foods translated into fewer donations to food banks. However, the high-volume, high-variety fresh produce supply chains could not exactly mimic the more precise "just-in-time" handling of nonperishable goods. Perishable products often fell outside of supermarket standards and were made available to food banks.

Under conditions of infrastructural uncertainty, neither the contexts nor any particular strategic actors provided the definitive paths forward. Infrastructural uncertainty was a necessary condition in the transformation of the food system, but it was not sufficient. It set in motion competing methods, materials, and standards of valuation, coordination, and connection. Shifting from infrastructural uncertainty to infrastructural interdependency occurred by way of collective intelligence and sociotechnical implementation. In this case, permeating market technologies filled the cracks of uncertainty.

Permeating Market Technologies

People plotted, under the constraints and conditions of infrastructural uncertainty, to use public resources to advance profit-making goals, organizational connections, technical innovations, and industry-wide standards. This process has been consistent throughout United States history since the rise of industrial capitalism. Public land was made available for private railroad corporations to lay down tracks that accelerated rural and urban development. The federal government subsidized suburbanization and sprawl, as well as highways and roads accommodating the auto, oil, and rubber industries, which led to new possibilities for spatial interdependencies. Federal agencies supplied the research and development for the original internet "web" on which private industries expanded in many directions, including into the management of distribution systems. The USDA, the FDA, and the Interstate Commerce Commission, among other government agencies, subsidized agricultural industries that led to higher yields of staple commodities that were converted into cheaper processed foods.

Michael Mann coined the term "infrastructural power" to refer to the autonomous role of the state to create systems of connection, coordination, literacy, and valuation. From this point of view, the state has played a central role in administering the profit-making logics of capitalism, for example, by investing in connective hardware, knowledge, and technology, and through taxation, industry regulations, and deregulations. Still, as Mann points out, such autonomous positions of power have been neither static nor directly converted into outcomes. Democracy under the conditions of capitalism has meant that the state must take into account the relatively autonomous inputs of civil society and interest groups, and of course, that includes changing economic interests as well.[8]

The material manifestation of the American food system was not the direct outcome of the state's "infrastructural power," but it also did not arise from "biopower." Biopower is Michel Foucault's term for the distributed rational administrative mechanisms aiming to optimize human life by controlling the biological features of the population.[9] It might seem logical that the state would set up a vital infrastructure according to a rational organizational logic geared toward optimizing population health, as occurred in managing domestic security threats over vital systems.[10] That is not to say that the American food system did not absorb any concerns about biological control and disciplining populations through a framework of public health and nutrition. All sorts of food safety regulations and standards diminished food-borne illnesses and supported nutrient fortification in staple products to address concerns about human sustenance.[11]

Yet managing human sustenance and protecting against security and contamination threats are different kinds of planning priorities than those for strategically optimizing population health. One major reason for persistent difficulties in elevating the role of nutrition in population health and in solving health disparities is that no mechanism was ever created for interlocking the American food system with public health, nutritional, and medical expertise. Nutritional expertise has played only a subordinate role in shaping human consumption and in treating illness and disease in the United States. Over time, pursuing profitability by way of fulfilling consumer convenience and tastes became more important than promoting human health. That is, the food system was set up to sustain populations and preserve markets but not to maximize the pursuit of the nation's health. And corporations and industry lobbyists took full advantage of this reality.[12]

However, there is an important distinction between political-economic strategy and permeating market technologies that maps onto the distinction drawn by Chandra Mukerji between infrastructural power and logistical power. Mukerji views the former as hierarchical and top down, in which administrative arms of the state were set up to control and discipline populations. In contrast, she views the latter as decentered and bottom-up, founded upon the technical logic of controlling nature and things.[13]

State-financed infrastructural projects gave rise to new physical connections and subsidized commodities and industries. Logistical knowledge facilitated the particular forms of territorial and land-use interdependencies, multiplied valuations and competitions through the established physical connections, and most importantly from Mukerji's perspective, advanced the primacy of technical problem-solving for responding to emerging uncertainties. Prior to building infrastructure connections, people did not have to worry about canals flooding, bridges getting washed out, or distribution systems failing. Yet once the physical connections were put in place, a "technocracy" built upon logistical expertise gained influence by managing risk and reinforcing the sociotechnical order.[14] Infrastructural work became the governing order of the day as the force of sociotechnical reproduction.

Unlike in Mukerji's account of hydraulics and canal building in seventeenth-century Southern France, building the United States food infrastructure was not the product of collective actions in a single time and place. The food system was constituted by heterogeneous organizations, supply chains, material resources, and regions. Nearly everyone in the United States is now reliant on this complex and spatially distributed system for sustenance. Those responsible for maintaining the food system and for solving its emergent problems have for more than a century filtered technical knowledge and practical competencies through the lens of managing market risk. They pushed calculative devices measuring profit/loss efficiencies into the invisible background of everyday food exchange interactions in ways that made market-based influences evermore difficult to comprehend or unravel.

Political-economic actors proposed ideological goals in terms of global trade, taxation, regulation, and securitization, but they did not implement the methods of framing and preserving corporate profitability as a top-down form of problem-solving.[15] Scientists, engineers, entrepreneurs, and executives evaluated the constraints on profit-based efficiencies and consumer conveniences. They came up with a range of organizational and technical prototypes. Actors with different interests and expertise negotiated over the designs and details of the new applications in order to facilitate more fluid interactions between exchange partners.[16] Through trial and error, they found "value-added" benefits that gradually changed supply chains.[17]

The power of logistical expertise comes from the collective and distributed work to turn infrastructural uncertainties into mutually reinforcing relationships between profits and efficiencies in situations. The rise of the supermarket is one example. By the end of the 1920s, grocery chains prospered, self-service stores were on the rise, and more canned and packaged products with longer shelf lives entered the market. During the Great Depression, entrepreneurs saw an opportunity to assemble different supply chains into one market space. The rise of "cheapy" warehouse markets was similar to the founding of early department stores that integrated multiple kinds of products and vendors into a single exchange location. Over time, supermarket buyers learned how to incorporate new product lines and cultivate relationships with hundreds and then thousands of different supply chains. They reconfigured the shared profit-seeking logic into a standard high-volume and high-variety distribution framework.

The creation of the UPC is another example. Scientists and engineers at technology firms like RCA and IBM carved out new connections between information technology, manufacturing, retailing, and wholesaling industries. They studied product codes, printing, scanning, lasers, automation, computerization, product packaging, accounting, and telecommunications. Scientists and engineers eventually marshaled these independent streams of knowledge into coherent market-based prototypes that manufacturers, retailers, and wholesalers could try out in their own facilities.

These historical situations were not just about actors pulling previous innovations together. Companies had to match up the social and practical competencies with technical innovations into everyday interaction situations. The two key components—the social and the technical—had to be synchronized for companies and supply chains to achieve the value-added rewards. For automated checkout systems to take off, many previous applications and details had to line up. Manufacturers figured out how to print bar codes on all of their products and take into account different kinds of packaging materials. Grocery clerks learned new ways of entering product information and operating automated checkout stands. Engineers worked out the missteps in the rhythms between scanners, bar code printing, and employee and consumer competencies. Corporations rearranged their inventory and restocking methods. Sometimes the codes did not scan, some manufacturers and retailers did not adopt the coding system, consumers did not like that they could not initially see the prices on products, and store managers were initially discouraged that the new system slowed down rather than accelerated the customer checkout process.

The relationships between the social and the technical were "tuned up" over time.[18] As benefits were realized, more and more supermarkets adopted the UPC system. Automated checkout stations became another part of mass consumerism, built into people's shopping routines. Once the sociotechnical methods were integrated, companies found additional applications in market research, storage, transportation, self-checkout, and online shopping. Market research firms learned how to assemble and study new consumer information, and retailers, wholesalers, and manufacturers applied the new techniques to better forecast the interdependencies between supply and demand. The sociotechnical apparatus served as the foundation on which big box stores eventually exploded onto the consumer landscape.

The infrastructural changes discussed throughout the book were dramatic: rail distribution was replaced by trucking; ice-based cooling was supplanted by refrigeration; corner grocery stores gave way to combination stores, supermarkets, and big box stores; seasonal fresh produce sections transitioned to standard produce aisles without seasons; in-store bookkeeping was replaced by computerized accounting operations; and the food system transformed at the aggregate level from feeding cities to feeding regions to feeding the nation.

However, no one imposed these systemic changes from the top down or from the outside in. At moments of infrastructural uncertainty, organizational actors carved out new directions and gradually built them into mutually reinforcing reward structures. New market technologies permeated everyday interactions. They created more information, additional ways of measuring and evaluating profit-based efficiency problems, new interactions between public, private, and nonprofit sectors, and new consumer expectations about abundance and convenience. There was neither a coherent political and economic plan to create optimal health conditions out of these permeating market technologies, nor a central organizational strategy for promoting unequal health outcomes.

Unintended Consequences of System Transformation

Businesses applied sociotechnical methods for controlling and calculating the link between profits and efficiencies into more and more situations. Over time, by managing infrastructural uncertainties in coordination and connection, they realigned the social and material conditions. This process shifted the dynamics between public and private investments; industries and market platforms; product qualities and supply chains; for-profit and nonprofit realms; and the sites and methods of production, storage, distribution, and consumption. Maybe most importantly, it repositioned the relationships between strategic means and collective outcomes by reinforcing a system for managing market risk instead of one for managing other forms of risk, like public health and environmental risks.

Focusing on the historical reconfiguration of infrastructural interdependencies creates challenges for how to explain collective outcomes. Attention to the history of system complexity directs the primary explanation away from centralized power holders. Instead, the explanation turns to permeating and accumulating processes through which strategic actors gained their positions and contributed to the "lasting asymmetries" of the "macrostructure."[19] Micro-level decision-making processes had to be converted into macro-level positions. In this case, grocery chains, supermarkets, big box stores, and online shopping amassed influence in relationship to geographic extensions of urbanization and suburbanization. As the infrastructural conditions changed, certain organizational actors took coercive steps to obtain and maintain positions at the top of the infrastructural regimes.

A&P, Kmart, Wal-Mart, and Amazon.com were not always monolithic retail agents of coercion, and of course, some of them waxed as others waned. A combination of public and private interests and investments reconfigured the infrastructural foundations on which Sam Walton turned his Ben Franklin five-and-dime retail chain into Wal-Mart and Jeff Bezos converted his upstart online bookstore into a shopping empire. There would be no Wal-Mart or Amazon.com without the prior organizational adjustments to repair the infrastructural uncertainties and revise the interdependencies in coordination and connection.

Investments in new market technologies did not immediately control the decisions of other actors distributed throughout the complex system. In this nonlinear system, strategic actors experienced difficulties controlling collective outcomes. As Robert Merton argues, "purposive behavior" can lead to "unanticipated consequences."[20] Harvey Molotch labels this process as an "iterative buildup."[21] Strategic organizations did not start at the macrolevel with the ability to survey the entirety of the system. They aggregated up to the macro-level. Other actors then had to respond and make decisions about whether or not to rearrange their own profit-making possibilities in the face of cumulative effects and changing conventions.

The result is that something can be a terrible outcome but not be the result of a plot to do something terrible. The creation of food deserts in the 1970s was an emergent outcome, not a capitalist plot. A distribution infrastructure with a distinct organizational logic and scale materialized out of suburban developments and auto-centered networks. Corporate decision-makers and shareholders made money by linking high-volume supplies to regional distribution, and so they continued moving in that direction. Some companies tried to hold onto the older urban wholesale and retail frameworks as the interdependencies were pulled apart. They were gradually taken down, because new distribution and market technologies permeated and changed the economic reward structure.

Executives framed the dozens of simultaneous urban-based grocery store closings in terms of market risk, not in terms of public health effects. It was not until years later that public health sectors finally entered into the discussion about food access, tying together changing market conventions with emerging concerns about unequal health outcomes. Political and nonprofit agencies tried to turn food access into a public health issue, but they were up against established industry conventions. Corporations that had climbed to the top of the infrastructural regime did not want to use their wealth, power, and positions to correct the urban food desert outcome. Instead, they accepted widespread industry assumptions that urban contexts constrained supermarket profitability. A major part of the problem was that these economic assumptions were accurate. Sustaining profitable supermarkets in cities came with a series of challenges.

Economic risks did not make profitability impossible, however. Such risks required different ways of addressing the potential problems. In prior decades, for instance, Wal-Mart bucked the industry trends. The corporation demonstrated economic success by bringing the mass-merchandising enterprise to small towns. Wal-Mart eventually integrated supermarkets and discount stores into a massive shopping platform that the company called the Super Center. However, large companies did not want to take similar leaps to redesign the food supply system for urban centers. Franchisees eventually opened profitable supermarkets in underserved locations, but they did it by bridging together local ownership, cooperative buying systems, and public subsidies supporting start-up costs.

New public/private partnerships solved the problem of the grocery gap in many towns and neighborhoods across the country. Social scientists then found that supermarket access, in and of itself, did not make people living nearby healthier. Managing public health risks by way of reducing market risks brought a unique and sobering problem to light: this profit-making food system was never designed to optimize public health. Supermarkets were simply good organizational vehicles for channeling lots of available products to large concentrations of consumers. Health outcomes were an afterthought.

A major problem with the transformation from feeding cities to feeding the nation was that so many different kinds of products, places, and people were repositioned through mutual adaptations. Sugar's place in the system of mass consumption offers one of the most important examples, especially as it relates to current debates in public health. Sidney Mintz explains that capitalists were involved in the global diffusion of sugar, but the relative autonomy of human desire was another prominent force. The spread of sugar was a story of "sweetness and power."[22] Sugar tastes good, and a significant consequence of the global spread of sugar was that it ritualized interactions and consumer expectations around the taste itself. Sweetness and its material expression in candy, cake, and ice cream eventually became inseparable from religious festivals and birthday celebrations.

The sugar industry broadened its infrastructural reach to meet the growing global demand. In the United States, the interdependencies between sugar, public subsidies, and food manufacturing industries rearranged the profit-making priorities, how sugar was sourced (sugar cane, beets, and corn), and how sweetness infiltrated everyday food products. Sweetness found its way into so many things consumers do not necessarily associate with having high sugar content, such as yogurt, salad dressing, and granola bars. The relationship between sweetness and power radically redefined sugar's influence on mass production and consumption, as well as how people framed the commodity as a problem. In an earlier capitalist iteration, sugar was a force of global imperialism, slavery, and mass violence. Sugar was a dangerous social poison well before it became labeled as a dangerous health poison.

Today, the problems with sugar are deeply tied into the problems with mass consumption. The expansive corn and soy economy makes highly processed products available nearly everywhere. Corn and soy have material versatility as cost-cutters, fillers, binders, and energy sources that have made them economically useful in promoting this high-volume system of cheap food. For example, scientists converted corn into high fructose corn syrup, dextrose, maltodextrin, corn oil, corn starch, corn flour, and alcohol. These highly processed ingredients were blended into the wide range of packaged and branded products lining the shelves of tens of thousands of supermarkets.

Cheap stuff with longer shelf lives grew into the backbone of the United States food economy, molding consumer desires for foods packed with inexpensive sources of sugar, salt, and fat.[23] Building the food infrastructure was initially about feeding cities, but over time, it became less about meeting the demands of any specific consumers in any specific places and more about finding new profit nodes in the system of abundance and low prices. The transformation of the food system created unanticipated public health consequences that opening more supermarkets in underserved places could never fix.

Yet the expansion of the supermarket produce aisle was as remarkable as the spread of sugar, corn, and soy was disconcerting. Building the contemporary supermarket produce aisle occurred one object at a time. Supply chains were assembled fruit by fruit, vegetable by vegetable, to match up with the mass-merchandising logic. Growers, cold storage operators, shipping ports, and wholesale and retail distribution centers were patched into and realigned with national and global political-economic frameworks.

Fresh and healthy options have grown ever more abundant. According to the USDA and the United Fresh Produce Association, 1,500 companies and 100 commodity boards with members in every US state and 25 different countries have contributed to the fruit and vegetable industry's market value of over $50 billion. Unlike the sugar, corn, and soy industries' dependencies on public subsidies to reinforce the infrastructural connections, the fresh fruit and vegetable industry growth has occurred with minimal government aid. Public investment into fresh produce industries was more discreet and indirect, by way of dismantling global trade barriers and building regional, national, and global transport and market infrastructures. The fresh system now operates as another part of the infrastructure of abundance and convenience. However, the public health issue that remains is how to make these products even more accessible and cost-effective so that they inform and alter what people choose to eat.

As the food system served the needs of more people in more places, it also became further enmeshed with other high-stakes situations and collective threats. The food system reinforced racial and economic health disparities, eroded the quality of soil, reduced biodiversity, and now it is deeply entangled with the dangers of climate change. Farmers, already struggling to stay financially afloat, experience recurring droughts and floods; shipping industries suffer through huge storms and damaged distribution networks; and politicians and planners the world over must prepare for major climate events and pandemics in order to sustain food supplies for massive concentrations of people.

For more than a century, public and private organizations filtered the logic of the market across food distribution sectors and into dispersed consumer regions. The result is that market risks are inextricably interwoven with health disparities and threats of environmental catastrophe. How public and private actors define the problems of the future and invest in their infrastructural solutions will shape collective outcomes for generations to come. Only by unraveling the history of the infrastructural interdependencies—and then bringing competing interests together into problem-solving relationships—can we figure out new ways to intervene that get us closer to meaningful reform.

ACKNOWLEDGMENTS

Over the years of working on this book, I have relied on the generosity and support of so many people and institutions. I am deeply indebted to those who do the daily work to produce, store, and transport the food we see almost everywhere we go. Complete strangers invited me into their workplaces and made ample time, often as much time as I needed, to answer my questions and show me their organizational and technical worlds. This book would not have been possible without their patience and guidance. I am also so grateful to the archivists, librarians, and staff at the Hagley Museum and Library, the ID History Museum, the Philadelphia City Archives, the Philadelphia Department of Records, the Temple University Urban Archives and Special Collections Research Center, and the University of Pennsylvania Van Pelt and Special Collections Libraries. They did so much of the hidden infrastructural work to make resources easily accessible and available. Parts of chapter 3 appeared in *Social Forces* 95, no. 3 (2017): 1285–309. I thank Oxford University Press for granting permission to reprint those sections, and anonymous reviewers for their insightful comments on the article.

The University of Connecticut provided me with the space to get this project off the ground and the support to continue it. At UConn, I have been teaching courses on qualitative methods, sociological theory, cities, consumption, and infrastructure for eight years, and along the way, many have helped me to think through new topics, theoretical debates, and research questions. I have benefited especially from conversations with Claudio Benzecry, Ruth Braunstein, Manisha Desai, Jeremy Pais, Bandana Purkayastha, Gaye Tuchman, and Dan Winchester, some of whom have since moved on to new places, but not without first making an indelible mark on this project. Jeremy Pais was a sounding board at one point or another for every chapter and for thinking through all things markets, cities, development, technology, and social science methods, even coming through with some game-saving map-making expertise.

I began the research for this book when I was a Robert Wood Johnson Foundation Health & Society Scholar at the University of Pennsylvania. I thank the foundation for supporting my research and for facilitating such a vibrant intellectual community. The program directors, David Asch, Robby Aronowitz, and Jason Schnittker, and the program coordinator, Melissa Kulynich, set the pitch-perfect tone of lots of laughs, constructive criticism, and serious work. I had incredibly good fortune to share my time there with such an inspiring group: Mike Bader, Alison Buttenheim, Amy Gonzales, Danya Keene, Jooyoung Lee, Laura Tach, and Van Tran. I owe them all an enormous debt of gratitude for helping me think through the process of getting this project off the ground.

A number of people graciously introduced me to Philadelphia, its history, its food systems, and the prospects of conducting ethnographic and historical research on these topics. I benefited from conversations with Elijah Anderson, David Barnes, Charles Bosk, Philippe Bourgois, Randal Collins, David Grazian, Amy Hillier, John Jackson, Michael Katz, Annette Lareau, Thomas Sugrue, Mary Summers, and Dominic Vitiello. Extraordinary research assistants helped me to understand Philadelphia's neighborhoods, organizations, markets, food movements, and research opportunities more quickly and thoroughly than I could have ever possibly done on my own. For all of their hard work and persistence, I thank Monica Amoo-Achampong, Daniel Aronowitz, To Nhu Huynh, Yasmin Roberti, Matthew Steele, and Anna Weisberg.

Many colleagues and friends helped out in numerous ways: offering encouragement, asking timely questions, reading chapter drafts, organizing and participating in conferences, workshops, and panels, introducing me to new sources and fields, or all of the above. I am grateful to Rene Almeling, A. Aneesh, Hillary Angelo, Christine Bachrach, Peter Bearman, Claudio Benzecry, Gianpaolo Baiocchi, Fernando Domínguez Rubio, Phil Gorski, Black Hawk Hancock, Lesli Hoey, Marcus Hunter, Rob Jansen, Gail Kligman, Eric Klinenberg, Fayuki Kurasawa, Andrew Lakoff, Pablo Lapegna, Annette Lareau, Matthew Mahler, Harvey Molotch, Alexandra Murphy, Richard Ocejo, Jeremy Pais, Juan Pablo Pardo-Guerra, Josh Pascewitz, Andrew Perrin, Jennifer Reich, Bill Roy, Hilary Silver, Van Tran, Diane Vaughan, Frederick Wherry, Owen Whooley, Dan Winchester, Jon Wynn, and Caitlin Zaloom.

The book's topics, methods, and framework combining the study of the built environment and the worlds and meanings of material objects would not exist without Harvey Molotch. Harvey's own work shaped this project in countless ways, but he also generously gave of his time and intellectual energy, from early conversations exploring the germ of an idea to providing late-stage feedback on a complete draft of the book. I cannot thank him enough for all of his support. Bill Roy's breadth of historical, economic, and sociological knowledge seems unbounded, and I benefited immensely from his careful chapter readings and suggestions. I also want to acknowledge an anonymous reviewer for helping me hammer out the book's bigger picture. I owe a special thanks to Black Hawk Hancock for partaking in many thought-provoking sessions of walking and talking through neighborhoods and cities that helped me to clarify key links between new and old ideas.

I owe so much to the late Doug Mitchell. He had a passion for ideas and authors, and a contagious enthusiasm for life as an editor. I was so fortunate to have his support twice, and I hope he would have liked the way this one turned out. Elizabeth Branch Dyson took over the Press's sociology list right in the middle of things and created a seamless experience. I'm so grateful for her crucial editorial insights and continued support for the project. I also want to thank Mary Corrado, Jenni Fry, Mollie McFee, Lauren Salas, and Kyle Wagner for putting up with many back and forth emails and for tackling the important details necessary for bringing the book into print.

There is a piece of the food equation this book does not directly address. Food contributes so much to how we enjoy life and experience the world with others. It uniquely connects family traditions and a curiosity and respect for the world. My parents, Debbie and Mal Deener, introduced that to me, and I am forever grateful to them for that and for their always unwavering support. It is also impossible for me to write a book about food and not thank the entire Dlubak crew, especially Frank. In a family where the appreciation and enjoyment of food is the glue, Frank was the least adventurous eater out of everyone but one of the most ingenious people I ever met. I miss him.

I simply could never have written this book without the love and support of Alana Dlubak who is the connoisseur, craftsperson, and all-around creative mind to which I can only aspire. Azalea and Echo have the magic to tone down my inner-critic and inspire the kind of optimism I did not previously know people could experience. My life with the three of them makes it all worthwhile.

Strategic Variation and Historical Excavation

I narrowed down the book's focus on the transformation of the food system by way of strategic variation and historical excavation. Strategic variation is the process of untangling the component parts that constitute a system by following the leads from one organization or location to the next. The goal is to identify new organizations and settings in search of variations on their contents and connections. Excavation is about researching the precursors of those organizations and connections in order to examine how previous component parts and interdependencies were put in place and transformed.

As an urban sociologist, I started in a specific place—Philadelphia. I initially thought of the book's topic as "neighborhood food access," but after spending time in neighborhoods, I inverted that focus. First, I knew that urban sociologists understood the decline of neighborhood amenities as a central feature of spatial isolation. Instead of studying what it was like to experience commercial decline, I switched the focus to the supply dynamics as they intersected with the city. I started to investigate how organizational actors shaped the system, which I thought could better explain when, how, and why spatial isolation happened. Secondly, as I read widely on the history of food, I realized so much had already been written about sugar, industrial food processing, and fast food. Given the contemporary policy concerns about "healthy food access," I took a different research angle on the production, storage, and transporting of fresh fruits and vegetables and their relationships to the mass-merchandising system.

Starting in Philadelphia but then turning to the supply dynamics led me in multiple directions at the same time. I met with city and state policymakers, people in nonprofit settings, activists, and industry stakeholders. Strategic variation was about working toward meeting new informants and observing new topics, as well as challenging the information I learned about organizational processes and connections from previous informants.

Although I expanded on people's networks, I was not simply following a snowball sample. I consistently sought out new nodes to open up different perspectives. I discovered these focal points by conducting interviews, by reading periodicals, and by searching the internet. For instance, I made a contact with a marketing representative of the Philadelphia Port Authority who gave me a day-long tour of Philadelphia ports. The content of the interview led me in new directions: to port managers, owners of cold storage facilities, logistics firms, freight forwarding services, fumigation services, and executives of multinational shipping corporations. During the tour, I learned more about the language and labels of the industry and how and where to conduct subsequent research. Likewise, I came across the New York Produce Show on an industry website. Attending the show led me to product innovation sectors, agricultural and product preservation technology firms, large cooperative farming organizations, and commodity board associations focusing on specific products like strawberries, mangoes, or blueberries.

Each research setting presented its own constraints. The Philadelphia Wholesale Market, the Reading Terminal Market, and farmers' markets were open to the public. Most of the action at the wholesale market occurred in early mornings, but during that rush it was difficult to interview people, and so I made appointments and visited in later mornings and afternoons. Other settings, like shipping ports, cold storage facilities, and private distribution centers, were closed to the public. I made contacts by phone or email, and then after setting up a time, interviewed people and toured facilities. The interviews and tours lasted hours, covering the history of businesses, management steps for moving, storing, sorting, and timing products, and how connections in supply chains were made and sustained.

My approach to studying the nonprofit side was similar, following the leads from one organization to the next. Some organizations allowed me to volunteer, like Philabundance, Philadelphia's food bank. Interviews with personnel in different nonprofit organizations pointed me to upstream and downstream connections—to farmers, shippers, grocery store managers, and others supplying food to food banks. Making contacts with executives of Feeding America, the national food bank network, allowed me to transcend the Philadelphia-based networks, opening up additional nodes in other states as points of comparison.

I framed my interview questions about each context in terms of emerging and intersecting processes related to organizational decision-making, investment, daily routines, and relationships with other sites. I asked people about how they started in their industries, what typical work days looked like, how they bridged together products and places, how they connected to upstream and downstream organizations, what kinds of changes they had experienced or observed in their businesses, what kinds of difficulties emerged, and how they managed those difficulties. I also followed up on their answers by asking more about the particularities of the settings, practical work, and supply linkages.

Unpacking these organizational routines and interdependencies was similar to an "ethnography of infrastructure."[1] However, my instinct and preference for research was to inquire into how the contemporary conditions came to be the way that they are. The historical and ethnographic research practices were intertwined. Building on what I was learning in the present allowed me to trace the organizational and technical precursors, which then further informed my investigation of the contemporary system. My methodological aspiration was that by representing highly varied phenomena—emerging and interacting components—I could then trace out the interdependencies to see when and how they were put together and how and why certain configurations led to collective effects.

Yet ethnographic and historical research methods have clear differences, too. Ethnographers and interviewers can shape their data. They can ask questions about processes, interpretations, and networks, and seek out subjects, sites, settings, and interactions that vary from previous observations. A central difficulty of ethnographic research is managing constraints on access, as potential subjects can act as gatekeepers. Historical research, in contrast, is at the whim of what has been documented and/or of finding people who have connections to the past features of the phenomena. In my case, it meant finding people and documents to shed light on previous market, distribution, and nonprofit operations, settings, and relationships.

Early on, I interviewed several wholesalers who had parents and grandparents in the industry. They contextualized market transformations and also introduced me to key topics and locations in the history of Philadelphia food distribution. I started looking into the history of the city's produce wholesale market at the Temple Urban Archives and the Philadelphia City Archives. The collections on Dock Street at both archives included policy reports and planning proposals that detailed the rise and decline of the market and multiple development projects, including the debates and plans for demolition of Dock Street and the construction of the new wholesale market. The city archives had political memoranda and communications of the mayor's office, the city council, and the department of commerce. These memoranda were important to see how competing political and economic sectors—local, regional, and national interests—communicated about the Philadelphia wholesale and retail dynamics. The Temple Urban Archives also housed the clippings of the *Philadelphia Evening Bulletin*, as well as additional clippings from the *Philadelphia Inquirer* and other newspapers. These sources linked the city transition to economic changes and political conflicts around urban and suburban development and food market policies.

This inquiry pointed me to the shifting relationships between wholesaling and retailing. I sought out files on each wholesale and retail store, different distribution methods, and their interdependencies with other food distribution industries. I traced the connections, transportation methods, corporate mergers, organizational innovation projects, and key moments of spatial development. Once again, the clippings of the *Evening Bulletin* provided the initial context for retail transitions in Philadelphia. As I found more information on each company, I created tables that demonstrated lowering profit margins and openings and closings of specific stores in the city. The Archives of the Hagley Museum and Library housed additional materials, including annual reports of corporations like Food Fair and A&P. I photocopied major planning and policy reports, as well as significant newspaper articles, so I could revisit them at a later time.

Living in Philadelphia between 2010 and 2012 allowed me to cover a lot of ethnographic and historical ground. Reading through documents, interview transcripts, and field notes, I identified themes, wrote memos about the themes, and analyzed how different types of data and themes were tied together. I narrowed down a key focus of the book to the historical transformation of food distribution and the social organization of infrastructure.

Narrowing down this focus drove me to read more broadly about urban development, demographic patterns, and infrastructural and cultural histories of cities to better situate Philadelphia. Various libraries held rare books, historical policy reports, and planning studies about Philadelphia and its neighborhoods, as well as the related history of food distribution. These included the University of Pennsylvania Annenberg Rare Books Library and Van Pelt Library, and the Philadelphia Public Library. I also benefited from digitized rare books and reports, either in library online collections or through Google Books. Additional resources included published dissertations, law review essays on legal aspects of retail and wholesale industries, economic and policy studies on food distribution, wholesaling, and food and urban planning, as well as dozens of marketing reports about the grocery and wholesaling industries written in different periods. The historical databases of the *New York Times*, the *Philadelphia Tribune*, the *Philadelphia Daily News*, and the *Philadelphia Inquirer* supplemented these sources.

While living in Philadelphia, I presented my work at a number of workshops, which provided the space for dialogue to move the project forward. In these settings, I was not trying to get the argument exactly right. In Merton's terms, I was trying to "establish the phenomena."[2] About a year into the research, I decided the best way forward was to begin writing chapters. I returned to my earliest empirical research question: what happened to Philadelphia's market amenities?

Building on the historical materials, I wrote drafts of chapters on wholesaling and retailing—what became chapters 2 and 3. Although the two industries were intersected, I could better capture contingent events, organizational trajectories, and decision-making priorities by separating them. I found that organizational actors made their decisions and investments in relation to changing patterns of population settlement, transportation, and development, but the two industries had reconfigured around similar conditions in quite different ways. I also found that the changing wholesale/retail dynamic was not coordinated, but instead, infrastructural shifts propelled market decline and collective consequences.

My next writing venture turned to analyzing the organizational and technical changes in wholesaling, cold storage, shipping, and retail distribution. Having spent previous months coding interviews and ethnographic materials, I found central themes related to product handling, technical innovations, storage and preservation methods, expansions of product varieties and volumes, and changing organizational/distribution scales. In 2013, I returned to Philadelphia and presented these materials (eventually chapter 5) at another workshop, where I identified and analyzed parallels with my previous historical chapters.

I found a common thread on infrastructure and scale, but I was still working out the central narrative links. Fresh produce was arriving into Philadelphia ports, where it was then shipped off to different regions. It was a variation on the theme of transforming the infrastructural system in terms of the locations and scales of distribution and the different technologies for storage and product handling. Viewing these three chapter drafts together allowed me to develop one of the book's foundational ideas on system transformation from feeding cities to feeding regions to feeding the nation.

Yet the narrative from "infrastructural exclusion" to "reassembling the produce aisle" did not seem exactly right—not chronologically, and also not in terms of the organizational and technical innovations and implementations that made the transformation possible. The chapters on the history of wholesale and retail decline did not fluidly lead into the contemporary fresh food distribution segments. The logic of strategic variation and historical excavation came back into play. This time, however, I knew the time period that was missing. Now I needed to figure out what materials would help me unravel that story.

Together, the three chapters revealed a paradox: low margins disrupted the retail industry and created food deserts in the 1970s, but then larger stores with more products appeared on the scene. These stores were even more dependent on higher volumes while their profit margins remained low. How did they become profitable? I knew logistical technologies were a common topic among business owners handling fresh produce. I wanted to know more about when logistics became a primary space of adding market value in food industries. I read more about the engineering of distribution methods and organizational models in periodicals about retail and logistics and came across work on the rise of the bar code and retail computerization.

Reading about these topics and searching online for more sources led me to the most significant one: the ID History Museum, an online digitized archive. The ID History Museum included 203 primary "artifacts" (documents and images) donated by people participating in the making and spreading of the bar code: engineers, technicians, computer salesman, retail and technology executives, and industry consultants. The site also held an oral history collection from industry participants, as well as the collection of 51 *UPC Newsletters* published between 1973 and 1977 and issues of the applied industry journal *Code and Symbol*, published by Distribution Codes Inc., which helped with the UPC rollout.

I downloaded, reviewed, and took notes on available documents. These materials went deeper into how the technology was invented and implemented into the grocery distribution structure. I also saw themes linking back to previous chapters: contextual contingencies, multiplicity of technical and organizational prototypes, and decision-making uncertainties around implementation. Understanding how the bar code and the sociotechnical apparatus supporting it were designed, negotiated, and implemented into the supermarket system explained how food industries entered into the information age and transformed the supply logic from "feeding regions" to "feeding the nation."

This focus also opened my eyes to another variation: the growing prominence of discount stores, especially Kmart and Wal-Mart. I read Sam Walton's autobiography, a range of memoirs by Wal-Mart executives, and various histories and academic accounts of Wal-Mart, Kmart, and the discount store industry. I also read articles about emerging dynamics between supermarkets, the bar code, and discount store development in *Supermarket Business, Chain*

Store Age, Harvard Business Review, Modern Materials Handling, and other periodicals. The outcome of this historical excavation was chapter 4.

Revisiting chapters 2, 3, 4, and 5 together allowed me to identify major themes across them: the social organization and disruption of infrastructure as represented by changes in technologies, product handling methods, and distribution scales; and organizational uncertainty, decision-making negotiations, and unexpected collective effects during moments of infrastructural transition. Across periods, these infrastructural disruptions had collective effects: business failures; a vital infrastructure increasingly dependent on market mechanisms; and emerging public health problems.

As I narrowed in on these themes, I realized I was no longer doing urban sociology in isolation from other subfields. I taught a series of undergraduate classes combining different topics: urban sociology; the history of food and consumption; and the sociology of infrastructure. Teaching these classes allowed me to see links between urban studies, science and technology studies, economic sociology, and the sociology of food and consumption. I found that the concept of "infrastructure" was like the concept of "culture" in that it had a common influence across sociological (and other social science) subfields, and yet it had not opened up communication across them.

I was interested in bridging together these subfields to explain infrastructural transformations and their unintended consequences. I edited the chapters to integrate these ideas and drafted the book's introduction. My analytic sensibilities were now geared toward explaining the reconfiguration of a vital infrastructure and how it intersected with Philadelphia. After writing the introduction and the first five chapters, I returned to the rest of my data with new eyes.

Research assistants and I had interviewed dozens of people across different local organizations and observed and researched the history of different market and nonprofit settings: farmers' markets, public markets, and nonprofit food centers. I returned to the same exact points of data but with a different orientation to why they mattered in the history of food distribution. In the beginning of my research, I thought local neighborhood conditions were a mismatch for the decentered, national, and global food system. After tracing the infrastructural transformation, however, I could see how local market-making and nonprofit organizations fit into the broader narrative structure as another strategic variation on the theme of infrastructural transformation.

Local farms, farmers' markets, family wholesale businesses, local brokerage firms, and nonprofit hunger relief organizations—while seemingly separate spheres of distribution—shared core attributes. They carved out local channels in response to broader food distribution trends. This strategic variation allowed me to highlight a second infrastructural inequality. The first was about the transition between abundance, convenience, and market access; the second was about the transition between abundance, product standardization, scales of operation, and object qualities. Chapters 4 and 5 explained the making of standard market dynamics, which then opened up the analysis of the second-tier markets and nonprofit structures for taking on different scales and product qualities.

The narrative structure had three empirical sections. The first part (chapters 2 and 3) was about the shift from feeding cities to feeding regions and the consequence of infrastructural exclusion. The second part (chapters 4 and 5) was about the transition of the distribution scale from feeding regions to feeding the nation and the effects of standardizing store and product volumes, varieties, and qualities. The third part (chapters 6 and 7) was about patching up the system through organizational methods outside of the standard infrastructure. This section explained how efforts to fix food access inequalities came with their own constraints related to managing market and public health risks at the same time. It reinforced the idea that the problems with feeding cities are inextricably intertwined with the transformation of infrastructure, abundance, and inequality.

CHAPTER ONE

1. See for example, Levinson 2011.

2. The tension between abundance and scarcity has been one of the central driving questions about the food system and market society more generally. Monica Prasad (2012) defined the paradox of poverty arising in a "land of too much." Harvey Levenstein (2003a) refers to the "paradox of plenty," as a relationship between food obsession, mass production, and regulation of diet. Raj Patel (2007) points out that although we produce more food than ever before in human history and over a billion people are obese, another billion suffer from hunger. Marion Nestle (2002) refers to the shift from scarcity to abundance as an underlying logic of the politics of food. Andrew Abbott (2016) refers to the problem of excess as equally if not more significant than the problem of scarcity.

3. For an account of the development of the United States electric system, see Hughes 1993. For studies of water supplies, see Gandy 2004 and Gandy 2014.

4. Even in the early 1800s, when public markets were prominent distribution methods, they were occupied by profit-driven vendors. As the public markets declined during that century, they contributed to creating two different food systems, one for the rich, another for the poor. See Baics 2016.

5. For more on the idea of "system building," see Hughes 1993, whose historical study of the modern electric grid demonstrates the distinct stages of innovation and system-building. A key part of his argument is that system-builders are part of a unique subset of organizational actors who convert the ad hoc process of innovation into systemic relationships. Also see Hughes 2012.

6. Most species have been altered in so many different ways, and are embedded in the process of global exploration and expansion that has resulted in international interconnections that then get obfuscated by the production of culture. Krishnendu Ray and Tulasi Srinivas (2012) argue that the rise and distinctions of regional and national cuisines are based on collective actors converting wide-ranging ingredients, originating from many points of origin, into place-based cultural, political, and economic production. That is, cuisine is neither local nor global, but rather, it is a situated point for the composite of cultural and political relationships and processes that over time crystallize as shared understandings, experiences, and representations. For instance, potatoes are not indigenous to India despite their centrality to Indian cuisine.

7. See Gordon 2017.
8. For more on historical approaches to "formation stories" as a methodological genre, see Hirschman and Reed 2014.
9. These "efficiency" features are artificial constructs related to the way that different organizations become interdependent through changing political and economic institutions and decisions. For historical accounts of the changing relationships between organizations, institutions, and infrastructure see Cronon 1991; for a focus on power dynamics in the relationship, see Roy 1997; for conventions of coordination see Thévenot 2001, Biggart and Beamish 2003, Boltanski and Thévenot 2006; for the embeddedness of mundane practice into economic infrastructure see Callon, Méadel, and Rabeharisoa 2002; for the relationship between conventions, qualities, and supply chains see Ponte and Gibbon 2005; Gibbon, Bair, and Ponte 2008.
10. Bowker and Star 2000.
11. See Mann 1984; Mann 2008. Also, the relationship between the state and economic infrastructures is commonplace in various kinds of studies, for instance, related to credit infrastructure and deregulation. See Prasad 2012; Harvey 2005; Brenner and Theodore 2002.
12. See Star 1999; Star and Ruhleder 1996; Bowker and Star 2000; Edwards 2003. Beniger 1986 labeled the changing relationship between technology and economy as both an industrial revolution and a "control revolution." He argued that the modes of mass production and economic organization were intertwined with methods of processing information, fostering communication, and coordinating markets across distances. Also see Mukerji 2015, and especially her conclusion, where she conceptualizes the distinctions between strategy and logistics as formal and informal modes of control.
13. Infrastructural regimes are different than "food regimes," which are theorized as "international relations of food production and consumption," as they intersect with "periods of capitalist accumulation." In its world system emphasis, the food regime literature is mostly characterized by the role and impact of agricultural systems in solidifying class relations and geographic capital accumulation between state sectors and industries. For more on food regimes, see especially Friedmann 1987; Friedmann and McMichael 1989; McMichael 2009.
14. See Heidegger 1977; Edwards 2003.
15. Malthus 1888 wrote about the delicate balance between population growth and agricultural production. He did not think that surpluses would improve the standard of living of the existing population, because it generated additional population surges. Economists have described this ecological constraint as the "Malthusian trap." The industrial revolution, however, overcame this trap, especially in sites of the most prosperous urban development. It propelled advances in machinery, storage, and mechanization to meet the food and nutritional needs of larger and denser population settlements. For a relationship between urban development and the "Malthusian trap," see Scott and Storper 2015.
16. Castells 2000 has pointed to this dual dimension of economic development. Latour 2005 argues actors, materials, and processes serve as "connectors" between the local and the extra-local. They mediate and frame how distinct places become interpreted as symbolically coherent. For a more thorough accounting of the relationship between urbanization and actor-network theory see Farías and Bender 2010. In studies of infrastructural interdependencies, the connections between places also create inequalities between places, especially in conflicts over the uses, control, and profits of resources. See, for example, Espeland 1998; Needham 2014.

17. For more on how infrastructure is comprised of both "hard" physical material and "soft" social elements, see Klinenberg 2018; Carse 2017.
18. See Cronon 1991. Infrastructure could be thought of as force of interdependency in the "ecological complex," Otis Dudley Duncan's term (1961) for the interlocking and mutually reinforcing relationships between population, organization, environment, and technology, or simply P.O.E.T.
19. For an overview of this perspective, see Brenner 2014; Angelo and Wachsmuth 2015.
20. See Simmel [1903] 1971.
21. See Wirth 1938.
22. See Angelo and Wachsmuth 2015.
23. An interesting space to see this conflict is in the changing uses of the term "ecology" in urban studies. Historically, the notion of urban and human ecology referred to place-based relationships between populations, neighborhoods, and unfolding patterns of social and economic differentiation, most notably in Chicago, but also applied more broadly thereafter. The most well-known examples are compiled in Park and Burgess 1925. In recent years, another field of inquiry into urban "political ecology" has gained momentum, which is a more critical field combining political economy with the focus on land-based resources like water distribution and the blurring of "urban" and "nature." See especially Swyngedouw 1996. For a good overview of urban political ecology, see Angelo and Wachsmuth 2015.
24. Well-known examples framing this debate in terms of "place matters" are found in Sassen 2001; Sampson 2012.
25. The best account of the distinction is in Logan and Molotch 1987.
26. Mumford 1938.
27. See Logan and Molotch 1987.
28. See Goddard 1996.
29. See Monkkonen 1988; Fischer 1992; Rae 2003.
30. Fishman 1990.
31. Jackson 1985; Cohen 1996; Rae 2003.
32. See Rae 2003.
33. See Jackson 1985; Hayden 2004.
34. Lefebvre 2003.
35. See Graham and Marvin 2002; Hughes 1993; Castells 2000; Gordon 2017.
36. See, for example, Holmes 2011; Ellickson and Grieco 2013; LeCavalier 2016.
37. The study of risk—and the protections against risk—are foundational to studies of vital infrastructures. In this case, the bridge between security and market has become deeply entrenched. For more on security and vital infrastructures, see Collier and Lakoff 2015.
38. Cronon 1991.
39. Jackson 1985.
40. Zukin 2004, p. 8.
41. For example, see Thompson 1967.
42. See Callon 1998.
43. This point is foundational to economic sociology's focus on embeddedness, institutions, and power. See, for example, Granovetter 1985; DiMaggio and Powell 1983; Fligstein 1993.
44. See Tilly 1983; Friedmann 1987; McMichael 2009.
45. See Bijker 1995.
46. See Becker 1995; Clarke and Star 2008.

47. See Jervis 1998; Padgett and Powell 2012; Thrift 1999; Urry 2005.
48. Jervis 1998.
49. See Mann 1984 and Mann 2008.
50. See Foucault 2009; also see Collier and Lakoff 2015.
51. See Prasad 2012.
52. See Fourcade 2017; Fourcade 2011.
53. See Mukerji 2015.
54. As Nigel Thrift (1999) puts it, there are a "multiplicity of sequences that lurk at every fork of the present." Also see Hughes 1993; Hughes 2012.
55. Pickering 1995.
56. See DiMaggio and Powell 1983.
57. Vaughan 1999. For more on organizational uncertainty, see Levitt and March 1988; March and Olsen 1975. Uncertainty is also one of the fundamental dynamics of the "normalization of risk" that routinize mistakes and accidents. See Perrow 2011; Vaughan 1997.
58. Complex systems are filled with these kinds of situations, making it possible to analyze them in terms of what Ermakoff 2015 calls the "structure of contingency."
59. Jervis 1998; Molotch 2004.
60. In discussing the case of Amazon.com, Warren Buffett said about Amazon's founder Jeff Bezos, "I was too dumb to realize. I did not think [Bezos] could succeed on the scale he has." https://www.cnbc.com/2018/01/30/warren-buffett-is-finally-getting-a-second-chance-to-partner-with-amazon-ceo-jeff-bezos-.html. For the Wal-Mart example, see Walton 1992.
61. Grinspoon 2016 refers to "long-chain complex recipe technology" as a series of steps that if "performed in just the right way," actors can accomplish the desired effect. Reliability through complexity requires this kind of long-chain technical recipe.
62. See Sheffi 2012.

CHAPTER TWO

1. Phillips and Fraser 1922. This report, titled *Wholesale Distribution of Fresh Fruits and Vegetables*, was a product of the Joint Council of the National League of Commission Merchants in the United States, the Western Fruit Jobbers Association of America, and the International Apple Shippers Association. See "Development of Fresh Fruit and Vegetable Industry as Revealed by Rail Movement," p. 188.
2. The focus on surplus as related to population expansion was fundamental to Malthus 1888, and has been taken up a great deal by scholars of food security. See for example, Ehrlich, Ehrlich, and Daily 1993. The issue of standardization and market expansion was central to Cronon 1991.
3. See Levenstein 2003a; Levenstein 2003b; Levinson 2011.
4. Upton Sinclair's 1906 novel, *The Jungle*, was a famous source of origin for exposing the difficulties of handling perishable foods. Also see Pacyga 2015; Otter 2005; MacLachlan 2001; Otter 2004; Freidberg 2009; Friedland, Barton, and Thomas 1981.
5. Friedland, Barton, and Thomas 1981; Sackman 2005.
6. See Freidberg 2009.
7. The scientific invention of "iceberg" lettuce coupled with refrigerated rail transport changed the possibilities of distribution and lettuce consumption—the product was "virtually indestructible," as reported by Levenstein 2003b. See also Freidberg 2009.
8. Leach 2011; Chandler 1993.
9. Drewnowski 1997.

10. Adams 1916.
11. Philipps and Fraser 1922, p. 163.
12. Leach 2011; Chandler 1993. For a critique of the efficiency thesis, see Roy 1997.
13. Friedland, Barton, and Thomas 1981; Sackman 2005.
14. See Harrison 2008; Baics 2016.
15. Harrison 2008.
16. Fletcher 1976.
17. Harrison 2008.
18. See Williams 1999. Also see Williams [1961] 2001.
19. See Zukin 1989; Vitiello 2008.
20. Harrison 2008.
21. *Philadelphia Inquirer* 1885.
22. *Philadelphia Inquirer* 1886.
23. Fletcher 1976.
24. See Logan and Molotch 1987; Sackman 2005.
25. Philips and Fraser 1922, p. 159.
26. White 2011.
27. Sackman 2005, p. 38.
28. Ibid.
29. See Striffler and Moberg 2003; Chapman 2007; Soluri 2005.
30. See Esposito 2014.
31. This chapter does not name specific employees who were interviewed or the private companies where they work. In interview data, I use pseudonyms.
32. *Philadelphia Inquirer* 1900.
33. See Duddy and Revzan 1939; Jumper 1974.
34. Philips and Fraser 1922.
35. All of these figures are cited in Adams 1916.
36. Levenstein 2003b.
37. Philips and Fraser 1922.
38. Philips and Fraser 1922, pp. 183–184.
39. Citing *Railway Age*, April 22, 1921 in Philips and Fraser 1922.
40. Philips and Fraser 1922, p. 47.
41. Levenstein 2003b.
42. Graham and Marvin 2002.
43. *Architectural Forum* 1947; Scott 1998.
44. *Perishable Products Terminal, Philadelphia* 1926; *Pennsylvania Farmer, Consolidated with Pennsylvania Stockman and Farmer* 1939.
45. *Perishable Products Terminal, Philadelphia* 1926; *Pennsylvania Farmer, Consolidated with Pennsylvania Stockman and Farmer* 1939.
46. *Evening Bulletin*, December 1, 1936.
47. Ibid.
48. *Evening Bulletin.* December 14, 1936.
49. Ibid.
50. *Philadelphia Inquirer* 1940.
51. *Wholesale Food Distribution Facilities for Philadelphia, PA* 1954; Brecht 1954.
52. Pennsylvania Farmer 1939.
53. Memorandum to Walter M. Phillips, Director of Commerce from Harold L. Enarson. Subject: "Dock Street and the Problems of Wholesale Marketing Facilities in Philadelphia." June 12, 1953. Philadelphia City Archives.

54. Graden 1952.
55. See Jackson 1985.
56. Groff 1950.
57. Werthner 1957.
58. *Wholesale Food Distribution Facilities for Philadelphia, PA* 1954.
59. Greater Philadelphia Movement 1954.
60. Ibid.
61. Groden 1952; Memorandum to Walter M. Phillips from Harold L. Enarson.
62. Selby 1954; Greater Philadelphia Movement [ca. 1950s].
63. Greater Philadelphia Movement [ca. 1950s].
64. William C. Crow, United States Department of Agriculture Production and Marketing Administration, Correspondence with Harold L. Enarson, Assistant Director of Commerce. June 8, 1953. Philadelphia City Archives.
65. *Wholesale Food Distribution Facilities for Philadelphia, PA* 1954.
66. Ibid.
67. Memorandum to Walter M. Phillips from Harold L. Enarson.
68. Brecht 1954.
69. Langan 1964.
70. Feist 1953.
71. Letter from Association of Wholesale Fruit and Vegetable Distributors to City Commissioner about sanitation and upkeep of Dock Street. Office of the Mayor, City Hall, Philadelphia, August 17, 1953 Philadelphia City Archives.
72. Greater Philadelphia Movement 1954.
73. Ibid.; Feist, September 4, 1953.
74. The major wholesale districts of downtowns are now mostly gone. Paris's Les Halles and London's Covent Garden Wholesale market were repositioned to areas that were less densely crowded and reimagined as popular shopping destinations.
75. This was before the tremendous interest in "behind the scenes" food issues. Wholesale markets have become tourist attractions, and public markets reflect the collective nostalgia for a different form of consumption. See Bestor 2004.
76. Greater Philadelphia Movement 1954.
77. Redevelopment Authority of the City of Philadelphia 1968.
78. Brecht, October 31, 1954.
79. Report no. 39. Citizens' Council on City Planning: The Proposed Food Distribution Center. December 1, 1954. Philadelphia City Archives.
80. City of Philadelphia Department of Commerce, Statement Regarding the Establishment of a Food Distribution Center before Councilmanic Hearings. Presented by Walter M. Phillips, Director of Commerce. December 5, 1955. Philadelphia City Archives.
81. Greater Philadelphia Movement 1954.
82. Allen 1954.
83. Groff 1950.
84. Allen 1954.
85. Memorandum to Walter M. Phillips from Harold L. Enarson.
86. Letter to the Honorable Joseph S. Clark, Jr., Mayor of the City of Philadelphia from Paul J. Cupp, Vice President of American Stores Company. October 23, 1953. Office of the Mayor, City Hall. Philadelphia City Archives.
87. Samuel Cooke, President of Penn Fruit Company, January 15, 1954. Remarks at a Luncheon in the Packard Building. Temple Urban Archives.

88. City of Philadelphia Department of Commerce, Statement Regarding the Establishment of a Food Distribution Center.

89. Brecht 1954.

90. Greater Philadelphia Movement 1954; *Toward Greater Prosperity in Philadelphia: The Story of the Department of Commerce of the City of Philadelphia, 1952–1955*. Philadelphia, PA. Mayor's Office. Department of Commerce. Philadelphia City Archives; Correspondence between William C. Crow, USDA and Harold L. Enarson, Philadelphia Department of Commerce. October 9, 1953. Philadelphia City Archives.

91. The Dock Street Case, Philadelphia, PA. House of Representatives, Committee on Education and Labor, Washington, DC. February 7, 1947. University of Pennsylvania Library.

92. City of Philadelphia Department of Commerce, Statement Regarding the Establishment of a Food Distribution Center.

93. City of Philadelphia Department of Commerce, Statement Regarding the Establishment of a Food Distribution Center.

94. Custis 1950.

95. *Evening Bulletin* 1954.

96. Langan 1964.

97. *Philadelphia Inquirer* 1955.

98. See Le Faivre-Rochester 2003.

99. Forsythe 1964.

100. Ibid.

101. Ibid.

CHAPTER THREE

1. See Deener 2017.

2. See Star 1995.

3. See Molotch 2004.

4. See Countryman 2007.

5. King 1915.

6. Levinson 2011, pp. 14–15, 19, 22, 24–26, 30–31.

7. *Evening Bulletin* 1917.

8. *Philadelphia Inquirer* 1915.

9. *Evening Bulletin* 1917.

10. Fry 1991.

11. Moeckel 1953, p. 184.

12. Levinson 2011, p. 53.

13. *Evening Bulletin* 1917.

14. *Evening Bulletin* 1917; *Evening Bulletin* 1969.

15. *Evening Bulletin* 1917.

16. Levinson 2011, pp. 48, 41.

17. Ibid.

18. *Evening Bulletin* 1912.

19. Ibid.

20. Shaw 1912; Moeckel 1953, pp. 177–179.

21. Levenstein 2003b, pp. 33–35.

22. Shaw 1912.

23. Abbott 1920.

24. Dimitri, Effland, and Conklin 2005.
25. Levenstein 2003b, p. 37.
26. Levinson 2011.
27. Ingram and Rao 2004; Rowe 1957; Greer et al. 1986; Levinson 2011; National Commission on Food Marketing 1966.
28. Rowe 1957.
29. Rowe 1957; Greer et al. 1986; Levinson 2011; National Commission on Food Marketing 1966.
30. "Statement on Signing the Agricultural Adjustment Act of 1938." February 16, 1938. http://www.presidency.ucsb.edu/ws/?pid=15599.
31. See Levenstein 2003b; USDA 1972; Greer et al. 1986, pp. 95–96; Ingram and Rao 2004; Manfredo and Libbin 1998.
32. Greer et al. 1986; Ingram and Rao 2004.
33. Quoted in Greer et al. 1986, p. 94.
34. Ibid., pp. 95–96.
35. Ingram and Rao 2004.
36. The USDA's Agricultural Marketing Services conducted market research and disseminated information about crop yields and commodity qualities. Participants and stakeholders from multiple sectors contributed to the Agricultural Marketing Act of 1946, which gave rise to the current grading system that provides information about the standard market qualities of different perishable commodities. http://national aglawcenter.org/overview/paca/
37. Hartford 1938.
38. United States Department of Commerce Report, 1946. "Establishing and Operating a Grocery Store," pp. 3–5. Hagley.
39. Mayo 1993, 77–87.
40. Charvat 1961.
41. Longstreth 1999, pp. 86–87.
42. See Charvat 1961; Pelroth 2009.
43. Pelroth 2009.
44. Zimmerman 1937.
45. Mayo 1993.
46. Charvat 1961, pp. 26–28.
47. Zimmerman 1941.
48. Pelroth 2009.
49. Gillespie 1978.
50. Ibid.
51. Fetridge 1951; Nagle 1955; *Evening Bulletin*, August 19, 1955; *Evening Bulletin*, August 22, 1958.
52. Food Fair Stores Inc. 1956 Annual Report.
53. Friedland and Cooke 1953.
54. Sikora 1971; Nagle 1955.
55. Food Fair Stores Inc. 1956 Annual Report.
56. Zimmerman 1941.
57. Newman 1957.
58. *New York Times* 1955; Newman 1957; *Evening Bulletin*, November 1, 1957.
59. Gaige 1958; *Evening Bulletin*, November 1, 1957.
60. Jackson 1985; also see Hayden 2004.
61. Grocery Industry Barometer 1970. Hagley.

62. Hamilton 2008.
63. *Evening Bulletin,* January 17, 1955; *Evening Bulletin,* November 13, 1958; *Evening Bulletin* 1959, p. F4.
64. City of Philadelphia Memorandum from Harold L. Enarson, Subject: Conversation with Mr. Capus, Market News Service, Department of Agriculture. May 29, 1953. Philadelphia City Archives.
65. *Evening Bulletin* 1956.
66. Garrison 2013.
67. Ibid.
68. Friedland and Cooke 1953.
69. *Evening Bulletin,* June 15, 1956; *Evening Bulletin* 1972.
70. *Evening Bulletin* 1962; *Evening Bulletin* 1964; *Evening Bulletin* 1965; *Evening Bulletin,* February 2, 1966; *Evening Bulletin,* March 23, 1966.
71. *Philadelphia Inquirer* 1957; *Evening Bulletin* 1957.
72. Rhodes 1970.
73. *Evening Bulletin* 1967.
74. *Philadelphia Inquirer* 1967.
75. *Evening Bulletin* 1961.
76. Stein, January 9, 1970. TUA.
77. Bijker 1995 for sociotechnical ensemble; LeCavalier 2016 on the distinctive "architecture of fulfillment" in Wal-Mart's distribution.
78. Stein 1970.
79. *Philadelphia Inquirer* 1954; Great Atlantic & Pacific Tea Company of America, 1962 Annual Report, "Heartbeat of Distribution: The A&P Warehouse." Hagley.
80. *Evening Bulletin* 1959.
81. Stein 1970.
82. Ibid.
83. Park 1971.
84. Ibid.
85. *Evening Bulletin* 1974.
86. Prokop 1972.
87. Ibid.; Holland, September 4, 1975; Milletti 1975; Sama 1975.
88. Drill 1976.
89. Knox, September 28, 1976; Prokop 1976; *Evening Bulletin* 1976; Herman 1975.
90. Newman, June 2, 1958.
91. Gaige 1958.
92. Knox 1978.
93. Ibid.
94. Eisen 1979.
95. *Evening Bulletin* 1978; Gillespie 1978; Eisen and Herman 1979; Eisen1979; Gillespie 1979.
96. Goff 1978.
97. Holland, March 23, 1975.
98. Gillespie 1979.
99. Ibid.
100. Newman 1975; Dalton 1975; Herman 1975.
101. Smith 1979.
102. *Philadelphia Tribune* 1979.
103. Logan and Molotch 1987.

CHAPTER FOUR

1. For the relationship between logistics and retail supply chains, see Wrigley and Lowe 2014; for the rise of logistics in geography, transportation, and shipping, see Allen 1997; Bonacich and Wilson 2008; Bonacich and Hardie 2006; Cowen 2014; for the rise of Wal-Mart's logistical apparatus see LeCavalier 2016.
2. Pickering 1995.
3. See Holmes 2011; Ellickson and Grieco 2013; Ellickson 2016; Le Cavalier 2016; Fishman 2006; Brunn 2006; Lichtenstein 2006.
4. Of course, Amazon.com is now putting pressure on the system again, as the emblem of the era of online shopping and direct-to-the-home distribution. See Stone 2013.
5. Liebowitz 1999; Fox 2012.
6. Liebowitz 1999; Fox 2012.
7. Liebowitz 1999; Fox 2012.
8. Woodland and Silver, 1952.
9. Bucklin and Sengupta 1993.
10. Fox 2012.
11. Townes 2010.
12. Selmeier 2008, pp. 78–79.
13. Brown 1997.
14. Grinspoon 2016.
15. Quoted in Nye 2013, p. 165.
16. See Bowker and Star 2000.
17. Ben Nelson, "Chapter 9. The Universal Product Code." Artifact 61, Idhistory.com.
18. Ibid.
19. Woodland's "Technical Memorandum, IBM: The Design of an Optical Scanner for Recognition of Code Patterns, 17–085," July 31, 1962. Artifact 22, Idhistory.com.
20. Dunlop and Rivkin 1997.
21. See Bromberg 1991; Bertolotti 1999.
22. Nelson, "Chapter 9. The University Product Code."
23. Liebowitz 1999; Fox 2012. For optical scanning, see Woodland's "Technical Memorandum, IBM: The Design of an Optical Scanner for Recognition of Code Patterns, 17–085," July 31, 1962. Artifact 22, Idhistory.com; Francis X. Beck Jr., "Some Reminiscing: A Few Years before the UPC." Artifact 108, Idhistory.com.
24. Nelson, "Chapter 9. The University Product Code."
25. Selmeier 2008.
26. Beck, "Some Reminiscing: A Few Years Before the UPC."
27. Nelson, "Chapter 9. The University Product Code."
28. Bijker 1995.
29. Barsky and Kilian 2004.
30. Liebowitz 1999.
31. Selmeier 2008; Brown 1997; Haberman 2001.
32. Wilson 2001.
33. UPC'72 Newsletter. "The Executive Summary of Timely Information about the Universal Product Code," issue 2, October 10, 1972, IDhistory.com; Meeting minutes, Ad Hoc Committee on a Uniform Grocery Product Code, Artifact 182, Idhistory.com.
34. UPC'72 Newsletter. "The Executive Summary of Timely Information about the Universal Product Code," issue 2, October 10, 1972, IDhistory.com; Meeting minutes, Ad Hoc Committee on a Uniform Grocery Product Code, Artifact 182, Idhistory.com.

35. UPC'72 Newsletter. "The Executive Summary of Timely Information about the Universal Product Code," issue 2, October 10, 1972, IDhistory.com; Meeting minutes, Ad Hoc Committee on a Uniform Grocery Product Code, Artifact 182, Idhistory.com.

36. UPC'72 Newsletter. "The Executive Summary of Timely Information about the Universal Product Code," issue 2, October 10, 1972, IDhistory.com; Meeting minutes, Ad Hoc Committee on a Uniform Grocery Product Code, Artifact 182, Idhistory.com.

37. See Timmermans and Epstein 2010.

38. Brown, 1997, p. 40; Haberman 2001, appendix; UPC'72 Newsletter, "The Executive Summary of Timely Information about the Universal Product Code."

39. Distribution Number Bank of the Uniform Grocery Product Code Council, "UPC Symbol Specification." May 1973, Artifact 86, Idhistory.com.

40. "Minutes of the Meeting of the Code Management Subcommittee and Board of Governors of the Uniform Grocery Product Code Council Inc. March 1, 1972. TWA Conference Room, O'Hare Airport, Chicago, Illinois," Artifact 183, Idhistory.com.

41. "Minutes of the Ad Hoc Committee Meeting, McKinsey and Company Inc. NY NY, October 10, 1972," Artifact 182, Idhistory.com.

42. "Recommended Standards for the Grocery Industry, 1973 Edition." Artifact 178, Idhistory.com.

43. *Business Week*, 1973.

44. Dunlop and Rivkin 1997.

45. Barry Franz, "Symbol Decision, March 6, 1973." Artifact 181, Idhistory.com.

46. Ibid.; Savir and Laurer 1975; Engineer symbol notes, Artifact 170, Idhistory.com; Symbol Selection Guide, Artifact 162, Idhistory.com.

47. Mann 2001; Haberman 2001, appendix; "Press Release Grocery Industry Selects a Standard Symbol," Artifact 177, Idhistory.com.

48. Mann 2001; Haberman 2001, appendix; "Press Release Grocery Industry Selects a Standard Symbol," Artifact 177, Idhistory.com.

49. Morton 1994.

50. Callon 1984.

51. Pickering 1995.

52. Walsh 1993.

53. Distribution Codes Inc., *UPC Newsletter*, Vol. 3–4, March 1, 1974. Idhistory.com.

54. Petrovic and Hamilton 2006, p. 306.

55. "Press Release Grocery Industry Selects a Standard Symbol."

56. See Busch 2011, pp. 117–119.

57. Distribution Codes Inc., *UPC Newsletter*, Vol. 10–4, October 1, 1974. Idhistory.com.

58. Distribution Codes Inc., *UPC Newsletter*, Vol. 5–4, May 1, 1974. Idhistory.com.

59. Distribution Codes Inc., *UPC Newsletter*, Vol. 12–4, December 1, 1974. Idhistory.com.

60. Distribution Codes Inc., *UPC Newsletter*, Vol. 9–4, September 1, 1974. Idhistory.com.

61. Uniform Product Code Council Inc., *UPC Newsletter*, Vol. 11–7, November 1977. Idhistory.com.

62. Whooley 2013 describes this kind of situation as an "epistemic contest."

63. Distribution Codes Inc., *UPC Newsletter*, Vol. 7–4, July 1, 1974. Idhistory.com.

64. Ibid.

65. "Recommended Standards for the Grocery Industry, 1973 Edition." Artifact 178, Idhistory.com; Uniform Product Code Council Inc., *Universal Product Code: A Guide to Manufacturers*, Dayton, OH, 1980. Artifact 93, Idhistory.com.

66. Selmeier 2008.

67. Ibid., p. 127.
68. Ibid., pp. 197–198.
69. Ibid., p. 98.
70. Ibid., p. 177.
71. ID Museum. P. V. McEnroe and J. E. Jones, "Identification Technology for the Retail Industry," October 1971. Artifact 107, Idhistory.com.
72. Ibid.
73. See DiMaggio and Powell 1983; Callon and Latour 1981.
74. Walton 1992.
75. Distribution Codes Inc., *UPC Newsletter*, Vol. 1–5, January 1, 1975. Idhistory.com.
76. Valerie DeMuro, "The SAMI Consumer Shopping Panel." *Code and Symbol: The Journal for the Applied Science of Product Identification*. September 1977, 3/9. Idhistory.com.
77. Ibid.
78. Peter V. Andrews, "What IBM Wrought at RTP: The Supermarket Scanner." *Other Views: The News and Observer*, April 29, 2012. Artifact 151, Idhistory.com.
79. Ibid.
80. Ibid.
81. Robert J. Peterson, "Uses of Automated Data Capture in Manufacturing Operations." *Code and Symbol: The Journal for the Applied Science of Product Identification*. September 1977, 3/9. Idhistory.com.
82. Ibid.
83. Ibid.
84. See for example, Levinson 2016; Bonacich and Wilson 2008.
85. Uniform Product Code Council Inc., *UPC Newsletter*, Vol. 11–7, November 1977. Idhistory.com.
86. Petrovic and Hamilton 2006, p. 306.
87. Bucklin and Sengupta 1993.
88. Dunlop 2001.
89. *Chain Store Age Executive* 1985.
90. Stalk, Evans, and Shulman 1992.
91. Quoted in *Chain Store Age Executive* 1985.
92. Walton 1992.
93. Stalk, Evans, and Shulman 1992.
94. Walton 1992, p. 116.
95. Abe Marks quoted in Walton 1992, p. 110–111.
96. Holmes 2011.
97. Ellickson and Grieco 2013.
98. See, for example, LeCavalier 2016; Cowen 2014.
99. Petrovic and Hamilton 2006.
100. Walton 1992, p. 272. See LeCavalier's 2016 account for a more thorough discussion of Wal-Mart's logistics capacities and capabilities and especially the architectural platforms.
101. Walton 1992.
102. Ibid., pp. 271–273.
103. Stalk, Evans, and Shulman 1992.
104. Martin 2001.
105. *Chain Store Age* 1999.
106. Ibid.
107. Ibid.

108. Wagar 1995.
109. *Atlantic* 1992.
110. Quoted in the *Atlantic* 1992, p. 36.
111. De Santa 1996.
112. Ellickson 2007.
113. Partch 1996; Partch 2000.
114. Martens 2008.
115. See https://corporate.walmart.com/our-story/our-business.
116. Kroger Company, *The Kroger Company 2012 Factbook*.
117. Trebilcock 2009.
118. http://www.supervalu.com/about/history-innovation.html
119. The Reinvestment Fund, "Understanding the Grocery Industry," *Financing Healthy Food Options: Implementation Handbook*, September 30, 2011; Martinez 2007.
120. Dunlop and Rivkin 1997.
121. Ibid.
122. GS 1 US, 2014, "Annual Review: 40 Years Back, 40 Years Forward." https://www.gs1us .org/about-gs1-us/corporate/annual-overview.
123. See Gereffi, Humphrey, and Sturgeon 2005; Gereffi, Korzeniewicz, and Korzeniewicz 1994; Bair 2009.
124. DiMaggio and Powell 1983.

CHAPTER FIVE

1. This chapter captures the collective process, but it does not name the specific employees who were interviewed or the private companies where they work. In interview and ethnographic data, I use pseudonyms.
2. See Callon, Méadel, and Rabeharisoa 2002.
3. Shapin 2016.
4. *Evening Bulletin* 1893. Also see O'Neil 2003, p. 13–14.
5. Sackman 2005.
6. Petrick 2006; Freidberg 2009, pp. 181–184.
7. Petrick 2006; Freidberg 2009, pp. 181–184.
8. Rees 2013; Hamilton 2008, p. 123; Freidberg 2009.
9. Griffin and White 1955. Also see Freidberg 2009, pp. 181–184.
10. US Department of Agriculture 1955; Griffin and White 1955.
11. Tanimura and Antle. http://www.taproduce.com/consumer/press-detail.php?id=23 &keywords=Iceberg_Lettuce_%E2%80%93_A_Cornerstone_Of_American_Cuisine; Friedland 1994.
12. *Packer* 1993, p. 164. Also see Freidberg 2009, p. 184.
13. US Department of Agriculture 1955, p. 1.
14. Griffin and White 1955.
15. Griffin and White 1955; Petrick 2006. Church established a company continually looking for technical innovations. Along with engineers at Whirlpool, he developed the bagged lettuce technology that grew into the company Fresh Express, the largest bagged lettuce distributor, dominating the lettuce market in the 1980s: http://www .transfresh.com/about-us/our-history.
16. Seabrook 2011.
17. Smock 1942.
18. Ibid.
19. See http://bestapples.com/facts/facts_controlled.aspx.

20. Seabrook 2011.
21. Love 1988.
22. Ibid.
23. Ibid.
24. Schotzko and Granatstein 2004.
25. Love 1988. Also see "The Journey of an Apple." http://yakimavalleymuseum.org/apple /journey08.cfm
26. Love 1988.
27. Schotzko and Granatstein 2004.
28. Seabrook 2011. Also see: http://www.agmrc.org/commodities__products/fruits/apples /commodity-apple-profile/; Schotzko and Granatstein 2004.
29. Levenstein 2003a, pp. 106–108; Kurlansky 2013.
30. See Estabrook 2011; also see Whiteside 1977.
31. Calvin and Barrios 1999.
32. Ibid.
33. Tinsman 2014.
34. Ibid.
35. Sheffi 2012.
36. Bonacich and Wilson 2008.
37. Sheffi 2012.
38. Calvin and Barrios 1999.
39. See Gereffi, Humphrey, and Sturgeon. 2005; Gereffi, Korzeniewicz, and Korzeniewicz 1994; Bair 2009.
40. USDA 1957; USDA 1973; USDA 2014. The total amount of cold storage in the United States continues to lead the world, but its major competitors are no longer in Europe. China, currently investing in its national mobility infrastructure, is catching up to the United States at least in its total cubic feet. Still, with such a large national population, it currently has nowhere near the amount of cold storage space per capita in comparison to the United States. Twilley (2014) puts it this way: "An artificial winter has begun to stretch across the country, through its fields and its ports, its logistics hubs and freeways. China had 250 million cubic feet of refrigerated storage capacity in 2007; by 2017, the country is on track to have 20 times that. At five billion cubic feet, China will surpass even the United States, which has led the world in cold storage ever since artificial refrigeration was invented. And even that translates to only 3.7 cubic feet of cold storage per capita, or roughly a third of what Americans currently have—meaning that the Chinese refrigeration boom is only just beginning."
41. See Kingsbury 2009.
42. Seabrook 2011.
43. https://www.pma.com/content/articles/2017/05/top-20-fruits-and-vegetables-sold -in-the-us, last accessed May 17, 2019.
44. https://www.ams.usda.gov/about-ams, accessed July 30, 2019.
45. US Department of Agriculture 1972, p. 13.
46. United States Department of Agriculture Agricultural Marketing Service Fruit and Vegetable Programs Fresh Products Branch, 2007, "United States Standards for Grades of Greenhouse Tomatoes." https://www.ams.usda.gov/sites/default/files/me dia/Greenhouse_Tomato_Standard%5B1%5D.pdf, last accessed August 16, 2018.
47. See Zuckerman 2012, p. 224.
48. Shapin 2016.
49. Bowker and Star 2000.

CHAPTER SIX

1. Gunders 2012.
2. As Foucault put it, historical periods present "regularities" in the dominant knowledge paradigm but not "uniformities" in the availability of knowledge. For Foucault, "subjugated" forms of knowledge always remain alongside the paradigmatic system. See Foucault 1972. Also see Timmermans and Epstein 2010.
3. For the biography of things, see Koptyoff 1986; Appadurai 1986; Marcus 1995. There is a good deal of work on material quality decline and adaptation in the social sciences. In the study of infrastructure, see Klinenberg 2002; Graham 2010; Amin 2014. For object decline and adaptation, see Keane 2003; Rubio 2014; McDonnell 2016.
4. Keane 2003. Also see Rubio 2014.
5. For an account of contingency with structure, see Ermakoff 2015.
6. Geertz 1978; also see Bestor 2004. The bazaar economy logic of grooved channels is also different from Karpik's (2010) economy of singularities, which focuses more on distinct types of unique objects that are incommensurable with standard markets. The bazaar system itself, not only the types of objects, holds the logic for reinforcing channels for handling indeterminate features.
7. See https://www.ams.usda.gov/rules-regulations/paca/education-training, last accessed May 18, 2019.
8. Timmermans and Epstein 2010.
9. United States Department of Agriculture 1972.
10. Keane 2003.
11. See Poppendieck 1999.
12. Ibid.
13. Fresh food rescue platforms arose independently of each other. Foodchain and Second Harvest merged in 2000, becoming the basis for a new direction in the food banking sector. See O'Brien et al. 2004.
14. PR Newswire 2001; PR Newswire 2005.
15. deCourcy Hinds 1990.
16. The growing fresh food channel led some organizations to adjust their understandings of "quality." Historically, food banks compared themselves on the basis of a simple metric of pounds of recovery and distribution. They still emphasize their total pounds, but many have internal evaluative methods using algorithms to address "qualities" and "quantities." Philabundance employs a Quality Adjusted Statistical Pounds system, which divides its distribution system into 360 categories. They adjust for "quality pounds," what Clark describes as a "jumble of nutritional value, economic value, and scarcity." In this valuation, 1,000 pounds of potato chips is equivalent to one "quality pound," which allows the food bank to assess how nutritional concerns correspond to total distribution.
17. See https://www.sfmfoodbank.org/programs/fresh-produce-initiative/, last accessed May 18, 2019.
18. Amin 2014.
19. Scholars of food studies have focused on the rise of national and ethnic cuisines as politically and economically charged categories turning certain specified objects, flavor profiles, and dishes into representations of regional and national cuisines. See Ray and Srinivas 2012. Researchers have also shown how historical categories can respond to changing geopolitical dynamics in food distribution, giving rise to a new kind of "gastronationalism," as was the case with foie gras in France. See DeSoucey 2010.

20. See, for example, DeSoucey 2010; Johnston and Baumann 2010; Miller 2017; Ocejo 2017.
21. Thompson 1971.
22. See Johnston and Baumann 2010.
23. See https://www.usda.gov/sites/default/files/documents/KYFCompass.pdf.
24. See https://www.ams.usda.gov/sites/default/files/media/NationalCountofFMDirectory 17.JPG; Brown 2001; McFadden et al. 2016.
25. Kent 1997.
26. *Produce Business* 2016.
27. De La Pradelle 2006.
28. Wicks 2013, pp. 88, 110.
29. Ibid.
30. See https://www.tog.coop/our-history/, last accessed May 18, 2019.
31. The Common Market, Feasibility Study, p. 10. https://www.thecommonmarket.org /assets/uploads/reports/CM-Full-Feasibility-Study.pdf.
32. DeBaise 2017.
33. Testimony of Haile Johnston, co-founder and co-director of The Common Market (of Philadelphia, PA and East Point, GA). To the United States Senate Committee on Agriculture, Nutrition and Forestry, At the Hearing on Opportunities in Global and Local Markets, Specialty Crops, and Organics: Perspectives for the 2018 Farm Bill Thursday, July 13, 2017. https://www.agriculture.senate.gov/imo/media/doc/Testi mony_Johnston.pdf.

CHAPTER SEVEN

1. See Romero 2017.
2. A partnership between *City Paper*, PlanPhilly, and *Technically Philly* led to a series called "The Abandoned City." See http://planphilly.com/series/abandoned-city. For an article on the topic, see Thompson 2011. Elijah Anderson's (2011) work addresses this very tension through the lens of the lived experience, boundaries, and spaces of this emerging uneven development, especially as it impacts and is reinforced by racial inequalities.
3. See, for example, Clark 2004.
4. See, for example, Anguelovski 2015.
5. See Cox 1994; Miller 2017.
6. See Miller 2017.
7. Lordan 1969; O'Leary 1971; Takiff 1972; Forman 1974; Rieder, April 3, 1975.
8. Hackney 1976.
9. Ibid.
10. Hackney 1977.
11. Rieder, May 4, 1975.
12. *Philadelphia Inquirer* 1976.
13. Harris 1972.
14. Hanania 1977.
15. Boyle 1976; Knox, October 22, 1976; Hanania 1977.
16. Ibid.
17. Porter 1977.
18. Ibid.
19. Highsmith and Holton 1994.
20. Capuzzo 1987.

21. Simon and Alnutt 2007.
22. Highsmith and Holton 1994; Simon and Alnutt 2007.
23. Highsmith and Holton 1994.
24. Simon and Alnutt 2007.
25. Capuzzo 1987.
26. Interview with Duane Perry, April 4, 2011.
27. Ibid.
28. Capuzzo 1987. Also see O'Neil 2005.
29. See Johnston and Baumann 2010.
30. Capuzzo 1987.
31. http://www.wholefoodsmarket.com/company-info/whole-foods-market-history #freshfields, last accessed May 19, 2019.
32. O'Neil 2005.
33. Gammage 2002.
34. Panaritis 2015.
35. Doyle 2017. For an account of the bridge between cultural consumption and growth machine politics see Zukin 1995.
36. Anderson 2011.
37. Ibid.
38. Wang et al. 2018.
39. Interview with Duane Perry, April 4, 2011.
40. Ibid.
41. deCourcy Hinds 1994.
42. Anthony 1994.
43. Cummins and Macintyre 2002. In fact, the term "food desert" was first used by a British Nutrition Task Force focused on health disparities in the 1990s. Others were also studying issues related to food access, and they started to use that term and debate the meaning and impact over the next decade.
44. Ibid.
45. Meltzer 1994.
46. Ibid.
47. Foster 1995.
48. Ibid.
49. Vobejda and Cohn 1995; for the original study see: Cotterill and Franklin 1995.
50. Interview with Duane Perry, April 4, 2011.
51. For an account of the creation of the Food Trust research protocol, see Perry et al. 2001; Also see Giang et al. 2008.
52. See Molotch 2014.
53. Interview with Duane Perry, April 4, 2011.
54. See Levitt and March 1988; March and Olsen 1975.
55. Cross 1970.
56. Worden 2003.
57. Brown 2012.
58. Burton and Perry 2004.
59. Giang et al. 2008.
60. Evans 2010; also see https://www.reinvestment.com/success-story/pennsylvania-fresh -food-financing-initiative/.
61. Evans 2010; also see https://www.reinvestment.com/success-story/pennsylvania-fresh -food-financing-initiative/.

62. Giang et al. 2008.
63. *Supermarket News* 1995; https://www.acmemarkets.com/our-company/newsroom/albertsons-llc-announces-definitive-agreement-for-purchase-of-877-stores-from-supervalu/; Reuters 2013.
64. The Reinvestment Fund 2011.
65. Evans and Weidman 2011.
66. Marter 2006.
67. Gates 2008.
68. Ibid.
69. Kinney 2016.
70. Singh 2015.
71. Treuhaft 2012.
72. Soursourian 2010/2011; Evans 2010.
73. Soursourian 2010/2011; Evans 2010.
74. Healthyfoodaccess.org 2017.
75. Ibid.
76. Rose et al. 2009.
77. Cooksey-Stowers, Schwartz, and Brownell 2017.
78. An and Maurer 2016.
79. Hunt, Diamond, and Dube 2017. They summarize their findings like this: "We study the causes of 'nutritional inequality': why the wealthy tend to eat more healthfully than the poor in the US. Using event study designs exploiting supermarket entry and households' moves to healthier neighborhoods, we reject that neighborhood environments have meaningful effects on healthy eating. Using a structural demand model, we find that exposing low-income households to the same availability and prices experienced by high-income households reduces nutritional inequality by only 9 percent, while the remaining 91 percent is driven by differences in demand. These findings contrast with discussions of nutritional inequality that emphasize supply-side factors such as food deserts."
80. Owens 2017; McCrystal 2019.
81. See Bender 2007.
82. DuBois 1899; Thomas and Znainecki 1918–1920; Drake and Cayton 1945.
83. See Small, Harding, and Lamont 2010; Aronowitz et al. 2015.
84. See Mukherjee 2018.

CHAPTER EIGHT
1. Heidegger 1977.
2. Cronon 1991.
3. Becker 1982.
4. Bowker and Star 2000.
5. Vaughan 1999.
6. Ermakoff 2015.
7. Whooley 2013.
8. Mann 1984; Mann 2008.
9. Foucault 2009.
10. Collier and Lakoff 2008; Collier and Lakoff 2015.
11. Bishai and Nalubola 2002.
12. Nestle 2002; Moss 2013.
13. Mukerji 2015.

14. Ibid.
15. Many corporations, through information technology, can seek out competitive vantage points to "see" how people consume in order to more profitably align supply and demand. One of the main features of the current infrastructural regime is what Fourcade and Healy (2016) label as the ability to "see like a market." It is based on a new power position to classify and forecast—and use that technical position toward profit incentive—based on bridging the infrastructural system with a more internally stratified classification of product and consumer characteristics.
16. Pickering 1995.
17. See Gereffi, Humphrey, and Sturgeon 2005; Hamilton and Gereffi 2009.
18. Pickering 1995.
19. Callon and Latour 1981. Callon and Latour put it in terms of a distinction—in their terms, a false distinction—between the macro- and the micro-levels. For them, everything is happening at the micro-level with certain actors able to put more networks in black boxes than other actors. Whether one believes that macro and micro are ontologically distinct levels of inquiry and/or analysis is beyond the scope of this conclusion. I'm more concerned with their relational characteristics in regards to the transformation of the food system. I agree with Callon and Latour that the making of macro-level coercion/power requires a wide range of micro-level processes to accumulate into durable organizational interdependencies.
20. Merton 1936.
21. Molotch 2004.
22. Mintz 1985.
23. Moss (2013) correctly points out that people got hooked on salt, sugar, and fat, but it was not only that the market "giants hooked us." It was a deeply complex historical and sociological process, built upon mutual adaptations between heterogeneous organizations reconfiguring supply and demand. It had as much to do with the transformation of the infrastructure of abundance, convenience, and consumer desire for cheap and tasty foods.

METHODS APPENDIX
1. Star 1999.
2. Merton 1987.

REFERENCES

ARCHIVAL COLLECTIONS
Hagley Museum and Library

Food Fair Stores
The Great Atlantic & Pacific Tea Company
Grocery Industry Barometer
National Commission on Food Marketing
Supermarket News

ID History Museum

Artifacts
Code and Symbol: The Journal for the Applied Science of Product Identification
UPC Newsletters

Philadelphia City Archives

Administration of Joseph S. Clark

    Dock Street Market
    Greater Philadelphia Movement
    The Philadelphia Housing Authority

Administration of Richardson Dilworth

    Food Distribution Center

Administration of James H. Tate

    Food Distribution Center

Temple Urban Archives

American Stores Company (Acme Market)
Atlantic & Pacific Tea Company
Dock Street Wholesale Market
Evening Bulletin and Newspaper Clippings
Food Fair Market
Greater Philadelphia Movement
Penn Fruit Market
Philadelphia Food Distribution Center
Reading Terminal Market

288 / References

PUBLISHED PRIMARY AND
SECONDARY SOURCES

Abbott, Andrew. 2016. *Processual Sociology*. Chicago: University of Chicago Press.

Abbott, William Lewis. 1920. *Competition and Combination in the Wholesale Grocery Trade in Philadelphia*. Menasha, WI: Collegiate Press, George Banta Publishing Company.

Adams, Artho Barto. 1916. *Marketing Perishable Farm Products*. New York: Columbia University Press.

Allen, Keith C. 1954. "New Dock St. Food Depot Site Picked." *Philadelphia Inquirer*, June 27, 1954.

Allen, W. Bruce. 1997. "The Logistics Revolution and Transportation." *Annals of the American Academy of Political and Social Science* 553, no. 1: 106–116.

Amin, Ash. 2014. "Lively Infrastructure." *Theory, Culture & Society* 31, no. 7–8: 137–161.

An, Ruopeng, and Grace Maurer. 2016. "Consumption of Sugar-Sweetened Beverages and Discretionary Foods among US Adults by Purchase Location." *European Journal of Clinical Nutrition* 70, no. 12: 1396–1400.

Anderson, Elijah. 2011. *The Cosmopolitan Canopy: Race and Civility in Everyday Life*. New York: W. W. Norton.

Angelo, Hillary, and David Wachsmuth. 2015. "Urbanizing Urban Political Ecology: A Critique of Methodological Cityism." *International Journal of Urban and Regional Research* 39, no. 1: 16–27.

Anguelovski, Isabelle. 2015. "Healthy Food Stores, Greenlining and Food Gentrification: Contesting New Forms of Privilege, Displacement and Locally Unwanted Land Uses in Racially Mixed Neighborhoods." *International Journal of Urban and Regional Research* 39, no. 6: 1209–1230.

Anthony, Ted. 1994. "Market Brings Fresh Produce to City's Impoverished Areas." *Associated Press*, October 4, 1994.

Appadurai, Arjun, ed. 1986. *The Social Life of Things: Commodities in Cultural Perspective*. New York: Cambridge University Press.

Architectural Forum. 1947. "Philadelphia Plans Again." December 1947.

Aronowitz, Robert, Andrew Deener, Danya Keene, Jason Schnittker, and Laura Tach. 2015. "Cultural Reflexivity in Health Research and Practice." *American Journal of Public Health* 105, no. S3: S403–S408.

Atlantic. 1992. "Adventures in the Food Chain." 269, no. 6 (June): 30–40.

Baics, Gergely. 2016. *Feeding Gotham: The Political Economy and Geography of Food in New York, 1790–1860*. Princeton: Princeton University Press.

Bair, Jennifer, ed. 2009. *Frontiers of Commodity Chain Research*. Stanford: Stanford University Press.

Barsky, Robert B., and Lutz Kilian. 2004. "Oil and the Macroeconomy since the 1970s." *Journal of Economic Perspectives* 18, no. 4: 115–134.

Becker, Howard S. 1982. *Art Worlds*. Berkeley: University of California Press.

Becker, Howard S. 1995. "The Power of Inertia." *Qualitative Sociology* 18, no. 3: 301–309.

Bender, Thomas. 2007. *The Unfinished City: New York and the Metropolitan Idea*. New York: NYU Press.

Beniger, James R. 1986. *The Control Revolution: Technological and Economic Origins of the Information Society*. Cambridge, MA: Harvard University Press.

Bertolotti, Mario. 1999. *The History of the Laser*. New York: Taylor and Francis Group.

Bestor, Theodore C. 2004. *Tsukiji: The Fish Market at the Center of the World*. Berkeley. University of California Press.

Biggart, Nicole Woolsey, and Thomas D. Beamish. 2003. "The Economic Sociology of Conventions: Habit, Custom, Practice, and Routine in Market Order." *Annual Review of Sociology* 29, no. 1: 443–464.

Bijker, Wiebe E. 1995. *Of Bicycles, Bakelites, and Bulbs: Toward a Theory of Sociotechnical Change*. Cambridge, MA: MIT Press.

Bishai, David, and Ritu Nalubola. 2002. "The History of Food Fortification in the United States: Its Relevance for Current Fortification Efforts in Developing Countries." *Economic Development and Cultural Change* 51, no. 1: 37–53.

Boltanski, Luc, and Laurent Thévenot. 2006. *On Justification: Economies of Worth*. Princeton, NJ: Princeton University Press.

Bonacich, Edna, and Khaleelah Hardie. 2006. "Wal-Mart and the Logistics Revolution." In *Wal-Mart: The Face of Twenty-First-Century Capitalism*, edited by Nelson Lichtenstein. New York: New Press.

Bonacich, Edna, and Jake B. Wilson. 2008. *Getting the Goods: Ports, Labor, and the Logistics Revolution*. Cornell University Press.

Bowker, Geoffrey C., and Susan Leigh Star. 2000. *Sorting Things Out: Classification and Its Consequences*. Cambridge, MA: MIT Press.

Boyle, Bruce. 1976. "New Landlord Terminates Leases: Merchants at Terminal Oppose Rent Increases." *Evening Bulletin*, October 6, 1976.

Brecht, Raymond C. 1954. "Vast South Phila. Project Will Replace Antiquated Markets of Dock St. Area." *Evening Bulletin*, October 31, 1954.

Brenner, Neil, ed. 2014. *Implosions/Explosions: Towards a Study of Planetary Urbanization*. Berlin: jovis Verlag.

Brenner, Neil, and Nik Theodore. 2002. "Cities and the Geographies of 'Actually Existing Neoliberalism.'" *Antipode* 34, no. 3: 349–379.

Bromberg, Joan Lisa. 1991. *The Laser in America, 1950–1970*. Cambridge, MA: MIT Press.

Brown, Allison. 2001. "Counting Farmers' Markets." *Geographical Review* 4: 655–674.

Brown, Jeff. 2012. "The Grocery Gap." *Nurturing Healthy Food Financing*. Opportunity Finance Network. December 12, 2012. https://ofn.org/sites/default/files/resources/PDFs/Presentations/GroceryGap_Final.pdf.

Brown, Stephen Allen. 1997. *Revolution at the Checkout Counter*. Cambridge, MA: Harvard University Press.

Brunn, Stanley D., ed. 2006. *The Wal-Mart World: The World's Biggest Corporation in the Global Economy*. New York: Routledge.

Bucklin, Louis P., and Sanjit Sengupta. 1993. "The Co-diffusion of Complementary Innovations: Supermarket Scanners and UPC Symbols." *Journal of Product Innovation Management* 10, no. 2: 148–160.

Burton, Hannah, and Duane Perry. 2004. *Stimulating Supermarket Development: A New Day for Philadelphia*. Philadelphia: Food Trust.

Busch, Lawrence. 2011. *Standards: Recipes for Reality*. Cambridge, MA: MIT Press.

Business Week. 1973. "A Standard Labeling Code for Food." April 7, 1973, 71–73.

Callon, Michel. 1984. "Some Elements of a Sociology of Translation: Domestication of the Scallops and the Fishermen of St Brieuc Bay." *Sociological Review* 32, no. 1: 196–233.

Callon, Michel. 1998. "Introduction: The Embeddedness of Economic Markets in Economics." *Sociological Review* 46, no. 1: 1–57.

Callon, Michel, and Bruno Latour. 1981. "Unscrewing the Big Leviathan: How Do Actors Macrostructure Reality." In *Advances in Social Theory and Methodology: Toward an*

Integration of Micro-and Macro-sociologies, edited by Karin Knorr-Cetina and Aaron Cicourel, 277–303. New York: Routledge.

Callon, Michel, Cécile Méadel, and Vololona Rabeharisoa. 2002. "The Economy of Qualities." *Economy and Society* 31, no. 2: 194–217.

Calvin, Linda, and Veronica Barrios. 1999. "Marketing Winter Vegetables from Mexico." *Journal of Food Distribution Research* 30: 50–62.

Capuzzo, Michael. 1987. "Renewal & the Reading." *Philadelphia Inquirer*, January 21, 1987.

Carse, Ashley. 2017. "Keyword: Infrastructure: How a Humble French Engineering Term Shaped the Modern World." In *Infrastructures and Social Complexity: A Routledge Companion*, edited by Harvey Penny, Casper Bruun Jensen, and Atsuro Morita, 27–39. London: Routledge.

Castells, Manuel. 2000. *The Rise of the Network Society: The Information Age*. 2nd ed. Malden, MA: Blackwell.

Chain Store Age. 1999. "The Big Box Decade." 75, no. 13: 98–101.

Chain Store Age Executive. 1985. "Discounters Commit to Bar-Code Scanning: K Mart and Wal-Mart Have Pledged to Install POS Bar-Code Scanning in All Stores by the End of the Decade." September 1985.

Chandler, Alfred D. 1993. *The Visible Hand: The Managerial Revolution in American Business*. Cambridge, MA: Harvard University Press.

Chapman, Peter. 2007. *Bananas: How the United Fruit Company Shaped the World*. New York: Canongate.

Charvat, Frank J. 1961. *Supermarketing*. New York: Macmillan.

Clark, Terry Nichols. 2004. "Chapter 3. Urban Amenities: Lakes, Opera, and Juice Bars: Do They Drive Development?" in *The City as an Entertainment Machine, Research in Urban Policy, Vol. 9*, edited by Terry Nichols Clark, 103–140. Boston: JAI/Elsevier.

Clarke, Adele E., and Susan Leigh Star. 2008. "The Social Worlds Framework: A Theory/Methods Package." In *The Handbook of Science and Technology Studies*, edited by Hackett, Edward J., Olga Amsterdamska, Michael Lynch, and Judy Wajcman, 113–137. Cambridge, MA: MIT Press.

Cohen, Lizabeth. 1996. "From Town Center to Shopping Center: The Reconfiguration of Community Marketplaces in Postwar America." *American Historical Review* 101, no. 4: 1050–1081.

Collier, Stephen J., and Andrew Lakoff. 2008. "Distributed Preparedness: The Spatial Logic of Domestic Security in the United States." *Environment and Planning D: Society and Space* 26, no. 1: 7–28.

Collier, Stephen J., and Andrew Lakoff. 2015. "Vital Systems Security: Reflexive Biopolitics and the Government of Emergency." *Theory, Culture, & Society* 32, no. 2: 19–51.

Cooksey-Stowers, Kristen, Marlene B. Schwartz, and Kelly D. Brownell. 2017. "Food Swamps Predict Obesity Rates Better than Food Deserts in the United States." *International Journal in Environmental Research and Public Health* 14, no. 1: 1366.

Cotterill, Ronald W., and Franklin, Andrew W. 1995. *The Urban Grocery Store Gap*. Issue Paper 8, University of Connecticut, Department of Agricultural and Resource Economics, Charles J. Zwick Center for Food and Resource Policy.

Countryman, Matthew J. 2007. *Up South: Civil Rights and Black Power in Philadelphia*. Philadelphia: University of Pennsylvania Press.

Cowen, Deborah. 2014. *The Deadly Life of Logistics: Mapping Violence in Global Trade*. Minneapolis: University of Minnesota Press.

Cox, Craig. 1994. *Storefront Revolution: Food Co-ops and the Counterculture*. New Brunswick: Rutgers University Press.

Cronon, William. 1991. *Nature's Metropolis: Chicago and the Great West*. New York: W. W. Norton.

Cross, Jennifer. 1970. *The Supermarket Trap: The Consumer and the Food Industry*. Bloomington: Indiana University Press.

Cummins, Steven, and Sally Macintyre. 2002. "'Food Deserts'—Evidence and Assumption in Health Policy Making." *British Medical Journal* 325, no. 7361: 436–438.

Custis, Emerson. 1950. [Untitled article on wholesale market]. *Evening Bulletin*, January 22, 1950.

Dalton, Lin. 1975. "The Closing of a Store Holds Special Meaning." *Evening Bulletin*, November 2, 1975.

DeBaise, Colleen. 2017. "This Philadelphia Entrepreneur Is Helping Fix a Broken Food System." *Story Exchange*, January 31, 2017. https://thestoryexchange.org/philadelphia-com pany-helping-fix-broken-food-system/.

deCourcy Hinds, Michael. 1990. "Leftovers Become Sustenance for Needy." *New York Times*, July 26, 1990.

deCourcy Hinds, Michael. 1994. "Philadelphia Journal: Inner City Market Blossoms." *New York Times*, May 14, 1994, section 1, 8.

Deener, Andrew. 2017. "The Origins of the Food Desert: Urban Inequality as Infrastructural Exclusion." *Social Forces* 95, no. 3: 1285–1309.

de La Pradelle, Michèle. 2006. *Market Day in Provence*. Chicago: University of Chicago Press.

De Santa, Richard. 1996. "A Most Measured Approach." *Supermarket Business* 51, no. 11 (November): 17–20.

DeSoucey, Michaela. 2010. "Gastronationalism: Food Traditions and Authenticity Politics in the European Union." *American Sociological Review* 75, no. 3: 432–455.

DiMaggio, Paul, and Walter W. Powell. 1983. "The Iron Cage Revisited: Collective Rationality and Institutional Isomorphism in Organizational Fields." *American Sociological Review* 48, no. 2: 147–160.

Dimitri, Carolyn, Anne Effland, and Neilson Conklin. 2005. "The 20th Century Transformation of U.S. Agriculture and Farm Policy." United States Department of Agriculture, Economic Research Service, Economic Information Bulletin no. 3. June 2005.

Doyle, Terrence B. 2017. "Quincy Market Food Crawl: Tasty Treats in a Tourist Trap." https://boston.eater.com/2017/11/22/16685330/best-food-quincy-market.

Drake, St. Clair, and H. Cayton. 1945. *Black Metropolis: A Study of Negro Life in a Northern City*. New York: Harcourt Brace.

Drewnowski, Adam. 1997. "Taste Preferences and Food Intake." *Annual Review of Nutrition* 17, no. 1: 237–253.

Drill, Herb. 1976. "Penn Fruit Co. Goes Show Biz." *Evening Bulletin*, June 4, 1976.

DuBois, W. E. B. 1899. *The Philadelphia Negro: A Social Study*. Philadelphia: University of Pennsylvania Press.

Duddy, E. A., and D. A. Revzan. 1939. "Transportation and Marketing Facilities for Fresh Fruits and Vegetables in Chicago." *Journal of Business of the University of Chicago* 12, no. 3: 280–297.

Duncan, Otis Dudley. 1961. "From Social System to Ecosystem." *Sociological Inquiry* 31, no. 2: 140–149.

Dunlop, John T. 2001. "The Diffusion of UCC Standards." In *Twenty-Five Years behind Bars: The Proceedings of the Twenty-Fifth Anniversary of the U.P.C. at the Smithsonian Institution, September 30, 1999*, edited by Alan L. Haberman, 12–24. Cambridge, MA: Harvard University Press.

Dunlop, John T., and Jan W. Rivkin. 1997. "Introduction." In *Revolution at the Checkout Counter*, edited by Stephen A. Brown, 1–38. Cambridge, MA: Harvard University Press.

Edwards, Paul N. 2003. "Infrastructure and Modernity: Force, Time, and Social Organization in the History of Sociotechnical Systems." *Modernity and Technology* 1: 185–226.

Ehrlich, Paul R., Anne H. Ehrlich, and Gretchen C. Daily. 1993. "Food Security, Population, and Environment." *Population and Development Review* 19, no. 1: 1–32.

Eisen, Edward N. "Food Fair Stores Shut for Good." *Evening Bulletin*, January 27, 1979.

Eisen, Edward N., and Martin J. Herman. 1979. "Judge Likely to OK Food Fair Closings." *Evening Bulletin*, January 26, 1979.

Ellickson, Paul B. 2007. "Does Sutton Apply to Supermarkets?" *RAND Journal of Economics* 38, no. 1: 43–59.

Ellickson, Paul B. 2016. "The Evolution of the Supermarket Industry: From A&P to Wal-Mart." In *Handbook on the Economics of Retailing and Distribution*, edited by Emek Basker, 368–391. Northampton, MA: Edward Elgar.

Ellickson, Paul B., and Paul L. E. Grieco. 2013. "Wal-Mart and the Geography of Grocery Retailing." *Journal of Urban Economics* 75: 1–14.

Ermakoff, Ivan. 2015. "The Structure of Contingency." *American Journal of Sociology* 121, no. 1: 64–125.

Espeland, Wendy Nelson. 1998. *The Struggle for Water: Politics, Rationality, and Identity in the American Southwest*. Chicago: University of Chicago Press.

Esposito, Nicolas. 2014. "It Started with Bananas." Hidden City Philadelphia website, May 20. https://hiddencityphila.org/2014/05/it-started-with-bananas/.

Estabrook, Barry. 2011. *Tomatoland: How Modern Industrial Agriculture Destroyed Our Most Alluring Fruit*. Kansas City, MI: Andrews McMeel.

Evans, Dwight. 2010. "Report on Key Issues from the House Appropriations Committee." *Budget Briefing*, March 4, 2010. http://www.ncsl.org/documents/labor/workingfamilies/PA_FFFI.pdf.

Evans, Dwight, and John Weidman. 2011. "Growing Network: Fresh Food Financing Initiative." Governing: The States and Localities website, July 11, 2011. http://www.governing.com/blogs/bfc/Fresh-Food-Financing-Initiative-070711.html.

Evening Bulletin. 1893. "Reading's New Terminal." October 14, 1893.

Evening Bulletin. 1912. "City to Establish Curb Markets to Cut Cost of Living in Frankford, West Philadelphia, and Chestnut Hill." November 24, 1912.

Evening Bulletin. 1917. "Chain Store Merger Details Announced." April 2, 1917.

Evening Bulletin. 1936. "U.S. Market Plan Baffles Dealers: Local Produce Merchants Ask Time to Study Proposal for Widespread Merger." December 1, 1936.

Evening Bulletin. 1936. "Men and Things: Inadequacy of Present Equipment for Wholesale Handling of Philadelphia's Daily Fruit and Vegetable Supply Is Shown in Plea for New Enterprise." December 14, 1936.

Evening Bulletin. 1954. "City Planners Approve Site for Food Center in S. Phila." November 18, 1954.

Evening Bulletin. 1955. "Food Fair Buys Surpass Plant: Will Demolish It for New Supermarket." January 17, 1955.

Evening Bulletin. 1955. "Food Fair Plans Firm to Run Shopping Centers." August 19, 1955.

Evening Bulletin. 1956. "High Principles Set by Founders Guide Vast Program of Penn Fruit." June 15, 1956.

Evening Bulletin. 1957. "Remodeled A&P Opens at 5234 N. 5th St." September 11, 1957. TUA

Evening Bulletin. 1957. "American Stores Net Up to $2.94." November 1, 1957.

Evening Bulletin. 1958. "Food Fair Announces Purchase of Best Markets." August 22, 1958.

Evening Bulletin. 1958. "Food Fair to Open Baltimore Av. Market." November 13, 1958.

Evening Bulletin. 1959. "Food Fair Takes Big Site at New Center." September 9, 1959, F4.

Evening Bulletin. 1961. "Center City Group Votes to Battle New Supermarket." March 29, 1961.

Evening Bulletin. 1962. "Acme Opens First Store in Swarthmorewood Center." June 6, 1962.

Evening Bulletin. 1964. "Acme Opening Store at 2132 E. Lehigh Av." December 2, 1964.

Evening Bulletin. 1965. "New Acme Market Planned on 25th St. near Wharton." January 20, 1965.

Evening Bulletin. 1966. "Acme Plans Shopping Mart in Eastwick." February 2, 1966.

Evening Bulletin. 1966. "New Acme Opened on Roosevelt Blvd." March 23, 1966.TUA

Evening Bulletin. 1967. "School in Shopping Center to Train Negro Businessmen." July 27, 1967.

Evening Bulletin. 1969. "78 and Still Growing: Billion Dollar Sales from Modest Beginning Is Story of Growth of Acme Markets." March 4, 1969.

Evening Bulletin. 1972. "Center City Penn Fruit Closes Friday." August 24, 1972.

Evening Bulletin. 1974. [Untitled article on food and nonfood products in grocery stores]. December 9, 1974.

Evening Bulletin. 1976. "Food Fair May Buy Penn Fruit." June 3, 1976, section E.

Evening Bulletin. 1978. "Suppliers Deserting Food Fair." October 5, 1978.

Farías, Ignacio, and Thomas Bender, eds. 2010. *Urban Assemblages: How Actor-Network Theory Changes Urban Studies.* New York: Routledge.

Feist, William F. 1953. "Big Terminal Planned to Supplant Dock St." *Philadelphia Inquirer,* September 4, 1953.

Fetridge, Robert H. 1951. "Along the Highways and Byways of Finance." *New York Times,* August 5, 1951.

Fischer, Claude S. 1994. *America Calling: The Social History of the Telephone to 1940.* Berkeley: University of California Press.

Fishman, Charles. 2006. *The Wal-Mart Effect: How the World's Most Powerful Company Really Works—and How It's Transforming the American Economy.* New York: Penguin.

Fishman, Robert. 1990. "America's New City: Megalopolis Unbound." *Wilson Quarterly* 14 (Winter): 25–45.

Fletcher, Stevenson Whitcomb. 1976. *The Philadelphia Society for Promoting Agriculture, 1785–1955.* Philadelphia, PA: Philadelphia Society for Promoting Agriculture.

Fligstein, Neil. 1993. *The Transformation of Corporate Control.* Cambridge, MA: Harvard University Press.

Forman, Nessa. 1974. "It's No Secret, We're a Throwaway Culture." *Evening Bulletin,* July 28, 1974.

Forsythe, William A. 1964. "Philadelphia's Larder for 4 1/5 Million People." *Evening Bulletin,* December 13, 1964.

Foster, Andrea. 1995. "For Philadelphia Poor, Groceries Scarce." *States News Service,* May 16, 1995.

Foucault, Michel. 1972. *The Archaeology of Knowledge.* Translated by A. M. Sheridan Smith. New York: Vintage Books.

Foucault, Michel. 2009. *Security, Territory, Population: Lectures at the Collège de France, 1977–78.* Translated by Graham Burchell. New York: Palgrave McMillan.

Fourcade, Marion. 2011. "Cents and Sensibility: Economic Valuation and the Nature of Nature." *American Journal of Sociology* 116, no. 6: 1721–1777.

Fourcade, Marion. 2017. "The Fly and the Cookie: Alignment and Unhingement in 21st-Century Capitalism." *Socio-Economic Review* 15, no. 3: 661–678.

Fourcade, Marion, and Kieran Healy. 2016. "Seeing like a Market." *Socio-Economic Review* 15, no. 1: 9–29.

Fox, Margalit. 2012. "N. Joseph Woodland, Inventor of the Bar Code, Dies at 91." *New York Times*, December 14, A1.

Freidberg, Susanne. 2009. *Fresh: A Perishable History*. Cambridge, MA: Harvard University Press.

Friedland, George, and Samuel Cooke. "Supermarket Growth Seen; New Sales Peak Predicted." *Evening Bulletin*, January 5, 1953.

Friedland, William H. 1994. "The Global Fresh Fruit and Vegetable System: An Industrial Organization Analysis." In *The Global Restructuring of Agro-Food Systems*, edited by Philip D. McMichael, 173–189. Ithaca: Cornell University Press.

Friedland, William H., Amy E. Barton, and Robert J. Thomas. 1981. *Manufacturing Green Gold*. New York: Cambridge University Press.

Friedmann, Harriet. 1987. "International Regimes of Food and Agriculture since 1870." In *Peasants and Peasant Societies*, edited by Teodor Shanin, 247–258. Oxford: Basil Blackwell.

Friedmann, Harriet, and Philip McMichael. 1989. "Agriculture and the State System: The Rise and Fall of National Agricultures, 1870 to the Present." *Sociologia Ruralis* 29, no. 2: 93–117.

Fry, Herbert C. 1991. "The House that Quality Built: A Brief History of the American Stores Company." Tredyffrin Easttown Historical Society *History Quarterly* 29, no. 2 (April): 43–64.

Gaige, Jeremy. 1958. "Acme Plans to Continue 'Making Up Lost Ground.'" *Evening Bulletin*, July 6, 1958.

Gammage, Jeff. 2002. "Fresh Ideas—Reading Terminal Market Is Healthy but Threatened, Its New Manager Says." *Philadelphia Inquirer*, April 21, 2002.

Gandy, Matthew. 2004. "Rethinking Urban Metabolism: Water, Space and the Modern City." *City* 8, no. 3: 363–379.

Gandy, Matthew. 2014. *The Fabric of Space: Water, Modernity, and the Urban Imagination*. Cambridge, MA: MIT Press.

Garrison, Shannon Teresa. 2013. "Penn Fruit and the Everyday Modern: Interpreting the Mid-century Supermarket." Master's thesis, University of Pennsylvania.

Gates, Kellie Patrick. 2008. "Challenge of Creating an Urban Supermarket." *PlanPhilly*, October 27, 2008.

Geertz, Clifford. 1978. "The Bazaar Economy: Information and Search in Peasant Marketing." *American Economic Review* 68, no. 2: 28–32.

Gereffi, Gary, John Humphrey, and Timothy Sturgeon. 2005. "The Governance of Global Value Chains." *Review of International Political Economy* 12, no. 1: 78–104.

Gereffi, Gary, Miguel Korzeniewicz, and Roberto P. Korzeniewicz. 1994. "Introduction: Global Commodity Chains." In *Commodity Chains and Global Capitalism*, edited by Gary Gereffi and Miguel Korzeniewicz, 1–14. Westport, CT: Praeger.

Giang, Tracey, Allison Karpyn, Hannah Burton Laurison, Amy Hillier, and Duayne Perry. 2008. "Closing the Grocery Gap in Underserved Communities: The Creation of the Pennsylvania Fresh Food Financing Initiative." *Journal of Public Health Management and Practice* 14, no. 3: 272–279.

Gibbon, Peter, Jennifer Bair, and Stefano Ponte. 2008. "Governing Global Value Chains: An Introduction." *Economy and Society* 37, no. 3: 315–338.

Gillespie, John T. 1978. "The Rise and Fall of Food Fair Chain." *Evening Bulletin*, October 8, 1978.

Gillespie, John T. 1979. "Food Fair Bosses Blamed." *Evening Bulletin,* January 28, 1979.

Goddard, Stephen B. 1996. *Getting There: The Epic Struggle between Road and Rail in the American Century.* Chicago: University of Chicago Press.

Goff, Kristin. 1978. "A&P, Food Fair Exceptions in Profitable Year for Chains." *Evening Bulletin,* October 9, 1978.

Gordon, Robert J. 2017. *The Rise and Fall of American Growth: The U.S. Standard of Living since the Civil War.* Princeton: Princeton University Press.

Graden, Thurston. 1952. "Philadelphia Wholesale Fruit and Vegetable Market." *Economics Business Bulletin* 5, no. 2: 10–16.

Graham, Stephen, ed. 2010. *Disrupted Cities: When Infrastructure Fails.* New York: Routledge.

Graham, Stephen, and Simon Marvin. 2002. *Splintering Urbanism: Networked Infrastructures, Technological Mobilities and the Urban Condition.* New York: Routledge.

Granovetter, Mark. 1985. "Economic Action and Social Structure: The Problem of Embeddedness." *American Journal of Sociology* 91, no. 3: 481–510.

Greater Philadelphia Movement. [ca. 1950s]. "How Philadelphia Created the World's First Complete Food Distribution Center." Manuscript.

Greater Philadelphia Movement. 1954. "New Food Distribution Center." October 27, 1954.

Greer, William, John A. Logan, and Paul S. Willis. 1986. *America the Bountiful: How the Supermarket Came to Main Street: An Oral History.* Washington, DC: Food Marketing Institute.

Griffin, Paul F., and C. Langdon White. 1955. "Lettuce Industry of the Salinas Valley." *Scientific Monthly* 81, no. 2: 77–84.

Grinspoon, David. 2016. *Earth in Human Hands: Shaping Our Planet's Future.* Hachette.

Groden, Thurston. 1952. "Philadelphia Wholesale Fruit and Vegetable Market." *Economics Business Bulletin* 5(2): 10–16.

Groff, Vernon. 1950. "Proposed Bill Would Pave Way for Huge Produce Market Here." *Evening Bulletin,* January 22, 1950.

Gunders, Dane. 2012. "Wasted: How America Is Losing Up to 4 Percent of Its Food from Farm to Fork to Landfill." Natural Resources Defense Council, Issue Paper, August.

Haberman, Alan L., ed. 2001. "Appendix: 17 Billion Reasons to Say Thanks." In *Twenty-Five Years behind Bars: The Proceedings of the Twenty-Fifth Anniversary of the UPC at the Smithsonian Institution, September 30, 1999.* Cambridge, MA: Harvard University Press.

Haberman, Alan L., ed. 2001. *Twenty-Five Years behind Bars: The Proceedings of the Twenty-Fifth Anniversary of the U.P.C. at the Smithsonian Institution, September 30, 1999.* Cambridge, MA: Harvard University Press.

Hackney, David C. 1976. "SEPTA Board Agrees to Buy 'Bargains' from Rail Lines." *Evening Bulletin,* January 7, 1976.

Hackney, David C. 1977. "Speedy Start Due on Tunnel." *Evening Bulletin,* January 13, 1977.

Hamilton, Gary G., and Gary Gereffi. 2009. "Global Commodity Chains, Market Makers, and the Rise of Demand-Responsive Economies." In *Frontiers of Commodity Chain Research,* edited by Jennifer Bair, 136–161. Stanford: Stanford University Press.

Hamilton, Shane. 2008. *Trucking Country: The Road to America's Wal-Mart Economy.* Princeton: Princeton University Press.

Hanania, Joseph. 1977. "Tales of a Great Marketplace." *Philadelphia Inquirer,* April 24, 1977.

Harris, Gene. 1972. "Reading Terminal Cited for City Code Violations." *Evening Bulletin,* February 27, 1972.

Harrison, Candice L. 2008. "The Contest of Exchange: Space, Power, and Politics in Philadelphia's Public Markets, 1770–1859." PhD diss., Emory University.

Hartford, George L. 1938. "A Statement of Public Policy by The Great Atlantic & Pacific Tea Company." *Evening Bulletin*, October 13, 1938.

Harvey, David. 2005. *Spaces of Neoliberalization: Towards a Theory of Uneven Geographical Development*. New York: Verso.

Hayden, Dolores. 2004. *Building Suburbia: Green Fields and Urban Growth, 1820–2000*. New York: Vintage.

Healthyfoodaccess.org. 2017. "The Healthy Food Financing Initiative: An Innovative Public-Private Partnership Sparking Economic Development and Improving Health." http://healthyfoodaccess.org/resources/library/healthy-food-financing-initiative-hffi.

Heidegger, Martin. 1977. *The Question Concerning Technology, and Other Essays*. New York: Harper & Row.

Herman, Martin J. 1975. "Market Closings Aimed at Unprofitable Stores." *Evening Bulletin*. September 18, 1975.

Highsmith, Carol M., and James L. Holton. 1994. *Reading Terminal and Market: Philadelphia's Historic Gateway and Grand Convention Center*. Washington, DC: Chelsea.

Hirschman, Daniel, and Isaac Ariail Reed. 2014. "Formation Stories and Causality in Sociology." *Sociological Theory* 32, no. 4: 259–282.

Holland, John. 1975. "A&P to Shut 62 Stores in 3 States." *Philadelphia Inquirer*, March 23, 1975.

Holland, John. 1975. "Insolvent, Penn Fruit Tells Court." *Philadelphia Inquirer*, September 4, 1975.

Holmes, Thomas J. 2011. "The Diffusion of Wal-Mart and Economies of Density." *Econometrica* 79, no. 1: 253–302.

Hughes, Thomas P. 2012. "The Evolution of Large Technical Systems." In *The Social Construction of Technological Systems: New Directions in the Sociology and History of Technology*, edited by Wiebe Bijker, Thomas Hughes, and Trevor Pinch, 45–76. Cambridge, MA: MIT Press.

Hughes, Thomas P. 1993. *Networks of Power: Electrification in Western Society, 1880–1930*. Baltimore: Johns Hopkins University Press.

Hunt, Allcott, Rebecca Diamond, and Jean-Pierre Dube. 2017. "The Geography of Poverty and Nutrition: Food Deserts and Food Choices across the United States." NBER Working Paper no. 24094.

Ingram, Paul, and Hayagreeva Rao. 2004. "Store Wars: The Enactment and Repeal of Anti-Chain-Store Legislation in America." *American Journal of Sociology* 110, no. 2: 446–487.

Jackson, Kenneth T. 1985. *Crabgrass Frontier: The Suburbanization of the United States*. New York: Oxford University Press.

Jervis, Robert. 1998. *System Effects: Complexity in Political and Social Life*. Princeton: Princeton University Press.

Johnston, Josée, and Shyon Baumann. 2010. *Foodies: Democracy and Distinction in the Gourmet Foodscape*. New York: Routledge.

Jumper, Sidney R. 1974. "Wholesale Marketing of Fresh Vegetables." *Annals of the Association of American Geographers* 64, no. 3: 387–396.

Karpik, Lucien. 2010. *Valuing the Unique: The Economies of Singularities*. Princeton: Princeton University Press.

Keane, Webb. 2003. "Semiotics and the Social Analysis of Material Things." *Language & Communication* 23, nos. 3–4: 409–425.

Kent, Bill. 1997. "In Vineland, a Marketplace Run by Farmers, for Farmers." *New York Times*, August 3, 1997.

King, Clyde Lyndon. 1915. *Lower Living Costs in Cities: A Constructive Programme for Urban Efficiency*. New York: D. Appleton.

Kingsbury, Noel. 2009. *Hybrid: The History and Science of Plant Breeding*. Chicago: University of Chicago.

Kinney, Jen. 2016. "Watching Philly Grocery Shoppers Is Changing How Cities Build Supermarkets." *Next City*, November 4, 2016. https://nextcity.org/features/view/phil adelphia-grocery-stores-changing-food-deserts.

Klinenberg, Eric. 2002. *Heat Wave: A Social Autopsy of Disaster in Chicago*. Chicago: University of Chicago Press.

Klinenberg, Eric. 2018. *Palaces for the People: How Social Infrastructure Can Help Fight Inequality, Polarization, and the Decline of Civic Life*. New York: Penguin.

Knox, Andrea. 1976. "Food Fair to Buy 17 Area Stores from Bankrupt Penn Fruit Co." *Philadelphia Inquirer*, September 28, 1976.

Knox, Andrea. 1976. "Lease Confirms Merchants' Fears at Reading Market." *Philadelphia Inquirer*, October 22, 1976.

Knox, Andrea. 1978. "Problem of Profits, Backlog." *Philadelphia Inquirer*, July 30, 1978.

Koptyoff, Igor. 1986. "The Cultural Biography of Things: Commoditization as Process." In *The Social Life of Things: Commodities in Cultural Perspective*, edited by Arjun Appadurai, 64–94. New York: Cambridge University Press.

Kurlansky, Mark. 2013. *Birdseye: The Adventures of a Curious Man*. New York: Anchor.

Langan, Daniel. 1964. "Smoldering Dump Is Transformed into Vast City Food Center." *Philadelphia Inquirer*, June 28, 1964.

Latour, Bruno. 2005. *Reassembling the Social: An Introduction to Actor-Network-Theory*. New York: Oxford University Press.

Leach, William R. 2011. *Land of Desire: Merchants, Power, and the Rise of a New American Culture*. New York: Vintage.

LeCavalier, Jesse. 2016. *The Rule of Logistics: Walmart and the Architecture of Fulfillment*. Minneapolis: University of Minnesota Press.

Le Faivre-Rochester, Carole. 2003. "Society Hill Towers: A Bold and Graceful Venture." In *I. M. Pei and Society Hill: A 40th Anniversary Celebration*, edited by Herman Baron, 35–36. Philadelphia: Diane.

Lefebvre, Henri. 2003. *The Urban Revolution*. Minneapolis: University of Minnesota Press.

Levenstein, Harvey. 2003a. *Paradox of Plenty: A Social History of Eating in Modern America*. Berkeley: University of California Press.

Levenstein, Harvey. 2003b. *Revolution at the Table: The Transformation of the American Diet*. Berkeley: University of California Press.

Levinson, Marc. 2011. *The Great A&P and the Struggle for Small Business in America*. New York: Hill and Wang.

Levinson, Marc. 2016. *The Box: How the Shipping Container Made the World Smaller and the World Economy Bigger*. Princeton: Princeton University Press.

Levitt, Barbara, and James G. March. 1988. "Organizational Learning." *Annual Review of Sociology* 14, no. 1: 319–338.

Lichtenstein, Nelson. 2006. *Wal-Mart: The Face of Twenty-First-Century Capitalism*. New York: New Press.

Liebowitz, Ed. 1999. "Bar Codes: Reading between the Lines." *Smithsonian* 29, no. 11: 130–146.

Logan, John R., and Harvey Molotch. 1987. *Urban Fortunes: The Political Economy of Place*. Berkeley: University of California Press.

Longstreth, Richard, 1999. *The Drive-In, the Supermarket, and the Transformation of Commercial Space in Los Angeles, 1914–1941*. Cambridge, MA: MIT Press.

Lordan, Francis M. 1969. "Reading Co. Plans Building: Part of Market East Complex." *Philadelphia Inquirer*, October 21, 1969.

Love, John M. 1988. "Robert Smock and the Diffusion of Controlled Atmosphere Technology in the U.S. Apple Industry, 1940–1960." August 1988, no. 88-20. Department of Agricultural Economics, Cornell University Agricultural Experiment Station. New York State College of Agriculture and Life Sciences.

MacLachlan, Ian. 2001. *Kill and Chill: Restructuring Canada's Beef Commodity Chain.* Toronto: University of Toronto Press.

Malthus, Thomas Robert. 1888. *An Essay on the Principle of Population: Or, A View of Its Past and Present Effects on Human Happiness.* London: Reeves & Turner.

Manfredo, Mark R., and James D. Libbin. 1998. "The Development of Index Futures Contracts for Fresh Fruits and Vegetables." *Journal of Agribusiness* 16: 1–22.

Mann, Marvin L. 2001. "Cracking the Code." In *Twenty-Five Years behind Bars: The Proceedings of the Twenty-Fifth Anniversary of the UPC at the Smithsonian Institution, September 30, 1999,* edited by Alan L. Haberman, XX–XX. Cambridge, MA: Harvard University Press.

Mann, Michael. 1984. "The Autonomous Power of the State: Its Origins, Mechanisms and Results." *European Journal of Sociology* 25, no. 2: 185–213.

Mann, Michael. 2008. "Infrastructural Power Revisited." *Studies in Comparative International Development* 43, nos. 3–4: 355–365.

March, James G., and Johan P. Olsen. 1975. "The Uncertainty of the Past: Organizational Learning under Ambiguity." *European Journal of Political Research* 3, no. 2: 147–171.

Marcus, George E. 1995. "Ethnography in/of the World System: The Emergence of Multi-sited Ethnography." *Annual Review of Anthropology* 24, no. 1: 95–117.

Martens, Bobby J. 2008. "The Effect of Entry by Wal-Mart Supercenters on Retail Grocery Concentration." *Journal of Food Distribution Research* 39, no. 3: 13–28.

Marter, Marilynn. 2006. "Special Request—More Grocery Stores, Especially Those in Ethnically Diverse Neighborhoods, Are Learning What Their Customers Like—and Stocking It." *Philadelphia Inquirer*, October 5, 2006.

Martin, Bob L. 2001. "From Vision to Reality." In *Twenty-Five Years behind Bars*, edited by Alan L. Haberman, 34–42. Cambridge, MA: Harvard University Press.

Martinez, Steve W. 2007. "The U.S. Food Marketing System: Recent Developments, 1997–2006." United States Department of Agriculture, Economic Research Service, Economic Research Report 42, May 2007.

Mayo, James M. 1993. *The American Grocery Store: The Business Evolution of an Architectural Space.* Westport, CT: Greenwood.

McCrystal, Laura. 2019. "Jeff Brown to Close West Philly ShopRite, Blames Soda Tax." *Philadelphia Inquirer.* January 2, 2019. https://www.philly.com/news/soda-tax-shoprite-kenney-jeff-brown-haverford-20190102.html.

McDonnell, Terence E. 2016. *Best Laid Plans: Cultural Entropy and the Unraveling of AIDS Media Campaigns.* Chicago: University of Chicago Press.

McFadden, Dawn Thilmany, David Conner, Steven Deller, David Hughes, Ken Meter, Alfonso Morales, Todd Schmit, et al. 2016. "The Economics of Local Food Systems: A Toolkit to Guide Community Discussions, Assessments, and Choices." US Department of Agriculture, Agricultural Marketing Service, March 2016. Web.

McMichael, Philip. 2009. "A Food Regime Genealogy." *Journal of Peasant Studies* 36, no. 1: 139–169.

Meltzer, Marc. 1994. "Reading Terminal Market Produces Relief for Mantua." *Philadelphia Daily News*, May 26, 1994, 8.

Merton, Robert K. 1936. "The Unanticipated Consequences of Purposive Social Action." *American Sociological Review* 1, no. 6: 894–904.

Merton, Robert K. 1987. "Three Fragments from a Sociologist's Notebooks: Establishing the Phenomenon, Specified Ignorance, and Strategic Research Materials." *Annual Review of Sociology* 13, no. 1: 1–29.

Miller, Laura J. 2017. *Building Nature's Market: The Business and Politics of Natural Foods.* Chicago: University of Chicago Press.

Milletti, Mario A. 1975. "Penn Fruit Files for Reorganization." *Evening Bulletin*, September 3, 1975.

Mintz, Sidney W. 1985. *Sweetness and Power.* New York: Penguin Press.

Moeckel, Bill Reid. 1953. *The Development of the Wholesaler in the United States, 1860–1900.* PhD diss., University of Illinois.

Molotch, Harvey. 2004. *Where Stuff Comes From: How Toasters, Toilets, Cars, Computers and Many Other Things Come to Be as They Are.* New York: Routledge.

Molotch, Harvey. 2014. "Zero-Sum Urbanism." *Public Books*, February 1. https://www.publicbooks.org/zero-sum-urbanism/.

Monkkonen, Eric H. 1988. *America Becomes Urban: The Development of U.S. Cities and Towns, 1780–1980.* Berkeley: University of California Press.

Morton, Alan Q. 1994. "Packaging History: The Emergence of the Uniform Product Code (UPC) in the United States, 1970–1975." *History and Technology* 11: 101–111.

Moss, Michael. 2013. *Salt, Sugar, Fat: How the Food Giants Hooked Us.* New York: Random House.

Mukerji, Chandra. 2015. *Impossible Engineering: Technology and Territoriality on the Canal du Midi.* Princeton: Princeton University Press.

Mukherjee, Sidhartha. 2018. "It's Time to Study Whether Eating Particular Diets Can Help Heal Us." *New York Times*, December 5, 2018. https://www.nytimes.com/2018/12/05/magazine/its-time-to-study-whether-eating-particular-diets-can-help-heal-us.html.

Mumford, Lewis. 1938. *The Culture of Cities.* New York: Harcourt, Brace.

Nagle, James J. 1955. "Food Fair to Open 4 Stores in a Day: Expansion of the Relatively Small Chain Attracts Industry's Notice." *New York Times*, November 13, 1955.

National Commission on Food Marketing. 1966. "Organization and Competition in Food Retailing." Technical Study no. 7, June 1966.

Needham, Andrew. 2014. *Power Lines: Phoenix and the Making of the Modern Southwest.* Princeton: Princeton University Press.

Nestle, Marion. 2002. *Food Politics: How the Food Industry Influences Nutrition and Health.* Berkeley: University of California Press.

Newman, A. Joseph, Jr. 1957. "Food for Thought in Acme Stock." *Evening Bulletin*, August 30, 1957.

Newman, A. Joseph, Jr. 1958. "Food Chain Tries 50% Non-Food." *Evening Bulletin.* June 2, 1958.

Newman, A. Joseph, Jr. 1975. "Signposts . . . at the American Stores Meeting: 'No Quick Solution' to Store Closings." *Evening Bulletin*, July 25, 1975.

New York Times. 1955. "Acme Chain to Add 92 Stores Upstate." December 10, 1955.

Nye, David E. 2013. *America's Assembly Line.* Cambridge, MA: MIT Press.

O'Brien, Doug, Erinn Staley, Stephanie Uchima, Eleanor Thompson, and Halley Torres Aldeen. 2004. "The Charitable Food Assistance System: The Sector's Role in Ending Hunger in America." Hunger Forum Discussion Paper, UPS Foundation and Congressional Hunger Center. www.hungercenter.org.

Ocejo, Richard E. 2017. *Masters of Craft: Old Jobs in the New Urban Economy.* Princeton: Princeton University Press.

O'Leary, Daniel F. 1971. "Firm May Raze Reading Rail Terminal." *Evening Bulletin*, March 11, 1971.

O'Neil, David. 2005. "Ten Qualities of Successful Public Markets." *The Project for Public Spaces*, September 30, 2005. https://www.pps.org/article/tencharacteristics-2.

O'Neil, David K. 2003. *Reading Terminal Market: An Illustrated History*. Philadelphia: Camino.

Otter, Christopher. 2004. "Cleansing and Clarifying: Technology and Perception in Nineteenth-Century London." *Journal of British Studies* 43, no. 1: 40–64.

Otter, Christopher. 2005. "Civilizing Slaughter: The Development of the British Public Abattoir, 1850–1910." *Food and History* 3, no. 2: 29–51.

Owens, Cassie. 2017. "How ShopRite's Jeff Brown Became a Progressive—and a Soda Tax Opponent." *Philadelphia Inquirer*, December 18, 2017.

The Packer. 1993. "A Century of Produce 1893–1993." Vol. 100, no. 56. Overland Park, KS: Vance.

Pacyga, Dominic A. 2015. *Slaughterhouse: Chicago's Union Stock Yard and the World It Made.* Chicago: University of Chicago Press.

Padgett, John F., and Walter W. Powell. 2012. *The Emergence of Organizations and Markets.* Princeton: Princeton University Press.

Panaritis, Maria. 2015. "(Greater) Center City's Population Second Only to Midtown Manhattan's." *Philadelphia Inquirer*, April 21, 2015.

Park, John R. 1971. "Food Supplies Large, So Prices Should Benefit." *Evening Bulletin*, January 11, 1971.

Park, Robert E., and Ernest W. Burgess. 1925. *The City.* Chicago: University of Chicago Press.

Partch, Ken. 1996. "Wal-Mart: Second Coming of the Old A&P?" *Supermarket Business* 51, no. 9 (September 1996).

Partch, Ken. 2000. "Is the Supermarket at an End?" *Supermarket Business* 55, no. 7 (July 15, 2000): 138.

Patel, Raj. 2007. *Stuffed and Starved: Markets, Power and the Hidden Battle for the World Food System.* Melbourne: Schwartz.

Pelroth, Nicole. 2009. "The Consumer's Temple." *Forbes*, April 30, 2009. http://www.forbes.com/2009/04/30/1930s-advertising-innovation-business-supermarket.html.

Pennsylvania Farmer, Consolidated with Pennsylvania Stockman and Farmer. 1939. 121, no. 7. September 23, 1939.

Perishable Products Terminal, Philadelphia. 1926. 1, no. 12. May 12, 1926.

Perrow, Charles. 2011. *Normal Accidents: Living with High Risk Technologies.* Princeton: Princeton University Press.

Perry, R. Duane, Sandy Sherman, Meredith Stone, Amy Hillier, and Georgia Pozoukidou. 2001. *The Need for More Supermarkets in Philadelphia: Special Report.* Philadelphia: The Food Trust.

Petrick, Gabriella M. 2006. "'Like Ribbons of Green and Gold': Industrializing Lettuce and the Quest for Quality in the Salinas Valley, 1920–1965." *Agricultural History* 80, no. 3: 269–329.

Petrovic, Misha, and Gary G. Hamilton. 2006. "Making Global Markets: Wal-Mart and Its Suppliers." In *Wal-Mart: The Face of Twenty-First Century Capitalism*, edited by Nelson Lichtenstein, p. 306. New York: New Press.

Philadelphia Inquirer. 1885. "Produce: A Business That Necessitates Early Rising." September 3, 1885.

Philadelphia Inquirer. 1886. "At Dock Street Wharf." September 23, 1886.

Philadelphia Inquirer. 1900. "Direct Trade with the South: Dock Street Merchants Unanimous in Their Demand for a New Line." March 14, 1900, 7.

Philadelphia Inquirer. 1915. "Thomas P. Hunter Dies, Ill 12 Days: Founder of Acme Tea Stores Succumbs to Heart Trouble at Summer Home—Came from Ireland." May 26, 1915.

Philadelphia Inquirer. 1940. "Market Plan Hit by U.S. Expert: Prices Called Needlessly High Here." January 26, 1940.

Philadelphia Inquirer. 1954. "A&P to Build New Warehouse." April 2, 1954.

Philadelphia Inquirer. 1955. "City Planners Put OK on Phila. Food Center." April 21, 1955.

Philadelphia Inquirer. 1957. "New A&P Store Will Open Today." November 13, 1957.

Philadelphia Inquirer. 1967. "A&P Will Build Supermarket in Negro Center: Sullivan Discloses Lease and Outlines Training Program." July 28, 1967.

Philadelphia Inquirer. 1976. "New Landmark: An Honor for the Old Reading Terminal." December 25, 1976.

Philadelphia Tribune. 1979. "Hearings on Supermarket Closings Set for July 31." July 20, 1979, 5.

Philipps, R. G., and Samuel Fraser. 1922. *Wholesale Distribution of Fresh Fruits and Vegetables.* Rochester, NY: Fish-Lyman.

Pickering, Andrew. 1995. *The Mangle of Practice: Time, Agency, and Science.* Chicago: University of Chicago Press.

Ponte, Stefano, and Peter Gibbon. 2005. "Quality Standards, Conventions and the Governance of Global Value Chains." *Economy and Society* 34, no. 1: 1–31.

Poppendieck, Janet. 1999. *Sweet Charity? Emergency Food and the End of Entitlement.* New York: Penguin.

Porter, Jill. "High Rent Terminating Market?" *Evening Bulletin,* August 4, 1977.

Prasad, Monica. 2012. *The Land of Too Much: American Abundance and the Paradox of Poverty.* Cambridge, MA: Harvard University Press.

Produce Business. 2016. "New Jersey Produce Increases Exposure." June 1, 2016. https://www.producebusiness.com/new-jersey-produce-exposure/.

Prokop, Trudy, 1972. "War Flares Up on All Fronts along Supermarket Row." *Philadelphia Inquirer,* July 8, 1972. TUA

Prokop, Trudy. 1976. "Penn Fruit Markets for Sale—Food Chains 'Biting.'" *Evening Bulletin,* August 26, 1976, section E.

PR Newswire. 2001. "Shelves Are Bare at the Greater Philadelphia Food Bank; Changes in Food Industry Leave Food Bank Struggling for Donations." April 24, 2001.

PR Newswire. 2005. "The Greater Philadelphia Food Bank and Philabundance Finalize Merger; New Philabundance to Provide the Largest Hunger Relief Service in Delaware Valley." January 27, 2005.

Rae, Douglas. 2003. *City: The End of Urbanism.* New Haven: Yale University Press.

Ray, Krishnendu, and Tulasi Srinivas. 2012. "Introduction." In *Curried Cultures: Globalization, Food, and South Asia.* Berkeley: University of California Press.

Redevelopment Authority of the City of Philadelphia. 1968. *Society Hill: A Modern Community That Lives with History.* Philadelphia: Redevelopment Authority.

Rees, Jonathan. 2013. *Refrigeration Nation: A History of Ice, Appliances, and Enterprise in America.* Baltimore: Johns Hopkins University Press.

The Reinvestment Fund. 2011. "Pennsylvania Fresh Food Financing Initiative." Food Desert Panel Summary.

Reuters. 2013. "Supervalu Selling 877 Supermarkets in $3.3 Billion Deal." January 10, 2013.

Rhodes, John. 1970. "First 'Our Market' Opening Huge Success in North Phila." *Philadelphia Tribune,* March 3, 1970, 2.

Rieder, Rem. 1975. "Reading Terminal Market Future Is Cloudy." *Evening Bulletin*, April 3, 1975.

Rieder, Rem. 1975. "Market St.'s Market: Oyster Stew, Too." *Evening Bulletin*, May 4, 1975.

Romero, Melissa. 2017. "Census: Philly Remains the Poorest Major US City." *Curbed Philadelphia*, September 14, 2017. https://philly.curbed.com/2017/9/14/16307258 /philadelphia-poverty-rate-versus-major-cities.

Rose, Donald, J. Nicholas Bodor, Chris M. Swalm, Janet C. Rice, Thomas A. Farley, and Paul L. Hutchinson. 2009. "Deserts in New Orleans? Illustrations of Urban Food Access and Implications for Policy." Paper prepared for the University of Michigan National Poverty Center and the USDA Economic Research Service Research, Ann Arbor, MI.

Rowe, Frederick M. 1957. "The Evolution of the Robinson-Patman Act: A Twenty-Year Perspective." *Columbia Law Review* 57, no. 8: 1059–1088.

Roy, William G. 1997. *Socializing Capital: The Rise of the Large Industrial Corporation in America*. Princeton: Princeton University Press.

Rubio, Fernando Domínguez. 2014. "Preserving the Unpreservable: Docile and Unruly Objects at MoMA." *Theory and Society* 43, no. 6: 617–645.

Sackman, Douglas Cazaux. 2005. *Orange Empire: California and the Fruits of Eden*. Berkeley: University of California Press.

Sama, Dominic. 1975. "Penn Fruit Reports $970,000 Quarter Loss." *Evening Bulletin*, June 26, 1975.

Sampson, Robert. 2012. *Great American City: Chicago and the Enduring Neighborhood Effect*. Chicago: University of Chicago Press.

Sassen, Saskia. 2001. *The Global City: New York, London, Tokyo*. Princeton: Princeton University Press.

Savir, David, and George J. Laurer. 1975. "The Characteristics and Decodability of the Universal Product Code." *IBM Systems Journal* 14, no. 1: 16–34.

Schotzko, R. Thomas, and David Granatstein. 2004. *A Brief Look at the Washington Apple Industry: Past and Present*. Washington State University, School of Economic Sciences, SES: 04–05.

Scott, Allen J., and Michael Storper. 2015. "The Nature of Cities: The Scope and Limits of Urban Theory." *International Journal of Urban and Regional Research* 39, no. 1: 1–15.

Scott, James C. 1998. *Seeing like a State: How Certain Schemes to Improve the Human Condition Have Failed*. New Haven: Yale University Press.

Seabrook, John. 2011. "Crunch." *New Yorker*, November 21, 2011.

Selby, Earl. 1954. "Huge Wholesale Food Center Planned Here: $15 Million Project Would Make Phila. East's 'Market Basket.'" *Evening Bulletin*, April 2, 1954.

Selmeier, William. 2008. *Spreading the Barcode*. Self-published memoir of IBM.

Shapin, Steven. 2016. "Invisible Science." *Hedgehog Review* 18: 34–46.

Shaw, Arch Wilkinson. 1912. "Some Problems in Market Distribution." *Quarterly Journal of Economics* 26: 725–730.

Sheffi, Yossi. 2012. *Logistics Clusters: Delivering Value and Driving Growth*. Cambridge, MA: MIT Press.

Sikora, Martin J. 1971. "Food Fair's Stein Credits Finance as Keytone to Firm's Successes." *Evening Bulletin*, March 28, 1971.

Simmel, Georg. [1903] 1971. "The Metropolis and Mental Life." In *Georg Simmel on Individuality and Social Forms*, edited by Donald Levin, XX–XX. Chicago: University of Chicago Press.

Simon, Roger D., and Brian Alnutt. 2007. "Philadelphia, 1982–2007: Toward the Postindustrial City." *Pennsylvania Magazine of History and Biography* 131, no. 4: 395–444.

Singh, Maanvi. 2015. "Why a Philadelphia Grocery Chain Is Thriving in Food Deserts." NPR: The Salt. May 14, 2015. https://www.npr.org/sections/thesalt/2015/05/14/406476968/why-one-grocery-chain-is-thriving-in-philadelphias-food-deserts.

Small, Mario Luis, David J. Harding, and Michèle Lamont. 2010. "Introduction: Reconsidering Culture and Poverty." *Annals of the American Academy of Political and Social Science* 629, no. 1: 6–27.

Smith, Pamela. 1979. "100,000 Affected by Closing of 58th and Baltimore Pantry Pride Supermarket." *Philadelphia Tribune*, February 9, 1979, 15.

Smock, Robert M. 1942. "Influence of Controlled-Atmosphere Storage on Respiration of McIntosh Apples." *Botanical Gazette* 104, no. 1: 178–184.

Soluri, John. 2005. *Banana Cultures: Agriculture, Consumption, and Environmental Change in Honduras and the United States.* Austin: University of Texas Press.

Soursourian, Matthew. 2010/2011. "Healthy Food Financing Initiatives: Increasing Access to Fresh Foods in Underserved Markets." *Community Investments* 22, no. 3: 19–20.

Stalk, George, Philip Evans, and Lawrence E. Shulman. 1992. "Competing on Capabilities: The New Rules of Corporate Strategy." *Harvard Business Review* (March–April).

Star, Susan Leigh. 1995. "Introduction." In *Ecologies of Knowledge: Work and Politics in Science and Technology*, edited by Susan Leigh Star, 1–38. Albany: State University of New York Press.

Star, Susan Leigh. 1999. "The Ethnography of Infrastructure." *American Behavioral Scientist* 43, no. 3: 377–391.

Star, Susan Leigh, and Karen Ruhleder. 1996. "Steps toward an Ecology of Infrastructure: Design and Access for Large Information Spaces." *Information Systems Research* 7, no. 1: 111–134.

Stein, Louis [chairman of the board, Food Fair Stores]. 1970. "Food Called the Best Buy in America." *Evening Bulletin.* January 9, 1970.

Stone, Brad. 2013. *The Everything Store: Jeff Bezos and the Age of Amazon.* New York: Random House.

Striffler, Steve, and Mark Moberg. 2003. *Banana Wars: Power, Production, and History in the Americas.* Durham, NC: Duke University Press.

Supermarket News. 1995. "Penn Traffic Closes 45 Acme Store Deal." January 30, 1995.

Swyngedouw, Erik. 1996. "The City as a Hybrid: On Nature, Society and Cyborg Urbanization." *Capitalism Nature Socialism* 7, no. 2: 65–80.

Takiff, Jonathan. 1972. "The Lady Lives On within Her Shell." *Evening Bulletin*, February 25, 1972.

Thévenot, Laurent. 2001. "Organized Complexity: Conventions of Coordination and the Composition of Economic Arrangements." *European Journal of Social Theory* 4, no. 4: 405–425.

Thomas, W. I., and Florian Znainecki. 1918–1920. *The Polish Peasant in Europe and America.* Chicago: University of Chicago Press.

Thompson, Edward P. 1967. "Time, Work-Discipline, and Industrial Capitalism." *Past & Present* 38: 56–97.

Thompson, Edward P. 1971. "The Moral Economy of the English Crowd in the Eighteenth Century." *Past & Present* 50: 76–136.

Thompson, Isaiah. 2011. "The Vacant Land Issue: Addressing the Problem That Permeates Every Facet of Philly Life." *Philadelphia City Paper*, July 21, 2011.

Thrift, Nigel. 1999. "The Place of Complexity." *Theory, Culture & Society* 16, no. 3: 31–69.

Tilly, Louise A. 1983. "Food Entitlement, Famine, and Conflict." *Journal of Interdisciplinary History* 14, no. 2: 333–349.

Timmermans, Stefan, and Steven Epstein. 2010. "A World of Standards but Not a Standard World: Toward a Sociology of Standards and Standardization." *Annual Review of Sociology* 36: 69–89.

Tinsman, Heidi. 2014. *Buying into the Regime: Grapes and Consumption in Cold War Chile and the United States*. Durham, NC: Duke University Press.

Townes, Charles H. 2010. "The First Laser." In *A Century of Nature: Twenty-One Discoveries That Changed Science and the World*, edited by Laura Garwin and Tim Lincoln, 105–114. Chicago: University of Chicago Press.

Trebilcock, Bob. 2009. "Kroger Changes the Game." *Modern Materials Handling*, May 2009, 16–22.

Treuhaft, Sarah. 2012. A Healthy (and Profitable) Oasis in Philly's Food Deserts." *Yes Magazine*, October 1, 2012.

Twilley, Nicola. 2014. "What Do Chinese Dumplings Have to Do with Global Warming?" *New York Times Magazine*, July 25, 2014.

United States Department of Agriculture. 1955. "Packing and Shipping Lettuce in Fiberboard Cartons and Wooden Crates, A Comparison. Marketing Research." Report no. 86. Washington, DC: US Department of Agriculture, Agricultural Marketing Service.

United States Department of Agriculture. 1957. "Capacity of Refrigerated Warehouses in the United States. October 1, 1957." *Cold Storage* 2, no. 58: 1–31. Washington, DC: CRCP Reporting Board, Agricultural Marketing Service.

United States Department of Agriculture. 1972. *This Is USDA's Agricultural Marketing Services*. Washington, DC: US Government Printing Office.

United States Department of Agriculture. 1973. "Capacity of Refrigerated Warehouses, October 1, 1973." *Cold Storage* 2, no. 74: 1–16. Washington, DC: USDA Statistical Reporting Service.

United States Department of Agriculture. 2014. "Capacity of Refrigerated Warehouses, 2013 Summary." January 2014. Washington, DC: National Agricultural Statistics Service.

Urry, John. 2005. "The Complexity Turn." *Theory, Culture & Society* 22, no. 5: 1–14.

Vaughan, Diane. 1997. *The Challenger Launch Decision: Risky Technology, Culture, and Deviance at NASA*. Chicago: University of Chicago Press.

Vaughan, Diane. 1999. "The Dark Side of Organizations: Mistake, Misconduct, and Disaster." *Annual Review of Sociology* 25, no. 1: 271–305.

Vitiello, Domenic. 2008. "Machine Building and City Building: Urban Planning and Industrial Restructuring in Philadelphia, 1894–1928." *Journal of Urban History* 34, no. 3: 399–434.

Vobejda, Barbara, and D'Vera Cohn. 1995. "Study Finds Inner City Grocery Gap." *Washington Post*, May 17, 1995.

Wagar, Ken. 1995. "The Logic of Flow-Through Logistics." *Supermarket Business* 50, no. 6 (June 1995): 29–35.

Walsh, John P. 1993. *Supermarkets Transformed: Understanding Organizational and Technological Innovations*. New Brunswick, NJ: Rutgers University Press.

Walton, Sam [with Jon Huey]. 1992. *Sam Walton: Made in America*. New York: Doubleday.

Wang, Qi, Nolan Edward Phillips, Mario L. Small, and Robert J. Sampson. 2018. "Urban Mobility and Neighborhood Isolation in America's 50 Largest Cities." *PNAS* 115, no. 30: 7735–7740.

Werthner, George. 1957. "GPM: Vigilantes Anonymous." *Greater Philadelphia Magazine*, April 1957.

White, Richard. 2011. *Railroaded: The Transcontinentals and the Making of Modern America*. New York: W. W. Norton.

Whiteside, Thomas. 1977. "Tomatoes." *New Yorker*, January 24, 1977.

Wholesale Food Distribution Facilities for Philadelphia, PA, 1954. Agricultural Transportation and Facilities Branch, Marketing Research Division, Agricultural Marketing Services, US Department of Agriculture, Washington, DC. Marketing Research Report no. 201. TUA.

Whooley, Owen. 2013. *Knowledge in the Time of Cholera: The Struggle over American Medicine in the Nineteenth Century.* Chicago: University of Chicago Press.

Wicks, Judy. 2013. *Good Morning Beautiful Business: The Unexpected Journey of an Activist Entrepreneur and Local Economy Pioneer.* White River Junction, VT: Chelsea Green.

Williams, Raymond. [1961] 2001. *The Long Revolution.* Orchard Park, NY: Broadview Press.

Williams, Raymond. 1999. "Consumer." In *Consumer Society in American History: A Reader*, edited by Lawrence B. Glickman, 17–18. Ithaca: Cornell University Press.

Wilson, Thomas W. 2001. "How a Low-Tech Industry Pulled Off the U.P.C. Standard." In *Twenty-Five Years behind Bars*, edited by Alan L. Haberman, XX–XX. Cambridge, MA: Harvard University Press.

Wirth, Louis. 1938. "Urbanism as a Way of Life." *American Journal of Sociology* 44, no. 1: 1–24.

Woodland, Norman J. and Silver, Bernard. 1952. "Classifying Apparatus and Method." United States Patent Office, Patent Number: 2,612,994. October 7, 1952.

Worden, Amy. 2003. "Wanted: Inner City Supermarkets." *Philadelphia Inquirer*, November 21, 2003, B0.

Wrigley, Neil, and Michelle Lowe. 2014. *Reading Retail: A Geographical Perspective on Retailing and Consumption Spaces.* New York: Routledge.

Zimmerman, Max Mendell. 1937. *Super Market: Spectacular Exponent of Mass Distribution.* New York: Super Market.

Zimmerman, Max Mendell. 1941. "The Supermarket and the Changing Retail Structure." *Journal of Marketing* 5, no. 4: 402–409.

Zuckerman, Ezra W. 2012. "Construction, Concentration, and (Dis)continuities in Social Valuations." *Annual Review of Sociology* 38: 223–245.

Zukin, Sharon. 1989. *Loft Living: Culture and Capital in Urban Change.* New Brunswick: Rutgers University Press.

Zukin, Sharon. 1995. *The Cultures of Cities.* Cambridge, MA: Blackwell.

Zukin, Sharon. 2004. *Point of Purchase: How Shopping Changed American Culture.* New York: Routledge.

INDEX